Verilog® HDL

A Guide to Digital Design and Synthesis

Second Edition

Samir Palnitkar

Portions of this product may be derived from the UNIX® system and from the Berkeley 4.3 BSD system, licensed from the University of California. Third-party software, including font technology in this product, is protected by copyright and licensed from Sun's Suppliers.

Trademarks

Sun, Sun Microsystems, the Sun logo, and Solaris are trademarks or registered trademarks of Sun Microsystems, Inc. in the United States and may be protected as trademarks in other countries. UNIX is a registered trademark in the United States and other countries, exclusively licensed through X/Open company, Ltd. OPEN LOOK is a registered trademark of Novell, Inc. PostScript and Display PostScript are trademarks od Adobe Systems, Inc. Verilog is a registered of Cadence Design Systems, Inc. Verilog-XL is a trademark of Cadence Design Systems, Inc. VCS is a trademark of Viewlogic Systems, Inc. Magellan is a registered trademark of Systems Science, Inc. VirSim is a trademark of Simulation Technologies, Inc. Signalscan is a trademark of Design Acceleration, Inc. All other product, Service, or company names mentioned herein are claimed as trademarks and trade names by their respective companies.

All SPARC trademarks, including the SCD Complaint Logo, are trademarks or registered trademarks of SPARC International, Inc. in the United States and may be protected as trademarks in other countries. SPARCcenter, SPARCcluster, SPARCompiler, SPARCdesign, SPARCengine, SPARCprinter, SPARCserver, SPARCstation, SPARCstorage, SPARCworks, microSPARC, microSPARC-II, and UltraSPARC are licensed exclusively to Sun Microsystems, Inc. Products bearing SPARC trademarks are based upon an architecture developed by Sun Microsystems, Inc.

The OPEN LOOK™ and Sun™ Graphical User Interface were developed by Sun Microsystems, Inc. for its users and licensees. Sun acknowledges the pioneering efforts of Xerox in researching and developing the concept of visual or graphical user interfaces for the computer industry. Sun holds a non-exclusive license from Xerox to the Xerox Graphical User Interface, which license also covers Sun's licensees who implement OPEN LOOK GUI's and otherwise comply with Sun's written license agreements.

X Window System is a trademark of X Consortium, Inc.

This edition is published by arrangement with Pearson Education, Inc. and Dorling Kindersley Publishing Inc.

ISBN 81-7758-918-0

First Impression, 2006
Second Impression, 2007
Third Impression, 2007
Fourth Impression, 2007
Fifth Impression, 2007
Sixth Impression, 2008

This edition is manufactured in India and is authorized for sale only in India, Bangladesh, Bhutan, Pakistan, Nepal, Sri Lanka and the Maldives. Circulation of this edition outside of these territories is UNAUTHORIZED.

Published by Dorling Kindersley (India) Pvt. Ltd., licensees of Pearson Education in South Asia.

Head Office: 482, F.I.E., Patparganj, Delhi 110 092, India.
Registered Office: 14 Local Shopping Centre, Panchsheel Park, New Delhi 110 017, India.

Printed in India by Anand Sons.

Dedication

To Anu, Aditya, and Sahil,

Thank you for everything.

To our families,

Thank you for your constant encouragement and support.

— Samir

About the Author

Samir Palnitkar is currently the President of Jambo Systems, Inc., a leading ASIC design and verification services company which specializes in high-end designs for microprocessor, networking, and communications applications. Mr. Palnitkar is a serial entrepreneur. He was the founder of Integrated Intellectual Property, Inc., an ASIC company that was acquired by Lattice Semiconductor, Inc. Later he founded Obongo, Inc., an e-commerce software firm that was acquired by AOL Time Warner, Inc.

Mr. Palnitkar holds a Bachelor of Technology in Electrical Engineering from Indian Institute of Technology, Kanpur, a Master's in Electrical Engineering from University of Washington, Seattle, and an MBA degree from San Jose State University, San Jose, CA.

Mr. Palnitkar is a recognized authority on Verilog HDL, modeling, verification, logic synthesis, and EDA-based methodologies in digital design. He has worked extensively with design and verification on various successful microprocessor, ASIC, and system projects. He was the lead developer of the Verilog framework for the shared memory, cache coherent, multiprocessor architecture, popularly known as the UltraSPARC™ Port Architecture, defined for Sun's next generation UltraSPARC-based desktop systems. Besides the UltraSPARC CPU, he has worked on a number of diverse design and verification projects at leading companies including Cisco, Philips, Mitsubishi, Motorola, National, Advanced Micro Devices, and Standard Microsystems.

Mr. Palnitkar was also a leading member of the group that first experimented with cycle-based simulation technology on joint projects with simulator companies. He has extensive experience with a variety of EDA tools such as Verilog-NC, Synopsys VCS, Specman, Vera, System Verilog, Synopsys, SystemC, Verplex, and Design Data Management Systems.

Mr. Palnitkar is the author of three US patents, one for a novel method to analyze finite state machines, a second for work on cycle-based simulation technology and a third(pending approval) for a unique e-commerce tool. He has also published several technical papers. In his spare time, Mr. Palnitkar likes to play cricket, read books, and travel the world.

Table of Contents

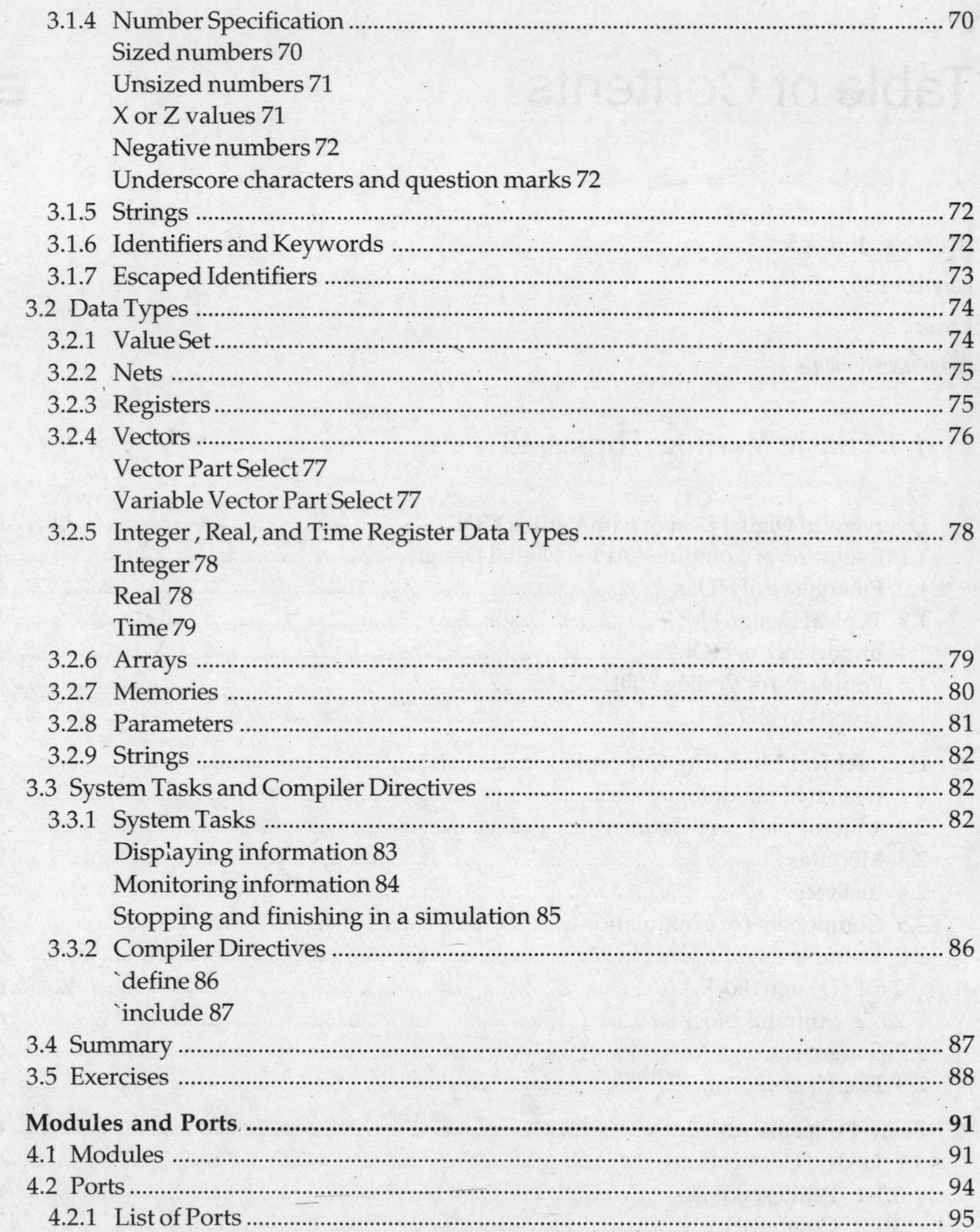

Part 2: Advanced Verilog Topics 255

Part 3: Appendices 403

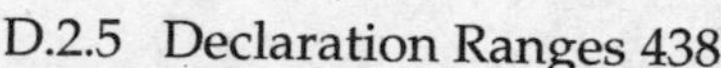

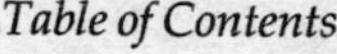

List of Figures

List of Tables

List of Examples

Foreword

From a modest beginning in early 1984 at Gateway Design Automation, the Verilog hardware description language has become an industry standard as a result of extensive use in the design of integrated circuit chips and digital systems. Verilog came into being as a proprietary language supported by a simulation environment that was the first to support mixed-level design representations comprising switches, gates, RTL, and higher levels of abstractions of digital circuits. The simulation environment provided a powerful and uniform method to express digital designs as well as tests that were meant to verify such designs.

There were three key factors that drove the acceptance and dominance of Verilog in the marketplace. First, the introduction of the Programming Language Interface (PLI) permitted users of Verilog to literally extend and customize the simulation environment. Since then, users have exploited the PLI and their success at adapting Verilog to their environment has been a real winner for Verilog. The second key factor which drove Verilog's dominance came from Gateways paying close attention to the needs of the ASIC foundries and enhancing Verilog in close partnership with Motorola, National, and UTMC in the 1987-1989 time-frame. The realization that the vast majority of logic simulation was being done by designers of ASIC chips drove this effort. With ASIC foundries blessing the use of Verilog and even adopting it as their internal sign-off simulator, the industry acceptance of Verilog was driven even further. The third and final key factor behind the success of Verilog was the introduction of Verilog-based synthesis technology by Synopsys in 1987. Gateway licensed its proprietary Verilog language to Synopsys for this purpose. The combination of the simulation and synthesis technologies served to make Verilog the language of choice for the hardware designers.

The arrival of the VHDL (VHSIC Hardware Description Language), along with the powerful alignment of the remaining EDA vendors driving VHDL as an IEEE standard, led to the placement of Verilog in the public domain. Verilog was inducted as the IEEE 1364 standard in 1995. Since 1995, many enhancements were made to Verilog HDL based on requests from Verilog users. These changes were incorporated into the latest IEEE 1364-2001 Verilog standard. Today, Verilog has become the language of choice for digital design and is the basis for synthesis, verification, and place and route technologies.

Samir's book is an excellent guide to the user of the Verilog language. Not only does it explain the language constructs with a rich variety of examples, it also goes into details of the usage of the PLI and the application of synthesis technology. The topics in the book are arranged logically and flow very smoothly. This book is written from a very practical design perspective rather than with a focus simply on the syntax aspects of the language.

This second edition of Samir's book is unique in two ways. Firstly, it incorporates all enhancements described in IEEE 1364-2001 standard. This ensures that the readers of the book are working with the latest information on Verilog. Secondly, a new chapter has been added on advanced verification techniques that are now an integral part of Verilog-based methodologies. Knowledge of these techniques is critical to Verilog users who design and verify multi-million gate systems.

I can still remember the challenges of teaching Verilog and its associated design and verification methodologies to users. By using Samir's book, beginning users of Verilog will become productive sooner, and experienced Verilog users will get the latest in a convenient reference book that can refresh their understanding of Verilog. This book is a must for any Verilog user.

Prabhu Goel

Former President of
Gateway Design Automation

Preface

During my earliest experience with Verilog HDL, I was looking for a book that could give me a "jump start" on using Verilog HDL. I wanted to learn basic digital design paradigms and the necessary Verilog HDL constructs that would help me build small digital circuits, using Verilog and run simulations. After I had gained some experience with building basic Verilog models, I wanted to learn to use Verilog HDL to build larger designs. At that time, I was searching for a book that broadly discussed advanced Verilog-based digital design concepts and *real* digital design methodologies. Finally, when I had gained enough experience with digital design and verification of real IC chips, though manuals of Verilog-based products were available, from time to time, I felt the need for a Verilog HDL book that would act as a handy reference. A desire to fill this need led to the publication of the first edition of this book.

It has been more than six years since the publication of the first edition. Many changes have occurred during these years. These years have added to the depth and richness of my design and verification experience through the diverse variety of ASIC and microprocessor projects that I have successfully completed in this duration. I have also seen state-of-the-art verification methodologies and tools evolve to a high level of maturity. The IEEE 1364-2001 standard for Verilog HDL has been approved. The purpose of this second edition is to incorporate the IEEE 1364-2001 additions and introduce to Verilog users the latest advances in verification. I hope to make this edition a richer learning experience for the reader.

This book emphasizes breadth rather than depth. The book imparts to the reader a working knowledge of a broad variety of Verilog-based topics, thus giving the reader a global understanding of Verilog HDL-based design. The book leaves the in-depth coverage of each topic to the Verilog HDL language reference manual and the reference manuals of the individual Verilog-based products.

This book should be classified not only as a Verilog HDL book but, more generally, as a digital design book. It is important to realize that Verilog HDL is only a tool used in digital design. It is the means to an end—*the digital IC chip*. Therefore, this book stresses the practical design perspective more than the mere language aspects of Verilog HDL. With HDL-based digital design having become a necessity, no digital designer can afford to ignore HDLs.

Who Should Use This Book

The book is intended primarily for beginners and intermediate-level Verilog users. However, for advanced Verilog users, the broad coverage of topics makes it an excellent reference book to be used in conjunction with the manuals and training materials of Verilog-based products.

The book presents a logical progression of Verilog HDL-based topics. It starts with the basics, such as HDL-based design methodologies, and then gradually builds on the basics to eventually reach advanced topics, such as PLI or logic synthesis. Thus, the book is useful to Verilog users with varying levels of expertise as explained below.

- **Students in logic design courses at universities**

  Part 1 of this book is ideal for a foundation semester course in Verilog HDL-based logic design. Students are exposed to hierarchical modeling concepts, basic Verilog constructs and modeling techniques, and the necessary knowledge to write small models and run simulations.

- **New Verilog users in the industry**

  Companies are moving to Verilog HDL-based design. Part 1 of this book is a perfect jump start for designers who want to orient their skills toward HDL-based design.

- **Users with basic Verilog knowledge who need to understand advanced concepts**

  Part 2 of this book discusses advanced concepts, such as UDPs, timing simulation, PLI, and logic synthesis, which are necessary for graduation from small Verilog models to larger designs.

- **Verilog experts**

  All Verilog topics are covered, from the basic modeling constructs to advanced topics like PLIs, logic synthesis, and advanced verification techniques. For Verilog experts, this book is a handy reference to be used along with the *IEEE Standard Verilog Hardware Description Language* reference manual.

The material in the book sometimes leans toward an Application Specific Integrated Circuit (ASIC) design methodology. However, the concepts explained in the book are general enough to be applicable to the design of FPGAs, PALs, buses, boards, and systems. The book uses Medium Scale Integration (MSI) logic examples to simplify discussion. The same concepts apply to VLSI designs.

How This Book Is Organized

This book is organized into three parts.

Part 1, Basic Verilog Topics, covers all information that a new user needs to build small Verilog models and run simulations. Note that in Part 1, gate-level modeling is addressed before behavioral modeling. I have chosen to do so because I think that it is easier for a new user to see a 1-1 correspondence between gate-level circuits and equivalent Verilog descriptions. Once gate-level modeling is understood, a new user can move to higher levels of abstraction, such as data flow modeling and behavioral modeling, without losing sight of the fact that Verilog HDL is a language for digital design and is not a programming language. Thus, a new user starts off with the idea that Verilog is a language for digital design. New users who start with behavioral modeling often tend to write Verilog the way they write their C programs. They sometimes lose sight of the fact that they are trying to represent hardware circuits by using Verilog. Part 1 contains nine chapters.

Part 2, Advanced Verilog Topics, contains the advanced concepts a Verilog user needs to know to graduate from small Verilog models to larger designs. Advanced topics such as timing simulation, switch-level modeling, UDPs, PLI, logic synthesis, and advanced verification techniques are covered. Part 2 contains six chapters.

Part 3, Appendices, contains information useful as a reference. Useful information, such as strength-level modeling, list of PLI routines, formal syntax definition, Verilog tidbits, and large Verilog examples is included. Part 3 contains six appendices.

Conventions Used in This Book

Table PR-1 describes the type changes and symbols used in this book.

Table PR-1 Typographic Conventions

Typeface or Symbol	Description	Examples
`AaBbCc123`	Keywords, system tasks and compiler directives that are a part of Verilog HDL	**`and`**, **`nand`**, **`$display`**, **`` `define ``**
AaBbCc123	Emphasis	*cell characterization, instantiation*
AaBbCc123	Names of signals, modules, ports, etc.	*fulladd4, D_FF, out*

A few other conventions need to be clarified:

- In the book, use of *Verilog* and *Verilog HDL* refers to the "Verilog Hardware Description Language." Any reference to a Verilog-based simulator is specifically mentioned, using words such as *Verilog simulator* or trademarks such as *Verilog-XL* or *VCS*.
- The word *designer* is used frequently in the book to emphasize the digital design perspective. However, it is a general term used to refer to a Verilog HDL user or a verification engineer.

Acknowledgments

The first edition of this book was written with the help of a great many people who contributed their energies to this project. Following were the primary contributors to my creation: *John Sanguinetti, Stuart Sutherland, Clifford Cummings, Robert Emberley, Ashutosh Mauskar, Jack McKeown, Dr. Arun Somani, Dr. Michael Ciletti, Larry Ke, Sunil Sabat, Cheng-I Huang, Maqsoodul Mannan, Ashok Mehta, Dick Herlein, Rita Glover, Ming-Hwa Wang, Subramanian Ganesan, Sandeep Aggarwal, Albert Lau, Samir Sanghani, Kiran Buch, Anshuman Saha, Bill Fuchs, Babu Chilukuri, Ramana Kalapatapu, Karin Ellison* and *Rachel Borden*. I would like to start by thanking all those people once again.

For this second edition, I give special thanks to the following people who helped me with the review process and provided valuable feedback:

Anders Nordstrom	ASIC Consultant
Stefen Boyd	Boyd Technology
Clifford Cummings	Sunburst Design
Harry Foster	Verplex Systems
Yatin Trivedi	Magma Design Automation
Rajeev Madhavan	Magma Design Automation
John Sanguinetti	Forte Design Systems
Dr. Arun Somani	Iowa State University
Michael McNamara	Verisity Design
Berend Ozceri	Cisco Systems
Shrenik Mehta	Sun Microsystems
Mike Meredith	Forte Design Systems

I also appreciate the help of the following individuals:

Richard Jones and John Williamson of Simucad Inc., for providing the free Verilog simulator SILOS 2001 to be packaged with the book.

Greg Doench of Prentice Hall and Myrna Rivera of Sun Microsystems for providing help in the publishing process.

Some of the material in this second edition of the book was inspired by conversations, email, and suggestions from colleagues in the industry. I have credited these sources where known, but if I have overlooked anyone, please accept my apologies.

Samir Palnitkar
Silicon Valley, California

Part 1 Basic Verilog Topics

Overview of Digital Design with Verilog HDL

1.1 Evolution of Computer-Aided Digital Design

Digital circuit design has evolved rapidly over the last 25 years. The earliest digital circuits were designed with vacuum tubes and transistors. Integrated circuits were then invented where logic gates were placed on a single chip. The first integrated circuit (IC) chips were SSI (*Small Scale Integration*) chips where the gate count was very small. As technologies became sophisticated, designers were able to place circuits with hundreds of gates on a chip. These chips were called MSI (*Medium Scale Integration*) chips. With the advent of LSI (*Large Scale Integration*), designers could put thousands of gates on a single chip. At this point, design processes started getting very complicated, and designers felt the need to automate these processes. *Electronic Design Automation* (EDA)[1] techniques began to evolve. Chip designers began to use circuit and logic simulation techniques to verify the functionality of building blocks of the order of about 100 transistors. The circuits were still tested on the breadboard, and the layout was done on paper or by hand on a graphic computer terminal.

With the advent of VLSI (*Very Large Scale Integration*) technology, designers could design single chips with more than 100,000 transistors. Because of the complexity of these circuits, it was not possible to verify these circuits on a breadboard. Computer-aided techniques became critical for verification and design of VLSI digital circuits. Computer programs to do automatic placement and routing of circuit layouts also became popular. The designers were now building gate-level digital circuits manually on graphic terminals. They would build small building blocks and then derive higher-

1. The earlier edition of the book used the term *CAD tools*. Technically, the term *Computer-Aided Design (CAD) tools* refers to back-end tools that perform functions related to place and route, and layout of the chip. The term *Computer-Aided Engineering (CAE) tools* refers to tools that are used for front-end processes such HDL simulation, logic synthesis, and timing analysis. Designers used the terms CAD and CAE interchangeably. Today, the term Electronic Design Automation is used for both CAD and CAE. For the sake of simplicity, in this book, we will refer to all design tools as *EDA tools*.

level blocks from them. This process would continue until they had built the top-level block. Logic simulators came into existence to verify the functionality of these circuits before they were fabricated on chip.

As designs got larger and more complex, logic simulation assumed an important role in the design process. Designers could iron out functional bugs in the architecture before the chip was designed further.

1.2 Emergence of HDLs

For a long time, programming languages such as FORTRAN, Pascal, and C were being used to describe computer programs that were sequential in nature. Similarly, in the digital design field, designers felt the need for a standard language to describe digital circuits. Thus, *Hardware Description Languages* (HDLs) came into existence. HDLs allowed the designers to model the concurrency of processes found in hardware elements. Hardware description languages such as *Verilog® HDL* and VHDL became popular. Verilog HDL originated in 1983 at Gateway Design Automation. Later, VHDL was developed under contract from DARPA. Using both Verilog and VHDL simulators to simulate large digital circuits quickly gained acceptance from designers.

Even though HDLs were popular for logic verification, designers had to manually translate the HDL-based design into a schematic circuit with interconnections between gates. The advent of logic synthesis in the late 1980s changed the design methodology radically. Digital circuits could be described at a *register transfer level (RTL)* by use of an HDL. Thus, the designer had to specify how the data flows between registers and how the design processes the data. The details of gates and their interconnections to implement the circuit were automatically extracted by logic synthesis tools from the RTL description.

Thus, logic synthesis pushed the HDLs into the forefront of digital design. Designers no longer had to manually place gates to build digital circuits. They could describe complex circuits at an abstract level in terms of functionality and data flow by designing those circuits in HDLs. Logic synthesis tools would implement the specified functionality in terms of gates and gate interconnections.

HDLs also began to be used for system-level design. HDLs were used for simulation of system boards, interconnect buses, FPGAs (Field Programmable Gate Arrays), and PALs (Programmable Array Logic). A common approach is to design each IC chip, using an HDL, and then verify system functionality via simulation.

Today, Verilog HDL is an accepted IEEE standard. In 1995, the original standard IEEE 1364-1995 was approved. IEEE 1364-2001 is the latest Verilog HDL standard that made significant improvements to the original standard.

1.3 Typical Design Flow

A typical design flow for designing VLSI IC circuits is shown in Figure 1-1. Unshaded blocks show the level of design representation; shaded blocks show processes in the design flow.

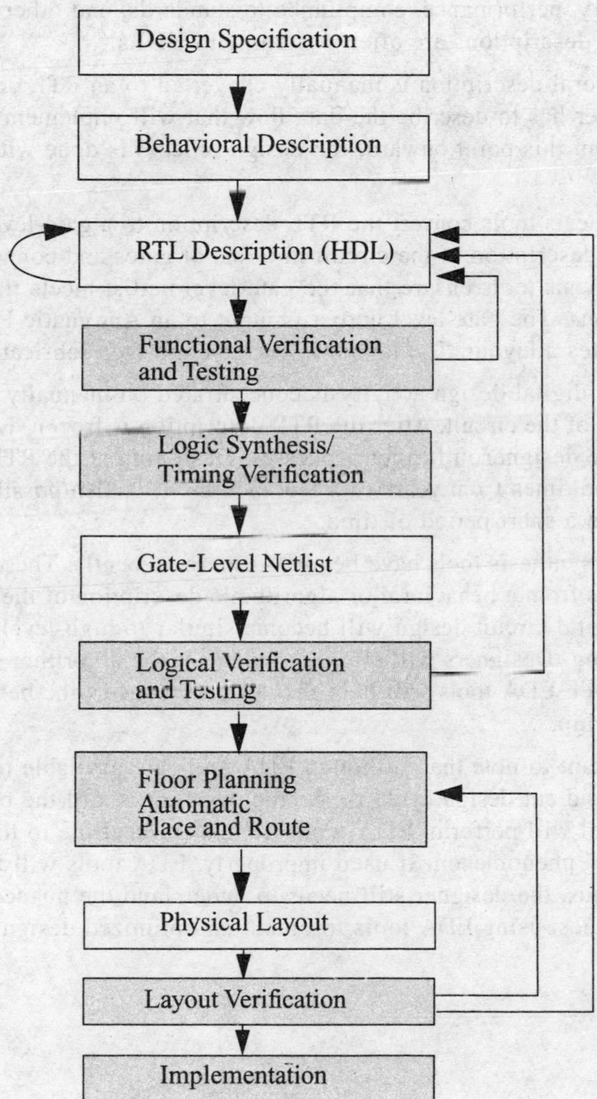

Figure 1-1 *Typical Design Flow*

The design flow shown in Figure 1-1 is typically used by designers who use HDLs. In any design, specifications are written first. Specifications describe abstractly the functionality, interface, and overall architecture of the digital circuit to be designed. At this point, the architects do not need to think about how they will implement this circuit. A behavioral description is then created to analyze the design in terms of functionality, performance, compliance to standards, and other high-level issues. Behavioral descriptions are often written with HDLs.[2]

The behavioral description is manually converted to an RTL description in an HDL. The designer has to describe the data flow that will implement the desired digital circuit. From this point onward, the design process is done with the assistance of EDA tools.

Logic synthesis tools convert the RTL description to a gate-level netlist. A gate-level netlist is a description of the circuit in terms of gates and connections between them. Logic synthesis tools ensure that the gate-level netlist meets timing, area, and power specifications. The gate-level netlist is input to an Automatic Place and Route tool, which creates a layout. The layout is verified and then fabricated on a chip.

Thus, most digital design activity is concentrated on manually optimizing the RTL description of the circuit. After the RTL description is frozen, EDA tools are available to assist the designer in further processes. Designing at the RTL level has shrunk the design cycle times from years to a few months. It is also possible to do many design iterations in a short period of time.

Behavioral synthesis tools have begun to emerge recently. These tools can create RTL descriptions from a behavioral or algorithmic description of the circuit. As these tools mature, digital circuit design will become similar to high-level computer programming. Designers will simply implement the algorithm in an HDL at a very abstract level. EDA tools will help the designer convert the behavioral description to a final IC chip.

It is important to note that, although EDA tools are available to automate the processes and cut design cycle times, the designer is still the person who controls how the tool will perform. EDA tools are also susceptible to the "*GIGO : Garbage In Garbage Out*" phenomenon. If used improperly, EDA tools will lead to inefficient designs. Thus, the designer still needs to understand the nuances of design methodologies, using EDA tools to obtain an optimized design.

---

2. New EDA tools have emerged to simulate behavioral descriptions of circuits. These tools combine the powerful concepts from HDLs and object oriented languages such as C++. These tools can be used instead of writing behavioral descriptions in Verilog HDL.

1.4 Importance of HDLs

HDLs have many advantages compared to traditional schematic-based design.

- Designs can be described at a very abstract level by use of HDLs. Designers can write their RTL description without choosing a specific fabrication technology. Logic synthesis tools can automatically convert the design to any fabrication technology. If a new technology emerges, designers do not need to redesign their circuit. They simply input the RTL description to the logic synthesis tool and create a new gate-level netlist, using the new fabrication technology. The logic synthesis tool will optimize the circuit in area and timing for the new technology.
- By describing designs in HDLs, functional verification of the design can be done early in the design cycle. Since designers work at the RTL level, they can optimize and modify the RTL description until it meets the desired functionality. Most design bugs are eliminated at this point. This cuts down design cycle time significantly because the probability of hitting a functional bug at a later time in the gate-level netlist or physical layout is minimized.
- Designing with HDLs is analogous to computer programming. A textual description with comments is an easier way to develop and debug circuits. This also provides a concise representation of the design, compared to gate-level schematics. Gate-level schematics are almost incomprehensible for very complex designs.

HDL-based design is here to stay.[3] With rapidly increasing complexities of digital circuits and increasingly sophisticated EDA tools, HDLs are now the dominant method for large digital designs. No digital circuit designer can afford to ignore HDL-based design.

1.5 Popularity of Verilog HDL

Verilog HDL has evolved as a standard hardware description language. Verilog HDL offers many useful features for hardware design.

- Verilog HDL is a general-purpose hardware description language that is easy to learn and easy to use. It is similar in syntax to the C programming language. Designers with C programming experience will find it easy to learn Verilog HDL.

3. New tools and languages focused on verification have emerged in the past few years. These languages are better suited for functional verification. However, for logic design, HDLs continue as the preferred choice.

- Verilog HDL allows different levels of abstraction to be mixed in the same model. Thus, a designer can define a hardware model in terms of switches, gates, RTL, or behavioral code. Also, a designer needs to learn only one language for stimulus and hierarchical design.
- Most popular logic synthesis tools support Verilog HDL. This makes it the language of choice for designers.
- All fabrication vendors provide Verilog HDL libraries for postlogic synthesis simulation. Thus, designing a chip in Verilog HDL allows the widest choice of vendors.
- The Programming Language Interface (PLI) is a powerful feature that allows the user to write custom C code to interact with the internal data structures of Verilog. Designers can customize a Verilog HDL simulator to their needs with the PLI.

1.6 Trends in HDLs

The speed and complexity of digital circuits have increased rapidly. Designers have responded by designing at higher levels of abstraction. Designers have to think only in terms of functionality. EDA tools take care of the implementation details. With designer assistance, EDA tools have become sophisticated enough to achieve a close-to-optimum implementation.

The most popular trend currently is to design in HDL at an RTL level, because logic synthesis tools can create gate-level netlists from RTL level design. Behavioral synthesis allowed engineers to design directly in terms of algorithms and the behavior of the circuit, and then use EDA tools to do the translation and optimization in each phase of the design. However, behavioral synthesis did not gain widespread acceptance. Today, RTL design continues to be very popular. Verilog HDL is also being constantly enhanced to meet the needs of new verification methodologies.

Formal verification and *assertion checking* techniques have emerged. Formal verification applies formal mathematical techniques to verify the correctness of Verilog HDL descriptions and to establish equivalency between RTL and gate-level netlists. However, the need to describe a design in Verilog HDL will not go away. Assertion checkers allow checking to be embedded in the RTL code. This is a convenient way to do checking in the most important parts of a design.

New verification languages have also gained rapid acceptance. These languages combine the parallelism and hardware constructs from HDLs with the object oriented nature of C++. These languages also provide support for automatic stimulus creation, checking, and coverage. However, these languages do not replace Verilog HDL. They simply boost the productivity of the verification process. Verilog HDL is still needed to describe the design.

For very high-speed and timing-critical circuits like microprocessors, the gate-level netlist provided by logic synthesis tools is not optimal. In such cases, designers often mix gate-level description directly into the RTL description to achieve optimum results. This practice is opposite to the high-level design paradigm, yet it is frequently used for high-speed designs because designers need to squeeze the last bit of timing out of circuits, and EDA tools sometimes prove to be insufficient to achieve the desired results.

Another technique that is used for system-level design is a mixed bottom-up methodology where the designers use either existing Verilog HDL modules, basic building blocks, or vendor-supplied core blocks to quickly bring up their system simulation. This is done to reduce development costs and compress design schedules. For example, consider a system that has a CPU, graphics chip, I/O chip, and a system bus. The CPU designers would build the next-generation CPU themselves at an RTL level, but they would use behavioral models for the graphics chip and the I/O chip and would buy a vendor-supplied model for the system bus. Thus, the system-level simulation for the CPU could be up and running very quickly and long before the RTL descriptions for the graphics chip and the I/O chip are completed.

Hierarchical Modeling Concepts

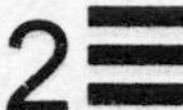

Before we discuss the details of the Verilog language, we must first understand basic hierarchical modeling concepts in digital design. The designer must use a "good" design methodology to do efficient Verilog HDL-based design. In this chapter, we discuss typical design methodologies and illustrate how these concepts are translated to Verilog. A digital simulation is made up of various components. We talk about the components and their interconnections.

Learning Objectives

- Understand top-down and bottom-up design methodologies for digital design.
- Explain differences between modules and module instances in Verilog.
- Describe four levels of abstraction—behavioral, data flow, gate level, and switch level—to represent the same module.
- Describe components required for the simulation of a digital design. Define a stimulus block and a design block. Explain two methods of applying stimulus.

2.1 Design Methodologies

There are two basic types of digital design methodologies: a *top-down* design methodology and a *bottom-up* design methodology. In a top-down design methodology, we define the top-level block and identify the sub-blocks necessary to build the top-level block. We further subdivide the sub-blocks until we come to leaf cells, which are the cells that cannot further be divided. Figure 2-1 shows the top-down design process.

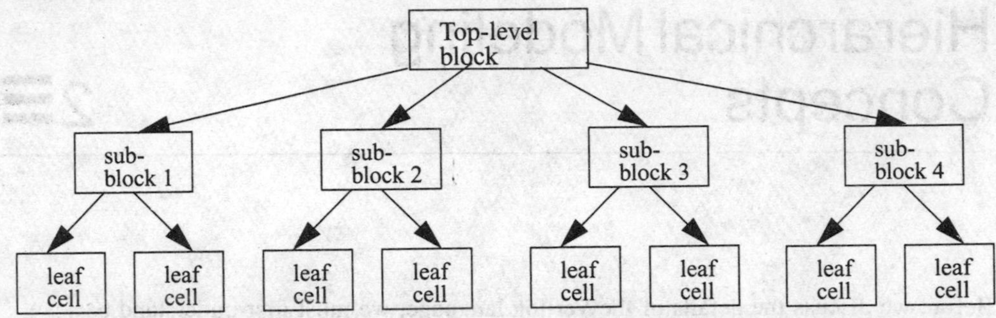

Figure 2-1 Top-down Design Methodology

In a bottom-up design methodology, we first identify the building blocks that are available to us. We build bigger cells, using these building blocks. These cells are then used for higher-level blocks until we build the top-level block in the design. Figure 2-2 shows the bottom-up design process.

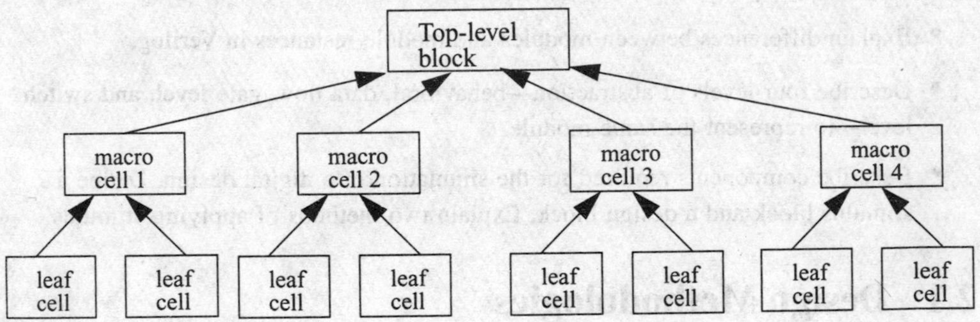

Figure 2-2 Bottom-up Design Methodology

Typically, a *combination* of top-down and bottom-up flows is used. Design architects define the specifications of the top-level block. Logic designers decide how the design should be structured by breaking up the functionality into blocks and sub-blocks. At the same time, circuit designers are designing optimized circuits for leaf-level cells. They build higher-level cells by using these leaf cells. The flow meets at an intermediate point where the switch-level circuit designers have created a library of leaf cells by using switches, and the logic level designers have designed from top-down until all modules are defined in terms of leaf cells.

To illustrate these hierarchical modeling concepts, let us consider the design of a negative edge-triggered 4-bit ripple carry counter described in Section 2.2, `4-bit Ripple Carry Counter`.

2.2 4-bit Ripple Carry Counter

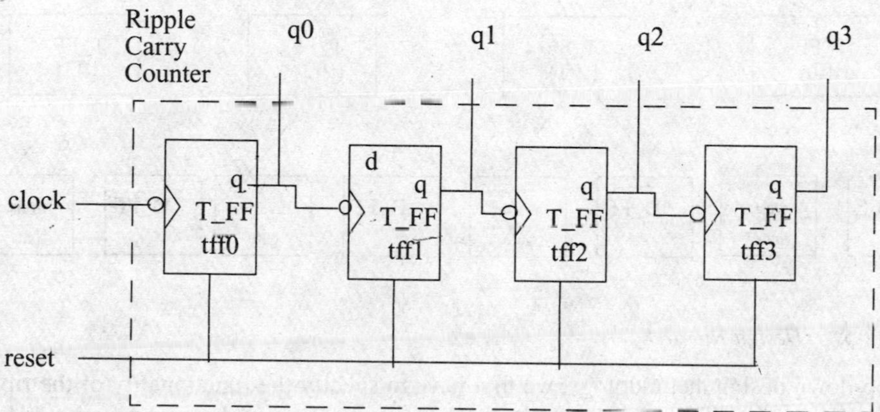

Figure 2-3 Ripple Carry Counter

The ripple carry counter shown in Figure 2-3 is made up of negative edge-triggered toggle flipflops (`T_FF`). Each of the *T_FFs* can be made up from negative edge-triggered D-flipflops (*D_FF*) and `inverters` (assuming *q_bar* output is not available on the *D_FF*), as shown in Figure 2-4.

reset	q_n	q_{n+1}
1	1	0
1	0	0
0	0	1
0	1	0
0	0	0

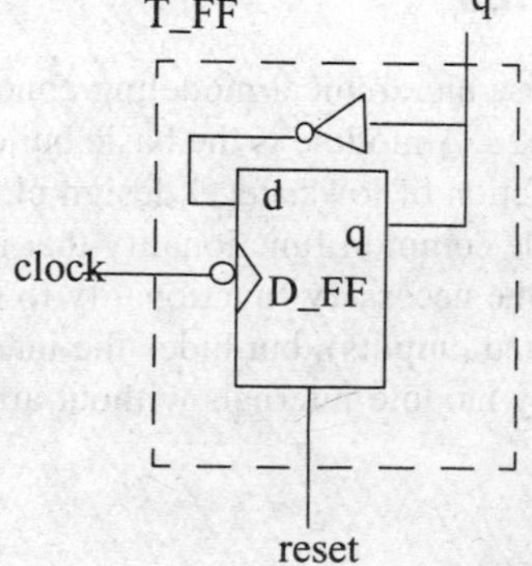

Figure 2-4 T-flipflop

Thus, the ripple carry counter is built in a hierarchical fashion by using building blocks. The diagram for the design hierarchy is shown in Figure 2-5.

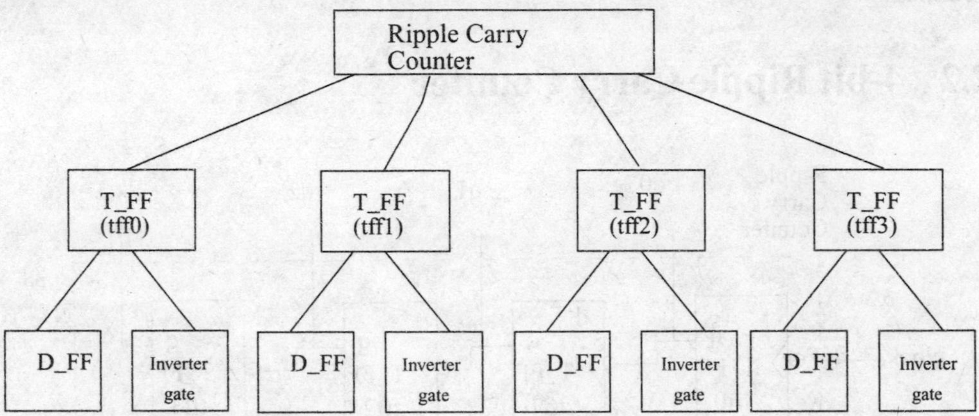

Figure 2-5 Design Hierarchy

In a top-down design methodology, we first have to specify the functionality of the ripple carry counter, which is the top-level block. Then, we implement the counter with *T_FF*s. We build the *T_FF*s from the *D_FF* and an additional inverter gate. Thus, we break bigger blocks into smaller building sub-blocks until we decide that we cannot break up the blocks any further. A bottom-up methodology flows in the opposite direction. We combine small building blocks and build bigger blocks; e.g., we could build *D_FF* from **`and`** and **`or`** gates, or we could build a custom *D_FF* from transistors. Thus, the bottom-up flow meets the top-down flow at the level of the *D_FF*.

2.3 Modules

We now relate these hierarchical modeling concepts to Verilog. Verilog provides the concept of a `module`. A module is the basic building block in Verilog. A module can be an element or a collection of lower-level design blocks. Typically, elements are grouped into modules to provide common functionality that is used at many places in the design. A module provides the necessary functionality to the higher-level block through its port interface (inputs and outputs), but hides the internal implementation. This allows the designer to modify module internals without affecting the rest of the design.

In Figure 2-5, *ripple carry counter*, *T_FF*, and `D_FF` are examples of modules. In Verilog, a module is declared by the keyword **`module`**. A corresponding keyword **`endmodule`** must appear at the end of the module definition. Each module must have a *module_name*, which is the identifier for the module, and a *module_terminal_list*, which describes the input and output terminals of the module.

```
module <module_name> (<module_terminal_list>);

...
<module internals>
...
...
endmodule
```

Specifically, the T-flipflop could be defined as a module as follows:

```
module T_FF (q, clock, reset);
.
.
<functionality of T-flipflop>
.
.
endmodule
```

Verilog is both a behavioral and a structural language. Internals of each module can be defined at `four` levels of abstraction, depending on the needs of the design. The module behaves identically with the external environment irrespective of the level of abstraction at which the module is described. The internals of the module are hidden from the environment. Thus, the level of abstraction to describe a module can be changed without any change in the environment. These levels will be studied in detail in separate chapters later in the book. The levels are defined below.

- **Behavioral or algorithmic level**
  This is the highest level of abstraction provided by Verilog HDL. A module can be implemented in terms of the desired design algorithm without concern for the hardware implementation details. Designing at this level is very similar to C programming.

- **Dataflow level**

  At this level, the module is designed by specifying the data flow. The designer is aware of how data flows between hardware registers and how the data is processed in the design.

- **Gate level**

  The module is implemented in terms of logic gates and interconnections between these gates. Design at this level is similar to describing a design in terms of a gate-level logic diagram.

- **Switch level**

  This is the lowest level of abstraction provided by Verilog. A module can be implemented in terms of switches, storage nodes, and the interconnections between them. Design at this level requires knowledge of switch-level implementation details.

Verilog allows the designer to mix and match all four levels of abstractions in a design. In the digital design community, the term `register transfer level (RTL)` is frequently used for a Verilog description that uses a combination of behavioral and dataflow constructs and is acceptable tc logic synthesis tools.

If a design contains four modules, Verilog allows each of the modules to be written at a different level of abstraction. As the design matures, most modules are replaced with gate-level implementations.

Normally, the higher the level of abstraction, the more flexible and technology-independent the design. As one goes lower toward switch-level design, the design becomes technology-dependent and inflexible. A small modification can cause a significant number of changes in the design. Consider the analogy with C programming and assembly language programming. It is easier to program in a higher-level language such as C. The program can be easily ported to any machine. However, if you design at the assembly level, the program is specific for that machine and cannot be easily ported to another machine.

2.4 Instances

A module provides a template from which you can create actual objects. When a module is invoked, Verilog creates a unique object from the template. Each object has its own name, variables, parameters, and I/O interface. The process of creating objects from a module template is called `instantiation`, and the objects are called `instances`. In

Example 2-1, the top-level block creates four instances from the T-flipflop (*T_FF*) template. Each *T_FF* instantiates a *D_FF* and an inverter gate. Each instance must be given a unique name. Note that `//` is used to denote single-line comments.

Example 2-1 Module Instantiation

```
// Define the top-level module called ripple carry
// counter. It instantiates 4 T-flipflops. Interconnections are
// shown in Section 2.2, 4-bit Ripple Carry Counter.
module ripple_carry_counter(q, clk, reset);

output [3:0] q; //I/O signals and vector declarations
                //will be explained later.
input clk, reset; //I/O signals will be explained later.

//Four instances of the module T_FF are created. Each has a unique
//name.Each instance is passed a set of signals. Notice, that
//each instance is a copy of the module T_FF.
T_FF tff0(q[0],clk, reset);
T_FF tff1(q[1],q[0], reset);
T_FF tff2(q[2],q[1], reset);
T_FF tff3(q[3],q[2], reset);

endmodule

// Define the module T_FF. It instantiates a D-flipflop. We assumed
// that module D-flipflop is defined elsewhere in the design. Refer
// to Figure 2-4 for interconnections.
module T_FF(q, clk, reset);

//Declarations to be explained later
output q;
input clk, reset;
wire d;

D_FF dff0(q, d, clk, reset); // Instantiate D_FF. Call it dff0.
not n1(d, q); // not gate is a Verilog primitive. Explained later.

endmodule
```

In Verilog, it is illegal to `nest` modules. One module definition cannot contain another module definition within the **`module`** and **`endmodule`** statements. Instead, a module definition can incorporate copies of other modules by instantiating them. It is important not to confuse module definitions and instances of a module. Module definitions simply specify how the module will work, its internals, and its interface. Modules must be instantiated for use in the design.

Example 2-2 shows an illegal module nesting where the module *T_FF* is defined inside the module definition of the ripple carry counter.

Example 2-2 *Illegal Module Nesting*

```
// Define the top-level module called ripple carry counter.
// It is illegal to define the module T_FF inside this module.
module ripple_carry_counter(q, clk, reset);
output [3:0] q;
input clk, reset;

    module T_FF(q, clock, reset);// ILLEGAL MODULE NESTING
    ...
    <module T_FF internals>
    ...
    endmodule // END OF ILLEGAL MODULE NESTING

endmodule
```

2.5 Components of a Simulation

Once a design block is completed, it must be tested. The functionality of the design block can be tested by applying stimulus and checking results. We call such a block the *stimulus* block. It is good practice to keep the stimulus and design blocks separate. The stimulus block can be written in Verilog. A separate language is not required to describe stimulus. The stimulus block is also commonly called a *test bench*. Different test benches can be used to thoroughly test the design block.

Two styles of stimulus application are possible. In the first style, the stimulus block instantiates the design block and directly drives the signals in the design block. In Figure 2-6, the stimulus block becomes the top-level block. It manipulates signals *clk* and *reset*, and it checks and displays output signal *q*.

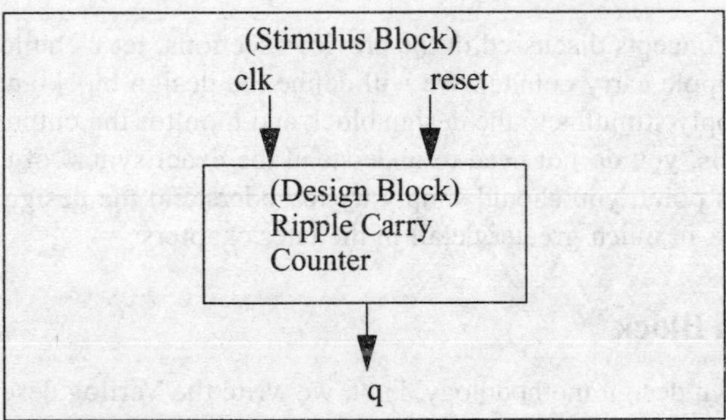

Figure 2-6 Stimulus Block Instantiates Design Block

The second style of applying stimulus is to instantiate both the stimulus and design blocks in a top-level dummy module. The stimulus block interacts with the design block only through the interface. This style of applying stimulus is shown in Figure 2-7. The stimulus module drives the signals *d_clk* and *d_reset*, which are connected to the signals *clk* and *reset* in the design block. It also checks and displays signal *c_q*, which is connected to the signal *q* in the design block. The function of top-level block is simply to instantiate the design and stimulus blocks.

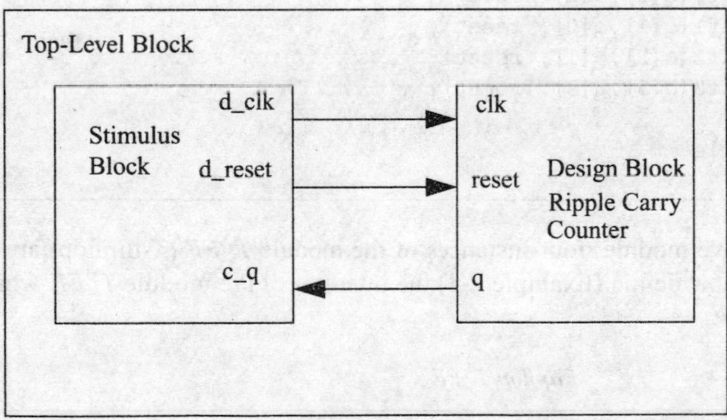

Figure 2-7 Stimulus and Design Blocks Instantiated in a Dummy Top-Level Module

Either stimulus style can be used effectively.

2.6 Example

To illustrate the concepts discussed in the previous sections, let us build the complete simulation of a ripple carry counter. We will define the design block and the stimulus block. We will apply stimulus to the design block and monitor the outputs. As we develop the Verilog models, you do not need to understand the exact syntax of each construct at this stage. At this point, you should simply try to understand the design process. We discuss the syntax in much greater detail in the later chapters.

2.6.1 Design Block

We use a top-down design methodology. First, we write the Verilog description of the top-level design block (Example 2-3), which is the `ripple carry counter` (*see* Section 2.2, `4-bit Ripple Carry Counter`).

Example 2-3 *Ripple Carry Counter Top Block*

```
module ripple_carry_counter(q, clk, reset);

output [3:0] q;
input clk, reset;

//4 instances of the module T_FF are created.
T_FF tff0(q[0],clk, reset);
T_FF tff1(q[1],q[0], reset);
T_FF tff2(q[2],q[1], reset);
T_FF tff3(q[3],q[2], reset);

endmodule
```

In the above module, four instances of the module *T_FF* (T-flipflop) are used. Therefore, we must now define (Example 2-4) the internals of the module *T_FF,* which was shown in Figure 2-4.

Example 2-4 *Flipflop T_FF*

```
module T_FF(q, clk, reset);

output q;
input clk, reset;
wire d;
```

Example 2-4 *Flipflop T_FF (Continued)*

```
D_FF dff0(q, d, clk, reset);
not n1(d, q); // not is a Verilog-provided primitive. case sensitive
endmodule
```

Since *T_FF* instantiates *D_FF*, we must now define (Example 2-5) the internals of module *D_FF*. We assume asynchronous reset for the *D_FF*.

Example 2-5 *Flipflop D_F*

```
// module D_FF with synchronous reset
module D_FF(q, d, clk, reset);

output q;
input d, clk, reset;
reg q;

// Lots of new constructs. Ignore the functionality of the
// constructs.
// Concentrate on how the design block is built in a top-down fashion.
always @(posedge reset or negedge clk)
if (reset)
    q <= 1'b0;
else
    q <= d;

endmodule
```

All modules have been defined down to the lowest-level leaf cells in the design methodology. The design block is now complete.

2.6.2 Stimulus Block

We must now write the stimulus block to check if the ripple carry counter design is functioning correctly. In this case, we must control the signals *clk* and *reset* so that the regular function of the ripple carry counter and the asynchronous reset mechanism are both tested. We use the waveforms shown in Figure 2-8 to test the design. Waveforms for *clk*, *reset*, and 4-bit output *q* are shown. The cycle time for *clk* is 10 units; the *reset* signal stays up from time 0 to 15 and then goes up again from time 195 to 205. Output *q* counts from 0 to 15.

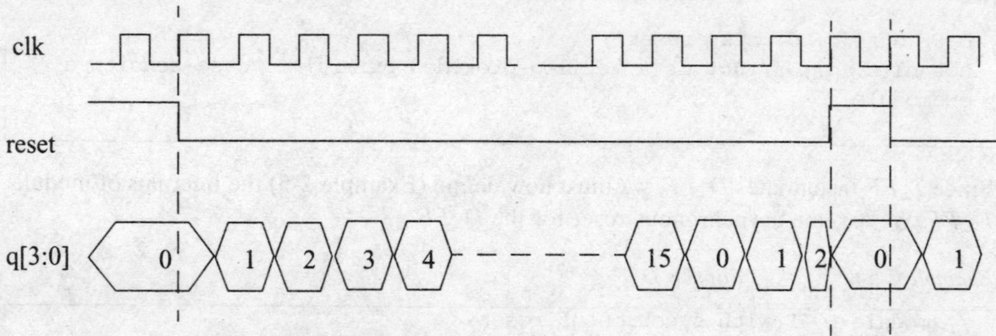

Figure 2-8 Stimulus and Output Waveforms

We are now ready to write the stimulus block (see 6Example 2-6) that will create the above waveforms. We will use the stimulus style shown in Figure 2-6. Do not worry about the Verilog syntax at this point. Simply concentrate on how the design block is instantiated in the stimulus block.

Example 2-6 Stimulus Block

```
module stimulus;

reg clk;
reg reset;
wire[3:0] q;

// instantiate the design block
ripple_carry_counter r1(q, clk, reset);

// Control the clk signal that drives the design block. Cycle time = 10
initial
    clk = 1'b0; //set clk to 0
always
    #5 clk = ~clk; //toggle clk every 5 time units

// Control the reset signal that drives the design block
// reset is asserted from 0 to 20 and from 200 to 220.
initial
begin
    reset = 1'b1;
    #15 reset = 1'b0;
    #180 reset = 1'b1;
```

Example 2-6 *Stimulus Block (Continued)*

```
    #10 reset = 1'b0;
    #20 $finish; //terminate the simulation
end

// Monitor the outputs
initial
    $monitor($time, " Output q = %d",  q);

endmodule
```

Once the stimulus block is completed, we are ready to run the simulation and verify the functional correctness of the design block. The output obtained when stimulus and design blocks are simulated is shown in Example 2-7.

Example 2-7 *Output of the Simulation*

```
                  0 Output q =  0
                 20 Output q =  1
                 30 Output q =  2
                 40 Output q =  3
                 50 Output q =  4
                 60 Output q =  5
                 70 Output q =  6
                 80 Output q =  7
                 90 Output q =  8
                100 Output q =  9
                110 Output q = 10
                120 Output q = 11
                130 Output q = 12
                140 Output q = 13
                150 Output q = 14
                160 Output q = 15
                170 Output q =  0
                180 Output q =  1
                190 Output q =  2
                195 Output q =  0
                210 Output q =  1
                220 Output q =  2
```

2.7 Summary

In this chapter we discussed the following concepts.

- Two kinds of design methodologies are used for digital design: top-down and bottom-up. A combination of these two methodologies is used in today's digital designs. As designs become very complex, it is important to follow these structured approaches to manage the design process.
- Modules are the basic building blocks in Verilog. Modules are used in a design by instantiation. An instance of a module has a unique identity and is different from other instances of the same module. Each instance has an independent copy of the internals of the module. It is important to understand the difference between modules and instances.
- There are two distinct components in a simulation: a design block and a stimulus block. A stimulus block is used to test the design block. The stimulus block is usually the top-level block. There are two different styles of applying stimulus to a design block.
- The example of the ripple carry counter explains the step-by-step process of building all the blocks required in a simulation.

This chapter is intended to give an understanding of the design process and how Verilog fits into the design process. The details of Verilog syntax are not important at this stage and will be dealt with in later chapters.

2.8 Exercises

1. An interconnect switch (*IS*) contains the following components, a shared memory (*MEM*), a system controller (*SC*), and a data crossbar (*Xbar*).
   a. Define the modules *MEM, SC*, and *Xbar*, using the **`module/endmodule`** keywords. You do not need to define the internals. Assume that the modules have no terminal lists.
   b. Define the module *IS*, using the **`module/endmodule`** keywords. Instantiate the modules *MEM, SC, and Xbar* and call the instances *mem1, sc1*, and *xbar1*, respectively. You do not need to define the internals. Assume that the module *IS* has no terminals.
   c. Define a stimulus block (Top), using the **`module/endmodule`** keywords. Instantiate the design block *IS* and call the instance *is1*. This is the final step in building the simulation environment.

2. A 4-bit ripple carry adder (*Ripple_Add*) contains four 1-bit full adders (*FA*).
   a. Define the module *FA*. Do not define the internals or the terminal list.
   b. Define the module *Ripple_Add*. Do not define the internals or the terminal list. Instantiate four full adders of the type *FA* in the module *Ripple_Add* and call them *fa0, fa1, fa2*, and *fa3*.

Basic Concepts 3

In this chapter, we discuss the basic constructs and conventions in Verilog. These conventions and constructs are used throughout the later chapters. These conventions provide the necessary framework for Verilog HDL. Data types in Verilog model actual data storage and switch elements in hardware very closely. This chapter may seem dry, but understanding these concepts is a necessary foundation for the successive chapters.

Learning Objectives

- Understand lexical conventions for operators, comments, whitespace, numbers, strings, and identifiers.
- Define the logic value set and data types such as nets, registers, vectors, numbers, simulation time, arrays, parameters, memories, and strings.
- Identify useful system tasks for displaying and monitoring information, and for stopping and finishing the simulation.
- Learn basic compiler directives to define macros and include files.

3.1 Lexical Conventions

The basic lexical conventions used by Verilog HDL are similar to those in the C programming language. Verilog contains a stream of tokens. Tokens can be comments, delimiters, numbers, strings, identifiers, and keywords. Verilog HDL is a case-sensitive language. All keywords are in lowercase.

3.1.1 Whitespace

Blank spaces (\b) , tabs (\t), and newlines (\n) comprise the whitespace. Whitespace is ignored by Verilog except when it separates tokens. Whitespace is not ignored in strings.

3.1.2 Comments

Comments can be inserted in the code for readability and documentation. There are two ways to write comments. A one-line comment starts with "//". Verilog skips from that point to the end of line. A multiple-line comment starts with "/*" and ends with "*/". Multiple-line comments cannot be nested. However, one-line comments can be embedded in multiple-line comments.

```
a = b && c; // This is a one-line comment

/* This is a multiple line
   comment */

/* This is /* an illegal */ comment */

/* This is //a legal comment */
```

3.1.3 Operators

Operators are of three types: *unary*, *binary*, and *ternary*. Unary operators precede the operand. Binary operators appear between two operands. Ternary operators have two separate operators that separate three operands.

```
a = ~ b; // ~ is a unary operator. b is the operand
a = b && c; // && is a binary operator. b and c are operands
a = b ? c : d; // ?: is a ternary operator. b, c and d are operands
```

3.1.4 Number Specification

There are two types of number specification in Verilog: sized and unsized.

Sized numbers

Sized numbers are represented as *<size>* '*<base format>* *<number>*.

<size> is written only in decimal and specifies the number of bits in the number. Legal base formats are decimal (*'d* or *'D*), hexadecimal (*'h* or *'H*), binary (*'b* or *'B*) and octal (*'o* or *'O*). The number is specified as consecutive digits from *0, 1, 2, 3, 4, 5, 6, 7, 8, 9, a, b, c, d, e, f*. Only a subset of these digits is legal for a particular base. Uppercase letters are legal for number specification.

```
4'b1111 // This is a 4-bit  binary number
12'habc // This is a 12-bit  hexadecimal number
16'd255 // This is a 16-bit  decimal number.
```

Unsized numbers

Numbers that are specified without a <*base format*> specification are decimal numbers by default. Numbers that are written without a <*size*> specification have a default number of bits that is simulator- and machine-specific (must be at least 32).

```
23456 // This is a 32-bit   decimal number by default
'hc3 // This is a 32-bit   hexadecimal number
'o21 // This is a 32-bit   octal number
```

X or Z values

Verilog has two symbols for unknown and high impedance values. These values are very important for modeling real circuits. An unknown value is denoted by an **x**. A high impedance value is denoted by **z**.

```
12'h13x // This is a 12-bit hex number; 4 least significant bits unknown
6'hx // This is a 6-bit hex number
32'bz // This is a 32-bit high impedance number
```

An **x** or **z** sets four bits for a number in the hexadecimal base, three bits for a number in the octal base, and one bit for a number in the binary base. If the most significant bit of a number is **0**, **x**, or **z**, the number is automatically extended to fill the most significant bits, respectively, with **0**, **x**, or **z**. This makes it easy to assign **x** or **z** to a whole vector. If the most significant digit is **1**, then it is also zero extended.

Negative numbers

Negative numbers can be specified by putting a minus sign before the size for a constant number. Size constants are always positive. It is illegal to have a minus sign between *<base format>* and *<number>*. An optional signed specifier can be added for signed arithmetic.

```
-6'd3 // 8-bit   negative number stored as 2's complement of 3
-6'sd3 // Used for performing signed integer math
4'd-2 // Illegal specification
```

Underscore characters and question marks

An underscore character "_" is allowed anywhere in a number except the first character. Underscore characters are allowed only to improve readability of numbers and are ignored by Verilog.

A question mark "**?**" is the Verilog HDL alternative for **z** in the context of numbers. The **?** is used to enhance readability in the **casex** and **casez** statements discussed in Chapter 7, where the high impedance value is a don't care condition. (Note that **?** has a different meaning in the context of user-defined primitives, which are discussed in Chapter 12, *User-Defined Primitives.*)

```
12'b1111_0000_1010 // Use of underline characters for readability
4'b10?? // Equivalent of a 4'b10zz
```

3.1.5 Strings

A string is a sequence of characters that are enclosed by double quotes. The restriction on a string is that it must be contained on a single line, that is, without a carriage return. It cannot be on multiple lines. Strings are treated as a sequence of one-byte ASCII values.

```
"Hello Verilog World" // is a string
"a / b" // is a string
```

3.1.6 Identifiers and Keywords

Keywords are special identifiers reserved to define the language constructs. Keywords are in lowercase. A list of all keywords in Verilog is contained in Appendix C, *List of Keywords, System Tasks, and Compiler Directives.*

Identifiers are names given to objects so that they can be referenced in the design. Identifiers are made up of alphanumeric characters, the underscore (_), or the dollar sign ($). Identifiers are case sensitive. Identifiers start with an alphabetic character or an underscore. They cannot start with a digit or a $ sign (The $ sign as the first character is reserved for system tasks, which are explained later in the book).

```
reg value; // reg is a keyword; value is an identifier
input clk; // input is a keyword, clk is an identifier
```

3.1.7 Escaped Identifiers

Escaped identifiers begin with the backslash (\ ) character and end with whitespace (space, tab, or newline). All characters between backslash and whitespace are processed literally. Any printable ASCII character can be included in escaped identifiers. Neither the backslash nor the terminating whitespace is considered to be a part of the identifier.

```
\a+b-c
\**my_name**
```

3.2 Data Types

This section discusses the data types used in Verilog.

3.2.1 Value Set

Verilog supports four values and eight strengths to model the functionality of real hardware. The four value levels are listed in Table 3-1.

Table 3-1 Value Levels

Value Level	Condition in Hardware Circuits
0	Logic zero, false condition
1	Logic one, true condition
x	Unknown logic value
z	High impedance, floating state

In addition to logic values, strength levels are often used to resolve conflicts between drivers of different strengths in digital circuits. Value levels `0` and `1` can have the strength levels listed in Table 3-2.

Table 3-2 Strength Levels

Strength Level	Type	Degree
supply	Driving	strongest
strong	Driving	▲
pull	Driving	
large	Storage	
weak	Driving	
medium	Storage	
small	Storage	
highz	High Impedance	weakest

If two signals of unequal strengths are driven on a wire, the stronger signal prevails. For example, if two signals of strength `strong1` and `weak0` contend, the result is resolved as a `strong1`. If two signals of equal strengths are driven on a wire, the result is unknown. If two signals of strength `strong1` and `strong0` conflict, the result is an `x`. Strength levels are particularly useful for accurate modeling of signal contention, MOS devices, dynamic

MOS, and other low-level devices. Only **trireg** nets can have storage strengths **large**, **medium**, and **small**. Detailed information about strength modeling is provided in Appendix A, *Strength Modeling and Advanced Net Definitions.*

3.2.2 Nets

Nets represent connections between hardware elements. Just as in real circuits, nets have values continuously driven on them by the outputs of devices that they are connected to. In Figure 3-1 net *a* is connected to the output of **and** gate *g1*. Net *a* will continuously assume the value computed at the output of gate *g1,* which is *b* & *c*.

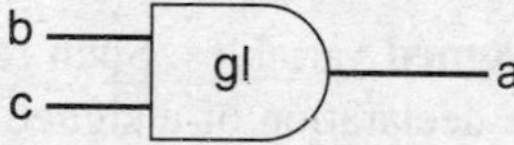

Figure 3-1 Example of Nets

Nets are declared primarily with the keyword **wire**. Nets are one bit values by default unless they are declared explicitly as vectors. The terms **wire** and net are often used interchangeably. The default value of a net is **z** (except the **trireg** net, which defaults to **x**). Nets get the output value of their drivers. If a net has no driver, it gets the value **z**.

```
wire a; // Declare net a for the above circuit
wire b,c; // Declare two wires b,c for the above circuit
wire d = 1'b0; // Net d is fixed to logic value 0 at declaration.
```

Note that *net* is not a keyword but represents a class of data types such as **wire**, **wand**, **wor**, **tri**, **triand**, **trior**, **trireg**, etc. The **wire** declaration is used most frequently. Other net declarations are discussed in Appendix A, *Strength Modeling and Advanced Net Definitions.*

3.2.3 Registers

Registers represent data storage elements. Registers retain value until another value is placed onto them. Do not confuse the term *registers* in Verilog with hardware registers built from edge-triggered flipflops in real circuits. In Verilog, the term *register* merely means a variable that can hold a value. Unlike a net, a register does not need a driver. Verilog registers do not need a clock as hardware registers do. Values of registers can be changed anytime in a simulation by assigning a new value to the register.

Register data types are commonly declared by the keyword **reg**. The default value for a **reg** data type is **x**. An example of how registers are used is shown Example 3-1.

Example 3-1 *Example of Register*

```
reg reset; // declare a variable reset that can hold its value
initial // this construct will be discussed later
begin
  reset = 1'b1; //initialize reset to 1 to reset the digital circuit.
  #100 reset = 1'b0; // after 100 time units reset is deasserted.
end
```

Registers can also be declared as **signed** variables. Such registers can be used for signed arithmetic. Example 3-2 shows the declaration of a signed register.

Example 3-2 *Signed Register Declaration*

```
reg signed [63:0] m; // 64 bit signed value
integer i; // 32 bit signed value
```

3.2.4 Vectors

Nets or **reg** data types can be declared as vectors (multiple bit widths). If bit width is not specified, the default is scalar (1-bit).

```
wire a; // scalar net variable, default
wire [7:0] bus; // 8-bit  bus
wire [31:0] busA,busB,busC; // 3 buses of 32-bit width.
reg clock; // scalar register, default
reg [0:40] virtual_addr; // Vector register, virtual address 41 bits wide
```

Vectors can be declared at *[high# : low#]* or *[low# : high#]*, but the left number in the squared brackets is always the most significant bit of the vector. In the example shown above, bit 0 is the most significant bit of vector *virtual_addr*.

Vector Part Select

For the vector declarations shown above, it is possible to address bits or parts of vectors.

```
busA[7] // bit # 7 of vector busA
bus[2:0] // Three least significant bits of vector bus,
 // using bus[0:2] is illegal because the significant bit should
 // always be on the left of a range specification
virtual_addr[0:1] // Two most significant bits of vector virtual_addr
```

Variable Vector Part Select

Another ability provided in Verilog HDl is to have variable part selects of a vector. This allows part selects to be put in for loops to select various parts of the vector. There are two special part-select operators:

[<starting_bit>+:width] - part-select increments from starting bit

[<starting_bit>-:width] - part-select decrements from starting bit

The starting bit of the part select can be varied, but the width has to be constant. The following example shows the use of variable vector part select:

```
reg [255:0] data1; //Little endian notation
reg [0:255] data2; //Big endian notation
reg [7:0] byte;

//Using a variable part select, one can choose parts
byte = data1[31-:8]; //starting bit = 31, width =8 => data[31:24]
byte = data1[24+:8]; //starting bit = 24, width =8 => data[31:24]
byte = data2[31-:8]; //starting bit = 31, width =8 => data[24:31]
byte = data2[24+:8]; //starting bit = 24, width =8 => data[24:31]

//The starting bit can also be a variable. The width has
//to be constant. Therefore, one can use the variable part select
//in a loop to select all bytes of the vector.
for (j=0; j<=31; j=j+1)
    byte = data1[(j*8)+:8]; //Sequence is [7:0], [15:8]... [255:248]

//Can initialize a part of the vector
data1[(byteNum*8)+:8] = 8'b0; //If byteNum = 1, clear 8 bits [15:8]
```

3.2.5 Integer , Real, and Time Register Data Types

`Integer`, **`real`**, and **`time`** register data types are supported in Verilog.

Integer

An integer is a general purpose register data type used for manipulating quantities. Integers are declared by the keyword **`integer`**. Although it is possible to use **`reg`** as a general-purpose variable, it is more convenient to declare an **`integer`** variable for purposes such as counting. The default width for an integer is the host-machine word size, which is implementation-specific but is at least 32 bits. Registers declared as data type **`reg`** store values as *unsigned* quantities, whereas integers store values as *signed* quantities.

```
integer counter; // general purpose variable used as a counter.
initial
    counter = -1; // A negative one is stored in the counter
```

Real

Real number constants and real register data types are declared with the keyword **`real`**. They can be specified in *decimal* notation (e.g., 3.14) or in *scientific* notation (e.g., 3e6, which is 3 x 10^6). Real numbers cannot have a range declaration, and their default value is 0. When a real value is assigned to an integer, the real number is rounded off to the nearest integer.

```
real delta; // Define a real variable called delta
initial
begin
    delta = 4e10; // delta is assigned in scientific notation
    delta = 2.13; // delta is assigned a value 2.13
end
integer i; // Define an integer i
initial
    i = delta; // i gets the value 2 (rounded value of 2.13)
```

Time

Verilog simulation is done with respect to *simulation time*. A special time register data type is used in Verilog to store simulation time. A time variable is declared with the keyword **time**. The width for time register data types is implementation-specific but is at least 64 bits.The system function **$time** is invoked to get the current simulation time.

```
time save_sim_time; // Define a time variable save_sim_time
initial
   save_sim_time = $time; // Save the current simulation time
```

Simulation time is measured in terms of *simulation seconds*. The unit is denoted by *s*, the same as real time. However, the relationship between real time in the digital circuit and simulation time is left to the user. This is discussed in detail in Section 9.4, *Time Scales*.

3.2.6 Arrays

Arrays are allowed in Verilog for **reg**, **integer**, **time**, **real**, **realtime** and *vector* register data types. Multi-dimensional arrays can also be declared with any number of dimensions. Arrays of nets can also be used to connect ports of generated instances. Each element of the array can be used in the same fashion as a scalar or vector net. Arrays are accessed by *<array_name>* [*<subscript>*]. For multi-dimensional arrays, indexes need to be provided for each dimension.

```
integer count[0:7]; //An array of 8 count variables

reg bool[31:0]; //Array of 32 one-bit boolean register variables

time chk_point[1:100]; //Array of 100 time checkpoint variables

reg [4:0] port_id[0:7]; //Array of 8 port_ids; each port_id is 5 bits wide

integer matrix[4:0][0:255]; //Two dimensional array of integers

reg [63:0] array_4d [15:0][7:0][7:0][255:0]; //Four dimensional array

wire [7:0] w_array2 [5:0]; //Declare an array of 8 bit vector wire

wire w_array1[7:0][5:0]; //Declare an array of single bit wires
```

It is important not to confuse arrays with net or register vectors. A vector is a single element that is *n*-bits wide. On the other hand, arrays are multiple elements that are *1*-bit or *n*-bits wide.

Examples of assignments to elements of arrays discussed above are shown below:

```
count[5] = 0; //Reset 5th element of array of count variables
chk_point[100] = 0; //Reset 100th time check point value
port_id[3] = 0; //Reset 3rd element (a 5-bit value) of port_id array.

matrix[1][0] = 33559; //Set value of element indexed by [1][0] to 33559
array_4d[0][0][0][0][15:0] = 0; //Clear bits 15:0 of the register
                                //accessed by indices [0][0][0][0]

port_id = 0; //Illegal syntax - Attempt to write the entire array
matrix [1] = 0; //Illegal syntax - Attempt to write [1][0]..[1][255]
```

3.2.7 Memories

In digital simulation, one often needs to model register files, RAMs, and ROMs. Memories are modeled in Verilog simply as a one-dimensional array of registers. Each element of the array is known as an *element* or *word* and is addressed by a single array index. Each word can be one or more bits. It is important to differentiate between *n* 1-bit registers and one *n*-bit register. A particular word in memory is obtained by using the address as a memory array subscript.

```
reg mem1bit[0:1023]; //Memory mem1bit with 1K 1-bit words
reg [7:0] membyte[0:1023]; //Memory membyte with 1K 8-bit words(bytes)
membyte[511] //Fetches 1 byte word whose address is 511.
```

3.2.8 Parameters

Verilog allows constants to be defined in a module by the keyword **parameter**. Parameters cannot be used as variables. Parameter values for each module instance can be overridden individually at compile time. This allows the module instances to be customized. This aspect is discussed later. Parameter types and sizes can also be defined.

```
parameter port_id = 5; //Defines a constant port_id
parameter cache_line_width=256; //Constant defines width of cache line
parameter signed [15:0] WIDTH; // Fixed sign and range for parameter
                                // WIDTH
```

Module definitions may be written in terms of parameters. Hardcoded numbers should be avoided. Parameters values can be changed at module instantiation or by using the **defparam** statement, which is discussed in detail in Chapter 9, *Useful Modeling Techniques*. Thus, the use of parameters makes the module definition flexible. Module behavior can be altered simply by changing the value of a parameter.

Verilog HDL local parameters (defined using keyword **localparam** -) are identical to parameters except that they cannot be directly modified with the **defparam** statement or by the ordered or named parameter value assignment. The **localparam** keyword is used to define parameters when their values should not be changed. For example, the state encoding for a state machine can be defined using **localparam**. The state encoding cannot be changed. This provides protection against inadvertent parameter redefinition.

```
localparam state1 = 4'b0001,
           state2 = 4'b0010,
           state3 = 4'b0100,
           state4 = 4'b1000;
```

3.2.9 Strings

Strings can be stored in **reg**. The width of the register variables must be large enough to hold the string. Each character in the string takes up 8 bits (1 byte). If the width of the register is greater than the size of the string, Verilog fills bits to the left of the string with zeros. If the register width is smaller than the string width, Verilog truncates the leftmost bits of the string. It is always safe to declare a string that is slightly wider than necessary.

```
reg [8*18:1] string_value; //Declare a variable that is 18 bytes wide
initial
    string_value = "Hello Verilog World"; // String can be stored
                                          // in variable
```

Special characters serve a special purpose in displaying strings, such as newline, tabs, and displaying argument values. Special characters can be displayed in strings only when they are preceded by escape characters, as shown in Table 3-3.

Table 3-3 Special Characters

Escaped Characters	Character Displayed
\n	newline
\t	tab
%%	%
\\	\
\"	"
\ooo	Character written in 1–3 octal digits

3.3 System Tasks and Compiler Directives

In this section, we introduce two special concepts used in Verilog: system tasks and compiler directives.

3.3.1 System Tasks

Verilog provides standard system tasks for certain routine operations. All system tasks appear in the form **$<keyword>**. Operations such as displaying on the screen, monitoring values of nets, stopping, and finishing are done by system tasks. We will discuss only the most useful system tasks. Other tasks are listed in Verilog manuals provided by your simulator vendor or in the *IEEE Standard Verilog Hardware Description Language* specification.

Displaying information

$display is the main system task for displaying values of variables or strings or expressions. This is one of the most useful tasks in Verilog.

Usage: **$display***(p1, p2, p3,....., pn);*

p1, p2, p3,..., pn can be quoted strings or variables or expressions. The format of **$display** is very similar to `printf` in C. A **$display** inserts a newline at the end of the string by default. A **$display** without any arguments produces a newline.

Strings can be formatted using the specifications listed in Table 3-4. For more detailed specifications, see *IEEE Standard Verilog Hardware Description Language* specification.

Table 3-4 String Format Specifications

Format	Display
%d or %D	Display variable in decimal
%b or %B	Display variable in binary
%s or %S	Display string
%h or %H	Display variable in hex
%c or %C	Display ASCII character
%m or %M	Display hierarchical name (no argument required)
%v or %V	Display strength
%o or %O	Display variable in octal
%t or %T	Display in current time format
%e or %E	Display real number in scientific format (e.g., 3e10)
%f or %F	Display real number in decimal format (e.g., 2.13)
%g or %G	Display real number in scientific or decimal, whichever is shorter

Example 3-3 shows some examples of the **$display** task. If variables contain **x** or **z** values, they are printed in the displayed string as "**x**" or "**z**".

Example 3-3 $display Task

```
//Display the string in quotes
$display("Hello Verilog World");
-- Hello Verilog World

//Display value of current simulation time 230
$display($time);
```

Example 3-3 *$display Task (Continued)*

```
-- 230

//Display value of 41-bit virtual address 1fe0000001c at time 200
reg [0:40] virtual_addr;
$display("At time %d virtual address is %h", $time, virtual_addr);
-- At time 200 virtual address is 1fe0000001c

//Display value of port_id 5 in binary
reg [4:0] port_id;
$display("ID of the port is %b", port_id);
-- ID of the port is 00101

//Display x characters
//Display value of 4-bit bus 10xx (signal contention) in binary
reg [3:0] bus;
$display("Bus value is %b", bus);
-- Bus value is 10xx

//Display the hierarchical name of instance p1 instantiated under
//the highest-level module called top. No argument is required. This
//is a useful feature)
$display("This string is displayed from %m level of hierarchy");
-- This string is displayed from top.p1 level of hierarchy
```

Special characters are discussed in Section 3.2.9, *Strings*. Examples of displaying special characters in strings as discussed are shown in Example 3-4.

Example 3-4 *Special Characters*

```
//Display special characters, newline and %
$display("This is a \n multiline string with a %% sign");
-- This is a
-- multiline string with a % sign

//Display other special characters
```

Monitoring information

Verilog provides a mechanism to monitor a signal when its value changes. This facility is provided by the **$monitor** task.

Usage: **$monitor**(*p1,p2,p3,....,pn*)**;**

The parameters *p1*, *p2*, ... , *pn* can be variables, signal names, or quoted strings. A format similar to the **`$display`** task is used in the **`$monitor`** task. **`$monitor`** continuously monitors the values of the variables or signals specified in the parameter list and displays all parameters in the list whenever the value of any one variable or signal changes. Unlike **`$display`**, **`$monitor`** needs to be invoked only once.

Only one monitoring list can be active at a time. If there is more than one **`$monitor`** statement in your simulation, the last **`$monitor`** statement will be the active statement. The earlier **`$monitor`** statements will be overridden.

Two tasks are used to switch monitoring on and off.

Usage: **`$monitoron;`**

`$monitoroff;`

The **`$monitoron`** tasks enables monitoring, and the **`$monitoroff`** task disables monitoring during a simulation. Monitoring is turned on by default at the beginning of the simulation and can be controlled during the simulation with the **`$monitoron`** and **`$monitoroff`** tasks. Examples of monitoring statements are given in Example 3-5. Note the use of **`$time`** in the **`$monitor`** statement.

Example 3-5 *Monitor Statement*

```
//Monitor time and value of the signals clock and reset
//Clock toggles every 5 time units and reset goes down at 10 time units
initial
begin
   $monitor($time,
            " Value of signals clock = %b reset = %b", clock,reset);
end
```

Partial output of the monitor statement:

```
-- 0 Value of signals clock = 0 reset = 1
-- 5 Value of signals clock = 1 reset = 1
-- 10 Value of signals clock = 0 reset = 0
```

Stopping and finishing in a simulation

The task **`$stop`** is provided to stop during a simulation.

Usage: **`$stop;`**

The **`$stop`** task puts the simulation in an interactive mode. The designer can then debug the design from the interactive mode. The **`$stop`** task is used whenever the designer wants to suspend the simulation and examine the values of signals in the design.

The **`$finish`** task terminates the simulation.

Usage: **$finish;**

Examples of **$stop** and **$finish** are shown in Example 3-6.

Example 3-6 Stop and Finish Tasks

```
// Stop at time 100 in the simulation and examine the results
// Finish the simulation at time 1000.
initial // to be explained later. time = 0
begin
clock = 0;
reset = 1;
#100 $stop; // This will suspend the simulation at time = 100
#900 $finish; // This will terminate the simulation at time = 1000
end
```

3.3.2 Compiler Directives

Compiler directives are provided in Verilog. All compiler directives are defined by using the **`<keyword>** construct. We deal with the two most useful compiler directives.

`define

The **`define** directive is used to define text macros in Verilog (see Example 3-7). The Verilog compiler substitutes the text of the macro wherever it encounters a `*<macro_name>*. This is similar to the *#define* construct in C. The defined constants or text macros are used in the Verilog code by preceding them with a ` (back tick).

Example 3-7 `define Directive

```
//define a text macro that defines default word size
//Used as 'WORD_SIZE in the code
'define WORD_SIZE 32

//define an alias. A $stop will be substituted wherever 'S appears
'define S $stop;

//define a frequently used text string
'define WORD_REG reg [31:0]
// you can then define a 32-bit register as 'WORD_REG reg32;
```

`include

The `` `include `` directive allows you to include entire contents of a Verilog source file in another Verilog file during compilation. This works similarly to the *#include* in the C programming language. This directive is typically used to include header files, which typically contain global or commonly used definitions (see Example 3-8).

Example 3-8 `include Directive

```
// Include the file header.v, which contains declarations in the
// main verilog file design.v.
'include header.v
...
...
<Verilog code in file design.v>
...
...
```

Two other directives, `` `ifdef `` and `` `timescale ``, are used frequently. They are discussed in Chapter 9, *Useful Modeling Techniques*.

3.4 Summary

We discussed the basic concepts of Verilog in this chapter. These concepts lay the foundation for the material discussed in the later chapters.

- Verilog is similar in syntax to the C programming language. Hardware designers with previous C programming experience will find Verilog easy to learn.
- Lexical conventions for operators, comments, whitespace, numbers, strings, and identifiers were discussed.
- Various data types are available in Verilog. There are four logic values, each with different strength levels. Available data types include nets, registers, vectors, numbers, simulation time, arrays, memories, parameters, and strings. Data types represent actual hardware elements very closely.
- Verilog provides useful system tasks to do functions like displaying, monitoring, suspending, and finishing a simulation.
- Compiler directive `` `define `` is used to define text macros, and `` `include `` is used to include other Verilog files.

3.5 Exercises

1. Practice writing the following numbers:

   a. Decimal number 123 as a sized 8-bit number in binary. Use _ for readability.

   b. A 16-bit hexadecimal unknown number with all **x**'s.

   c. A 4-bit negative 2 in decimal . Write the 2's complement form for this number.

   d. An unsized hex number *1234*.

2. Are the following legal strings? If not, write the correct strings.

   a. *"This is a string displaying the % sign"*

   b. *"out = in1 + in2"*

   c. *"Please ring a bell \007"*

   d. *"This is a backslash \ character\n"*

3. Are these legal identifiers?

   a. *system1*

   b. *1reg*

   c. *$latch*

   d. *exec$*

4. Declare the following variables in Verilog:

   a. An 8-bit vector net called *a_in*.

   b. A 32-bit storage register called *address*. Bit 31 must be the most significant bit. Set the value of the register to a 32-bit decimal number equal to 3.

   c. An integer called *count*.

   d. A time variable called *snap_shot*.

   e. An array called *delays*. Array contains 20 elements of the type **integer**.

   f. A memory *MEM* containing 256 words of 64 bits each.

   g. A parameter *cache_size* equal to 512.

5. What would be the output/effect of the following statements?

   a. *latch = 4'd12;*
   $display(*"The current value of latch = %b\n", latch);*

   b. *in_reg = 3'd2;*
   **$monitor**(*$time, " In register value = %b\n", in_reg[2:0]);*

   c. **`define** *MEM_SIZE 1024*
   $display(*"The maximum memory size is %h", 'MEM_SIZE);*

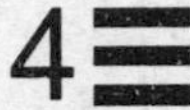

Modules and Ports 4

In the previous chapters, we acquired an understanding of the fundamental hierarchical modeling concepts, basic conventions, and Verilog constructs. In this chapter, we take a closer look at modules and ports from the Verilog language point of view.

Learning Objectives

- Identify the components of a Verilog module definition, such as module names, port lists, parameters, variable declarations, dataflow statements, behavioral statements, instantiation of other modules, and tasks or functions.
- Understand how to define the port list for a module and declare it in Verilog.
- Describe the port connection rules in a module instantiation.
- Understand how to connect ports to external signals, by ordered list, and by name.
- Explain hierarchical name referencing of Verilog identifiers.

4.1 Modules

We discussed how a module is a basic building block in Chapter 2, *Hierarchical Modeling Concepts.* We ignored the internals of modules and concentrated on how modules are defined and instantiated. In this section, we analyze the internals of the module in greater detail.

A module in Verilog consists of distinct parts, as shown in Figure 4-1.

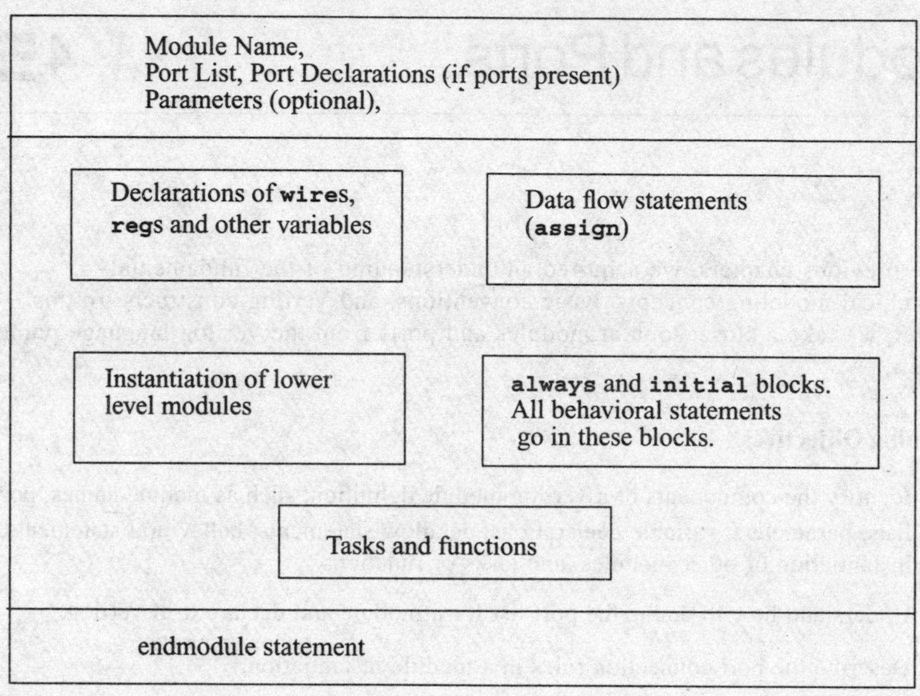

Figure 4-1 Components of a Verilog Module

A module definition always begins with the keyword **`module`**. The *module name, port list, port declarations*, and optional *parameters* must come first in a module definition. *Port list* and *port declarations* are present only if the module has any ports to interact with the external environment.The five components within a module are: *variable declarations, dataflow statements, instantiation of lower modules, behavioral blocks*, and *tasks* or *functions*. These components can be in any order and at any place in the module definition. The **`endmodule`** statement must always come last in a module definition. All components except **`module`**, *module name*, and **`endmodule`** are optional and can be mixed and matched as per design needs. Verilog allows multiple modules to be defined in a single file. The modules can be defined in any order in the file.

To understand the components of the module shown above, let us consider a simple example of an *SR latch*, as shown in Figure 4-2.

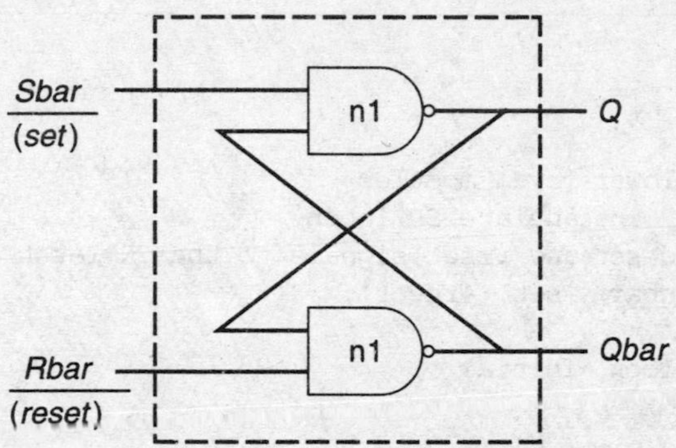

Figure 4-2 *SR Latch*

The *SR latch* has *S* and *R* as the input ports and *Q* and *Qbar* as the output ports. The *SR latch* and its stimulus can be modeled as shown in Example 4-1.

Example 4-1 ***Components of SR Latch***

```
// This example illustrates the different components of a module

// Module name and port list
// SR_latch module
module SR_latch(Q, Qbar, Sbar, Rbar);

//Port declarations
output Q, Qbar;
input Sbar, Rbar;

// Instantiate lower-level modules
// In this case, instantiate Verilog primitive nand gates
// Note, how the wires are connected in a cross-coupled fashion.
nand n1(Q, Sbar, Qbar);
nand n2(Qbar, Rbar, Q);

// endmodule statement
endmodule

// Module name and port list
// Stimulus module
module Top;

// Declarations of wire, reg, and other variables
```

Example 4-1 Components of SR Latch (Continued)

```
wire q, qbar;
reg set, reset;

// Instantiate lower-level modules
// In this case, instantiate SR_latch
// Feed inverted set and reset signals to the SR latch
SR_latch m1(q, qbar, ~set, ~reset);

// Behavioral block, initial
initial
begin
  $monitor($time, " set = %b, reset= %b, q= %b\n",set,reset,q);
  set = 0; reset = 0;
  #5 reset = 1;
  #5 reset = 0;
  #5 set = 1;
end

// endmodule statement
endmodule
```

Notice the following characteristics about the modules defined above:

- In the *SR latch* definition above, notice that all components described in Figure 4-1 need not be present in a module. We do not find *variable declarations, dataflow* (**assign**) *statements*, or *behavioral blocks* (**always** or **initial**).
- However, the stimulus block for the SR latch contains *module name, wire, reg*, and *variable declarations, instantiation of lower level modules, behavioral block* (**initial**), and **endmodule** statement but does not contain *port list, port declarations*, and *data flow* (**assign**) statements.
- Thus, all parts except **module**, *module name*, and **endmodule** are optional and can be mixed and matched as per design needs.

4.2 Ports

Ports provide the interface by which a module can communicate with its environment. For example, the *input/output* pins of an IC chip are its ports. The environment can interact with the module only through its ports. The internals of the module are not visible to the environment. This provides a very powerful flexibility to the designer. The internals of the module can be changed without affecting the environment as long as the interface is not modified. Ports are also referred to as *terminals.*

4.2.1 List of Ports

A module definition contains an optional list of ports. If the module does not exchange any signals with the environment, there are no ports in the list. Consider a 4-bit full adder that is instantiated inside a top-level module *Top*. The diagram for the *input/output* ports is shown in Figure 4-3.

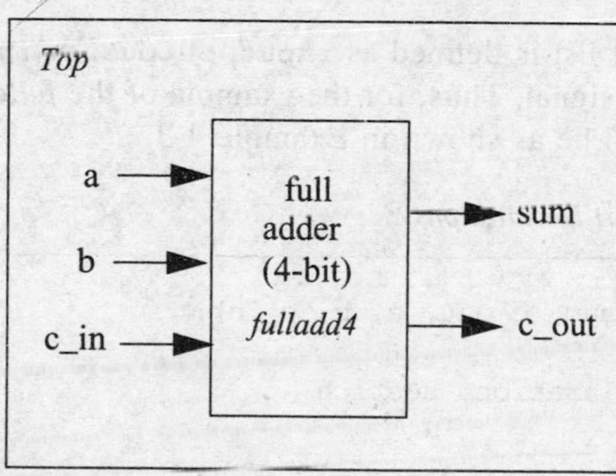

Figure 4-3 I/O Ports for Top and Full Adder

Notice that in the above figure, the module *Top* is a top-level module. The module *fulladd4* is instantiated below *Top*. The module *fulladd4* takes input on ports *a, b,* and *c_in* and produces an output on ports *sum* and *c_out*. Thus, module *fulladd4* performs an addition for its environment. The module *Top* is a top-level module in the simulation and does not need to pass signals to or receive signals from the environment. Thus, it does not have a list of ports. The module names and port lists for both module declarations in Verilog are as shown in Example 4-2.

Example 4-2 List of Ports

```
module fulladd4(sum, c_out, a, b, c_in); //Module with a list of ports
module Top; // No list of ports, top-level module in simulation
```

4.2.2 Port Declaration

All ports in the list of ports must be declared in the module. Ports can be declared as follows:

Verilog Keyword	Type of Port
input	Input port
output	Output port
inout	Bidirectional port

Each port in the port list is defined as **input**, **output**, or **inout**, based on the direction of the port signal. Thus, for the example of the *fulladd4* in Example 4-2, the port declarations will be as shown in Example 4-3.

Example 4-3 Port Declarations

```
module fulladd4(sum, c_out, a, b, c_in);

//Begin port declarations section
output[3:0] sum;
output c_cout;

input [3:0] a, b;
input c_in;
//End port declarations section
...
<module internals>
...
endmodule
```

Note that all port declarations are implicitly declared as **wire** in Verilog. Thus, if a port is intended to be a **wire**, it is sufficient to declare it as **output**, **input**, or **inout**. **Input** or **inout** ports are normally declared as **wires**. However, if **output** ports hold their value, they must be declared as **reg**. For example, in the definition of *DFF*, in Example 2-5, we wanted the output *q* to retain its value until the next clock edge. The port declarations for *DFF* will look as shown in Example 4-4.

Example 4-4 Port Declarations for DFF

```
module DFF(q, d, clk, reset);
output q;
reg q; // Output port q holds value; therefore it is declared as reg.
input d, clk, reset;
...
...
endmodule
```

Ports of the type **input** and **inout** cannot be declared as **reg** because **reg** variables store values and input ports should not store values but simply reflect the changes in the external signals they are connected to.

Note that the module *fulladd4* in Example 4-3 can be declared using an ANSI C style syntax to specify the ports of that module. Each declared port provides the complete information about the port. Example 4-5 shows this alternate syntax. This syntax avoids the duplication of naming the ports in both the module definition statement and the module port list definitions. If a port is declared but no data type is specified, then, under specific circumstances, the signal will default to a *wire* data type.

Example 4-5 ANSI C Style Port Declaration Syntax

```
module fulladd4(output reg [3:0] sum,
                output reg c_out,
                input [3:0] a, b, //wire by default
                input c_in); //wire by default
...
<module internals>
...
endmodule
```

4.2.3 Port Connection Rules

One can visualize a port as consisting of two units, one unit that is *internal* to the module and another that is *external* to the module. The internal and external units are connected. There are rules governing port connections when modules are instantiated within other modules. The Verilog simulator complains if any port connection rules are violated. These rules are summarized in Figure 4-4.

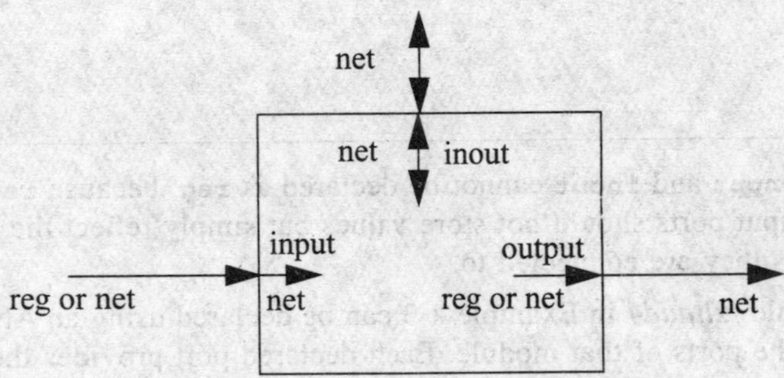

Figure 4-4 Port Connection Rules

Inputs

Internally, input ports must always be of the type *net*. Externally, the inputs can be connected to a variable which is a `reg` or a *net*.

Outputs

Internally, outputs ports can be of the type `reg` or *net*. Externally, outputs must always be connected to a *net*. They cannot be connected to a `reg`.

Inouts

Internally, inout ports must always be of the type *net*. Externally, inout ports must always be connected to a *net*.

Width matching

It is legal to connect internal and external items of different sizes when making inter-module port connections. However, a warning is typically issued that the widths do not match.

Unconnected ports

Verilog allows ports to remain unconnected. For example, certain output ports might be simply for debugging, and you might not be interested in connecting them to the external signals. You can let a port remain unconnected by instantiating a module as shown below.

```
fulladd4 fa0(SUM, , A, B, C_IN); // Output port c_out is unconnected
```

Example of illegal port connection

To illustrate port connection rules, assume that the module *fulladd4* in Example 4-3 is instantiated in the stimulus block *Top*. Example 4-6 shows an illegal port connection.

Example 4-6 Illegal Port Connection

```
module Top;

//Declare connection variables
reg [3:0]A,B;
reg C_IN;
reg [3:0] SUM;
wire C_OUT;

    //Instantiate fulladd4, call it fa0
    fulladd4 fa0(SUM, C_OUT, A, B, C_IN);
    //Illegal connection because output port sum in module fulladd4
    //is connected to a register variable SUM in module Top.
    .
    .
    <stimulus>
    .
    .
endmodule
```

This problem is rectified if the variable *SUM* is declared as a *net* (**wire**).

4.2.4 Connecting Ports to External Signals

There are two methods of making connections between signals specified in the module instantiation and the ports in a module definition. These two methods cannot be mixed. These methods are discussed in the following sections.

Connecting by ordered list

Connecting by ordered list is the most intuitive method for most beginners. The signals to be connected must appear in the module instantiation in the same order as the ports in the port list in the module definition. Once again, consider the module *fulladd4* defined in Example 4-3. To connect signals in module *Top* by ordered list, the Verilog code is shown in Example 4-7. Notice that the external signals *SUM, C_OUT, A, B,* and *C_IN* appear in exactly the same order as the ports *sum, c_out, a, b,* and *c_in* in the module definition of *fulladd4*.

Example 4-7 *Connection by Ordered List*

```
module Top;

//Declare connection variables
reg [3:0]A,B;
reg C_IN;
wire [3:0] SUM;
wire C_OUT;

    //Instantiate fulladd4, call it fa_ordered.
    //Signals are connected to ports in order (by position)
    fulladd4 fa_ordered(SUM, C_OUT, A, B, C_IN);
    ...
    <stimulus>
    ...
endmodule


module fulladd4(sum, c_out, a, b, c_in);
output[3:0] sum;
output c_cout;
input [3:0] a, b;
input c_in;
    ...
    <module internals>
    ...
endmodule
```

Connecting ports by name

For large designs where modules have, say, 50 ports, remembering the order of the ports in the module definition is impractical and error-prone. Verilog provides the capability to connect external signals to ports by the port names, rather than by position. We could connect the ports by name in Example 4-7 above by instantiating the module *fulladd4*, as follows. Note that you can specify the port connections in any order as long as the port name in the module definition correctly matches the external signal.

```
// Instantiate module fa_byname and connect signals to ports by name
fulladd4 fa_byname(.c_out(C_OUT), .sum(SUM), .b(B), .c_in(C_IN), .a(A),);
```

Note that only those ports that are to be connected to external signals must be specified in port connection by name. Unconnected ports can be dropped. For example, if the port *c_out* were to be kept unconnected, the instantiation of *fulladd4* would look as follows. The port *c_out* is simply dropped from the port list.

```
// Instantiate module fa_byname and connect signals to ports by name
fulladd4 fa_byname(.sum(SUM), .b(B), .c_in(C_IN), .a(A),);
```

Another advantage of connecting ports by name is that as long as the port name is not changed, the order of ports in the port list of a module can be rearranged without changing the port connections in module instantiations.

4.3 Hierarchical Names

We described earlier how Verilog supports a hierarchical design methodology. Every module instance, signal, or variable is defined with an *identifier*. A particular identifier has a unique place in the design hierarchy. *Hierarchical name referencing* allows us to denote every identifier in the design hierarchy with a unique name. A *hierarchical name* is a list of identifiers separated by dots ("**.**") for each level of hierarchy. Thus, any identifier can be addressed from any place in the design by simply specifying the complete hierarchical name of that identifier.

The top-level module is called the *root* module because it is not instantiated anywhere. It is the starting point. To assign a unique name to an identifier, start from the top-level module and trace the path along the design hierarchy to the desired identifier. To clarify this process, let us consider the simulation of SR latch in Example 4-1. The design hierarchy is shown in Figure 4-5.

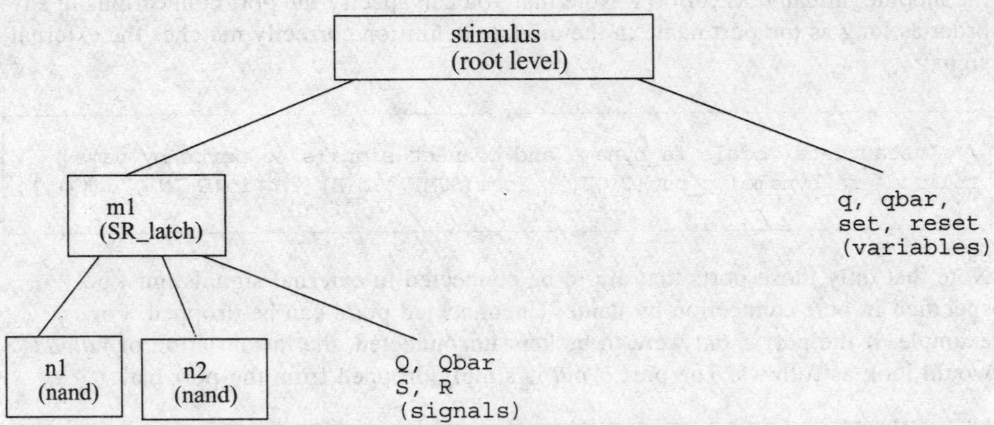

Figure 4-5 Design Hierarchy for SR Latch Simulation

For this simulation, *stimulus* is the top-level module. Since the top-level module is not instantiated anywhere, it is called the *root* module. The identifiers defined in this module are *q, qbar, set,* and *reset*. The root module instantiates *m1,* which is a module of type *SR_latch*. The module *m1* instantiates **nand** gates *n1* and *n2*. *Q, Qbar, S,* and *R* are port signals in instance *m1*. Hierarchical name referencing assigns a unique name to each identifier. To assign hierarchical names, use the module name for root module and instance names for all module instances below the root module. Example 4-8 shows hierarchical names for all identifiers in the above simulation. Notice that there is a dot (`.`) for each level of hierarchy from the *root* module to the desired identifier.

Example 4-8 Hierarchical Names

```
stimulus                        stimulus.q
stimulus.qbar                   stimulus.set
stimulus.reset                  stimulus.m1
stimulus.m1.Q                   stimulus.m1.Qbar
stimulus.m1.S                   stimulus.m1.R
stimulus.n1                     stimulus.n2
```

Each identifier in the design is uniquely specified by its hierarchical path name. To display the level of hierarchy, use the special character *%m* in the **`$display`** task. See Table 3-4, *String Format Specifications*, for details.

4.4 Summary

In this chapter, we discussed the following aspects of Verilog:

- Module definitions contain various components. Keywords **`module`** and **`endmodule`** are mandatory. Other components—*port list*, *port declarations*, *variable* and *signal declarations*, *dataflow statements*, *behavioral blocks*, *lower-level module instantiations,* and *tasks* or *functions*—are optional and can be added as needed.
- Ports provide the module with a means to communicate with other modules or its environment. A module can have a port list. Ports in the port list must be declared as **`input`**, **`output`**, or **`inout`**. When instantiating a module, port connection rules are enforced by the Verilog simulator. An ANSI C style embeds the port declarations in the module definition statement.
- Ports can be connected by *name* or by *ordered list.*
- Each identifier in the design has a unique hierarchical name. Hierarchical names allow us to address any identifier in the design from any other level of hierarchy in the design.

4.5 Exercises

1. What are the basic components of a module? Which components are mandatory?
2. Does a module that does not interact with its environment have any I/O ports? Does it have a port list in the module definition?
3. A 4-bit parallel shift register has I/O pins as shown in the figure below. Write the module definition for this module *shift_reg*. Include the list of ports and port declarations. You do not need to show the internals.

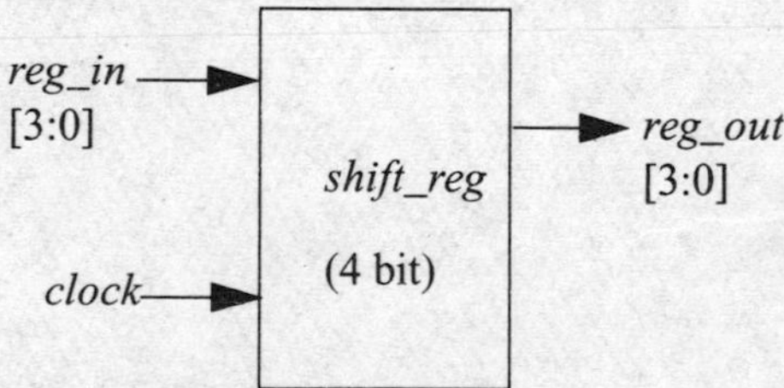

4. Declare a top-level module *stimulus*. Define *REG_IN* (4 bit) and *CLK* (1 bit) as **`reg`** register variables and *REG_OUT* (4 bit) as **`wire`**. Instantiate the module *shift_reg* and call it *sr1*. Connect the ports by ordered list.

5. Connect the ports in Step 4 by name.
6. Write the hierarchical names for variables *REG_IN*, *CLK*, and *REG_OUT*.
7. Write the hierarchical name for the instance *sr1*. Write the hierarchical names for its ports *clock* and *reg_in*.

Gate-Level Modeling

In the earlier chapters, we laid the foundations of Verilog design by discussing design methodologies, basic conventions and constructs, modules and port interfaces. In this chapter, we get into modeling actual hardware circuits in Verilog.

We discussed the four levels of abstraction used to describe hardware. In this chapter, we discuss a design at a low level of abstraction—*gate* level. Most digital design is now done at gate level or higher levels of abstraction. At gate level, the circuit is described in terms of gates (e.g., **and**, **nand**). Hardware design at this level is intuitive for a user with a basic knowledge of digital logic design because it is possible to see a one-to-one correspondence between the logic circuit diagram and the Verilog description. Hence, in this book, we chose to start with gate-level modeling and move to higher levels of abstraction in the succeeding chapters.

Actually, the lowest level of abstraction is *switch-* (transistor-) level modeling. However, with designs getting very complex, very few hardware designers work at switch level. Therefore, we will defer switch-level modeling to Chapter 11, *Switch-Level Modeling*, in Part 2 of this book.

Learning Objectives

- Identify logic gate primitives provided in Verilog.
- Understand instantiation of gates, gate symbols, and truth tables for *and/or* and *buf/not* type gates.
- Understand how to construct a Verilog description from the logic diagram of the circuit.
- Describe *rise, fall*, and *turn-off* delays in the gate-level design.
- Explain *min, max*, and *typ* delays in the gate-level design.

5.1 Gate Types

A logic circuit can be designed by use of logic gates. Verilog supports basic logic gates as predefined *primitives*. These primitives are instantiated like modules except that they are predefined in Verilog and do not need a module definition. All logic circuits can be designed by using basic gates. There are two classes of basic gates: *and/or* gates and *buf/not* gates.

5.1.1 And/Or Gates

and/or gates have *one* scalar output and *multiple* scalar inputs. The first terminal in the list of gate terminals is an output and the other terminals are inputs. The output of a gate is evaluated as soon as one of the inputs changes. The **and/or** gates available in Verilog are shown below.

```
and     or     xor
nand    nor    xnor
```

The corresponding logic symbols for these gates are shown in Figure 5-1. We consider gates with two inputs. The output terminal is denoted by *out*. Input terminals are denoted by *i1* and *i2*.

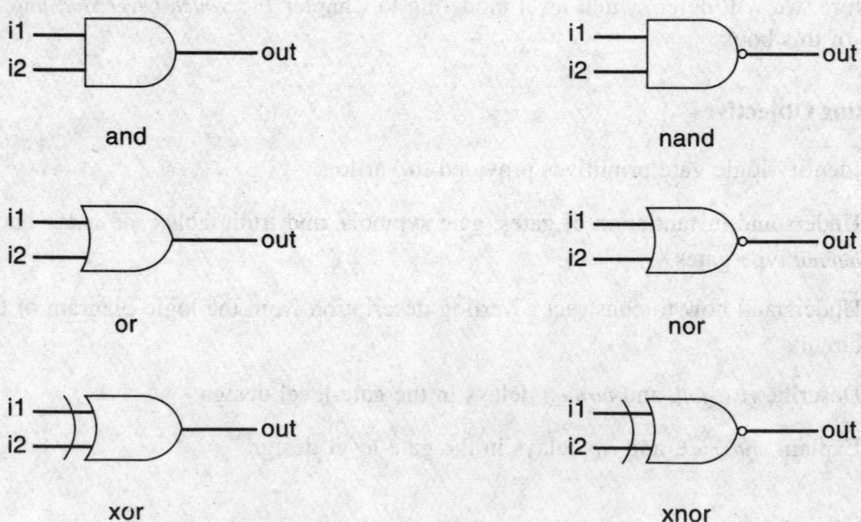

Figure 5-1 Basic Gates

These gates are instantiated to build logic circuits in Verilog. Examples of gate instantiations are shown below. In Example 5-1, for all instances, *OUT* is connected to the output *out*, and *IN1* and *IN2* are connected to the two inputs *i1* and *i2* of the gate primitives. Note that the instance name does not need to be specified for primitives. This lets the designer instantiate hundreds of gates without giving them a name.

More than two inputs can be specified in a gate instantiation. Gates with more than two inputs are instantiated by simply adding more input ports in the gate instantiation (see Example 5-1). Verilog automatically instantiates the appropriate gate.

Example 5-1 *Gate Instantiation of And/Or Gates*

```
wire OUT, IN1, IN2;

// basic gate instantiations.
and a1(OUT, IN1, IN2);
nand na1(OUT, IN1, IN2);
or or1(OUT, IN1, IN2);
nor nor1(OUT, IN1, IN2);
xor x1(OUT, IN1, IN2);
xnor nx1(OUT, IN1, IN2);

// More than two inputs; 3 input nand gate
nand na1_3inp(OUT, IN1, IN2, IN3);

// gate instantiation without instance name
and (OUT, IN1, IN2); // legal gate instantiation
```

The truth tables for these gates define how outputs for the gates are computed from the inputs. Truth tables are defined assuming two inputs. The truth tables for these gates are shown in Table 5-1. Outputs of gates with more than two inputs are computed by applying the truth table iteratively.

Table 5-1 Truth Tables for And/Or Gates

and		i1			
		0	1	x	z
i2	0	0	0	0	0
	1	0	1	x	x
	x	0	x	x	x
	z	0	x	x	x

nand		i1			
		0	1	x	z
i2	0	1	1	1	1
	1	1	0	x	x
	x	1	x	x	x
	z	1	x	x	x

or		i1			
		0	1	x	z
i2	0	0	1	x	x
	1	1	1	1	1
	x	x	1	x	x
	z	x	1	x	x

nor		i1			
		0	1	x	z
i2	0	1	0	x	x
	1	0	0	0	0
	x	x	0	x	x
	z	x	0	x	x

xor		i1			
		0	1	x	z
i2	0	0	1	x	x
	1	1	0	x	x
	x	x	x	x	x
	z	x	x	x	x

xnor		i1			
		0	1	x	z
i2	0	1	0	x	x
	1	0	1	x	x
	x	x	x	x	x
	z	x	x	x	x

5.1.2 Buf/Not Gates

Buf/not gates have one scalar input and one or more scalar outputs. The last terminal in the port list is connected to the input. Other terminals are connected to the outputs. We will discuss gates that have one input and one output.

Two basic *buf/not* gate primitives are provided in Verilog.

```
buf         not
```

The symbols for these logic gates are shown in Figure 5-2.

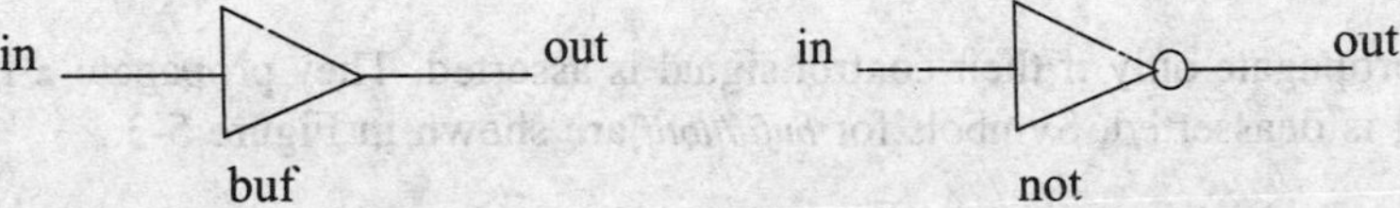

Figure 5-2 Buf and Not Gates

These gates are instantiated in Verilog as shown Example 5-2. Notice that these gates can have multiple outputs but exactly one input, which is the last terminal in the port list.

Example 5-2 Gate Instantiations of Buf/Not Gates

```
// basic gate instantiations.
buf b1(OUT1, IN);
not n1(OUT1, IN);

// More than two outputs
buf b1_2out(OUT1, OUT2, IN);

// gate instantiation without instance name
not (OUT1, IN); // legal gate instantiation
```

The truth tables for these gates are very simple. Truth tables for gates with one input and one output are shown in Table 5-2.

Table 5-2 Truth Tables for Buf/Not Gates

buf	in	out
	0	0
	1	1
	x	x
	z	x

not	in	out
	0	1
	1	0
	x	x
	z	x

Bufif/notif

Gates with an additional control signal on **buf** and **not** gates are also available.

```
bufif1        notif1
bufif0        notif0
```

These gates propagate only if their control signal is asserted. They propagate **z** if their control signal is deasserted. Symbols for *bufif/notif* are shown in Figure 5-3.

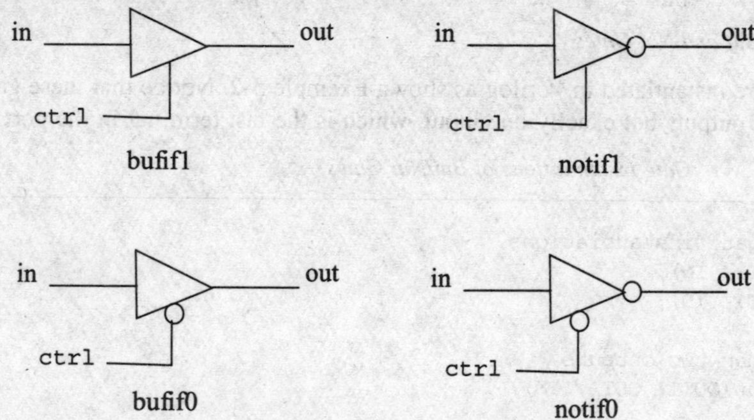

Figure 5-3 Gates Bufif and Notif

The truth tables for these gates are shown in Table 5-3.

Table 5-3 Truth Tables for Bufif/Notif Gates

bufif1		ctrl 0	1	x	z
in	0	z	0	L	L
	1	z	1	H	H
	x	z	x	x	x
	z	z	x	x	x

bufif0		ctrl 0	1	x	z
in	0	0	z	L	L
	1	1	z	H	H
	x	x	z	x	x
	z	x	z	x	x

notif1		ctrl 0	1	x	z
in	0	z	1	H	H
	1	z	0	L	L
	x	z	x	x	x
	z	z	x	x	x

notif0		ctrl 0	1	x	z
in	0	1	z	H	H
	1	0	z	L	L
	x	x	z	x	x
	z	x	z	x	x

These gates are used when a signal is to be driven only when the control signal is asserted. Such a situation is applicable when multiple drivers drive the signal. These drivers are designed to drive the signal on mutually exclusive control signals. Example 5-3 shows examples of instantiation of **bufif** and **notif** gates.

Example 5-3 Gate Instantiations of Bufif/Notif Gates

```
//Instantiation of bufif gates.
bufif1 b1 (out, in, ctrl);
bufif0 b0 (out, in, ctrl);

//Instantiation of notif gates
notif1 n1 (out, in, ctrl);
notif0 n0 (out, in, ctrl);
```

5.1.3 Array of Instances

There are many situations when repetitive instances are required. These instances differ from each other only by the index of the vector to which they are connected. To simplify specification of such instances, Verilog HDL allows an array of primitive instances to be defined.[1] Example 5-4 shows an example of an array of instances.

Example 5-4 *Simple Array of Primitive Instances*

```
wire [7:0] OUT, IN1, IN2;

// basic gate instantiations.
nand n_gate[7:0](OUT, IN1, IN2);

// This is equivalent to the following 8 instantiations
nand n_gate0(OUT[0], IN1[0], IN2[0]);
nand n_gate1(OUT[1], IN1[1], IN2[1]);
nand n_gate2(OUT[2], IN1[2], IN2[2]);
nand n_gate3(OUT[3], IN1[3], IN2[3]);
nand n_gate4(OUT[4], IN1[4], IN2[4]);
nand n_gate5(OUT[5], IN1[5], IN2[5]);
nand n_gate6(OUT[6], IN1[6], IN2[6]);
nand n_gate7(OUT[7], IN1[7], IN2[7]);
```

1. Refer to the IEEE Standard Verilog Hardware Description Language document for detailed information on the use of an array of instances.

5.1.4 Examples

Having understood the various types of gates available in Verilog, we will discuss a real example that illustrates design of gate-level digital circuits.

Gate-level multiplexer

We will design a *4-to-1 multiplexer* with 2 select signals. Multiplexers serve a useful purpose in logic design. They can connect two or more sources to a single destination. They can also be used to implement boolean functions. We will assume for this example that signals *s1* and *s0* do not get the value **x** or **z**. The I/O diagram and the truth table for the multiplexer are shown in Figure 5-4. The I/O diagram will be useful in setting up the port list for the multiplexer.

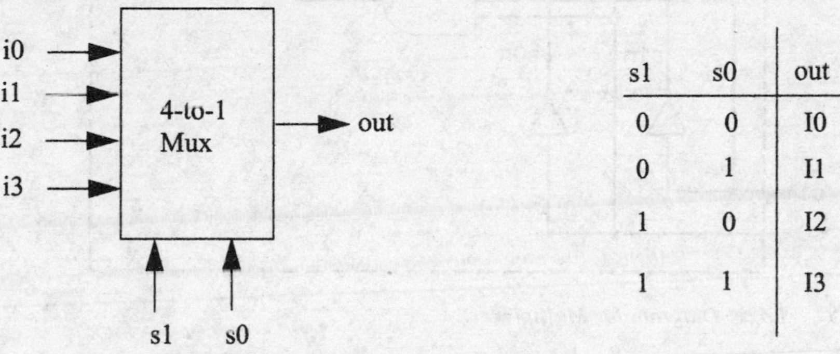

s1	s0	out
0	0	I0
0	1	I1
1	0	I2
1	1	I3

Figure 5-4 4-to-1 Multiplexer

We will implement the logic for the multiplexer using basic logic gates. The logic diagram for the multiplexer is shown in Figure 5-5.

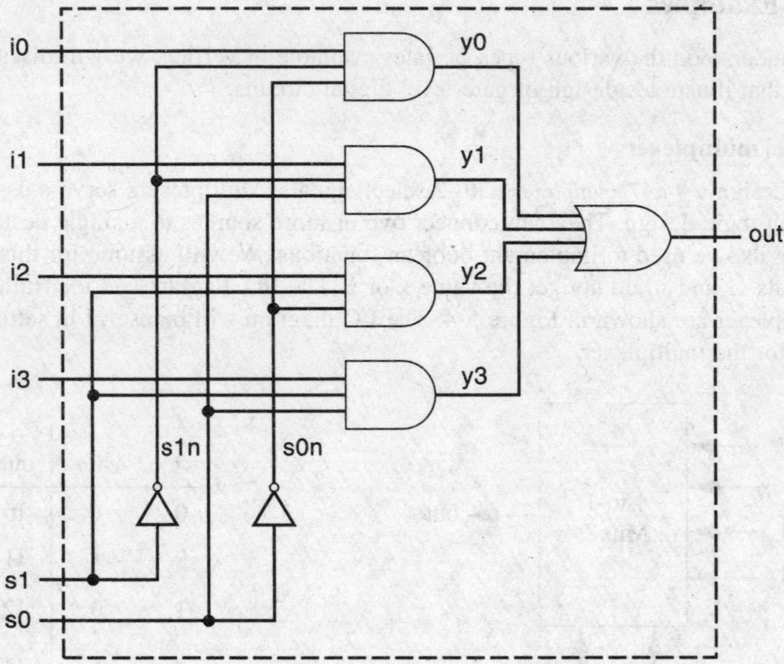

Figure 5-5 Logic Diagram for Multiplexer

The logic diagram has a one-to-one correspondence with the Verilog description. The Verilog description for the multiplexer is shown in Example 5-5. Two intermediate nets, *s0n* and *s1n*, are created; they are complements of input signals *s1* and *s0*. Internal nets *y0, y1, y2,* and *y3* are also required. Note that instance names are not specified for primitive gates, **not**, **and**, and **or**. Instance names are optional for Verilog primitives but are mandatory for instances of user-defined modules.

Example 5-5 Verilog Description of Multiplexer

```
// Module 4-to-1 multiplexer. Port list is taken exactly from
// the I/O diagram.
module mux4_to_1 (out, i0, i1, i2, i3, s1, s0);

// Port declarations from the I/O diagram
output out;
input i0, i1, i2, i3;
input s1, s0;

// Internal wire declarations
```

Example 5-5 *Verilog Description of Multiplexer (Continued)*

```
wire s1n, s0n;
wire y0, y1, y2, y3;

// Gate instantiations

// Create s1n and s0n signals.
not (s1n, s1);
not (s0n, s0);

// 3-input and gates instantiated
and (y0, i0, s1n, s0n);
and (y1, i1, s1n, s0);
and (y2, i2, s1, s0n);
and (y3, i3, s1, s0);

// 4-input or gate instantiated
or (out, y0, y1, y2, y3);

endmodule
```

This multiplexer can be tested with the stimulus shown in Example 5-6. The stimulus checks that each combination of select signals connects the appropriate input to the output. The signal *OUTPUT* is displayed one time unit after it changes. System task **$monitor** could also be used to display the signals when they change values.

Example 5-6 *Stimulus for Multiplexer*

```
// Define the stimulus module (no ports)
module stimulus;

// Declare variables to be connected
// to inputs
reg IN0, IN1, IN2, IN3;
reg S1, S0;

// Declare output wire
wire OUTPUT;

// Instantiate the multiplexer
mux4_to_1 mymux(OUTPUT, IN0, IN1, IN2, IN3, S1, S0);

// Stimulate the inputs
```

Example 5-6 Stimulus for Multiplexer (Continued)

```
// Define the stimulus module (no ports)
initial
begin
  // set input lines
  IN0 = 1; IN1 = 0; IN2 = 1; IN3 = 0;
  #1 $display("IN0= %b, IN1= %b, IN2= %b, IN3= %b\n",IN0,IN1,IN2,IN3);

  // choose IN0
  S1 = 0; S0 = 0;
  #1 $display("S1 = %b, S0 = %b, OUTPUT = %b \n", S1, S0, OUTPUT);

  // choose IN1
  S1 = 0; S0 = 1;
  #1 $display("S1 = %b, S0 = %b, OUTPUT = %b \n", S1, S0, OUTPUT);

  // choose IN2
  S1 = 1; S0 = 0;
  #1 $display("S1 = %b, S0 = %b, OUTPUT = %b \n", S1, S0, OUTPUT);

  // choose IN3
  S1 = 1; S0 = 1;
  #1 $display("S1 = %b, S0 = %b, OUTPUT = %b \n", S1, S0, OUTPUT);
end

endmodule
```

The output of the simulation is shown below. Each combination of the select signals is tested.

```
IN0= 1, IN1= 0, IN2= 1, IN3= 0

S1 = 0, S0 = 0, OUTPUT = 1

S1 = 0, S0 = 1, OUTPUT = 0

S1 = 1, S0 = 0, OUTPUT = 1

S1 = 1, S0 = 1, OUTPUT = 0
```

4-bit Ripple Carry Full Adder

In this example, we design a 4-bit full adder whose port list was defined in Section 4.2.1, *List of Ports*. We use primitive logic gates, and we apply stimulus to the 4-bit full adder to check functionality . For the sake of simplicity, we will implement a ripple carry adder. The basic building block is a 1-bit full adder. The mathematical equations for a 1-bit full adder are shown below.

$$sum = (a \oplus b \oplus cin)$$

$$cout = (a \cdot b) + cin \cdot (a \oplus b)$$

The logic diagram for a 1-bit full adder is shown in Figure 5-6.

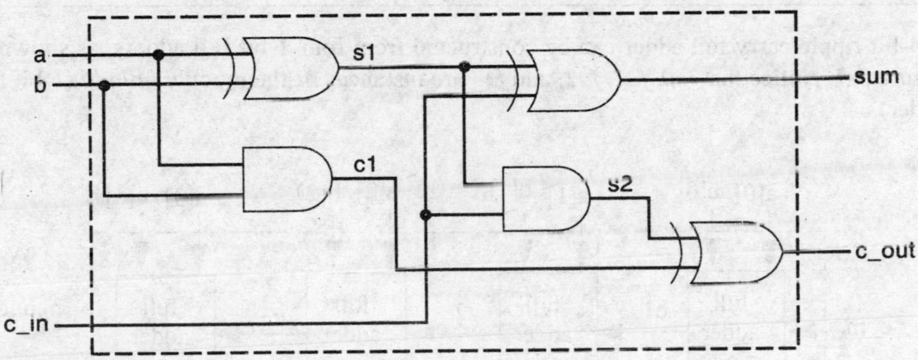

Figure 5-6 1 bit Full Adder

This logic diagram for the 1-bit full adder is converted to a Verilog description, shown in Example 5-7.

Example 5-7 Verilog Description for 1-bit Full Adder

```
// Define a 1-bit full adder
module fulladd(sum, c_out, a, b, c_in);

// I/O port declarations
output sum, c_out;
input a, b, c_in;

// Internal nets
wire s1, c1, c2;
```

Example 5-7 *Verilog Description for 1-bit Full Adder (Continued)*

```
// Instantiate logic gate primitives
xor (s1, a, b);
and (c1, a, b);

xor (sum, s1, c_in);
and (c2, s1, c_in);

xor  (c_out, c2, c1);

endmodule
```

A 4-bit ripple carry full adder can be constructed from four 1-bit full adders, as shown in Figure 5-7. Notice that *fa0, fa1, fa2*, and *fa3* are instances of the module *fulladd* (1-bit full adder).

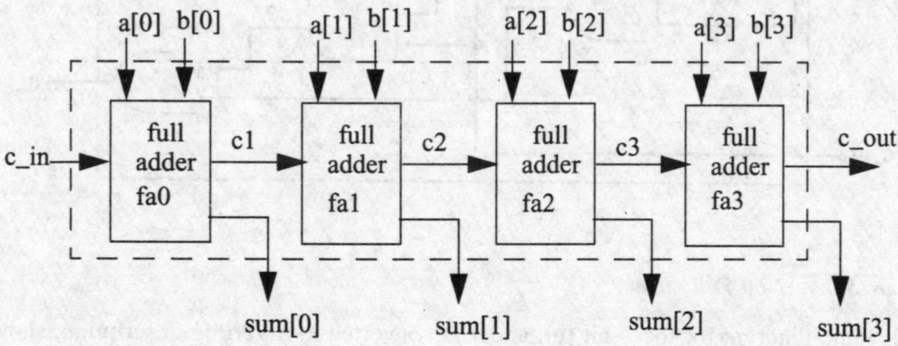

Figure 5-7 *4-bit Ripple Carry Full Adder*

This structure can be translated to Verilog as shown in Example 5-8. Note that the port names used in a 1-bit full adder and a 4-bit full adder are the same but they represent different elements. The element *sum* in a 1-bit adder is a scalar quantity and the element *sum* in the 4-bit full adder is a 4-bit vector quantity. Verilog keeps names local to a module. Names are not visible outside the module unless hierarchical name referencing is used. Also note that instance names must be specified when defined modules are instantiated, but when instantiating Verilog primitives, the instance names are optional.

Example 5-8 *Verilog Description for 4-bit Ripple Carry Full Adder*

```
// Define a 4-bit full adder
module fulladd4(sum, c_out, a, b, c_in);

// I/O port declarations
output [3:0] sum;
output c_out;
input[3:0] a, b;
input c_in;

// Internal nets
wire c1, c2, c3;

// Instantiate four 1-bit full adders.
fulladd fa0(sum[0], c1, a[0], b[0], c_in);
fulladd fa1(sum[1], c2, a[1], b[1], c1);
fulladd fa2(sum[2], c3, a[2], b[2], c2);
fulladd fa3(sum[3], c_out, a[3], b[3], c3);

endmodule
```

Finally, the design must be checked by applying stimulus, as shown in Example 5-9. The module *stimulus* stimulates the 4-bit full adder by applying a few input combinations and monitors the results.

Example 5-9 *Stimulus for 4 bit Ripple Carry Full Adder*

```
// Define the stimulus (top level module)
module stimulus;

// Set up variables
reg [3:0] A, B;
reg C_IN;
wire [3:0] SUM;
wire C_OUT;

// Instantiate the 4-bit full adder. call it FA1_4
fulladd4 FA1_4(SUM, C_OUT, A, B, C_IN);


// Set up the monitoring for the signal values
```

Example 5-9 Stimulus for 4-bit Ripple Carry Full Adder (Continued)

```
initial
begin
  $monitor($time," A= %b, B=%b, C_IN= %b, --- C_OUT= %b, SUM= %b\n",
                          A, B, C_IN, C_OUT, SUM);
end

// Stimulate inputs
initial
begin
  A = 4'd0; B = 4'd0; C_IN = 1'b0;

  #5 A = 4'd3; B = 4'd4;

  #5 A = 4'd2; B = 4'd5;

  #5 A = 4'd9; B = 4'd9;

  #5 A = 4'd10; B = 4'd15;

  #5 A = 4'd10; B = 4'd5; C_IN = 1'b1;
end

endmodule
```

The output of the simulation is shown below.

```
0 A= 0000, B=0000, C_IN= 0, --- C_OUT= 0, SUM= 0000

5 A= 0011, B=0100, C_IN= 0, --- C_OUT= 0, SUM= 0111

10 A= 0010, B=0101, C_IN= 0, --- C_OUT= 0, SUM= 0111

15 A= 1001, B=1001, C_IN= 0, --- C_OUT= 1, SUM= 0010

20 A= 1010, B=1111, C_IN= 0, --- C_OUT= 1, SUM= 1001

25 A= 1010, B=0101, C_IN= 1,, C_OUT= 1, SUM= 0000
```

5.2 Gate Delays

Until now, we described circuits without any delays (i.e., zero delay). In real circuits, logic gates have delays associated with them. Gate delays allow the Verilog user to specify delays through the logic circuits. Pin-to-pin delays can also be specified in Verilog. They are discussed in Chapter 10, *Timing and Delays*.

5.2.1 Rise, Fall, and Turn-off Delays

There are three types of delays from the inputs to the output of a primitive gate.

Rise delay

The rise delay is associated with a gate output transition to a `1` from another value.

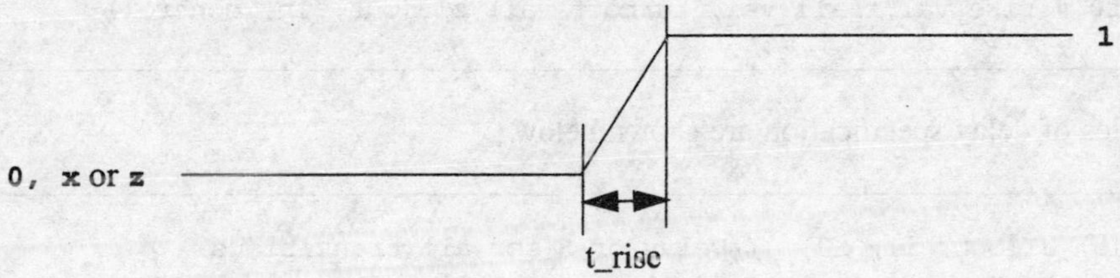

Fall delay

The fall delay is associated with a gate output transition to a `0` from another value.

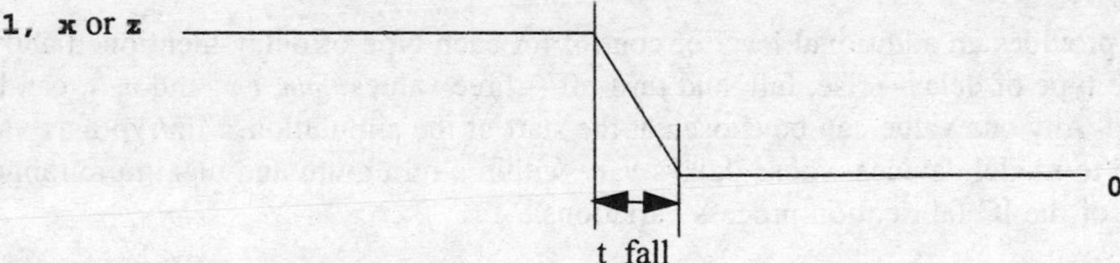

Turn-off delay

The turn-off delay is associated with a gate output transition to the high impedance value (`z`) from another value.

If the value changes to `x`, the minimum of the three delays is considered.

Three types of delay specifications are allowed. If only *one* delay is specified, this value is used for all transitions. If *two* delays are specified, they refer to the rise and fall delay values. The turn-off delay is the minimum of the two delays. If all *three* delays are specified, they refer to rise, fall, and turn-off delay values. If no delays are specified, the default value is zero. Examples of delay specification are shown in Example 5-10.

Example 5-10 Types of Delay Specification

```
// Delay of delay_time for all transitions
and #(delay_time) a1(out, i1, i2);

// Rise and Fall Delay Specification.
and #(rise_val, fall_val) a2(out, i1, i2);

// Rise, Fall, and Turn-off Delay Specification
bufif0 #(rise_val, fall_val, turnoff_val) b1 (out, in, control);
```

Examples of delay specification are shown below.

```
and #(5) a1(out, i1, i2); //Delay of 5 for all transitions
and #(4,6) a2(out, i1, i2); // Rise = 4, Fall = 6
bufif0 #(3,4,5) b1 (out, in, control); //Rise = 3, Fall = 4, Turn-off = 5
```

5.2.2 Min/Typ/Max Values

Verilog provides an additional level of control for each type of delay mentioned above. For each type of delay—rise, fall, and turn-off—three values, *min*, *typ*, and *max,* can be specified. Any one value can be chosen at the start of the simulation. Min/typ/max values are used to model devices whose delays vary within a minimum and maximum range because of the IC fabrication process variations.

Min value

The min value is the minimum delay value that the designer expects the gate to have.

Typ val

The typ value is the typical delay value that the designer expects the gate to have.

Max value

The max value is the maximum delay value that the designer expects the gate to have.

Min, typ, or max values can be chosen at Verilog run time. The method of choosing a min/typ/max value may vary for different simulators or operating systems. (For Verilog-XL™, the values are chosen by specifying options **+maxdelays**, **+ typdelays**, and **+mindelays** at run time. If no option is specified, the typical delay value is the default). This allows the designers the flexibility of building three delay values for each transition into their design. The designer can experiment with delay values without modifying the design.

Examples of min, typ, and max value specification for Verilog-XL are shown in Example 5-11.

Example 5-11 *Min, Max, and Typical Delay Values*

```
// One delay
// if +mindelays, delay= 4
// if +typdelays, delay= 5
// if +maxdelays, delay= 6
and #(4:5:6) a1(out, i1, i2);

// Two delays
// if +mindelays, rise= 3, fall= 5, turn-off = min(3,5)
// if +typdelays, rise= 4, fall= 6, turn-off = min(4,6)
// if +maxdelays, rise= 5, fall= 7, turn-off = min(5,7)
and #(3:4:5, 5:6:7) a2(out, i1, i2);

// Three delays
// if +mindelays, rise= 2 fall= 3 turn-off = 4
// if +typdelays, rise= 3 fall= 4 turn-off = 5
// if +maxdelays, rise= 4 fall= 5 turn-off = 6
and #(2:3:4, 3:4:5, 4:5:6) a3(out, i1,i2);
```

Examples of invoking the Verilog-XL simulator with the command-line options are shown below. Assume that the module with delays is declared in the file *test.v*.

```
//invoke simulation with maximum delay
> verilog test.v +maxdelays

//invoke simulation with minimum delay
> verilog test.v +mindelays

//invoke simulation with typical delay
> verilog test.v +typdelays
```

5.2.3 Delay Example

Let us consider a simple example to illustrate the use of gate delays to model timing in the logic circuits. A simple module called *D* implements the following logic equations:

$$out = (a \cdot b) + c$$

The gate-level implementation is shown in *Module D* (Figure 5-8). The module contains two gates with delays of 5 and 4 time units.

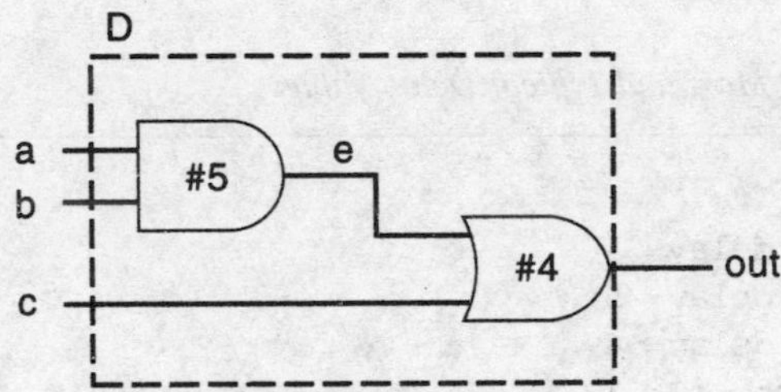

Figure 5-8 Module D

The module *D* is defined in Verilog as shown in Example 5-12.

Example 5-12 Verilog Definition for Module D with Delay

```
// Define a simple combination module called D
module D (out, a, b, c);

// I/O port declarations
output out;
input a,b,c;

// Internal nets
wire e;

// Instantiate primitive gates to build the circuit
and #(5) a1(e, a, b); //Delay of 5 on gate a1
or  #(4) o1(out, e,c); //Delay of 4 on gate o1

endmodule
```

This module is tested by the stimulus file shown in Example 5-13.

Example 5-13 Stimulus for Module D with Delay

```
// Stimulus (top-level module)
module stimulus;

// Declare variables
reg A, B, C;
wire OUT;

// Instantiate the module D
D d1( OUT, A, B, C);

// Stimulate the inputs. Finish the simulation at 40 time units.
initial
begin
  A= 1'b0; B= 1'b0; C= 1'b0;

  #10 A= 1'b1; B= 1'b1; C= 1'b1;

  #10 A= 1'b1; B= 1'b0; C= 1'b0;

  #20 $finish;
end

endmodule
```

The waveforms from the simulation are shown in Figure 5-9 to illustrate the effect of specifying delays on gates. The waveforms are not drawn to scale. However, simulation time at each transition is specified below the transition.

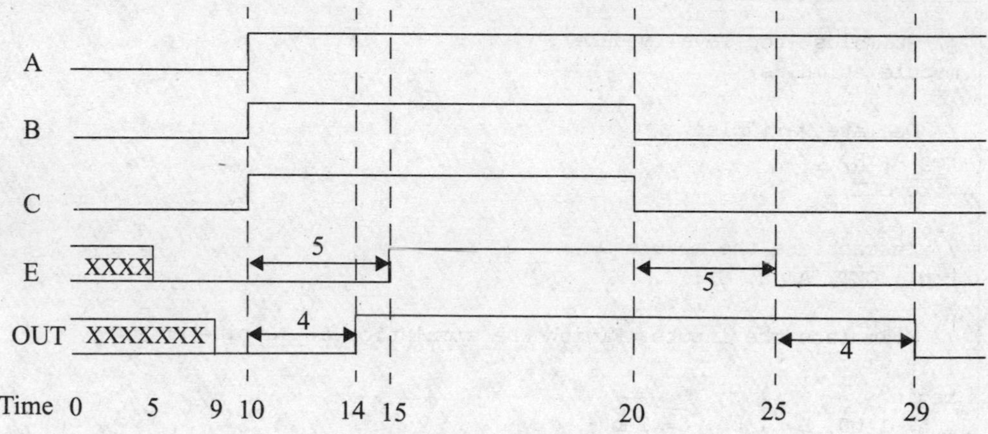

Figure 5-9 Waveforms for Delay Simulation

1. The outputs *E* and *OUT* are initially unknown.
2. At time 10, after *A, B,* and *C* all transition to `1`, *OUT* transitions to `1` after a delay of 4 time units and E changes value to `1` after 5 time units.
3. At time 20, *B* and *C* transition to `0`. *E* changes value to `0` after 5 time units, and *OUT* transitions to `0`, 4 time units after *E* changes.

It is a useful exercise to understand how the timing for each transition in the above waveform corresponds to the gate delays shown in *Module D*.

5.3 Summary

In this chapter, we discussed how to model gate-level logic in Verilog. We also discussed different aspects of gate-level design.

- The basic types of gates are **`and`**, **`or`**, **`xor`**, **`buf`**, and **`not`**. Each gate has a logic symbol, truth table, and a corresponding Verilog primitive. Primitives are instantiated like modules except that they are predefined in Verilog. The output of a gate is evaluated as soon as one of its inputs changes.
- Arrays of built-in primitive instances and user-defined modules can be defined in Verilog.

- For gate-level design, start with the logic diagram, write the Verilog description for the logic by using gate primitives, provide stimulus, and look at the output. Two design examples, a 4-to-1 multiplexer and a 4-bit full adder, were discussed. Each step of the design process was explained.
- Three types of delays are associated with gates: *rise*, *fall*, and *turn-off*. Verilog allows specification of one, two, or three delays for each gate. Values of rise, fall, and turn-off delays are computed by Verilog, based on the *one, two*, or *three* delays specified.
- For each type of delay, a *minimum, typical*, and *maximum* value can be specified. The user can choose which value to apply at simulation time. This provides the flexibility to experiment with three delay values without changing the Verilog code.
- The effect of propagation delay on waveforms was explained by the simple, two-gate logic example. For each gate with a delay of *t*, the output changes *t* time units after any of the inputs change.

5.4 Exercises

1. Create your own 2-input Verilog gates called *my-or, my-and* and *my-not* from 2-input **nand** gates. Check the functionality of these gates with a stimulus module.
2. A 2-input **xor** gate can be built from *my_and*, *my_or* and *my_not* gates. Construct an **xor** module in Verilog that realizes the logic function, $z = xy' + x'y$. Inputs are x and y, and z is the output. Write a stimulus module that exercises all four combinations of x and y inputs.
3. The 1-bit full adder described in the chapter can be expressed in a sum of products form.

   sum = a.b.c_in + a'.b.c_in' + a'.b'.c_in + a.b'.c_in'

   c_out = a.b + b.c_in + a.c_in

   Assuming *a, b, c_in* are the inputs and *sum* and *c_out* are the outputs, design a logic circuit to implement the 1-bit full adder, using only **and**, **not**, and **or** gates. Write the Verilog description for the circuit. You may use up to 4-input Verilog primitive **and** and **or** gates. Write the stimulus for the full adder and check the functionality for all input combinations.

4. The logic diagram for an *RS latch* with delay is shown below.

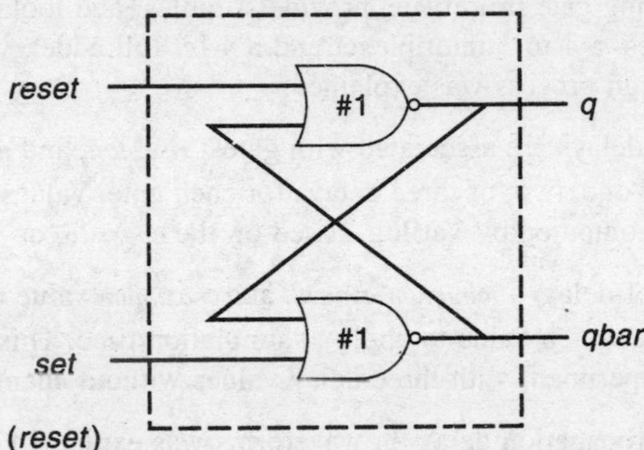

Write the Verilog description for the RS latch. Include delays of 1 unit when instantiating the **nor** gates. Write the stimulus module for the RS latch, using the following table, and verify the outputs.

set	reset	q_{n+1}
0	0	q_n
0	1	0
1	0	1
1	1	?

5. Design a 2-to-1 multiplexer using `bufif0` and `bufif1` gates as shown below.

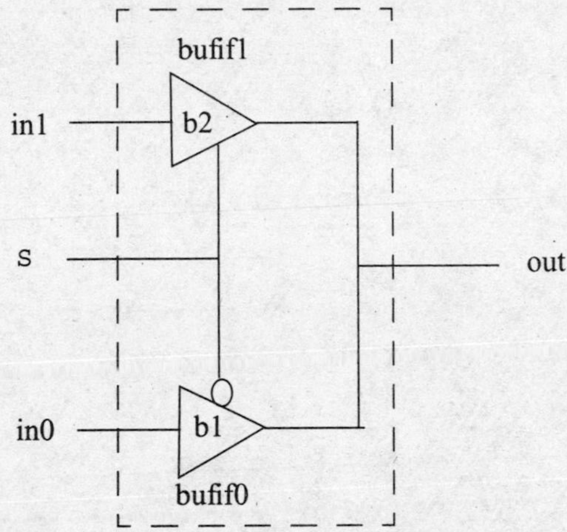

The delay specification for gates *b1* and *b2* are as follows:

	Min	**Typ**	**Max**
Risc	1	2	3
Fall	3	4	5
Turnoff	5	6	7

Apply stimulus and test the output values.

Dataflow Modeling 6

For small circuits, the gate-level modeling approach works very well because the number of gates is limited and the designer can instantiate and connect every gate individually. Also, gate-level modeling is very intuitive to a designer with a basic knowledge of digital logic design. However, in complex designs the number of gates is very large. Thus, designers can design more effectively if they concentrate on implementing the function at a level of abstraction higher than gate level. Dataflow modeling provides a powerful way to implement a design. Verilog allows a circuit to be designed in terms of the data flow between registers and how a design processes data rather than instantiation of individual gates. Later in this chapter, the benefits of dataflow modeling will become more apparent.

With gate densities on chips increasing rapidly, dataflow modeling has assumed great importance. No longer can companies devote engineering resources to handcrafting entire designs with gates. Currently, automated tools are used to create a gate-level circuit from a dataflow design description. This process is called *logic synthesis*. Dataflow modeling has become a popular design approach as logic synthesis tools have become sophisticated. This approach allows the designer to concentrate on optimizing the circuit in terms of data flow. For maximum flexibility in the design process, designers typically use a Verilog description style that combines the concepts of gate-level, data flow, and behavioral design. In the digital design community, the term RTL (Register Transfer Level) design is commonly used for a combination of dataflow modeling and behavioral modeling.

Learning Objectives

- Describe the continuous assignment (**`assign`**) statement, restrictions on the **`assign`** statement, and the implicit continuous assignment statement.
- Explain assignment delay, implicit assignment delay, and net declaration delay for continuous assignment statements.
- Define expressions, operators, and operands.
- List operator types for all possible operations—arithmetic, logical, relational, equality, bitwise, reduction, shift, concatenation, and conditional.
- Use dataflow constructs to model practical digital circuits in Verilog.

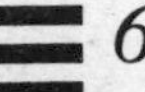

6.1 Continuous Assignments

A *continuous assignment* is the most basic statement in dataflow modeling, used to drive a value onto a net. This assignment replaces gates in the description of the circuit and describes the circuit at a higher level of abstraction. The assignment statement starts with the keyword **assign**. The syntax of an **assign** statement is as follows.

```
continuous_assign ::= assign [ drive_strength ] [ delay3 ]
                         list_of_net_assignments ;
list_of_net_assignments ::= net_assignment { , net_assignment }
net_assignment ::= net_lvalue = expression
```

Notice that drive strength is optional and can be specified in terms of strength levels discussed in Section 3.2.1, `Value Set`. We will not discuss drive strength specification in this chapter. The default value for drive strength is **strong1** and **strong0**. The delay value is also optional and can be used to specify delay on the **assign** statement. This is like specifying delays for gates. Delay specification is discussed in this chapter. Continuous assignments have the following characteristics:

1. The lefthand side of an assignment must always be a scalar or vector net or a concatenation of scalar and vector nets. It cannot be a scalar or vector register. Concatenations are discussed in Section 6.4.8, `Concatenation Operator`.
2. Continuous assignments are always active. The assignment expression is evaluated as soon as one of the right-hand-side operands changes and the value is assigned to the left-hand-side net.
3. The operands on the right-hand side can be registers or nets or function calls. Registers or nets can be scalars or vectors.
4. Delay values can be specified for assignments in terms of time units. Delay values are used to control the time when a net is assigned the evaluated value. This feature is similar to specifying delays for gates. It is very useful in modeling timing behavior in real circuits.

Examples of continuous assignments are shown below. Operators such as &, ^, |, {, } and + used in the examples are explained in Section 6.4, `Operator Types`. At this point, concentrate on how the **assign** statements are specified.

Example 6-1 *Examples of Continuous Assignment*

```
// Continuous assign. out is a net. i1 and i2 are nets.
assign out = i1 & i2;

// Continuous assign for vector nets. addr is a 16-bit vector net
// addr1 and addr2 are 16-bit vector registers.
assign addr[15:0] = addr1_bits[15:0] ^ addr2_bits[15:0];

// Concatenation. Left-hand side is a concatenation of a scalar
// net and a vector net.
assign {c_out, sum[3:0]} = a[3:0] + b[3:0] + c_in;
```

We now discuss a shorthand method of placing a continuous assignment on a net.

6.1.1 Implicit Continuous Assignment

Instead of declaring a net and then writing a continuous assignment on the net, Verilog provides a shortcut by which a continuous assignment can be placed on a net when it is declared. There can be only one implicit declaration assignment per net because a net is declared only once.

In the example below, an implicit continuous assignment is contrasted with a regular continuous assignment.

```
//Regular continuous assignment
wire out;
assign out = in1 & in2;

//Same effect is achieved by an implicit continuous assignment
wire out = in1 & in2;
```

6.1.2 Implicit Net Declaration

If a signal name is used to the left of the continuous assignment, an implicit net declaration will be inferred for that signal name. If the net is connected to a module port, the width of the inferred net is equal to the width of the module port.

```
// Continuous assign. out is a net.
wire i1, i2;
assign out = i1 & i2; //Note that out was not declared as a wire
                      //but an implicit wire declaration for out
                      //is done by the simulator
```

6.2 Delays

Delay values control the time between the change in a right-hand-side operand and when the new value is assigned to the left-hand side. Three ways of specifying delays in continuous assignment statements are *regular assignment delay, implicit continuous assignment delay*, and *net declaration delay.*

6.2.1 Regular Assignment Delay

The first method is to assign a delay value in a continuous assignment statement. The delay value is specified after the keyword **assign**. Any change in values of *in1* or *in2* will result in a delay of 10 time units before recomputation of the expression *in1* & *in2,* and the result will be assigned to *out*. If *in1* or *in2* changes value again before 10 time units when the result propagates to *out*, the values of *in1* and *in2* at the time of recomputation are considered. This property is called *inertial delay*. An input pulse that is shorter than the delay of the assignment statement does not propagate to the output.

```
assign #10 out = in1 & in2; // Delay in a continuous assign
```

The waveform in Figure 6-1 is generated by simulating the above **assign** statement. It shows the delay on signal *out*. Note the following change:

1. When signals *in1* and *in2* go high at time 20, *out* goes to a high 10 time units later (time = 30).
2. When *in1* goes low at 60, *out* changes to low at 70.

3. However, *in1* changes to high at 80, but it goes down to low before 10 time units have elapsed.
4. Hence, at the time of recomputation, 10 units after time 80, *in1* is 0. Thus, *out* gets the value 0. A pulse of width less than the specified assignment delay is not propagated to the output.

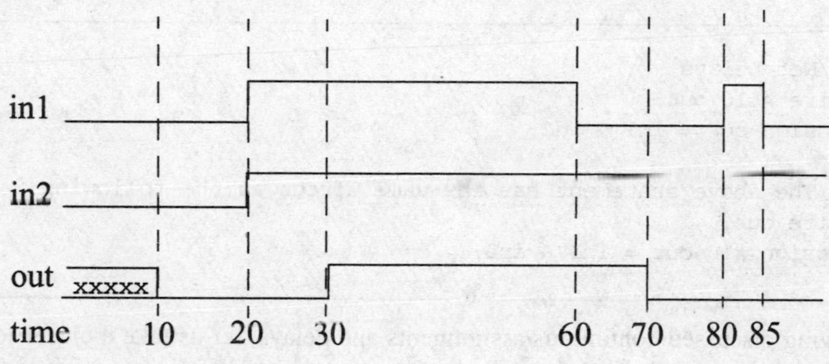

Figure 6-1 *Delays*

Inertial delays also apply to gate delays, discussed in Chapter 5, `Gate-Level Modeling`.

6.2.2 Implicit Continuous Assignment Delay

An equivalent method is to use an implicit continuous assignment to specify both a delay and an assignment on the net.

```
//implicit continuous assignment delay
wire #10 out = in1 & in2;

//same as
wire out;
assign #10 out = in1 & in2;
```

The declaration above has the same effect as defining a *wire out* and declaring a continuous assignment on *out*.

6.2.3 Net Declaration Delay

A delay can be specified on a net when it is declared without putting a continuous assignment on the net. If a delay is specified on a net *out*, then any value change applied to the net *out* is delayed accordingly. Net declaration delays can also be used in gate-level modeling.

```
//Net Delays
wire # 10 out;
assign out = in1 & in2;

//The above statement has the same effect as the following.
wire out;
assign #10 out = in1 & in2;
```

Having discussed continuous assignments and delays, let us take a closer look at expressions, operators, and operands that are used inside continuous assignments.

6.3 Expressions, Operators, and Operands

Dataflow modeling describes the design in terms of expressions instead of primitive gates. *Expressions, operators*, and *operands* form the basis of dataflow modeling.

6.3.1 Expressions

Expressions are constructs that combine operators and operands to produce a result.

```
// Examples of expressions. Combines operands and operators
a ^ b
addr1[20:17] + addr2[20:17]
in1 | in2
```

6.3.2 Operands

Operands can be any one of the data types defined in Section 3.2, `Data Types`. Some constructs will take only certain types of operands. Operands can be *constants, integers, real numbers, nets, registers, times, bit-select* (one bit of vector net or a vector register), *part-select* (selected bits of the vector net or register vector), and *memories* or *function calls* (functions are discussed later).

```
integer count, final_count;
final_count = count + 1;//count is an integer operand

real a, b, c;
c = a - b; //a and b are real operands

reg [15:0] reg1, reg2;
reg [3:0] reg_out;
reg_out = reg1[3:0] ^ reg2[3:0];//reg1[3:0] and reg2[3:0] are
                                //part-select register operands

reg ret_value;
ret_value = calculate_parity(A, B);//calculate_parity is a
                                   //function type operand
```

6.3.3 Operators

Operators act on the operands to produce desired results. Verilog provides various types of operators. Operator types are discussed in detail in Section 6.4, `Operator Types`.

```
d1 && d2 // && is an operator on operands d1 and d2
!a[0] // ! is an operator on operand a[0]
B >> 1 // >> is an operator on operands B and 1
```

6.4 Operator Types

Verilog provides many different operator types. Operators can be *arithmetic, logical, relational, equality, bitwise, reduction, shift, concatenation,* or *conditional*. Some of these operators are similar to the operators used in the C programming language. Each operator type is denoted by a symbol. Table 6-1 shows the complete listing of operator symbols classified by category.

Table 6-1 Operator Types and Symbols

<table>
<tr><th>Operator Type</th><th>Operator Symbol</th><th>Operation Performed</th><th>Number of Operands</th></tr>
<tr><td>Arithmetic</td><td>*
/
+
-
%
**</td><td>multiply
divide
add
subtract
modulus
power (exponent)</td><td>two
two
two
two
two
two</td></tr>
<tr><td>Logical</td><td>!
&&
||</td><td>logical negation
logical and
logical or</td><td>one
two
two</td></tr>
<tr><td>Relational</td><td>>
<
>=
<=</td><td>greater than
less than
greater than or equal
less than or equal</td><td>two
two
two
two</td></tr>
<tr><td>Equality</td><td>==
!=
===
!==</td><td>equality
inequality
case equality
case inequality</td><td>two
two
two
two</td></tr>
<tr><td>Bitwise</td><td>~
&
|
^
^~ or ~^</td><td>bitwise negation
bitwise and
bitwise or
bitwise xor
bitwise xnor</td><td>one
two
two
two
two</td></tr>
<tr><td>Reduction</td><td>&
~&
|
~|
^
^~ or ~^</td><td>reduction and
reduction nand
reduction or
reduction nor
reduction xor
reduction xnor</td><td>one
one
one
one
one
one</td></tr>
</table>

Table 6-1 Operator Types and Symbols (Continued)

Operator Type	Operator Symbol	Operation Performed	Number of Operands
Shift	>> << >>> <<<	Right shift Left shift Arithmetic right shift Arithmetic left shift	Two Two Two Two
Concatenation	{ }	Concatenation	Any number
Replication	{ { } }	Replication	Any number
Conditional	?:	Conditional	Three

Let us now discuss each operator type in detail.

6.4.1 Arithmetic Operators

There are two types of arithmetic operators: binary and unary.

Binary operators

Binary arithmetic operators are *multiply (*), divide (/), add (+), subtract (-), power (**),* and *modulus (%)*. Binary operators take two operands.

```
A = 4'b0011; B = 4'b0100; // A and B are register vectors
D = 6; E = 4; F=2// D and E are integers

A * B // Multiply A and B. Evaluates to 4'b1100
D / E // Divide D by E. Evaluates to 1. Truncates any fractional part.
A + B // Add A and B. Evaluates to 4'b0111
B - A // Subtract A from B. Evaluates to 4'b0001
F = E ** F; //E to the power F, yields 16
```

If any operand bit has a value **x**, then the result of the entire expression is **x**. This seems intuitive because if an operand value is not known precisely, the result should be an unknown.

```
in1 = 4'b101x;
in2 = 4'b1010;
sum = in1 + in2; // sum will be evaluated to the value 4'bx
```

Modulus operators produce the *remainder* from the division of two numbers. They operate similarly to the modulus operator in the C programming language.

```
13 % 3 // Evaluates to 1
16 % 4 // Evaluates to 0
-7 % 2 // Evaluates to -1, takes sign of the first operand
7 % -2 // Evaluates to +1, takes sign of the first operand
```

Unary operators

The operators + and - can also work as *unary* operators. They are used to specify the positive or negative sign of the operand. Unary + or – operators have higher precedence than the binary + or – operators.

```
-4 // Negative 4
+5 // Positive 5
```

Negative numbers are represented as 2's complement internally in Verilog. It is advisable to use negative numbers only of the type integer or real in expressions. Designers should avoid negative numbers of the type *<sss>* '*<base>* *<nnn>* in expressions because they are converted to unsigned 2's complement numbers and hence yield unexpected results.

```
//Advisable to use integer or real numbers
-10 / 5// Evaluates to -2

//Do not use numbers of type <sss> '<base> <nnn>
-'d10 / 5// Is equivalent (2's complement of 10)/5 = (2^32 - 10)/5
// where 32 is the default machine word width.
// This evaluates to an incorrect and unexpected result
```

6.4.2 Logical Operators

Logical operators are *logical-and* (&&), *logical-or* (||) and *logical-not* (!). Operators && and || are binary operators. Operator ! is a unary operator. Logical operators follow these conditions:

1. Logical operators always evaluate to a 1-bit value, `0` (false), `1` (true), or `x` (ambiguous).
2. If an operand is not equal to zero, it is equivalent to a logical `1` (true condition). If it is equal to zero, it is equivalent to a logical `0` (false condition). If any operand bit is `x` or `z`, it is equivalent to `x` (ambiguous condition) and is normally treated by simulators as a false condition.
3. Logical operators take variables or expressions as operands.

Use of parentheses to group logical operations is highly recommended to improve readability. Also, the user does not have to remember the precedence of operators.

```
// Logical operations
A = 3; B = 0;
A && B // Evaluates to 0. Equivalent to (logical-1 && logical-0)
A || B // Evaluates to 1. Equivalent to (logical-1 || logical-0)
!A// Evaluates to 0. Equivalent to not(logical-1)
!B// Evaluates to 1. Equivalent to not(logical-0)

// Unknowns
A = 2'b0x; B = 2'b10;
A && B // Evaluates to x. Equivalent to (x && logical 1)

// Expressions
(a == 2) && (b == 3) // Evaluates to 1 if both a == 2 and b == 3 are
true.
 // Evaluates to 0 if either is false.
```

6.4.3 Relational Operators

Relational operators are *greater-than (>), less-than (<), greater-than-or-equal-to (>=),* and *less-than-or-equal-to* (<=). If relational operators are used in an expression, the expression returns a logical value of `1` if the expression is true and `0` if the expression is false. If there are any unknown or `z` bits in the operands, the expression takes a value `x`. These operators function exactly as the corresponding operators in the C programming language.

```
// A = 4, B = 3
// X = 4'b1010, Y = 4'b1101, Z = 4'b1xxx

A <= B // Evaluates to a logical 0
A > B // Evaluates to a logical 1
```

(Continued...)

```
Y >= X // Evaluates to a logical 1
Y < Z // Evaluates to an x
```

6.4.4 Equality Operators

Equality operators are *logical equality* (==), *logical inequality* (!=), *case equality* (===), and *case inequality* (!==). When used in an expression, equality operators return logical value `1` if true, `0` if false. These operators compare the two operands bit by bit, with zero filling if the operands are of unequal length. Table 6-2 lists the operators.

Table 6-2 Equality Operators

Expression	Description	Possible Logical Value
a == b	a equal to b, result unknown if **x** or **z** in a or b	0, 1, x
a != b	a not equal to b, result unknown if **x** or **z** in a or b	0, 1, x
a === b	a equal to b, including **x** and **z**	0, 1
a !== b	a not equal to b, including **x** and **z**	0, 1

It is important to note the difference between the logical equality operators (`==`, `!=`) and case equality operators (`===`, `!==`). The logical equality operators (`==`, `!=`) will yield an **x** if either operand has **x** or **z** in its bits. However, the case equality operators (`===`, `!==`) compare both operands bit by bit and compare all bits, including **x** and **z**. The result is `1` if the operands match exactly, including **x** and **z** bits. The result is `0` if the operands do not match exactly. Case equality operators never result in an **x**.

```
// A = 4, B = 3
// X = 4'b1010, Y = 4'b1101
// Z = 4'b1xxz, M = 4'b1xxz, N = 4'b1xxx

A == B // Results in logical 0
X != Y // Results in logical 1
X == Z // Results in x
Z === M //Results in logical 1 (all bits match, including x and z)
Z === N //Results in logical 0 (least significant bit does not match)
M !== N // Results in logical 1
```

6.4.5 Bitwise Operators

Bitwise operators are *negation* (`~`), *and*(`&`), *or* (`|`), *xor* (`^`), *xnor* (`^~`, `~^`). Bitwise operators perform a bit-by-bit operation on two operands. They take each bit in one operand and perform the operation with the corresponding bit in the other operand. If one operand is shorter than the other, it will be bit-extended with zeros to match the length of the longer operand. Logic tables for the bit-by-bit computation are shown in Table 6-3. A **z** is treated as an **x** in a bitwise operation. The exception is the unary negation operator (~), which takes only one operand and operates on the bits of the single operand.

Table 6-3 Truth Tables for Bitwise Operators

bitwise and	0	1	x
0	0	0	0
1	0	1	x
x	0	x	x

bitwise or	0	1	x
0	0	1	x
1	1	1	1
x	x	1	x

bitwise xor	0	1	x
0	0	1	x
1	1	0	x
x	x	x	x

bitwise xnor	0	1	x
0	1	0	x
1	0	1	x
x	x	x	x

bitwise negation	result
0	1
1	0
x	x

Examples of bitwise operators are shown below.

```
// X = 4'b1010, Y = 4'b1101
// Z = 4'b10x1

~X      // Negation. Result is 4'b0101
X & Y   // Bitwise and. Result is 4'b1000
X | Y   // Bitwise or. Result is 4'b1111
X ^ Y   // Bitwise xor. Result is 4'b0111
```

```
(Continued...)
X ^~ Y // Bitwise xnor. Result is 4'b1000
X & Z // Result is 4'b10x0
```

It is important to distinguish bitwise operators `~`, `&`, and `|` from logical operators `!`, `&&`, `||`. Logical operators always yield a logical value `0`, `1`, `x`, whereas bitwise operators yield a bit-by-bit value. Logical operators perform a logical operation, not a bit-by-bit operation.

```
// X = 4'b1010, Y = 4'b0000

X | Y // bitwise operation. Result is 4'b1010
X || Y // logical operation. Equivalent to 1 || 0. Result is 1.
```

6.4.6 Reduction Operators

Reduction operators are *and* (`&`), *nand* (`~&`), *or* (`|`), *nor* (`~|`), *xor* (`^`), and *xnor* (`~^`, `^~`). Reduction operators take only one operand. Reduction operators perform a bitwise operation on a single vector operand and yield a 1-bit result. The logic tables for the operators are the same as shown in Section 6.4.5, `Bitwise Operators`. The difference is that bitwise operations are on bits from two different operands, whereas reduction operations are on the bits of the same operand. Reduction operators work bit by bit from right to left. *Reduction nand*, *reduction nor*, and *reduction xnor* are computed by inverting the result of the *reduction and*, *reduction or*, and *reduction xor*, respectively.

```
// X = 4'b1010

&X //Equivalent to 1 & 0 & 1 & 0. Results in 1'b0
|X//Equivalent to 1 | 0 | 1 | 0. Results in 1'b1
^X//Equivalent to 1 ^ 0 ^ 1 ^ 0. Results in 1'b0
//A reduction xor or xnor can be used for even or odd parity
//generation of a vector.
```

The use of a similar set of symbols for logical (`!`, `&&`, `||`), bitwise (`~`, `&`, `|`, `^`), and reduction operators (`&`, `|`, `^`) is somewhat confusing initially. The difference lies in the number of operands each operator takes and also the value of results computed.

6.4.7 Shift Operators

Shift operators are *right shift* (>>), *left shift* (<<), arithmetic *right shift* (>>>), and arithmetic *left shift* (<<<). Regular shift operators shift a vector operand to the right or the left by a specified number of bits. The operands are the vector and the number of bits to shift. When the bits are shifted, the vacant bit positions are filled with zeros. Shift operations do not wrap around. Arithmetic shift operators use the context of the expression to determine the value with which to fill the vacated bits.

```
// X = 4'b1100

Y = X >> 1; //Y is 4'b0110. Shift right 1 bit. 0 filled in MSB position.
Y = X << 1; //Y is 4'b1000. Shift left 1 bit. 0 filled in LSB position.
Y = X << 2; //Y is 4'b0000. Shift left 2 bits.

integer a, b, c; //Signed data types
a = 0;
b = -10; // 00111...10110 binary
c = a + (b >>> 3); //Results in -2 decimal, due to arithmetic shift
```

Shift operators are useful because they allow the designer to model shift operations, *shift-and-add* algorithms for multiplication, and other useful operations.

6.4.8 Concatenation Operator

The *concatenation* operator ({, }) provides a mechanism to append multiple operands. The operands must be sized. Unsized operands are not allowed because the size of each operand must be known for computation of the size of the result.

Concatenations are expressed as operands within braces, with commas separating the operands. Operands can be scalar nets or registers, vector nets or registers, bit-select, part-select, or sized constants.

```
// A = 1'b1, B = 2'b00, C = 2'b10, D = 3'b110

Y = {B , C} // Result Y is 4'b0010
Y = {A , B , C , D , 3'b001} // Result Y is 11'b10010110001
Y = {A , B[0], C[1]} // Result Y is 3'b101
```

6.4.9 Replication Operator

Repetitive concatenation of the same number can be expressed by using a replication constant. A replication constant specifies how many times to replicate the number inside the brackets ({ }).

```
reg A;
reg [1:0] B, C;
reg [2:0] D;
A = 1'b1; B = 2'b00; C = 2'b10; D = 3'b110;

Y = { 4{A} } // Result Y is 4'b1111
Y = { 4{A} , 2{B} } // Result Y is 8'b11110000
Y = { 4{A} , 2{B} , C } // Result Y is 8'b1111000010
```

6.4.10 Conditional Operator

The *conditional* operator(`?:`) takes three operands.

Usage: condition_expr ? true_expr : false_expr ;

The condition expression (*condition_expr*) is first evaluated. If the result is true (logical `1`), then the *true_expr* is evaluated. If the result is false (logical `0`), then the *false_expr* is evaluated. If the result is **x** (ambiguous), then both *true_expr* and *false_expr* are evaluated and their results are compared, bit by bit, to return for each bit position an **x** if the bits are different and the value of the bits if they are the same.

The action of a conditional operator is similar to a multiplexer. Alternately, it can be compared to the *if-else* expression.

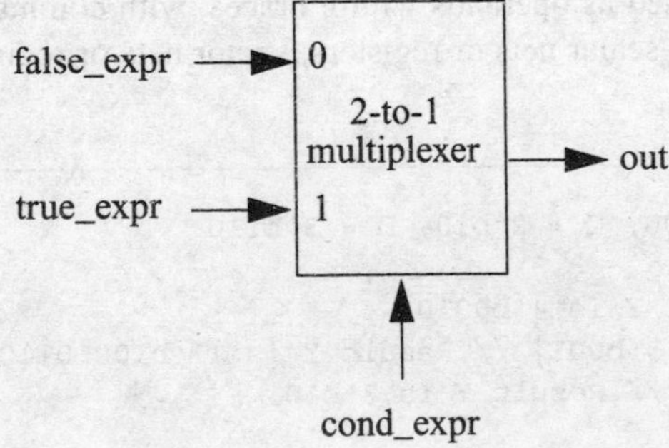

Conditional operators are frequently used in dataflow modeling to model conditional assignments. The conditional expression acts as a switching control.

```
//model functionality of a tristate buffer
assign addr_bus = drive_enable ? addr_out : 36'bz;

//model functionality of a 2-to-1 mux
assign out = control ? in1 : in0;
```

Conditional operations can be nested. Each *true_expr* or *false_expr* can itself be a conditional operation. In the example that follows, convince yourself that (*A==3*) and control are the two select signals of 4-to-1 multiplexer with *n, m, y, x* as the inputs and *out* as the output signal.

```
assign out = (A == 3) ? ( control ? x : y ): ( control ? m : n) ;
```

6.4.11 Operator Precedence

Having discussed the operators, it is now important to discuss operator precedence. If no parentheses are used to separate parts of expressions, Verilog enforces the following precedence. Operators listed in Table 6-4 are in order from highest precedence to lowest precedence. It is recommended that parentheses be used to separate expressions except in the case of unary operators or when there is no ambiguity.

Table 6-4 Operator Precedence

Operators	Operator Symbols	Precedence
Unary	+ - ! ~	Highest precedence
Multiply, Divide, Modulus	* / %	
Add, Subtract	+ -	
Shift	<< >>	
Relational	< <= > >=	
Equality	== != === !==	

Table 6-4 Operator Precedence (Continued)

Operators	Operator Symbols	Precedence
Reduction	&, ~& ^ ^~ |, ~|	
Logical	&& ||	
Conditional	? :	Lowest precedence

6.5 Examples

A design can be represented in terms of gates, data flow, or a behavioral description. In this section, we consider the 4-to-1 multiplexer and 4-bit full adder described in Section 5.1.4, `Examples`. Previously, these designs were directly translated from the logic diagram into a gate-level Verilog description. Here, we describe the same designs in terms of data flow. We also discuss two additional examples: a *4-bit full adder using carry lookahead* and a *4-bit counter using negative edge-triggered D-flipflops.*

6.5.1 4-to-1 Multiplexer

Gate-level modeling of a 4-to-1 multiplexer is discussed in Section 5.1.4, `Examples`. The logic diagram for the multiplexer is given in Figure 5-5 and the gate-level Verilog description is shown in Example 5-5. We describe the multiplexer, using dataflow statements. Compare it with the gate-level description. We show two methods to model the multiplexer by using dataflow statements.

Method 1: logic equation

We can use assignment statements instead of gates to model the logic equations of the multiplexer (see Example 6-2). Notice that everything is the same as the gate-level Verilog description except that computation of *out* is done by specifying one logic equation by using operators instead of individual gate instantiations. I/O ports remain the same. This is important so that the interface with the environment does not change. Only the internals of the module change. Notice how concise the description is compared to the gate-level description.

Example 6-2 4-to-1 Multiplexer, Using Logic Equations

```
// Module 4-to-1 multiplexer using data flow. logic equation
// Compare to gate-level model
module mux4_to_1 (out, i0, i1, i2, i3, s1, s0);
```

Example 6-2 4-to-1 Multiplexer, Using Logic Equations (Continued)

```
// Port declarations from the I/O diagram
output out;
input i0, i1, i2, i3;
input s1, s0;

//Logic equation for out
assign out =    (~s1 & ~s0 & i0)|
                 (~s1 & s0 & i1) |
                 (s1 & ~s0 & i2) |
                 (s1 & s0 & i3) ;

endmodule
```

Method 2: conditional operator

There is a more concise way to specify the 4-to-1 multiplexers. In Section 6.4.10, `Conditional Operator`, we described how a conditional statement corresponds to a multiplexer operation. We will use this operator to write a 4-to-1 multiplexer. Convince yourself that this description (Example 6-3) correctly models a multiplexer.

Example 6-3 4-to-1 Multiplexer, Using Conditional Operators

```
// Module 4-to-1 multiplexer using data flow. Conditional operator.
// Compare to gate-level model
module multiplexer4_to_1 (out, i0, i1, i2, i3, s1, s0);

// Port declarations from the I/O diagram
output out;
input i0, i1, i2, i3;
input s1, s0;
// Use nested conditional operator
assign out = s1 ? ( s0 ? i3 : i2) : (s0 ? i1 : i0) ;

endmodule
```

In the simulation of the multiplexer, the gate-level module in Example 5-5 can be substituted with the dataflow multiplexer modules described above. The stimulus module will not change. The simulation results will be identical. By encapsulating functionality inside a module, we can replace the gate-level module with a dataflow module without affecting the other modules in the simulation. This is a very powerful feature of Verilog.

6.5.2 4-bit Full Adder

The 4-bit full adder in Section 5.1.4, `Examples`, was designed by using gates; the logic diagram is shown in Figure 5-7 and Figure 5-6. In this section, we write the dataflow description for the 4-bit adder. Compare it with the gate-level description in Figure 5-7. In gates, we had to first describe a 1-bit full adder. Then we built a 4-bit full ripple carry adder. We again illustrate twc methods to describe a 4-bit full adder by means of dataflow statements.

Method 1: dataflow operators

A concise description of the adder (Example 6-4) is defined with the + and { } operators.

Example 6-4 4-bit Full Adder, Using Dataflow Operators

```
// Define a 4-bit full adder by using dataflow statements.
module fulladd4(sum, c_out, a, b, c_in);

// I/O port declarations
output [3:0] sum;
output c_out;
input[3:0] a, b;
input c_in;

// Specify the function of a full adder
assign {c_out, sum} = a + b + c_in;

endmodule
```

If we substitute the gate-level 4-bit full adder with the dataflow 4-bit full adder, the rest of the modules will not change. The simulation results will be identical.

Method 2: full adder with carry lookahead

In ripple carry adders, the carry must propagate through the gate levels before the sum is available at the output terminals. An n-bit ripple carry adder will have $2n$ gate levels. The propagation time can be a limiting factor on the speed of the circuit. One of the most popular methods to reduce delay is to use a *carry lookahead* mechanism. Logic equations for implementing the carry lookahead mechanism can be found in any logic design book.

The propagation delay is reduced to *four gate levels,* irrespective of the number of bits in the adder. The Verilog description for a carry lookahead adder is shown in Example 6-5. This module can be substituted in place of the full adder modules described before without changing any other component of the simulation. The simulation results will be unchanged.

Example 6-5 4-bit Full Adder with Carry Lookahead

```
module fulladd4(sum, c_out, a, b, c_in);
// Inputs and outputs
output [3:0] sum;
output c_out;
input [3:0] a,b;
input c_in;

// Internal wires
wire p0,g0, p1,g1, p2,g2, p3,g3;
wire c4, c3, c2, c1;

// compute the p for each stage
assign p0 = a[0] ^ b[0],
       p1 = a[1] ^ b[1],
       p2 = a[2] ^ b[2],
       p3 = a[3] ^ b[3];

// compute the g for each stage
assign g0 = a[0] & b[0],
       g1 = a[1] & b[1],
       g2 = a[2] & b[2],
       g3 = a[3] & b[3];

// compute the carry for each stage
// Note that c_in is equivalent c0 in the arithmetic equation for
// carry lookahead computation
assign c1 = g0 | (p0 & c_in),
       c2 = g1 | (p1 & g0) | (p1 & p0 & c_in),
       c3 = g2 | (p2 & g1) | (p2 & p1 & g0) | (p2 & p1 & p0 & c_in),
       c4 = g3 | (p3 & g2) | (p3 & p2 & g1) | (p3 & p2 & p1 & g0) |
                             (p3 & p2 & p1 & p0 & c_in);

// Compute Sum
assign sum[0] = p0 ^ c_in,
       sum[1] = p1 ^ c1,
       sum[2] = p2 ^ c2,
       sum[3] = p3 ^ c3;
```

Example 6-5 4-bit Full Adder with Carry Lookahead (Continued)

```
// Assign carry output
assign c_out = c4;

endmodule
```

6.5.3 Ripple Counter

We now discuss an additional example that was not discussed in the gate-level modeling chapter. We design a 4-bit ripple counter by using negative edge-triggered flipflops. This example was discussed at a very abstract level in Chapter 2, `Hierarchical Modeling Concepts`. We design it using Verilog dataflow statements and test it with a stimulus module. The diagrams for the 4-bit ripple carry counter modules are shown below.

Figure 6-2 shows the counter being built with *four T-flipflops.*

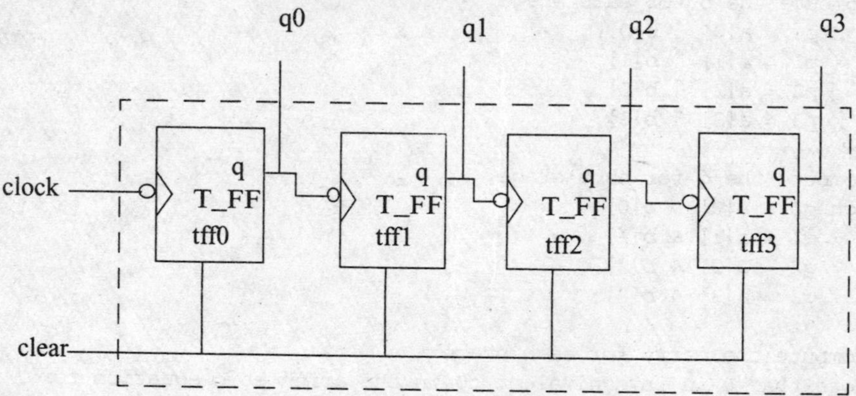

Figure 6-2 4-bit Ripple Carry Counter

Figure 6-3 shows that the *T-flipflop* is built with one *D-flipflop* and an inverter gate.

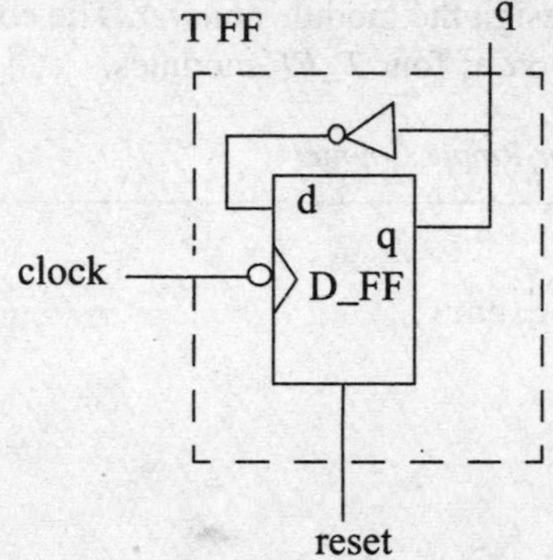

Figure 6-3 T-flipflop

Finally, Figure 6-4 shows the *D flipflop* constructed from basic logic gates.

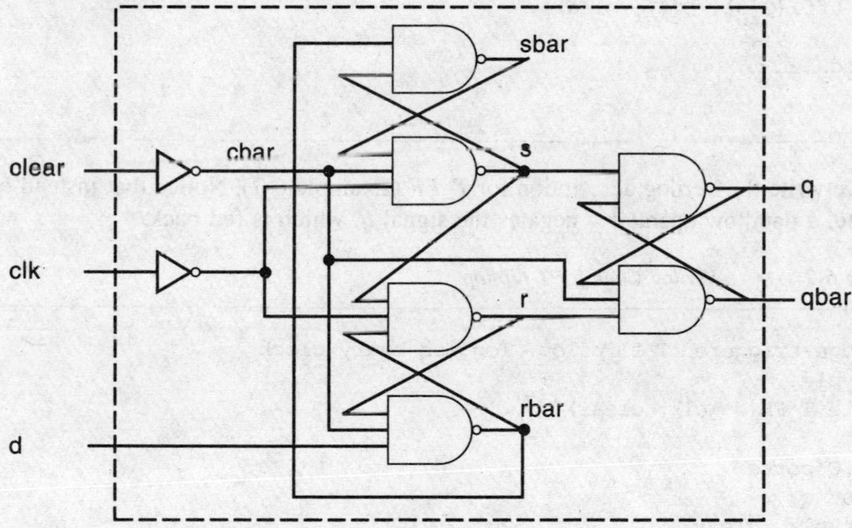

Figure 6-4 Negative Edge-Triggered D-flipflop with Clear

Given the above diagrams, we write the corresponding Verilog, using dataflow statements in a top-down fashion. First we design the module *counter*. The code is shown in Example 6-6. The code contains instantiation of four *T_FF* modules.

Example 6-6 Verilog Code for Ripple Counter

```
// Ripple counter
module counter(Q , clock, clear);

// I/O ports
output [3:0] Q;
input clock, clear;

// Instantiate the T flipflops
T_FF tff0(Q[0], clock, clear);
T_FF tff1(Q[1], Q[0], clear);
T_FF tff2(Q[2], Q[1], clear);
T_FF tff3(Q[3], Q[2], clear);

endmodule
```

Next, we write the Verilog description for *T_FF* (Example 6-7). Notice that instead of the **not** gate, a dataflow operator ~ negates the signal *q*, which is fed back.

Example 6-7 Verilog Code for T-flipflop

```
// Edge-triggered T-flipflop. Toggles every clock
// cycle.
module T_FF(q, clk, clear);

// I/O ports
output q;
input clk, clear;

// Instantiate the edge-triggered DFF
// Complement of output q is fed back.
// Notice qbar not needed. Unconnected port.
edge_dff ff1(q, ,~q, clk, clear);

endmodule
```

Finally, we define the lowest level module *D_FF* (*edge_dff*), using dataflow statements (Example 6-8). The dataflow statements correspond to the logic diagram shown in Figure 6-4. The nets in the logic diagram correspond exactly to the declared nets.

Example 6-8 *Verilog Code for Edge-Triggered D-flipflop*

```
// Edge-triggered D flipflop
module edge_dff(q, qbar, d, clk, clear);

// Inputs and outputs
output q,qbar;
input d, clk, clear;

// Internal variables
wire s, sbar, r, rbar,cbar;

// dataflow statements
//Create a complement of signal clear
assign cbar = ~clear;

// Input latches; A latch is level sensitive. An edge-sensitive
// flip-flop is implemented by using 3 SR latches.
assign  sbar = ~(rbar & s),
        s = ~(sbar & cbar & ~clk),
        r = ~(rbar & ~clk & s),
        rbar = ~(r & cbar & d);

// Output latch
assign  q = ~(s & qbar),
        qbar = ~(q & r & cbar);

endmodule
```

The design block is now ready. Now we must instantiate the design block inside the stimulus block to test the design. The stimulus block is shown in Example 6-9. The clock has a time period of 20 with a 50% duty cycle.

Example 6-9 *Stimulus Module for Ripple Counter*

```
// Top level stimulus module
module stimulus;

// Declare variables for stimulating input
```

Example 6-9 *Stimulus Module for Ripple Counter (Continued)*

```
reg CLOCK, CLEAR;
wire [3:0] Q;

initial
      $monitor($time, " Count Q = %b Clear= %b",  Q[3:0],CLEAR);

// Instantiate the design block counter
counter c1(Q, CLOCK, CLEAR);

// Stimulate the Clear Signal
initial
begin
      CLEAR = 1'b1;
      #34 CLEAR = 1'b0;
      #200 CLEAR = 1'b1;
      #50 CLEAR = 1'b0;
end
// Set up the clock to toggle every 10 time units
initial
begin
      CLOCK = 1'b0;
      forever #10 CLOCK = ~CLOCK;
end

// Finish the simulation at time 400
initial
begin
      #400 $finish;
end

endmodule
```

The output of the simulation is shown below. Note that the clear signal resets the count to zero.

```
  0 Count Q = 0000 Clear= 1
 34 Count Q = 0000 Clear= 0
 40 Count Q = 0001 Clear= 0
 60 Count Q = 0010 Clear= 0
 80 Count Q = 0011 Clear= 0
100 Count Q = 0100 Clear= 0
```

(Continued...)

```
120 Count Q = 0101 Clear= 0
140 Count Q = 0110 Clear= 0
160 Count Q = 0111 Clear= 0
180 Count Q = 1000 Clear= 0
200 Count Q = 1001 Clear= 0
220 Count Q = 1010 Clear= 0
234 Count Q = 0000 Clear= 1
284 Count Q = 0000 Clear= 0
300 Count Q = 0001 Clear= 0
320 Count Q = 0010 Clear= 0
340 Count Q = 0011 Clear= 0
360 Count Q = 0100 Clear= 0
380 Count Q = 0101 Clear= 0
```

6.6 Summary

- *Continuous assignment* is one of the main constructs used in dataflow modeling. A continuous assignment is always active and the assignment expression is evaluated as soon as one of the right hand-side variables changes. The left-hand side of a continuous assignment must be a net. Any logic function can be realized with continuous assignments.
- Delay values control the time between the change in a right-hand-side variable and when the new value is assigned to the left-hand side. Delays on a net can be defined in the **`assign`** statement, implicit continuous assignment, or net declaration.
- Assignment statements contain expressions, operators, and operands.
- The operator types are *arithmetic, logical, relational, equality, bitwise, reduction, shift, concatenation, replication,* and *conditional*. Unary operators require one operand, binary operators require two operands, and ternary require three operands. The concatenation operator can take any number of operands.
- The *conditional operator* behaves like a multiplexer in hardware or like the if-then-else statement in programming languages.
- Dataflow description of a circuit is more concise than a gate-level description. The 4-to-1 multiplexer and the 4-bit full adder discussed in the gate-level modeling chapter can also be designed by use of dataflow statements. Two dataflow implementations for both circuits were discussed. A 4-bit ripple counter using negative edge-triggered D-flipflops was designed.

6.7 Exercises

1. A *full subtractor* has three 1-bit inputs *x, y,* and *z* (previous borrow) and two 1-bit outputs *D* (difference) and *B* (borrow). The logic equations for D and B are as follows:

   $D = x'.y'.z + x'.y.z' + x.y'.z' + x.y.z$

   $B = x'.y + x'.z + y.z$

   Write the full Verilog description for the full subtractor module, including I/O ports (remember that + in logic equations corresponds to a logical or operator (| |) in dataflow). Instantiate the subtractor inside a stimulus block and test all eight possible combinations of *x, y,* and *z* given in the following truth table.

x	y	z	B	D
0	0	0	0	0
0	0	1	1	1
0	1	0	1	1
0	1	1	1	0
1	0	0	0	1
1	0	1	0	0
1	1	0	0	0
1	1	1	1	1

2. A *magnitude comparator* checks if one number is greater than or equal to or less than another number. A 4-bit magnitude comparator takes two 4-bit numbers, *A* and *B*, as input. We write the bits in *A* and *B* as follows. The leftmost bit is the most significant bit.

   $A = A(3)\ A(2)\ A(1)\ A(0)$

   $B = B(3)\ B(2)\ B(1)\ B(0)$

   The magnitude can be compared by comparing the numbers bit by bit, starting with the most significant bit. If any bit mismatches, the number with bit 0 is the lower number. To realize this functionality in logic equations, let us define an intermediate variable. Notice that the function below is an **xnor** function.

   $x(i) = A(i).B(i) + A(i)'.B(i)'$

   The three outputs of the magnitude comparator are *A_gt_B, A_lt_B, A_eq_B*. They are defined with the following logic equations:

   $A\_gt\_B = A(3).B(3)' + x(3).A(2).B(2)' + x(3).x(2).A(1).B(1)' + x(3).x(2).x(1).A(0).B(0)'$

   $A\_lt\_B = A(3)'.B(3) + x(3).A(2)'.B(2) + x(3).x(2).A(1)'.B(1) + x(3).x(2).x(1).A(0)'.B(0)$

$A\_eq\_B = x(3).x(2).x(1).x(0)$

Write the Verilog description of the module *magnitude_comparator*. Instantiate the magnitude comparator inside the stimulus module and try out a few combinations of *A* and *B*.

3. A *synchronous counter* can be designed by using *master-slave JK flipflops*. Design a 4-bit synchronous counter. Circuit diagrams for the synchronous counter and the JK flipflop are given in Figures 6-5 and 6-6. The *clear* signal is active low. Data gets latched on the positive edge of *clock*, and the output of the flipflop appears on the negative edge of *clock*. Counting is disabled when *count_enable* signal is low. Write the dataflow description for the synchronous counter. Write a stimulus file that exercises *clear* and *count_enable*. Display the output count *Q[3:0]*.

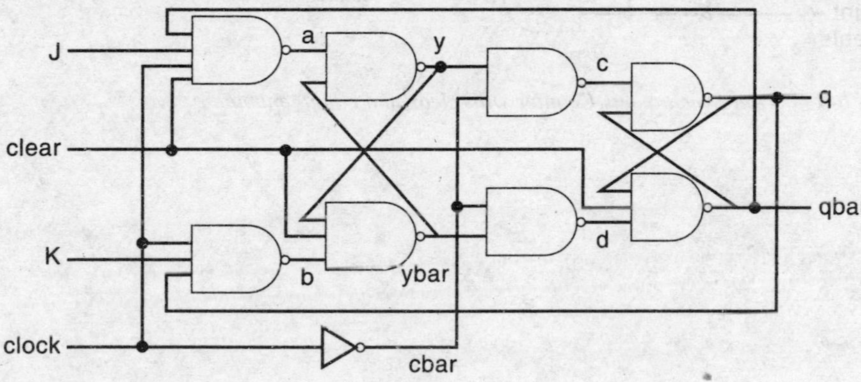

Figure 6-5 Master-Slave JK-flipflop

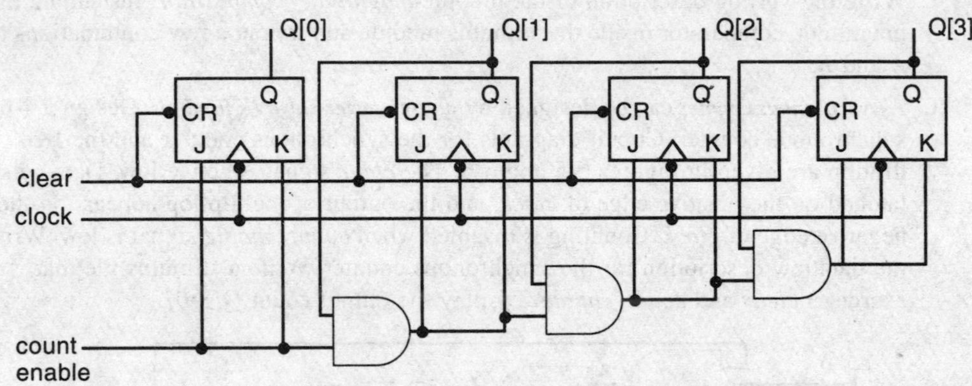

Figure 6-6 4-bit Synchronous Counter with clear and count_enable

Behavioral Modeling

With the increasing complexity of digital design, it has become vitally important to make wise design decisions early in a project. Designers need to be able to evaluate the trade-offs of various architectures and algorithms before they decide on the optimum architecture and algorithm to implement in hardware. Thus, architectural evaluation takes place at an algorithmic level where the designers do not necessarily think in terms of logic gates or data flow but in terms of the algorithm they wish to implement in hardware. They are more concerned about the behavior of the algorithm and its performance. Only after the high-level architecture and algorithm are finalized, do designers start focusing on building the digital circuit to implement the algorithm.

Verilog provides designers the ability to describe design functionality in an algorithmic manner. In other words, the designer describes the *behavior* of the circuit. Thus, behavioral modeling represents the circuit at a very high level of abstraction. Design at this level resembles C programming more than it resembles digital circuit design. Behavioral Verilog constructs are similar to C language constructs in many ways. Verilog is rich in behavioral constructs that provide the designer with a great amount of flexibility.

Learning Objectives

- Explain the significance of structured procedures `always` and `initial` in behavioral modeling.
- Define *blocking* and *nonblocking* procedural assignments.
- Understand the delay-based timing control mechanism in behavioral modeling. Use *regular delays, intra-assignment delays*, and *zero delays.*
- Describe the event-based timing control mechanism in behavioral modeling. Use *regular event control, named event control*, and *event OR control.*
- Use the level-sensitive timing control mechanism in behavioral modeling.
- Explain conditional statements using `if` and `else`.
- Describe multiway branching, using `case`, `casex`, and `casez` statements.

- Understand looping statements such as **while**, **for**, **repeat**, and **forever**.
- Define *sequential* and *parallel* blocks.
- Understand *naming of blocks* and *disabling* of named blocks.
- Use behavioral modeling statements in practical examples.

7.1 Structured Procedures

There are two structured procedure statements in Verilog: **always** and **initial**. These statements are the two most basic statements in behavioral modeling. All other behavioral statements can appear only inside these structured procedure statements.

Verilog is a concurrent programming language unlike the C programming language, which is sequential in nature. Activity flows in Verilog run in parallel rather than in sequence. Each **always** and **initial** statement represents a separate activity flow in Verilog. Each activity flow starts at simulation time 0. The statements **always** and **initial** cannot be nested. The fundamental difference between the two statements is explained in the following sections.

7.1.1 initial Statement

All statements inside an **initial** statement constitute an **initial** block. An **initial** block starts at time 0, executes exactly once during a simulation, and then does not execute again. If there are multiple **initial** blocks, each block starts to execute concurrently at time 0. Each block finishes execution independently of other blocks. Multiple behavioral statements must be grouped, typically using the keywords **begin** and **end**. If there is only one behavioral statement, grouping is not necessary. This is similar to the *begin-end* blocks in Pascal programming language or the *{ }* grouping in the C programming language. Example 7-1 illustrates the use of the **initial** statement.

Example 7-1 initial Statement

```
module stimulus;

reg x,y, a,b, m;

initial
    m = 1'b0; //single statement; does not need to be grouped

initial
```

Example 7-1 initial Statement (Continued)

```
begin
   #5 a = 1'b1; //multiple statements; need to be grouped
   #25 b = 1'b0;
end

initial
begin
   #10 x = 1'b0;
   #25 y = 1'b1;
end

initial
   #50 $finish;

endmodule
```

In the above example, the three initial statements start to execute in parallel at time 0. If a delay #<*delay*> is seen before a statement, the statement is executed <*delay*> time units after the current simulation time. Thus, the execution sequence of the statements inside the **initial** blocks will be as follows:

```
time            statement executed
0               m = 1'b0;
5               a = 1'b1;
10              x = 1'b0;
30              b = 1'b0;
35              y = 1'b1;
50              $finish;
```

The **initial** blocks are typically used for initialization, monitoring, waveforms and other processes that must be executed only once during the entire simulation run. The following subsections discuss how to initialize values using alternate shorthand syntax. The use of such shorthand syntax has the same effect as an **initial** block combined with a variable declaration.

Combined Variable Declaration and Initialization

Variables can be initialized when they are declared. Example 7-2 shows such a declaration.

Example 7-2 *Initial Value Assignment*

```
//The clock variable is defined first
reg clock;
//The value of clock is set to 0
initial clock = 0;

//Instead of the above method, clock variable
//can be initialized at the time of declaration
//This is allowed only for variables declared
//at module level.
reg clock = 0;
```

Combined Port/Data Declaration and Initialization

The combined port/data declaration can also be combined with an initialization. Example 7-3 shows such a declaration.

Example 7-3 *Combined Port/Data Declaration and Variable Initialization*

```
module adder (sum, co, a, b, ci);
output reg [7:0] sum = 0; //Initialize 8 bit output sum
output reg       co  = 0; //Initialize 1 bit output co
input      [7:0] a, b;
input            ci;

--
--
endmodule
```

Combined ANSI C Style Port Declaration and Initialization

ANSI C style port declaration can also be combined with an initialization. Example 7-4 shows such a declaration.

Example 7-4 *Combined ANSI C Port Declaration and Variable Initialization*

```
module adder (output reg [7:0] sum = 0, //Initialize 8 bit output
              output reg       co  = 0, //Initialize 1 bit output co
              input      [7:0] a, b,
              input            ci
              );
--
--
endmodule
```

7.1.2 always Statement

All behavioral statements inside an **always** statement constitute an **always** block. The **always** statement starts at time 0 and executes the statements in the **always** block continuously in a looping fashion. This statement is used to model a block of activity that is repeated continuously in a digital circuit. An example is a clock generator module that toggles the clock signal every half cycle. In real circuits, the clock generator is active from time 0 to as long as the circuit is powered on. Example 7-5 illustrates one method to model a clock generator in Verilog.

Example 7-5 *always Statement*

```
module clock_gen (output reg clock);

//Initialize clock at time zero
initial
        clock = 1'b0;

//Toggle clock every half-cycle (time period = 20)
always
        #10 clock = ~clock;

initial
        #1000 $finish;

endmodule
```

In Example 7-5, the **always** statement starts at time 0 and executes the statement *clock = ~clock* every 10 time units. Notice that the initialization of *clock* has to be done inside a separate **initial** statement. If we put the initialization of clock inside the **always** block, *clock* will be initialized every time the **always** is entered. Also, the simulation must be halted inside an **initial** statement. If there is no **$stop** or **$finish** statement to halt the simulation, the clock generator will run forever.

C programmers might draw an analogy between the **always** block and an infinite loop. But hardware designers tend to view it as a continuously repeated activity in a digital circuit starting from power on. The activity is stopped only by power off (**$finish**) or by an interrupt (**$stop**).

7.2 Procedural Assignments

Procedural assignments update values of **reg**, **integer**, **real**, or **time** variables. The value placed on a variable will remain unchanged until another procedural assignment updates the variable with a different value. These are unlike continuous assignments discussed in Chapter 6, *Dataflow Modeling*, where one assignment statement can cause the value of the right-hand-side expression to be continuously placed onto the left-hand-side net. The syntax for the simplest form of procedural assignment is shown below.

```
assignment ::= variable_lvalue = [ delay_or_event_control ]
           expression
```

The left-hand side of a procedural assignment *<lvalue>* can be one of the following:

- A **reg**, integer, real, or time register variable or a memory element
- A bit select of these variables (e.g., *addr[0]*)
- A part select of these variables (e.g., *addr[31:16]*)
- A concatenation of any of the above

The right-hand side can be any expression that evaluates to a value. In behavioral modeling, all operators listed in Table 6-1 on page 96 can be used in behavioral expressions.

There are two types of procedural assignment statements: *blocking* and *nonblocking*.

7.2.1 Blocking Assignments

Blocking assignment statements are executed in the order they are specified in a sequential block. A blocking assignment will not block execution of statements that follow in a parallel block. Both parallel and sequential blocks are discussed in Section 7.7, `Sequential and Parallel Blocks`. The = operator is used to specify blocking assignments.

Example 7-6 *Blocking Statements*

```
reg x, y, z;
reg [15:0] reg_a, reg_b;
integer count;

//All behavioral statements must be inside an initial or always block
initial
begin
        x = 0; y = 1; z = 1; //Scalar assignments
        count = 0; //Assignment to integer variables
        reg_a = 16'b0; reg_b = reg_a; //initialize vectors

        #15 reg_a[2] = 1'b1; //Bit select assignment with delay
        #10 reg_b[15:13] = {x, y, z} //Assign result of concatenation to
                                     // part select of a vector
        count = count + 1; //Assignment to an integer (increment)
end
```

In Example 7-6, the statement *y = 1* is executed only after *x = 0* is executed. The behavior in a particular block is sequential in a *begin-end* block if blocking statements are used, because the statements can execute only in sequence. The statement *count = count + 1* is executed last. The simulation times at which the statements are executed are as follows:

- All statements *x = 0* through *reg_b = reg_a* are executed at time 0
- Statement *reg_a[2] = 0* at time = 15
- Statement *reg_b[15:13] = {x, y, z}* at time = 25
- Statement *count = count + 1* at time = 25
- Since there is a delay of 15 and 10 in the preceding statements, *count = count + 1* will be executed at time = 25 units

Note that for procedural assignments to register, if the right-hand side has more bits than the register variable, the right-hand side is truncated to match the width of the register variable. The least significant bits are selected and the most significant bits are discarded. If the right-hand side has fewer bits, zeros are filled in the most significant bits of the register variable.

7.2.2 Nonblocking Assignments

Nonblocking assignments allow scheduling of assignments without blocking execution of the statements that follow in a sequential block. A **<=** operator is used to specify nonblocking assignments. Note that this operator has the same symbol as a relational operator, *less_than_equal_to*. The operator **<=** is interpreted as a relational operator in an expression and as an assignment operator in the context of a nonblocking assignment. To illustrate the behavior of nonblocking statements and its difference from blocking statements, let us consider Example 7-7, where we convert some blocking assignments to nonblocking assignments, and observe the behavior.

Example 7-7 *Nonblocking Assignments*

```
reg x, y, z;
reg [15:0] reg_a, reg_b;
integer count;


//All behavioral statements must be inside an initial or always block
initial
begin
      x = 0; y = 1; z = 1; //Scalar assignments
      count = 0; //Assignment to integer variables
      reg_a = 16'b0; reg_b = reg_a; //Initialize vectors

      reg_a[2] <= #15 1'b1; //Bit select assignment with delay
     reg_b[15:13] <= #10 {x, y, z}; //Assign result of concatenation
                                //to part select of a vector
      count <= count + 1; //Assignment to an integer (increment)
end
```

In this example, the statements *x = 0* through *reg_b = reg_a* are executed sequentially at time 0. Then the three nonblocking assignments are processed at the same simulation time.

1. *reg_a[2] = 0* is scheduled to execute after 15 units (i.e., time = 15)
2. *reg_b[15:13] = {x, y, z}* is scheduled to execute after 10 time units (i.e., time = 10)
3. *count = count + 1* is scheduled to be executed without any delay (i.e., time = 0)

Thus, the simulator schedules a *nonblocking* assignment statement to execute and continues to the next statement in the block without waiting for the nonblocking statement to complete execution. Typically, nonblocking assignment statements are executed last in the time step in which they are scheduled, that is, after all the blocking assignments in that time step are executed.

In the example above, we mixed blocking and nonblocking assignments to illustrate their behavior. However, it is recommended that blocking and nonblocking assignments not be mixed in the same always block.

Application of nonblocking assignments

Having described the behavior of nonblocking assignments, it is important to understand why they are used in digital design. They are used as a method to model several concurrent data transfers that take place after a common event. Consider the following example where three concurrent data transfers take place at the positive edge of clock.

```
always @(posedge clock)
begin
    reg1 <= #1 in1;
    reg2 <= @(negedge clock) in2 ^ in3;
    reg3 <= #1 reg1; //The old value of reg1
end
```

At each positive edge of clock, the following sequence takes place for the nonblocking assignments.

1. A *read* operation is performed on each right-hand-side variable, *in1*, *in2*, *in3*, and *reg1,* at the positive edge of clock. The right-hand-side expressions are evaluated, and the results are stored internally in the simulator.
2. The *write* operations to the left-hand-side variables are scheduled to be executed at the time specified by the intra-assignment delay in each assignment, that is, schedule "*write*" to *reg1* after 1 time unit, to *reg2* at the next negative edge of clock, and to *reg3* after 1 time unit.
3. The *write* operations are executed at the scheduled time steps. The order in which the write operations are executed is not important because the internally stored right-hand-side expression values are used to assign to the left-hand-side values. For

example, note that *reg3* is assigned the old value of *reg1* that was stored after the read operation, even if the write operation wrote a new value to *reg1* before the write operation to *reg3* was executed.

Thus, the final values of *reg1*, *reg2*, and *reg3* are not dependent on the order in which the assignments are processed.

To understand the read and write operations further, consider Example 7-8, which is intended to swap the values of registers *a* and *b* at each positive edge of clock, using two concurrent **always** blocks.

Example 7-8 Nonblocking Statements to Eliminate Race Conditions

```
//Illustration 1: Two concurrent always blocks with blocking
//statements
always @(posedge clock)
        a = b;

always @(posedge clock)
        b = a;

//Illustration 2: Two concurrent always blocks with nonblocking
//statements
always @(posedge clock)
        a <= b;

always @(posedge clock)
        b <= a;
```

In Example 7-8, in Illustration 1, there is a race condition when blocking statements are used. Either *a = b* would be executed before *b = a*, or vice versa, depending on the simulator implementation. Thus, values of registers *a* and *b* will not be swapped. Instead, both registers will get the same value (previous value of *a* or *b*), based on the Verilog simulator implementation.

However, nonblocking statements used in Illustration 2 eliminate the race condition. At the positive edge of clock, the values of all right-hand-side variables are "*read,*" and the right-hand-side expressions are evaluated and stored in *temporary* variables. During the write operation, the values stored in the temporary variables are assigned to the left-hand-side variables. Separating the read and write operations ensures that the values of registers *a* and *b* are swapped correctly, regardless of the order in which the write operations are performed. Example 7-9 shows how nonblocking assignments shown in Illustration 2 could be emulated using blocking assignments.

Example 7-9 Implementing Nonblocking Assignments using Blocking Assignments

```
//Emulate the behavior of nonblocking assignments by
//using temporary variables and blocking assignments
always @(posedge clock)
begin
   //Read operation
   //store values of right-hand-side expressions in temporary variables
   temp_a = a;
   temp_b = b;
   //Write operation
   //Assign values of temporary variables to left-hand-side variables
   a = temp_b;
   b = temp_a;
end
```

For digital design, use of nonblocking assignments in place of blocking assignments is highly recommended in places where concurrent data transfers take place after a common event. In such cases, blocking assignments can potentially cause race conditions because the final result depends on the order in which the assignments are evaluated. Nonblocking assignments can be used effectively to model concurrent data transfers because the final result is not dependent on the order in which the assignments are evaluated. Typical applications of nonblocking assignments include pipeline modeling and modeling of several mutually exclusive data transfers. On the downside, nonblocking assignments can potentially cause a degradation in the simulator performance and increase in memory usage.

7.3 Timing Controls

Various behavioral timing control constructs are available in Verilog. In Verilog, if there are no timing control statements, the simulation time does not advance. Timing controls provide a way to specify the simulation time at which procedural statements will execute. There are three methods of timing control: *delay-based timing control*, *event-based timing control*, and *level-sensitive timing control.*

7.3.1 Delay-Based Timing Control

Delay-based timing control in an expression specifies the time duration between when the statement is encountered and when it is executed. We used delay-based timing control statements when writing a few modules in the preceding chapters but did not explain them in detail. In this section, we will discuss delay-based timing control statements. Delays are specified by the symbol #. Syntax for the delay-based timing control statement is shown below.

```
delay3 ::= # delay_value | # ( delay_value [ , delay_value [ ,
         delay_value ] ] )
delay2 ::= # delay_value | # ( delay_value [ , delay_value ] )
delay_value ::=
        unsigned_number
      | parameter_identifier
      | specparam_identifier
      | mintypmax_expression
```

Delay-based timing control can be specified by a *number, identifier*, or a *mintypmax_expression*. There are three types of delay control for procedural assignments: *regular delay control, intra-assignment delay control*, and *zero delay control*.

Regular delay control

Regular delay control is used when a non-zero delay is specified to the left of a procedural assignment. Usage of regular delay control is shown in Example 7-10.

Example 7-10 *Regular Delay Control*

```
//define parameters
parameter latency = 20;
parameter delta = 2;
//define register variables
reg x, y, z, p, q;

initial
begin
      x = 0; // no delay control
      #10 y = 1; // delay control with a number. Delay execution of
                                    // y = 1 by 10 units

      #latency z = 0; //Delay control with identifier. Delay of 20 units
      #(latency + delta) p = 1; // Delay control with expression

      #y x = x + 1; // Delay control with identifier. Take value of y.

      #(4:5:6) q = 0; // Minimum, typical and maximum delay values.
```

Example 7-10 Regular Delay Control (Continued)

```
                        //Discussed in gate-level modeling chapter.
end
```

In Example 7-10, the execution of a procedural assignment is delayed by the number specified by the delay control. For begin-end groups, delay is always relative to time when the statement is encountered. Thus, *y =1* is executed 10 units after it is encountered in the activity flow.

Intra-assignment delay control

Instead of specifying delay control to the left of the assignment, it is possible to assign a delay to the right of the assignment operator. Such delay specification alters the flow of activity in a different manner. Example 7-11 shows the contrast between intra-assignment delays and regular delays.

Example 7-11 Intra-assignment Delays

```
//define register variables
reg x, y, z;

//intra assignment delays
initial
begin
        x = 0; z = 0;
        y = #5 x + z; //Take value of x and z at the time=0, evaluate
                   //x + z and then wait 5 time units to assign value
                  //to y.

end

//Equivalent method with temporary variables and regular delay control
initial
begin
        x = 0; z = 0;
        temp_xz = x + z;
        #5 y = temp_xz; //Take value of x + z at the current time and
                 //store it in a temporary variable. Even though x and z
                 //might change between 0 and 5,
                 //the value assigned to y at time 5 is unaffected.
end
```

Note the difference between intra-assignment delays and regular delays. Regular delays defer the execution of the entire assignment. Intra-assignment delays compute the right-hand-side expression at the current time and defer the assignment of the computed value to the left-hand-side variable. Intra-assignment delays are like using regular delays with a temporary variable to store the current value of a right-hand-side expression.

Zero delay control

Procedural statements in different *always-initial* blocks may be evaluated at the same simulation time. The order of execution of these statements in different *always-initial* blocks is nondeterministic. Zero delay control is a method to ensure that a statement is executed last, after all other statements in that simulation time are executed. This is used to eliminate race conditions. However, if there are multiple zero delay statements, the order between them is nondeterministic. Example 7-12 illustrates zero delay control.

Example 7-12 *Zero Delay Control*

```
initial
begin
    x = 0;
    y = 0;
end

initial
begin
    #0 x = 1; //zero delay control
    #0 y = 1;
end
```

In Example 7-12, four statements—*x = 0, y = 0, x = 1, y = 1*—are to be executed at simulation time 0. However, since *x = 1* and *y = 1* have *#0*, they will be executed last. Thus, at the end of time 0, x will have value `1` and y will have value `1`. The order in which *x = 1* and *y = 1* are executed is not deterministic.

The above example was used as an illustration. However, using *#0* is not a recommended practice.

7.3.2 Event-Based Timing Control

An *event* is the change in the value on a register or a net. Events can be utilized to trigger execution of a statement or a block of statements. There are four types of event-based timing control: *regular event control, named event control, event OR control,* and *level-sensitive timing control*.

Regular event control

The `@` symbol is used to specify an event control. Statements can be executed on changes in signal value or at a *positive* or *negative* transition of the signal value. The keyword **posedge** is used for a positive transition, as shown in Example 7-13.

Example 7-13 Regular Event Control

```
@(clock) q = d; //q = d is executed whenever signal clock changes value
@(posedge clock) q = d; //q = d is executed whenever signal clock does
                        //a positive transition ( 0 to 1,x or z,
                        // x to 1, z to 1 )
@(negedge clock) q = d; //q = d is executed whenever signal clock does
                        //a negative transition ( 1 to 0,x or z,
                        //x to 0, z to 0)
q = @(posedge clock) d; //d is evaluated immediately and assigned
                        //to q at the positive edge of clock
```

Named event control

Verilog provides the capability to *declare* an event and then *trigger* and *recognize* the occurrence of that event (see Example 7-14). The event does not hold any data. A named event is declared by the keyword **event**. An event is triggered by the symbol `->`. The triggering of the event is recognized by the symbol `@`.

Example 7-14 Named Event Control

```
//This is an example of a data buffer storing data after the
//last packet of data has arrived.

event received_data; //Define an event called received_data

always @(posedge clock) //check at each positive clock edge
begin
        if(last_data_packet) //If this is the last data packet
                ->received_data; //trigger the event received_data
end
```

Example 7-14 Named Event Control (Continued)

```
always @(received_data) //Await triggering of event received_data
                    //When event is triggered, store all four
                    //packets of received data in data buffer
                  //use concatenation operator { }
      data_buf = {data_pkt[0], data_pkt[1], data_pkt[2], data_pkt[3]};
```

Event OR Control

Sometimes a transition on any one of multiple signals or events can trigger the execution of a statement or a block of statements. This is expressed as an OR of events or signals. The list of events or signals expressed as an OR is also known as a *sensitivity* list. The keyword **or** is used to specify multiple triggers, as shown in Example 7-15.

Example 7-15 Event OR Control (Sensitivity List)

```
//A level-sensitive latch with asynchronous reset
always @( reset or clock or d)
                                  //Wait for reset or clock or d to change
begin
      if (reset)                  //if reset signal is high, set q to 0.
            q = 1'b0;
      else  if(clock)             //if clock is high, latch input
            q = d;
end
```

Sensitivity lists can also be specified using the "," (comma) operator instead of the **or** operator. Example 7-16 shows how the above example can be rewritten using the comma operator. Comma operators can also be applied to sensitivity lists that have edge-sensitive triggers.

Example 7-16 Sensitivity List with Comma Operator

```
//A level-sensitive latch with asynchronous reset
always @( reset, clock, d)
                                  //Wait for reset or clock or d to change
begin
      if (reset)                  //if reset signal is high, set q to 0.
            q = 1'b0;
```

(Continued)

```
        else    if(clock)     //if clock is high, latch input
                q = d;
end


//A positive edge triggered D flipflop with asynchronous falling
//reset can be modeled as shown below
always @(posedge clk, negedge reset) //Note use of comma operator
if(!reset)
   q <=0;
else
   q <=d;
```

When the number of input variables to a combination logic block are very large, sensitivity lists can become very cumbersome to write. Moreover, if an input variable is missed from the sensitivity list, the block will not behave like a combinational logic block. To solve this problem, Verilog HDL contains two special symbols: @* and @(*). Both symbols exhibit identical behavior. These special symbols are sensitive to a change on any signal that may be read by the statement group that follows this symbol.[1] Example 7-17 shows an example of this special symbol for combinational logic sensitivity lists.

1. See *IEEE Standard Verilog Hardware Description Language* document for details and restrictions on the @* and @(*) symbols.

Example 7-17 *Use of @* Operator*

```
//Combination logic block using the or operator
//Cumbersome to write and it is easy to miss one input to the block
always @(a or b or c or d or e or f or g or h or p or m)

begin
out1 = a ? b+c : d+e;
out2 = f ? g+h : p+m;
end

//Instead of the above method, use @(*) symbol
//Alternately, the @* symbol can be used
//All input variables are automatically included in the
//sensitivity list.
always @(*)
begin
out1 = a ? b+c : d+e;
out2 = f ? g+h : p+m;
end
```

7.3.3 Level-Sensitive Timing Control

Event control discussed earlier waited for the change of a signal value or the triggering of an event. The symbol `@` provided edge-sensitive control. Verilog also allows level-sensitive timing control, that is, the ability to wait for a certain condition to be true before a statement or a block of statements is executed. The keyword **`wait`** is used for level-sensitive constructs.

```
always
    wait (count_enable) #20 count = count + 1;
```

In the above example, the value of *count_enable* is monitored continuously. If *count_enable* is `0`, the statement is not entered. If it is logical `1`, the statement *count = count + 1* is executed after 20 time units. If *count_enable* stays at 1, count will be incremented every 20 time units.

7.4 Conditional Statements

Conditional statements are used for making decisions based upon certain conditions. These conditions are used to decide whether or not a statement should be executed. Keywords **if** and **else** are used for conditional statements. There are three types of conditional statements. Usage of conditional statements is shown below. For formal syntax, see Appendix D, *Formal Syntax Definition.*

```
//Type 1 conditional statement. No else statement.
//Statement executes or does not execute.
if (<expression>) true_statement ;

//Type 2 conditional statement. One else statement
//Either true_statement or false_statement is evaluated
if (<expression>) true_statement ; else false_statement ;

//Type 3 conditional statement. Nested if-else-if.
//Choice of multiple statements. Only one is executed.
if (<expression1>) true_statement1 ;
else if (<expression2>) true_statement2 ;
else if (<expression3>) true_statement3 ;
else default_statement ;
```

The *<expression>* is evaluated. If it is true (1 or a non-zero value), the *true_statement* is executed. However, if it is false (zero) or ambiguous (**x**), the *false_statement* is executed. The *<expression>* can contain any operators mentioned in Table 6-1 on page 96. Each *true_statement* or *false_statement* can be a single statement or a block of multiple statements. A block must be grouped, typically by using keywords **begin** and **end**. A single statement need not be grouped. See Example 7-18.

Example 7-18 Conditional Statement Examples

```
//Type 1 statements
if(!lock) buffer = data;
if(enable) out = in;

//Type 2 statements
if (number_queued < MAX_Q_DEPTH)
begin
        data_queue = data;
        number_queued = number_queued + 1;
end
```

Example 7-18 *Conditional Statement Examples (Continued)*

```
else
        $display("Queue Full. Try again");

//Type 3 statements
//Execute statements based on ALU control signal.
if (alu_control == 0)
        y = x + z;
else if(alu_control == 1)
        y = x - z;
else if(alu_control == 2)
        y = x * z;
else
        $display("Invalid ALU control signal");
```

7.5 Multiway Branching

In *type 3* conditional statement in Section 7.4, `Conditional Statements`, there were many alternatives, from which one was chosen. The nested *if-else-if* can become unwieldy if there are too many alternatives. A shortcut to achieve the same result is to use the **`case`** statement.

7.5.1 case Statement

The keywords **`case`**, **`endcase`**, and **`default`** are used in the *case* statement. .

```
case (expression)
    alternative1: statement1;
    alternative2: statement2;
    alternative3: statement3;
        ...
        ...
    default: default_statement;
endcase
```

Each of *statement1, statement2 ..., default_statement* can be a single statement or a block of multiple statements. A block of multiple statements must be grouped by keywords **`begin`** and **`end`**. The expression is compared to the alternatives in the order they are written. For the first alternative that matches, the corresponding statement or block is executed. If none of the alternatives matches, the *default_statement* is executed. The *default_statement* is optional. Placing of multiple default statements in one **case** statement is not allowed. The **case** statements can be nested. The following Verilog code implements the type 3 conditional statement in Example 7-18.

```
//Execute statements based on the ALU control signal
reg [1:0] alu_control;
...
...
case (alu_control)
  2'd0 : y = x + z;
  2'd1 : y = x - z;
  2'd2 : y = x * z;
  default : $display("Invalid ALU control signal");
endcase
```

The **case** statement can also act like a many-to-one multiplexer. To understand this, let us model the 4-to-1 multiplexer in Section 6.5, *Examples,* on page 106, using case statements. The I/O ports are unchanged. Notice that an 8-to-1 or 16-to-1 multiplexer can also be easily implemented by **case** statements.

Example 7-19 4-to-1 Multiplexer with Case Statement

```
module mux4_to_1 (out, i0, i1, i2, i3, s1, s0);

// Port declarations from the I/O diagram
output out;
input i0, i1, i2, i3;
input s1, s0;
reg out;

always @(s1 or s0 or i0 or i1 or i2 or i3)
case ({s1, s0}) //Switch based on concatenation of control signals
        2'd0 : out = i0;
        2'd1 : out = i1;
        2'd2 : out = i2;
        2'd3 : out = i3;
        default: $display("Invalid control signals");
endcase

endmodule
```

The **case** statement compares **0**, **1**, **x**, and **z** values in the expression and the alternative bit for bit. If the expression and the alternative are of unequal bit width, they are zero filled to match the bit width of the widest of the expression and the alternative. In Example 7-20, we will define a 1-to-4 demultiplexer for which outputs are completely specified, that is, definitive results are provided even for **x** and **z** values on the select signal.

Example 7-20 Case Statement with x and z

```
module demultiplexer1_to_4 (out0, out1, out2, out3, in, s1, s0);

// Port declarations from the I/O diagram
output out0, out1, out2, out3;
reg  out0,  out1,  out2,  out3;
input in;
input s1, s0;

always @(s1 or s0 or in)
case ({s1, s0}) //Switch based on control signals
    2'b00 : begin  out0 = in;  out1 = 1'bz;  out2 = 1'bz; out3 = 1'bz; end
    2'b01 : begin  out0 = 1'bz;  out1 = in;  out2 = 1'bz; out3 = 1'bz; end
    2'b10 : begin  out0 = 1'bz;  out1 = 1'bz;  out2 = in; out3 = 1'bz; end
    2'b11 : begin  out0 = 1'bz;  out1 = 1'bz;  out2 = 1'bz; out3 = in; end

    //Account for unknown signals on select. If any select signal is x
    //then outputs are x. If any select signal is z, outputs are z.
    //If one is x and the other is z, x gets higher priority.
    2'bx0, 2'bx1, 2'bxz, 2'bxx, 2'b0x, 2'b1x, 2'bzx :
        begin
            out0 = 1'bx;  out1 = 1'bx;  out2 = 1'bx;  out3 = 1'bx;
        end
    2'bz0, 2'bz1, 2'bzz, 2'b0z, 2'b1z :
        begin
            out0 = 1'bz;  out1 = 1'bz;  out2 = 1'bz;  out3 = 1'bz;
        end
    default: $display("Unspecified control signals");
endcase

endmodule
```

In the demultiplexer shown above, multiple input signal combinations such as *2'bz0, 2'bz1, 2,bzz, 2'b0z*, and *2'b1z* that cause the same block to be executed are put together with a *comma* (**,**) symbol.

7.5.2 casex, casez Keywords

There are two variations of the **case** statement. They are denoted by keywords, **casex** and **casez**.

- **casez** treats all **z** values in the case alternatives or the case expression as don't cares. All bit positions with **z** can also represented by **?** in that position.
- **casex** treats all **x** and **z** values in the case item or the case expression as don't cares.

The use of **casex** and **casez** allows comparison of only non-**x** or -**z** positions in the case expression and the case alternatives. Example 7-21 illustrates the decoding of state bits in a finite state machine using a **casex** statement. The use of **casez** is similar. Only one bit is considered to determine the next state and the other bits are ignored.

Example 7-21 *casex Use*

```
reg [3:0] encoding;
integer state;

casex (encoding) //logic value x represents a don't care bit.
4'b1xxx : next_state = 3;
4'bx1xx : next_state = 2;
4'bxx1x : next_state = 1;
4'bxxx1 : next_state = 0;
default : next_state = 0;
endcase
```

Thus, an input *encoding = 4'b10xz* would cause *next_state = 3* to be executed.

7.6 Loops

There are four types of looping statements in Verilog: *while, for, repeat*, and *forever*. The syntax of these loops is very similar to the syntax of loops in the C programming language. All looping statements can appear only inside an **initial** or **always** block. Loops may contain delay expressions.

7.6.1 While Loop

The keyword **while** is used to specify this loop. The **while** loop executes until the *while-expression* is not true. If the loop is entered when the *while-expression* is not true, the loop is not executed at all. Each expression can contain the operators in Table 6-1 on page 96.

Any logical expression can be specified with these operators. If multiple statements are to be executed in the loop, they must be grouped typically using keywords **begin** and **end**. Example 7-22 illustrates the use of the **while** loop.

Example 7-22 *While Loop*

```
//Illustration 1: Increment count from 0 to 127. Exit at count 128.
//Display the count variable.
integer count;

initial
begin
        count = 0;

        while (count < 128) //Execute loop till count is 127.
                            //exit at count 128
        begin
                $display("Count = %d", count);
                count = count + 1;
        end
end


//Illustration 2: Find the first bit with a value 1 in flag (vector
variable)
`define TRUE 1'b1';
`define FALSE 1'b0;
reg [15:0] flag;
integer i; //integer to keep count
reg continue;

initial
begin
  flag = 16'b 0010_0000_0000_0000;
  i = 0;
  continue = `TRUE;

  while((i < 16) && continue ) //Multiple conditions using operators.
  begin
    if (flag[i])
    begin
      $display("Encountered a TRUE bit at element number %d", i);
      continue = `FALSE;
    end
    i = i + 1;
```

Example 7-22 *While Loop (Continued)*

```
  end
end
```

7.6.2 For Loop

The keyword **for** is used to specify this loop. The **for** loop contains three parts:

- An initial condition
- A check to see if the terminating condition is true
- A procedural assignment to change value of the control variable

The counter described in Example 7-22 can be coded as a **for** loop (Example 7-23). The initialization condition and the incrementing procedural assignment are included in the **for** loop and do not need to be specified separately. Thus, the **for** loop provides a more compact loop structure than the **while** loop. Note, however, that the **while** loop is more general-purpose than the **for** loop. The for loop cannot be used in place of the **while** loop in all situations.

Example 7-23 *For Loop*

```
integer count;

initial
   for ( count=0; count < 128; count = count + 1)
         $display("Count = %d", count);
```

`for` loops can also be used to initialize an array or memory, as shown below.

```
//Initialize array elements
`define MAX_STATES 32
integer state [0: `MAX_STATES-1]; //Integer array state with elements 0:31
integer i;

initial
begin
    for(i = 0; i < 32; i = i + 2) //initialize all even locations with 0
        state[i] = 0;
    for(i = 1; i < 32; i = i + 2) //initialize all odd locations with 1
        state[i] = 1;
end
```

`for` loops are generally used when there is a fixed beginning and end to the loop. If the loop is simply looping on a certain condition, it is better to use the `while` loop.

7.6.3 Repeat Loop

The keyword **`repeat`** is used for this loop. The **`repeat`** construct executes the loop a fixed number of times. A **`repeat`** construct cannot be used to loop on a general logical expression. A `while` loop is used for that purpose. A **`repeat`** construct must contain a number, which can be a constant, a variable or a signal value. However, if the number is a variable or signal value, it is evaluated only when the loop starts and not during the loop execution.

The counter in Example 7-22 can be expressed with the repeat loop, as shown in Illustration 1 in Example 7-24. Illustration 2 shows how to model a data buffer that latches data at the positive edge of clock for the next eight cycles after it receives a data start signal.

Example 7-24 Repeat Loop

```
//Illustration 1 : increment and display count from 0 to 127
integer count;

initial
begin
   count = 0;
   repeat(128)
   begin
```

Example 7-24   Repeat Loop (Continued)

```
        $display("Count = %d", count);
        count = count + 1;
    end
end

//Illustration 2 : Data buffer module example
//After it receives a data_start signal.
//Reads data for next 8 cycles.

module data_buffer(data_start, data, clock);

parameter cycles = 8;
input data_start;
input [15:0] data;
input clock;

reg [15:0] buffer [0:7];
integer i;

always @(posedge clock)
begin
  if(data_start) //data start signal is true
  begin
    i = 0;
    repeat(cycles) //Store data at the posedge of next 8 clock
                   //cycles
    begin
      @(posedge clock) buffer[i] = data; //waits till next
                                          // posedge to latch data
      i = i + 1;
    end
  end
end

endmodule
```

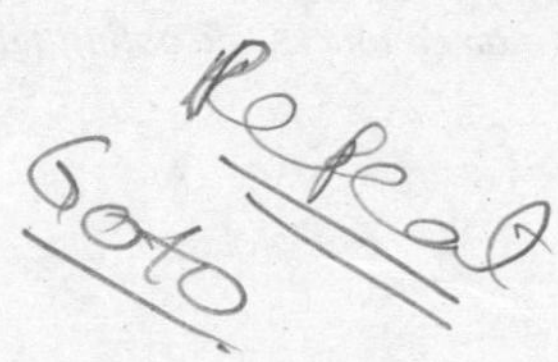

7.6.4 Forever loop

The keyword **forever** is used to express this loop. The loop does not contain any expression and executes forever until the **$finish** task is encountered. The loop is equivalent to a `while` loop with an expression that always evaluates to true, e.g., *while (1)*. A forever loop can be exited by use of the **disable** statement.

A `forever` loop is typically used in conjunction with timing control constructs. If timing control constructs are not used, the Verilog simulator would execute this statement infinitely without advancing simulation time and the rest of the design would never be executed. Example 7-25 explains the use of the **forever** statement.

Example 7-25 *Forever Loop*

```
//Example 1: Clock generation
//Use forever loop instead of always block
reg clock;

initial
begin
        clock = 1'b0;
        forever #10 clock = ~clock; //Clock with period of 20 units
end

//Example 2: Synchronize two register values at every positive edge of
//clock
reg clock;
reg x, y;

initial
        forever @(posedge clock) x = y;
```

7.7 Sequential and Parallel Blocks

Block statements are used to group multiple statements to act together as one. In previous examples, we used keywords **begin** and **end** to group multiple statements. Thus, we used sequential blocks where the statements in the block execute one after another. In this section we discuss the block types: *sequential* blocks and *parallel* blocks. We also discuss three special features of blocks: *named blocks*, *disabling named* blocks, and *nested* blocks.

7.7.1 Block Types

There are two types of blocks: *sequential* blocks and *parallel* blocks.

Sequential blocks

The keywords **begin** and **end** are used to group statements into sequential blocks. Sequential blocks have the following characteristics:

- The statements in a sequential block are processed in the order they are specified. A statement is executed only after its preceding statement completes execution (except for nonblocking assignments with intra-assignment timing control).
- If delay or event control is specified, it is relative to the simulation time when the previous statement in the block completed execution.

We have used numerous examples of sequential blocks in this book. Two more examples of sequential blocks are given in Example 7-26. Statements in the sequential block execute in order. In Illustration 1, the final values are x = 0, y= 1, z = 1, w = 2 at simulation time 0. In Illustration 2, the final values are the same except that the simulation time is 35 at the end of the block.

Example 7-26 *Sequential Blocks*

```
//Illustration 1: Sequential block without delay
reg x, y;
reg [1:0] z, w;

initial
begin
        x = 1'b0;
        y = 1'b1;
        z = {x, y};
        w = {y, x};
end

//Illustration 2: Sequential blocks with delay.
reg x, y;
reg [1:0] z, w;

initial
begin
        x = 1'b0; //completes at simulation time 0
        #5 y = 1'b1; //completes at simulation time 5
        #10 z = {x, y}; //completes at simulation time 15
```

Example 7-26 Sequential Blocks (Continued)

```
        #20 w = {y, x}; //completes at simulation time 35
end
```

Parallel blocks

Parallel blocks, specified by keywords **fork** and **join**, provide interesting simulation features. Parallel blocks have the following characteristics:

- Statements in a parallel block are executed concurrently.
- Ordering of statements is controlled by the delay or event control assigned to each statement.
- If delay or event control is specified, it is relative to the time the block was entered.

Notice the fundamental difference between sequential and parallel blocks. All statements in a parallel block start at the time when the block was entered. Thus, the order in which the statements are written in the block is not important.

Let us consider the sequential block with delay in Example 7-26 and convert it to a parallel block. The converted Verilog code is shown in Example 7-27. The result of simulation remains the same except that all statements start in *parallel* at time 0. Hence, the block finishes at time 20 instead of time 35.

Example 7-27 Parallel Blocks

```
//Example 1: Parallel blocks with delay.
reg x, y;
reg [1:0] z, w;

initial
fork
        x = 1'b0; //completes at simulation time 0
        #5 y = 1'b1; //completes at simulation time 5
        #10 z = {x, y}; //completes at simulation time 10
        #20 w = {y, x}; //completes at simulation time 20
join
```

Parallel blocks provide a mechanism to execute statements in parallel. However, it is important to be careful with parallel blocks because of implicit race conditions that might arise if two statements that affect the same variable complete at the same time. Shown below is the parallel version of Illustration 1 from Example 7-26. Race conditions have been deliberately introduced in this example. All statements start at simulation time 0. The order in which the statements will execute is not known. Variables *z* and *w* will get values *1* and *2* if *x = 1'b0* and *y = 1'b1* execute first. Variables *z* and *w* will get values *2'bxx* and *2'bxx* if *x = 1'b0* and *y = 1'b1* execute last. Thus, the result of *z* and *w* is nondeterministic and dependent on the simulator implementation. In simulation time, all statements in the fork-join block are executed at once. However, in reality, CPUs running simulations can execute only one statement at a time. Different simulators execute statements in different order. Thus, the race condition is a limitation of today's simulators, not of the fork-join block.

```
//Parallel blocks with deliberate race condition
reg x, y;
reg [1:0] z, w;

initial
fork
        x = 1'b0;
        y = 1'b1;
        z = {x, y};
        w = {y, x};
join
```

The keyword **`fork`** can be viewed as splitting a single flow into independent flows. The keyword **`join`** can be seen as joining the independent flows back into a single flow. Independent flows operate concurrently.

7.7.2 Special Features of Blocks

We discuss three special features available with block statements: *nested blocks, named blocks*, and *disabling of named blocks.*

Nested blocks

Blocks can be nested. Sequential and parallel blocks can be mixed, as shown in Example 7-28.

Example 7-28 *Nested Blocks*

```
//Nested blocks
initial
begin
        x = 1'b0;
```

Example 7-28 *Nested Blocks (Continued)*

```
    fork
            #5 y = 1'b1;
            #10 z = {x, y};
    join
    #20 w = {y, x};
end
```

Named blocks

Blocks can be given names.

- Local variables can be declared for the named block.
- Named blocks are a part of the design hierarchy. Variables in a named block can be accessed by using hierarchical name referencing.
- Named blocks can be disabled, i.e., their execution can be stopped.

Example 7-29 shows naming of blocks and hierarchical naming of blocks.

Example 7-29 *Named Blocks*

```
//Named blocks
module top;

initial
begin: block1 //sequential block named block1
integer i; //integer i is static and local to block1
          // can be accessed by hierarchical name, top.block1.i
...
...
end

initial
fork: block2 //parallel block named block2
reg i; // register i is static and local to block2
                // can be accessed by hierarchical name, top.block2.i
...
...
join
```

Disabling named blocks

The keyword **`disable`** provides a way to terminate the execution of a named block. **`disable`** can be used to get out of loops, handle error conditions, or control execution of pieces of code, based on a control signal. Disabling a block causes the execution control to be passed to the statement immediately succeeding the block. For C programmers, this is very similar to the `break` statement used to exit a loop. The difference is that a `break` statement can break the current loop only, whereas the keyword **`disable`** allows disabling of any named block in the design.

Consider the illustration in Example 7-22 on page 142, which looks for the first true bit in the flag. The **while** loop can be recoded, using the disable statement as shown in Example 7-30. The disable statement terminates the `while` loop as soon as a true bit is seen.

Example 7-30 Disabling Named Blocks

```
//Illustration: Find the first bit with a value 1 in flag (vector
//variable)
reg [15:0] flag;
integer i; //integer to keep count

initial
begin
  flag = 16'b 0010_0000_0000_0000;
  i = 0;
  begin: block1 //The main block inside while is named block1
  while(i < 16)
    begin
        if (flag[i])
        begin
             $display("Encountered a TRUE bit at element number %d", i);
             disable block1; //disable block1 because you found true bit.
        end
        i = i + 1;
    end
  end
end
```

7.8 Generate Blocks

Generate statements allow Verilog code to be generated dynamically at elaboration time before the simulation begins. This facilitates the creation of parametrized models. Generate statements are particularly convenient when the same operation or module instance is repeated for multiple bits of a vector, or when certain Verilog code is conditionally included based on parameter definitions.

Generate statements allow control over the declaration of variables, functions, and tasks, as well as control over instantiations. All generate instantiations are coded with a module scope and require the keywords **`generate`** - **`endgenerate`**.

Generated instantiations can be one or more of the following types:

- Modules
- User defined primitives
- Verilog gate primitives
- Continuous assignments
- **`initial`** and **`always`** blocks

Generated declarations and instantiations can be conditionally instantiated into a design. Generated variable declarations and instantiations can be multiply instantiated into a design. Generated instances have unique identifier names and can be referenced hierarchically. To support interconnection between structural elements and/or procedural blocks, generate statements permit the following Verilog data types to be declared within the generate scope:

- **`net, reg`**
- **`integer, real, time, realtime`**
- **`event`**

Generated data types have unique identifier names and can be referenced hierarchically.

Parameter redefinition using ordered or named assignment or a **`defparam`** statement can be declared with the generate scope. However, a **`defparam`** statement within a generate scope is allowed to modify the value of a parameter only in the same generate scope or within the hierarchy instantiated within the generate scope.

Task and function declarations are permitted within the generate scope but not within a generate loop. Generated tasks and functions have unique identifier names and can be referenced hierarchically.

Some module declarations and module items are not permitted in a generate statement. They include:

- parameters, local parameters
- input, output, inout declarations
- specify blocks

Connections to generated module instances are handled in the same way as with normal module instances.

There are three methods to create generate statements:

- Generate loop
- Generate conditional
- Generate case

The following sections explain these methods in detail:

7.8.1 Generate Loop

A generate loop permits one or more of the following to be instantiated multiple times using a for loop:

- Variable declarations
- Modules
- User defined primitives, gate primitives
- Continuous assignments
- **initial** and **always** blocks

Example 7-31 shows a simple example of how to generate a bit-wise xor of two N-bit buses. Note that this implementation can be done in a simpler fashion by using vector nets instead of bits. However, we choose this example to illustrate the use of generate loop.

Example 7-31 Bit-wise Xor of Two N-bit Buses

```
// This module generates a bit-wise xor of two N-bit buses

module bitwise_xor (out, i0, i1);
// Parameter Declaration. This can be redefined
parameter N = 32; // 32-bit bus by default
```

(Continued...)

```
// Port declarations
output [N-1:0] out;
input [N-1:0] i0, i1;

// Declare a temporary loop variable. This variable is used only
// in the evaluation of generate blocks. This variable does not
// exist during the simulation of a Verilog design
genvar j;

//Generate the bit-wise Xor with a single loop
generate for (j=0; j<N; j=j+1) begin: xor_loop
 xor g1 (out[j], i0[j], i1[j]);
end //end of the for loop inside the generate block
endgenerate //end of the generate block

// As an alternate style,
// the xor gates could be replaced by always blocks.
// reg [N-1:0] out;
//generate for (j=0; j<N; j=j+1) begin: bit
// always @(i0[j] or i1[j]) out[j] = i0[j] ^ i1[j];
//end
//endgenerate

endmodule
```

Some interesting observations for Example 7-31 are listed below.

- Prior to the beginning of the simulation, the simulator *elaborates* (*unrolls*) the code in the generate blocks to create a flat representation without the generate blocks. The *unrolled* code is then simulated. Thus, generate blocks are simply a convenient way of replacing multiple repetitive Verilog statements with a single statement inside a loop.
- **genvar** is a keyword used to declare variables that are used only in the evaluation of generate block. **Genvars** do not exist during simulation of the design.
- The value of a **genvar** can be defined only by a generate loop.
- Generate loops can be nested. However, two generate loops using the same **genvar** as an index variable cannot be nested.

- The name *xor_loop* assigned to the generate loop is used for hierarchical name referencing of the variables inside the generate loop. Therefore, the relative hierarchical names of the xor gates will be *xor_loop[0].g1*, *xor_loop[1].g1*, ..., *xor_loop[31].g1*.

Generate loops are fairly flexible. Various Verilog constructs can be used inside the generate loops. It is important to imagine the Verilog description after the generate loop is *unrolled*. That gives a clearer picture of the behavior of generate loops. Example 7-32 shows a generated ripple adder with the net declaration inside the generate loop.

Example 7-32 *Generated Ripple Adder*

```
// This module generates a gate level ripple adder

module ripple_adder(co, sum, a0, a1, ci);
// Parameter Declaration. This can be redefined
parameter N = 4; // 4-bit bus by default

// Port declarations
output [N-1:0] sum;
output co;
input [N-1:0] a0, a1;
input ci;

//Local wire declaration
wire [N-1:0] carry;

//Assign 0th bit of carry equal to carry input
assign carry[0] = ci;

// Declare a temporary loop variable. This variable is used only
// in the evaluation of generate blocks. This variable does not
// exist during the simulation of a Verilog design because the
// generate loops are unrolled before simulation.
genvar i;

//Generate the bit-wise Xor with a single loop
generate for (i=0; i<N; i=i+1) begin: r_loop
```

(Continued...)
```
   wire t1, t2, t3;
   xor g1 (t1, a0[i], a1[i]);
   xor g2 (sum[i], t1, carry[i]);
   and g3 (t2, a0[i], a1[i]);
   and g4 (t3, t1, carry[i]);
   or  g5 (carry[i+1], t2, t3);
end //end of the for loop inside the generate block
endgenerate //end of the generate block

// For the above generate loop, the following relative hierarchical
// instance names are generated
// xor : r_loop[0].g1, r_loop[1].g1, r_loop[2].g1, r_loop[3].g1
         r_loop[0].g2, r_loop[1].g2, r_loop[2].g2, r_loop[3].g2
// and : r_loop[0].g3, r_loop[1].g3, r_loop[2].g3, r_loop[3].g3
         r_loop[0].g4, r_loop[1].g4, r_loop[2].g4, r_loop[3].g4
// or :  r_loop[0].g5, r_loop[1].g5, r_loop[2].g5, r_loop[3].g5

// Generated instances are connected with the following
// generated nets
// Nets:  r_loop[0].t1, r_loop[0].t2, r_loop[0].t3
//        r_loop[1].t1, r_loop[1].t2, r_loop[1].t3
//        r_loop[2].t1, r_loop[2].t2, r_loop[2].t3
//        r_loop[3].t1, r_loop[3].t2, r_loop[3].t3

assign co = carry[N];

endmodule
```

7.8.2 Generate Conditional

A generate conditional is like an if-else-if generate construct that permits the following Verilog constructs to be conditionally instantiated into another module based on an expression that is deterministic at the time the design is elaborated:

- Modules
- User defined primitives, gate primitives
- Continuous assignments
- **`initial`** and **`always`** blocks

Example 7-33 shows the implementation of a parametrized multiplier. If either *a0_width* or *a1_width* parameters are less than 8 bits, a carry-look-ahead (CLA) multiplier is instantiated. If both *a0_width* or *a1_width* parameters are greater than or equal to 8 bits, a tree multiplier is instantiated.

Example 7-33 *Parametrized Multiplier Using Generate Conditional*

```
// This module implements a parametrized multiplier

module multiplier (product, a0, a1);
// Parameter Declaration. This can be redefined
parameter a0_width = 8; // 8-bit bus by default
parameter a1_width = 8; // 8-bit bus by default

// Local Parameter declaration.
// This parameter cannot be modified with defparam or
// with module instance # statement.
localparam product_width = a0_width + a1_width;

// Port declarations
output [product_width -1:0] product;
input [a0_width-1:0] a0;
input [a1_width-1:0] a1;


// Instantiate the type of multiplier conditionally.
// Depending on the value of the a0_width and a1_width
// parameters at the time of instantiation, the appropriate
// multiplier will be instantiated.
generate
 if (a0_width <8) || (a1_width < 8)
    cla_multiplier #(a0_width, a1_width) m0 (product, a0, a1);
 else
    tree_multiplier #(a0_width, a1_width) m0 (product, a0, a1);
endgenerate //end of the generate block

endmodule
```

7.8.3 Generate Case

A generate case permits the following Verilog constructs to be conditionally instantiated into another module based on a select-one-of-many case construct that is deterministic at the time the design is elaborated:

- Modules
- User defined primitives, Gate primitives
- Continuous assignments
- **`initial`** and **`always`** blocks

Example 7-34 shows the implementation of an N-bit adder using a generate case block.

Example 7-34 *Generate Case Example*

```
// This module generates an N-bit adder

module adder(co, sum, a0, a1, ci);
// Parameter Declaration. This can be redefined
parameter N = 4; // 4-bit bus by default

// Port declarations
output [N-1:0] sum;
output co;
input [N-1:0] a0, a1;
input ci;

// Instantiate the appropriate adder based on the width of the bus.
// This is based on parameter N that can be redefined at
// instantiation time.
generate
case (N)
  //Special cases for 1 and 2 bit adders
  1: adder_1bit adder1(c0, sum, a0, a1, ci); //1-bit implementation
  2: adder_2bit adder2(c0, sum, a0, a1, ci); //2-bit implementation
  // Default is N-bit carry look ahead adder
  default: adder_cla #(N) adder3(c0, sum, a0, a1, ci);
endcase
endgenerate //end of the generate block

endmodule
```

7.9 Examples

In order to illustrate the use of behavioral constructs discussed earlier in this chapter, we consider three examples in this section. The first two, *4-to-1 multiplexer* and *4-bit counter,* are taken from Section 6.5, *Examples.* Earlier, these circuits were designed by using dataflow statements. We will model these circuits with behavioral statements. The third example is a new example. We will design a *traffic signal controller*, using behavioral constructs, and simulate it.

7.9.1 4-to-1 Multiplexer

We can define a 4-to-1 multiplexer with the behavioral case statement. This multiplexer was defined, in Section 6.5.1, *4-to-1 Multiplexer*, by dataflow statements. It is described in Example 7-35 by behavioral constructs. The behavioral multiplexer can be substituted for the dataflow multiplexer; the simulation results will be identical.

Example 7-35 Behavioral 4-to-1 Multiplexer

```
// 4-to-1 multiplexer. Port list is taken exactly from
// the I/O diagram.
module mux4_to_1 (out, i0, i1, i2, i3, s1, s0);

// Port declarations from the I/O diagram
output out;
input i0, i1, i2, i3;
input s1, s0;
//output declared as register
reg out;

//recompute the signal out if any input signal changes.
//All input signals that cause a recomputation of out to
//occur must go into the always @(...)  sensitivity list.
always @(s1 or s0 or i0 or i1 or i2 or i3)
begin
  case ({s1, s0})
  2'b00: out = i0;
  2'b01: out = i1;
  2'b10: out = i2;
  2'b11: out = i3;
  default: out = 1'bx;
  endcase
end
```

Example 7-35 *Behavioral 4-to-1 Multiplexer (Continued)*

```
endmodule
```

7.9.2 4-bit Counter

In Section 6.5.3, *Ripple Counter*, we designed a 4-bit ripple carry counter. We will now design the 4-bit counter by using behavioral statements. At dataflow or gate level, the counter might be designed in hardware as ripple carry, synchronous counter, etc. But, at a behavioral level, we work at a very high level of abstraction and do not care about the underlying hardware implementation. We will design only functionality. The counter can be designed by using behavioral constructs, as shown in Example 7-36. Notice how concise the behavioral counter description is compared to its dataflow counterpart. If we substitute the counter in place of the dataflow counter, the simulation results will be exactly the same, assuming that there are no **x** and **z** values on the inputs.

Example 7-36 *Behavioral 4-bit Counter Description*

```
//4-bit Binary  counter
module counter(Q , clock, clear);

// I/O ports
output [3:0] Q;
input clock, clear;
//output defined as register
reg [3:0] Q;

always @( posedge clear  or negedge clock)
begin
  if (clear)
     Q <= 4'd0;  //Nonblocking assignments are recommended
                 //for creating sequential logic such as flipflops
  else
     Q <= Q + 1;// Modulo 16 is not necessary because Q is a
                // 4-bit value and wraps around.
end

endmodule
```

7.9.3 Traffic Signal Controller

This example is fresh and has not been discussed before in the book. We will design a *traffic signal controller*, using a *finite state machine* approach.

Specification

Consider a controller for traffic at the intersection of a main highway and a country road.

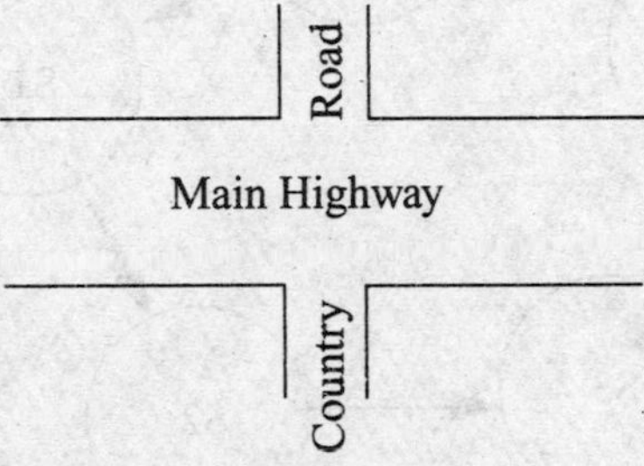

The following specifications must be considered:

- The traffic signal for the main highway gets highest priority because cars are continuously present on the main highway. Thus, the main highway signal remains green by default.
- Occasionally, cars from the country road arrive at the traffic signal. The traffic signal for the country road must turn green only long enough to let the cars on the country road go.
- As soon as there are no cars on the country road, the country road traffic signal turns yellow and then red and the traffic signal on the main highway turns green again.
- There is a sensor to detect cars waiting on the country road. The sensor sends a signal X as input to the controller. $X = 1$ if there are cars on the country road; otherwise, $X = 0$.
- There are delays on transitions from $S1$ to $S2$, from $S2$ to $S3$, and from $S4$ to $S0$. The delays must be controllable.

The state machine diagram and the state definitions for the traffic signal controller are shown in Figure 7-1.

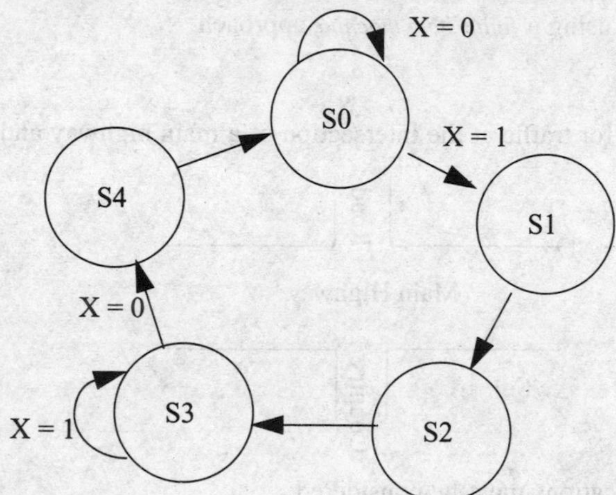

State	**Signals**
S0	*Hwy = G Cntry = R*
S1	*Hwy = Y Cntry = R*
S2	*Hwy = R Cntry = R*
S3	*Hwy = R Cntry = G*
S4	*Hwy = R Cntry = Y*

Figure 7-1 FSM for Traffic Signal Controller

Verilog description

The traffic signal controller module can be designed with behavioral Verilog constructs, as shown in Example 7-37.

Example 7-37 Traffic Signal Controller

```
`define TRUE  1'b1
`define FALSE 1'b0

//Delays
`define Y2RDELAY  3 //Yellow to red delay
`define R2GDELAY  2 //Red to green delay

module sig_control
    (hwy, cntry, X, clock, clear);

//I/O ports
output [1:0] hwy, cntry;
        //2-bit output for 3 states of signal
```

Example 7-37 Traffic Signal Controller (Continued)

```
        //GREEN, YELLOW, RED;
reg [1:0] hwy, cntry;
        //declared output signals are registers

input X;
        //if TRUE, indicates that there is car on
        //the country road, otherwise FALSE

input clock, clear;

parameter RED = 2'd0,
          YELLOW = 2'd1,
          GREEN = 2'd2;

//State definition      HWY           CNTRY
parameter S0 = 3'd0, //GREEN           RED
          S1 = 3'd1, //YELLOW          RED
          S2 = 3'd2, //RED             RED
          S3 = 3'd3, //RED             GREEN
          S4 = 3'd4; //RED             YELLOW

//Internal state variables
reg [2:0] state;
reg [2:0] next_state;


//state changes only at positive edge of clock
always @(posedge clock)
  if (clear)
      state <= S0; //Controller starts in S0 state
  else
      state <= next_state; //State change


//Compute values of main signal and country signal
always @(state)
begin
  hwy = GREEN; //Default Light Assignment for Highway light
  cntry = RED; //Default Light Assignment for Country light
  case(state)
     S0: ; // No change, use default
     S1: hwy = YELLOW;
     S2: hwy = RED;
```

Example 7-37 Traffic Signal Controller (Continued)

```
     S3:  begin
            hwy = RED;
            cntry = GREEN;
          end
     S4:  begin
            hwy = RED;
            cntry = `YELLOW;
          end
  endcase
end

//State machine using case statements
always @(state or  X)
begin
    case (state)
      S0: if(X)
            next_state = S1;
          else
            next_state = S0;
      S1: begin //delay some positive edges of clock
            repeat(`Y2RDELAY) @(posedge clock) ;
            next_state = S2;
          end
      S2: begin //delay some positive edges of clock
            repeat(`R2GDELAY) @(posedge clock);
            next_state = S3;
          end
      S3: if(X)
            next_state = S3;
          else
            next_state = S4;
      S4: begin //delay some positive edges of clock
            repeat(`Y2RDELAY) @(posedge clock) ;
            next_state = S0;
          end
     default: next_state = S0;
    endcase
end

endmodule
```

Stimulus

Stimulus can be applied to check if the traffic signal transitions correctly when cars arrive on the country road. The stimulus file in Example 7-38 instantiates the traffic signal controller and checks all possible states of the controller.

Example 7-38 Stimulus for Traffic Signal Controller

```
//Stimulus Module
module stimulus;

wire [1:0] MAIN_SIG, CNTRY_SIG;
reg CAR_ON_CNTRY_RD;
      //if TRUE, indicates that there is car on
      //the country road
reg CLOCK, CLEAR;

//Instantiate signal controller
sig_control SC(MAIN_SIG, CNTRY_SIG, CAR_ON_CNTRY_RD, CLOCK, CLEAR);

//Set up monitor
initial
  $monitor($time, " Main Sig = %b Country Sig = %b Car_on_cntry = %b",
                        MAIN_SIG, CNTRY_SIG, CAR_ON_CNTRY_RD);

//Set up clock
initial
begin
    CLOCK = `FALSE;
    forever #5 CLOCK = ~CLOCK;
end

//control clear signal
initial
begin
    CLEAR = `TRUE;
    repeat (5) @(negedge CLOCK);
    CLEAR = `FALSE;
end

//apply stimulus
initial
begin
    CAR_ON_CNTRY_RD = `FALSE;

    repeat(20)@(negedge CLOCK); CAR_ON_CNTRY_RD = `TRUE;
```

Example 7-38 Stimulus for Traffic Signal Controller (Continued)

```
    repeat(10)@(negedge CLOCK); CAR_ON_CNTRY_RD = `FALSE;

    repeat(20)@(negedge CLOCK); CAR_ON_CNTRY_RD = `TRUE;
    repeat(10)@(negedge CLOCK); CAR_ON_CNTRY_RD = `FALSE;

    repeat(20)@(negedge CLOCK); CAR_ON_CNTRY_RD = `TRUE;
    repeat(10)@(negedge CLOCK); CAR_ON_CNTRY_RD = `FALSE;

    repeat(10)@(negedge CLOCK); $stop;
end
endmodule
```

Note that we designed only the behavior of the controller without worrying about how it will be implemented in hardware.

7.10 Summary

We discussed digital circuit design with behavioral Verilog constructs.

- A behavioral description expresses a digital circuit in terms of the algorithms it implements. A behavioral description does not necessarily include the hardware implementation details. Behavioral modeling is used in the initial stages of a design process to evaluate various design-related trade-offs. Behavioral modeling is similar to C programming in many ways.

- Structured procedures **`initial`** and **`always`** form the basis of behavioral modeling. All other behavioral statements can appear only inside **`initial`** or **`always`** blocks. An **`initial`** block executes once; an **`always`** block executes continuously until simulation ends.

- Procedural assignments are used in behavioral modeling to assign values to register variables. *Blocking* assignments must complete before the succeeding statement can execute. *Nonblocking* assignments schedule assignments to be executed and continue processing to the succeeding statement.

- *Delay-based timing control*, *event-based timing control*, and *level-sensitive timing control* are three ways to control timing and execution order of statements in Verilog. *Regular delay, zero delay*, and *intra-assignment delay* are three types of delay-based timing control. *Regular event, named event,* and *event OR* are three types of event-based timing control. The **`wait`** statement is used to model level-sensitive timing control.

- Conditional statements are modeled in behavioral Verilog with **`if`** and **`else`** statements. If there are multiple branches, use of **`case`** statements is recommended. **`casex`** and **`casez`** are special cases of the **`case`** statement.

- Keywords **`while`**, **`for`**, **`repeat`**, and **`forever`** are used for four types of looping statements in Verilog.

- *Sequential* and *parallel* are two types of blocks. Sequential blocks are specified by keywords **`begin`** and **`end`**. Parallel blocks are expressed by keywords **`fork`** and **`join`**. Blocks can be *nested* and *named.* If a block is named, the execution of the block can be disabled from anywhere in the design. Named blocks can be referenced by hierarchical names

- Generate statements allow Verilog code to be generated dynamically at elaboration time before the simulation begins. This facilitates the creation of parametrized models. Generate statements are particularly convenient when the same operation or module instance is repeated for multiple bits of a vector, or when certain Verilog code is conditionally included based on parameter definitions. Generate loop, generate conditional, and generate case are the three types of generate statements.

7.11 Exercises

1. Declare a register called *oscillate*. Initialize it to 0 and make it toggle every 30 time units. Do not use an **`always`** statement. (Hint: Use the **`forever`** loop).
2. Design a *clock* with time period = 40 and a duty cycle of 25% by using the **`always`** and **`initial`** statements. The value of *clock* at time = 0 should be initialized to 0.
3. Given below is an **`initial`** block with blocking procedural assignments. At what simulation time is each statement executed? What are the intermediate and final values of *a, b, c, d*?

```
initial
begin
    a = 1'b0;
    b = #10 1'b1;
    c = #5 1'b0;
    d = #20 {a, b, c};
end
```

4. Repeat exercise 3 if *nonblocking* procedural assignments were used.

5. What is the order of execution of statements in the following Verilog code? Is there any ambiguity in the order of execution? What are the final values of *a, b, c, d*?

```
initial
begin
        a = 1'b0;
        #0 c = b;
end
initial
begin
        b = 1'b1;
        #0 d = a;
end
```

6. What is the final value of *d* in the following example? (Hint: See ***intra-assignment delays.***)

```
initial
begin
        b = 1'b1; c = 1'b0;
        #10 b = 1'b0;
initial
begin
        d = #25 (b | c);
end
```

7. Design a negative edge-triggered D-flipflop (*D_FF*) with synchronous clear, active high (*D_FF* clears only at a negative edge of *clock* when clear is high). Use behavioral statements only. (Hint: Output *q* of *D_FF* must be declared as `reg`.) Design a *clock* with a period of 10 units and test the *D_FF*.

8. Design the D-flipflop in exercise 7 with asynchronous clear (*D_FF* clears whenever *clear* goes high. It does not wait for next negative edge). Test the *D_FF*.

9. Using the `wait` statement, design a level-sensitive latch that takes *clock* and *d* as inputs and *q* as output. *q* = *d* whenever *clock* = *1*.

10. Design the 4-to-1 multiplexer in Example 7-19 by using `if` and `else` statements. The port interface must remain the same.

11. Design the traffic signal controller discussed in this chapter by using `if` and `else` statements.

12. Using a **case** statement, design an 8-function ALU that takes 4-bit inputs *a* and *b* and a 3-bit input signal *select*, and gives a 5-bit output *out*. The ALU implements the following functions based on a 3-bit input signal *select*. Ignore any overflow or underflow bits.

Select Signal	Function
3'b000	out = a
3'b001	out = a + b
3'b010	out = a - b
3'b011	out = a / b
3'b100	out = a % b (remainder)
3'b101	out = a << 1
3'b110	out = a >> 1
3'b111	out = (a > b) (magnitude compare)

13. Using a **while** loop, design a clock generator. Initial value of *clock* is 0. Time period for the clock is 10.

14. Using the **for** loop, initialize locations 0 to 1023 of a 4-bit register array *cache_var* to 0.

15. Using a **forever** statement, design a *clock* with time period = 10 and duty cycle = 40%. Initial value of *clock* is 0.

16. Using the **repeat** loop, delay the statement *a = a + 1* by 20 positive edges of *clock*.

17. Below is a block with nested *sequential* and *parallel* blocks. When does the block finish and what is the order of execution of events? At what simulation times does each statement finish execution?

```
initial
begin
        x = 1'b0;
        #5 y = 1'b1;
        fork
                 #20 a = x;
                 #15 b = y;
        join
        #40 x = 1'b1;
        fork
                #10 p = x;
                begin
                        #10 a = y;
                        #30 b = x;
                end
```

```
            #5 m = y;
    join
end
```

18. Design an 8-bit *counter* by using a **`forever`** loop, *named block*, and *disabling of named block*. The *counter* starts counting at count = 5 and finishes at count = 67. The count is incremented at positive edge of *clock*. The *clock* has a time period of 10. The *counter* counts through the loop only once and then is disabled. (Hint: Use the **`disable`** statement.)

Tasks and Functions

A designer is frequently required to implement the same functionality at many places in a behavioral design. This means that the commonly used parts should be abstracted into routines and the r outines must be invoked instead of repeating the code. Most programming languages provide procedures or subroutines to accomplish this. Verilog provides *tasks* and *functions* to break up large behavioral designs into smaller pieces. Tasks and functions allow the designer to abstract Verilog code that is used at many places in the design.

Tasks have **`input`**, **`output`**, and **`inout`** arguments; functions have **`input`** arguments. Thus, values can be passed into and out from tasks and functions. Considering the analogy of FORTRAN, tasks are similar to *SUBROUTINE* and functions are similar to *FUNCTION*.

Tasks and functions are included in the design hierarchy. Like named blocks, tasks or functions can be addressed by means of hierarchical names.

Learning Objectives

- Describe the differences between tasks and functions.
- Identify the conditions required for tasks to be defined. Understand task declaration and invocation.
- Explain the conditions necessary for functions to be defined. Understand function declaration and invocation.

8.1 Differences between Tasks and Functions

Tasks and functions serve different purposes in Verilog. We discuss tasks and functions in greater detail in the following sections. However, first it is important to understand differences between tasks and functions, as outlined in Table 8-1.

Table 8-1 Tasks and Functions

Functions	Tasks
A function can enable another function but not another task.	A task can enable other tasks and functions.
Functions always execute in 0 simulation time.	Tasks may execute in non-zero simulation time.
Functions must not contain any delay, event, or timing control statements.	Tasks may contain delay, event, or timing control statements.
Functions must have at least one **input** argument. They can have more than one **input**.	Tasks may have zero or more arguments of type **input, output**, or **inout**.
Functions always return a single value. They cannot have **output** or **inout** arguments.	Tasks do not return with a value, but can pass multiple values through **output** and **inout** arguments.

Both tasks and functions must be defined in a module and are local to the module. Tasks are used for common Verilog code that contains delays, timing, event constructs, or *multiple* output arguments. Functions are used when common Verilog code is purely combinational, executes in zero simulation time, and provides exactly *one* output. Functions are typically used for conversions and commonly used calculations.

Tasks can have `input`, `output`, and `inout` arguments; functions can have `input` arguments. In addition, they can have local variables, registers, time variables, integers, real, or events. Tasks or functions cannot have wires. Tasks and functions contain behavioral statements only. Tasks and functions do not contain `always` or `initial` statements but are called from `always` blocks, `initial` blocks, or other tasks and functions.

8.2 Tasks

Tasks are declared with the keywords `task` and `endtask`. Tasks must be used if any one of the following conditions is true for the procedure:

- There are delay, timing, or event control constructs in the procedure.
- The procedure has zero or more than one output arguments.
- The procedure has no input arguments.

8.2.1 Task Declaration and Invocation

Task declaration and task invocation syntax are as follows.

Example 8-1 *Syntax for Tasks*

```
task_declaration ::=
          task [ automatic ] task_identifier ;
          { task_item_declaration }
          statement
          endtask
        | task [ automatic ] task_identifier ( task_port_list ) ;
          { block_item_declaration }
          statement
          endtask

task_item_declaration ::=
         block_item_declaration
       | { attribute_instance } tf_input_declaration ;
       | { attribute_instance } tf_output_declaration ;
       | { attribute_instance } tf_inout_declaration ;
task_port_list ::= task_port_item { , task_port_item }
task_port_item ::=
         { attribute_instance } tf_input_declaration
       | { attribute_instance } tf_output_declaration
       | { attribute_instance } tf_inout_declaration
tf_input_declaration  ::=
          input [ reg ] [ signed ] [ range ] list_of_port_identifiers
        | input [ task_port_type ] list_of_port_identifiers
tf_output_declaration ::=
          output [ reg ] [ signed ] [ range ] list_of_port_identifiers
        | output [ task_port_type ] list_of_port_identifiers
tf_inout_declaration  ::=
          inout [ reg ] [ signed ] [ range ] list_of_port_identifiers
        | inout [ task_port_type ] list_of_port_identifiers
task_port_type ::=
          time | real | realtime | integer
```

I/O declarations use keywords **input**, **output**, or **inout**, based on the type of argument declared. *Input* and *inout* arguments are passed into the task. *Input* arguments are processed in the task statements. *Output* and *inout* argument values are passed back to the variables in the task invocation statement when the task is completed. Tasks can invoke other tasks or functions.

Although the keywords **input**, **inout**, and **output** used for I/O arguments in a task are the same as the keywords used to declare ports in modules, there is a difference. Ports are used to connect external signals to the module. I/O arguments in a task are used to pass values to and from the task.

8.2.2 Task Examples

We discuss two examples of tasks. The first example illustrates the use of input and output arguments in tasks. The second example models an asymmetric sequence generator that generates an asymmetric sequence on the clock signal.

Use of input and output arguments

Example 8-2 illustrates the use of **input** and **output** arguments in tasks. Consider a task called *bitwise_oper*, which computes the *bitwise and, bitwise or*, and *bitwise ex-or* of two 16-bit numbers. The two 16-bit numbers *a* and *b* are inputs and the three outputs are 16-bit numbers *ab_and*, *ab_or*, *ab_xor*. A parameter *delay* is also used in the task.

Example 8-2 *Input and Output Arguments in Tasks*

```
//Define a module called operation that contains the task bitwise_oper
module operation;
...
...
parameter delay = 10;
reg [15:0] A, B;
reg [15:0] AB_AND, AB_OR, AB_XOR;

always @(A or B) //whenever A or B changes in value
begin
        //invoke the task bitwise_oper. provide 2 input arguments A, B
        //Expect 3 output arguments AB_AND, AB_OR, AB_XOR
        //The arguments must be specified in the same order as they
        //appear in the task declaration.
        bitwise_oper(AB_AND, AB_OR, AB_XOR, A, B);
end
...
...
//define task bitwise_oper
task bitwise_oper;
output [15:0] ab_and, ab_or, ab_xor; //outputs from the task
input [15:0] a, b; //inputs to the task
begin
        #delay ab_and = a & b;
        ab_or = a | b;
```

Example 8-2 *Input and Output Arguments in Tasks (Continued)*

```
        ab_xor = a ^ b;
end
endtask
...
endmodule
```

In the above task, the input values passed to the task are *A* and *B*. Hence, when the task is entered, *a* = *A* and *b* = *B*. The three output values are computed after a delay. This delay is specified by the parameter *delay*, which is 10 units for this example. When the task is completed, the output values are passed back to the calling output arguments. Therefore, *AB_AND* = *ab_and, AB_OR* = *ab_or,* and *AB_XOR* = *ab_xor* when the task is completed.

Another method of declaring arguments for tasks is the ANSI C style. Example 8-3 shows the *bitwise_oper* task defined with an ANSI C style argument declaration.

Example 8-3 *Task Definition using ANSI C Style Argument Declaration*

```
//define task bitwise_oper
task bitwise_oper (output [15:0] ab_and, ab_or, ab_xor,
                   input [15:0] a, b);
begin
        #delay ab_and = a & b;
        ab_or = a | b;
        ab_xor = a ^ b;
end
endtask
```

Asymmetric Sequence Generator

Tasks can directly operate on **reg** variables defined in the module. Example 8-4 directly operates on the **reg** variable *clock* to continuously produce an asymmetric sequence. The *clock* is initialized with an initialization sequence.

Example 8-4 *Direct Operation on reg Variables*

```
//Define a module that contains the task asymmetric_sequence
module sequence;
...
reg clock;
...
initial
```

Example 8-4 *Direct Operation on reg Variables (Continued)*

```
        init_sequence; //Invoke the task init_sequence
...
always
begin
        asymmetric_sequence; //Invoke the task asymmetric_sequence
end
...
...
//Initialization sequence
task init_sequence;
begin
        clock = 1'b0;
end
endtask

//define task to generate asymmetric sequence
//operate directly on the clock defined in the module.
task asymmetric_sequence;
begin
        #12 clock = 1'b0;
        #5 clock = 1'b1;
        #3 clock = 1'b0;
        #10 clock = 1'b1;
end
endtask
...
...
endmodule
```

8.2.3 Automatic (Re-entrant) Tasks

Tasks are normally static in nature. All declared items are statically allocated and they are shared across all uses of the task executing concurrently. Therefore, if a task is called concurrently from two places in the code, these task calls will operate on the same task variables. It is highly likely that the results of such an operation will be incorrect.

To avoid this problem, a keyword **`automatic`** is added in front of the **`task`** keyword to make the tasks re-entrant. Such tasks are called *automatic* tasks. All items declared inside automatic tasks are allocated dynamically for each invocation. Each task call operates in an independent space. Thus, the task calls operate on independent copies of the task variables. This results in correct operation. It is recommended that automatic tasks be used if there is a chance that a task might be called concurrently from two locations in the code.

Example 8-5 shows how an automatic task is defined and used.

Example 8-5 *Re-entrant (Automatic) Tasks*

```
// Module that contains an automatic (re-entrant) task
// Only a small portion of the module that contains the task definition
// is shown in this example. There are two clocks.
// clk2 runs at twice the frequency of clk and is synchronous
// with clk.
module top;
reg [15:0] cd_xor, ef_xor; //variables in module top
reg [15:0] c, d, e, f; //variables in module top
-
task automatic bitwise_xor;
output [15:0] ab_xor; //output from the task
input [15:0] a, b; //inputs to the task
begin
    #delay ab_and = a & b;
    ab_or = a | b;
    ab_xor = a ^ b;
end
endtask
...
-
// These two always blocks will call the bitwise_xor task
// concurrently at each positive edge of clk. However, since
// the task is re-entrant, these concurrent calls will work correctly.
always @(posedge clk)
    bitwise_xor(ef_xor, e, f);
-
always @(posedge clk2) // twice the frequency as the previous block
    bitwise_xor(cd_xor, c, d);

-
-
endmodule
```

8.3 Functions

Functions are declared with the keywords **function** and **endfunction**. Functions are used if all of the following conditions are true for the procedure:

- There are no delay, timing, or event control constructs in the procedure.
- The procedure returns a single value.
- There is at least one input argument.
- There are no output or inout arguments.
- There are no nonblocking assignments.

8.3.1 Function Declaration and Invocation

The syntax for functions follows in Example 8-6:

Example 8-6 *Syntax for Functions*

```
function_declaration ::=
            function [ automatic ] [ signed ] [ range_or_type ]
            function_identifier ;
            function_item_declaration { function_item_declaration }
            function_statement
            endfunction
           | function [ automatic ] [ signed ] [ range_or_type ]
            function_identifier (function_port_list ) ;
            block_item_declaration { block_item_declaration }
            function_statement
            endfunction
function_item_declaration ::=
          block_item_declaration
        | tf_input_declaration ;
function_port_list ::= { attribute_instance } tf_input_declaration {,
                      { attribute_instance } tf_input_declaration }
range_or_type ::= range | integer | real | realtime | time
```

There are some peculiarities of functions. When a function is declared, a register with name *function_identifier* is declared implicitly inside Verilog. The output of a function is passed back by setting the value of the register *function_identifier* appropriately. The function is invoked by specifying function name and input arguments. At the end of function execution, the return value is placed where the function was invoked. The optional *range_or_type* specifies the width of the internal register. If no range or type is specified, the default bit width is 1. Functions are very similar to *FUNCTION* in FORTRAN.

Notice that at least one input argument must be defined for a function. There are no output arguments for functions because the implicit register *function_identifier* contains the output value. Also, functions *cannot* invoke other tasks. They can invoke only other functions.

8.3.2 Function Examples

We will discuss two examples. The first example models a parity calculator that returns a 1-bit value. The second example models a 32-bit left/right shift register that returns a 32-bit shifted value.

Parity calculation

Let us discuss a function that calculates the parity of a 32-bit *address* and returns the value. We assume even parity. Example 8-7 shows the definition and invocation of the function *calc_parity*.

Example 8-7 *Parity Calculation*

```
//Define a module that contains the function calc_parity
module parity;
...
reg [31:0] addr;
reg parity;

//Compute new parity whenever address value changes
always @(addr)
begin
        parity = calc_parity(addr); //First invocation of calc_parity
        $display("Parity calculated = %b", calc_parity(addr) );
                                    //Second invocation of calc_parity
end
...
...
//define the parity calculation function
function calc_parity;
input [31:0] address;
begin
        //set the output value appropriately. Use the implicit
        //internal register calc_parity.
        calc_parity = ^address; //Return the xor of all address bits.
end
endfunction
...
...
endmodule
```

Note that in the first invocation of *calc_parity*, the returned value was used to set the **reg** *parity*. In the second invocation, the value returned was directly used inside the **$display** task. Thus, the returned value is placed wherever the function was invoked.

Another method of declaring arguments for functions is the ANSI C style. Example 8-8 shows the *calc_parity* function defined with an ANSI C style argument declaration.

Example 8-8 *Function Definition Using ANSI C Style Argument Declaration*

```
//define the parity calculation function using ANSI C Style arguments
function calc_parity (input [31:0] address);
begin
        //set the output value appropriately. Use the implicit
        //internal register calc_parity.
        calc_parity = ^address; //Return the xor of all address bits.
end
endfunction
```

Left/right shifter

To illustrate how a range for the output value of a function can be specified, let us consider a function that shifts a 32-bit value to the left or right by one bit, based on a *control* signal. Example 8-9 shows the implementation of the left/right shifter.

Example 8-9 *Left/Right Shifter*

```
//Define a module that contains the function shift
module shifter;
...
//Left/right shifter
`define LEFT_SHIFT       1'b0
`define RIGHT_SHIFT      1'b1
reg [31:0] addr, left_addr, right_addr;
reg control;

//Compute the right- and left-shifted values whenever
//a new address value appears
always @(addr)
begin
       //call the function defined below to do left and right shift.
        left_addr = shift(addr, `LEFT_SHIFT);
        right_addr = shift(addr, `RIGHT_SHIFT);
end
```

Example 8-9 *Left/Right Shifter (Continued)*

```
...
...
//define shift function. The output is a 32-bit value.
function [31:0] shift;
input [31:0] address;
input control;
begin
        //set the output value appropriately based on a control signal.
        shift = (control == `LEFT_SHIFT) ?(address << 1) : (address >> 1);

end
endfunction
...
...
endmodule
```

8.3.3 Automatic (Recursive) Functions

Functions are normally used non-recursively. If a function is called concurrently from two locations, the results are non-deterministic because both calls operate on the same variable space.

However, the keyword **automatic** can be used to declare a recursive (automatic) function where all function declarations are allocated dynamically for each recursive call. Each call to an automatic function operates in an independent variable space. Automatic function items cannot be accessed by hierarchical references. Automatic functions can be invoked through the use of their hierarchical name.

Example 8-10 shows how an automatic function is defined to compute a factorial.

Example 8-10 *Recursive (Automatic) Functions*

```
//Define a factorial with a recursive function
module top;
...
// Define the function
function automatic integer factorial;
input [31:0] oper;
integer i;
begin
```

(Continued...)

```
if (operand >= 2)
   factorial = factorial (oper -1) * oper; //recursive call
else
   factorial = 1 ;
end
endfunction



// Call the function
integer result;
initial
begin
    result = factorial(4); // Call the factorial of 7
    $display("Factorial of 4 is %0d", result); //Displays 24
end
...
...
endmodule
```

8.3.4 Constant Functions

A *constant function*[1] is a regular Verilog HDL function, but with certain restrictions. These functions can be used to reference complex values and can be used instead of constants.

Example 8-11 shows how a constant function can be used to compute the width of the address bus in a module.

1. See *IEEE Standard Verilog Hardware Description Language* document for details on constant function restrictions.

Example 8-11 Constant Functions

```
//Define a RAM model
module ram (...);
parameter RAM_DEPTH = 256;
input [clogb2(RAM_DEPTH)-1:0] addr_bus; //width of bus computed
                                        //by calling constant
                                        //function defined below
                                        //Result of clogb2 = 8
                                        //input [7:0] addr_bus;
--
--
//Constant function
function integer clogb2(input integer depth);
begin
   for(clogb2=0; depth >0; clogb2=clogb2+1)
      depth = depth >> 1;
end
endfunction
--
--
endmodule
```

8.3.5 Signed Functions

Signed functions allow signed operations to be performed on the function return values. Example 8-12 shows an example of a signed function.

Example 8-12 Signed Functions

```
module top;
--
//Signed function declaration
//Returns a 64 bit signed value
function signed [63:0] compute_signed(input [63:0] vector);
--
--
endfunction
--
//Call to the signed function from the higher module
if(compute_signed(vector) < -3)
begin
--
end

--
endmodule
```

8.4 Summary

In this chapter, we discussed tasks and functions used in behavior Verilog modeling.

- *Tasks* and *functions* are used to define common Verilog functionality that is used at many places in the design. Tasks and functions help to make a module definition more readable by breaking it up into manageable subunits. Tasks and functions serve the same purpose in Verilog as subroutines do in C.
- Tasks can take any number of **`input`**, **`inout`**, or **`output`** arguments. Delay, event, or timing control constructs are permitted in tasks. Tasks can enable other tasks or functions.
- Re-entrant tasks defined with the keyword **`automatic`** allow each task call to operate in an independent space. Therefore, re-entrant tasks work correctly even with concurrent tasks calls.
- Functions are used when exactly one return value is required and at least one input argument is specified. Delay, event, or timing control constructs are not permitted in functions. Functions can invoke other functions but cannot invoke other tasks.

- A register with name as the function name is declared implicitly when a function is declared. The return value of the function is passed back in this register.
- Recursive functions defined with the keyword `automatic` allow each function call to operate in an independent space. Therefore, recursive or concurrent calls to such functions will work correctly.
- Tasks and functions are included in a design hierarchy and can be addressed by hierarchical name referencing.

8.5 Exercises

1. Define a **`function`** to calculate the `factorial` of a 4-bit number. The output is a 32-bit value. Invoke the function by using stimulus and check results.
2. Define a **`function`** to multiply two 4-bit numbers *a* and *b*. The output is an 8-bit value. Invoke the function by using stimulus and check results.
3. Define a **`function`** to design an 8-function ALU that takes two 4-bit numbers *a* and *b* and computes a 5-bit result *out* based on a 3-bit *select* signal. Ignore overflow or underflow bits.

Select Signal	Function Output
3'b000	a
3'b001	a + b
3'b010	a - b
3'b011	a / b
3'b100	a % 1 (remainder)
3'b101	a << 1
3'b110	a >> 1
3'b111	(a > b) (magnitude compare)

4. Define a **`task`** to compute the factorial of a 4-bit number. The output is a 32-bit value. The result is assigned to the output after a delay of 10 time units.
5. Define a **`task`** to compute even parity of a 16-bit number. The result is a 1-bit value that is assigned to the output after three positive edges of clock. (Hint: Use a **`repeat`** loop in the task.)
6. Using named events, tasks, and functions, design the traffic signal controller in `Traffic Signal Controller` on page 161.

Useful Modeling Techniques 9

We learned the basic features of Verilog in the preceding chapters. In this chapter we will discuss additional features that enhance the Verilog language, making it powerful and flexible for modeling and analyzing a design.

Learning Objectives

- Describe procedural continuous assignment statements **`assign`**, **`deassign`**, **`force`**, and **`release`**. Explain their significance in modeling and debugging.
- Understand how to override parameters by using the **`defparam`** statement at the time of module instantiation.
- Explain conditional compilation and execution of parts of the Verilog description.
- Identify system tasks for *`file output, displaying hierarchy, strobing, random number generation, memory initialization,`* and *`value change dump`*.

9.1 Procedural Continuous Assignments

We studied procedural assignments in Section 7.2, `Procedural Assignments`. Procedural assignments assign a value to a register. The value stays in the register until another procedural assignment puts another value in that register. *`Procedural continuous assignments`* behave differently. They are procedural statements which allow values of expressions to be driven continuously onto registers or nets for limited periods of time. Procedural continuous assignments override existing assignments to a register or net. They provide a useful extension to the regular procedural assignment statement.

9.1.1 assign and deassign

The keywords **`assign`** and **`deassign`** are used to express the first type of procedural continuous assignment. The left-hand side of procedural continuous assignments can be only be a *`register`* or a *`concatenation of registers`*. It cannot be a *`part`* or *`bit`* *select of a net* or an *array of registers*. Procedural continuous assignments override the effect of regular procedural assignments. Procedural continuous assignments are normally used for controlled periods of time.

A simple example is the negative edge-triggered D-flipflop with asynchronous reset that we modeled in Example 6-8. In Example 9-1, we now model the same *D_FF*, using **assign** and **deassign** statements.

Example 9-1 D-Flipflop with Procedural Continuous Assignments

```
// Negative edge-triggered D-flipflop with asynchronous reset
module edge_dff(q, qbar, d, clk, reset);

// Inputs and outputs
output q,qbar;
input d, clk, reset;
reg q, qbar; //declare q and qbar are registers

always @(negedge clk) //assign value of q & qbar at active edge of clock.
begin
      q = d;
      qbar = ~d;
end

always @(reset) //Override the regular assignments to q and qbar
            //whenever reset goes high. Use of procedural continuous
            //assignments.
      if(reset)
      begin  //if reset is high, override regular assignments to q with
             //the new values, using procedural continuous assignment.
             assign q = 1'b0;
             assign qbar = 1'b1;
      end
      else
      begin  //If reset goes low, remove the overriding values by
             //deassigning the registers. After this the regular
             //assignments q = d and qbar = ~d will be able to change
            //the registers on the next negative edge of clock.
             deassign q;
             deassign qbar;
      end

endmodule
```

In Example 9-1, we overrode the assignment on *q* and `qbar` and assigned new values to them when the *reset* signal went high. The register variables retain the continuously assigned value after the **`deassign`** until they are changed by a future procedural assignment. The **`assign`** and **`deassign`** constructs are now considered to be a bad coding style and it is recommended that alternative styles be used in Verilog HDL code.

9.1.2 force and release

Keywords **`force`** and **`release`** are used to express the second form of the procedural continuous assignments. They can be used to override assignments on both registers and nets. **`force`** and **`release`** statements are typically used in the interactive debugging process, where certain registers or nets are forced to a value, and the effect on other registers and nets is noted. It is recommended that **`force`** and **`release`** statements not be used inside design blocks. They should appear only in stimulus or as debug statements.

force and release on registers

A **`force`** on a register overrides any procedural assignments or procedural continuous assignments on the register until the register is released. The register variables will continue to store the forced value after being released, but can then be changed by a future procedural assignment. To override the values of *q* and *qbar* in Example 9-1 for a limited period of time, we could do the following:

```
module stimulus;
...
...
//instantiate the d-flipflop
edge_dff dff(Q, Qbar, D, CLK, RESET);
...
...
initial
begin
    //these statements force value of 1 on dff.q between time 50 and
    //100, regardless of the actual output of the edge_dff.
    #50 force dff.q = 1'b1; //force value of q to 1 at time 50.
    #50 release dff.q;  //release the value of q at time 100.
end
...
...
endmodule
```

force and release on nets

force on nets overrides any continuous assignments until the net is released. The net will immediately return to its normal driven value when it is released. A net can be forced to an expression or a value.

```
module top;
...
...
assign out = a & b & c; //continuous assignment on net out
...
initial
    #50 force out = a | b & c;
    #50 release out;
end
...
...
endmodule
```

In the example above, a new expression is forced on the net from time 50 to time 100. From time 50 to time 100, when the **force** statement is active, the expression `a | b & c` will be re-evaluated and assigned to *out* whenever values of signals *a* or *b* or *c* change. Thus, the **force** statement behaves like a continuous assignment except that it is active for only a limited period of time.

9.2 Overriding Parameters

Parameters can be defined in a module definition, as was discussed earlier in Section 3.2.8, *Parameters*. However, during compilation of Verilog modules, parameter values can be altered separately for each module instance. This allows us to pass a distinct set of parameter values to each module during compilation regardless of predefined parameter values.

There are two ways to override parameter values: through the *defparam statement* or through *module instance parameter value assignment*.

9.2.1 defparam Statement

Parameter values can be changed in any module instance in the design with the keyword **defparam**. The hierarchical name of the module instance can be used to override parameter values. Consider Example 9-2, which uses **defparam** to override the parameter values in module instances.

Example 9-2 Defparam Statement

```
//Define a module hello_world
module hello_world;
parameter id_num = 0; //define a module identification number = 0

initial //display the module identification number
      $display("Displaying hello_world id number = %d", id_num);
endmodule


//define top-level module
module top;
//change parameter values in the instantiated modules
//Use defparam statement
defparam w1.id_num = 1, w2.id_num = 2;

//instantiate two hello_world modules
hello_world w1();
hello_world w2();

endmodule
```

In Example 9-2, the module *hello_world* was defined with a default *id_num* = 0. However, when the module instances *w1* and *w2* of the type *hello_world* are created, their *id_num* values are modified with the **defparam** statement. If we simulate the above design, we would get the following output:

```
Displaying hello_world id number = 1
Displaying hello_world id number = 2
```

Multiple **defparam** statements can appear in a module. Any parameter can be overridden with the **defparam** statement. The **defparam** construct is now considered to be a bad coding style and it is recommended that alternative styles be used in Verilog HDL code.

Note that the module *hello_world* can also be defined using an ANSI C style parameter declaration. Example 9-3 shows the ANSI C style parameter declaration for the module *hello_world*.

Example 9-3 ANSI C Style Parameter Declaration

```
//Define a module hello_world
module hello_world #(parameter id_num = 0) ;//ANSI C Style Parameter

initial //display the module identification number
        $display("Displaying hello_world id number = %d", id_num);
endmodule
```

9.2.2 Module_Instance Parameter Values

Parameter values can be overridden when a module is instantiated. To illustrate this, we will use Example 9-2 and modify it a bit. The new parameter values are passed during module instantiation. The top-level module can pass parameters to the instances *w1* and *w2,* as shown below. Notice that **defparam** is not needed. The simulation output will be identical to the output obtained with the **defparam** statement.

```
//define top-level module
module top;

//instantiate two hello_world modules; pass new parameter values
//Parameter value assignment by ordered list
hello_world #(1) w1; //pass value 1 to module w1

//Parameter value assignment by name
hello_world #(.id_num(2)) w2; //pass value 2 to id_num parameter
                                       //for module w2

endmodule
```

If multiple parameters are defined in the module, during module instantiation, they can be overridden by specifying the new values in the same order as the parameter declarations in the module. If an overriding value is not specified, the default parameter declaration values are taken. Alternately, one can override specific values by naming the parameters and the corresponding values. This is called parameter value assignment by name. Consider Example 9-4.

Example 9-4 *Module Instance Parameter Values*

```
//define module with delays
module bus_master;
parameter delay1 = 2;
parameter delay2 = 3;
parameter delay3 = 7;
...
<module internals>
...
endmodule

//top-level module; instantiates two bus_master modules
module top;

//Instantiate the modules with new delay values

//Parameter value assignment by ordered list
bus_master #(4, 5, 6) b1(); //b1: delay1 = 4, delay2 = 5, delay3 = 6
bus_master #(9,4) b2(); //b2: delay1 = 9, delay2 = 4, delay3 = 7(default)

//Parameter value assignment by name
bus_master #(.delay2(4), delay3(7)) b3(); //b2: delay2 = 4, delay3 = 7
                                          //delay1=2 (default)
// It is recommended to use the parameter value assignment by name
// This minimizes the chance of error and parameters can be added
// or deleted without worrying about the order.

endmodule
```

Module-instance parameter value assignment is a very useful method used to override parameter values and to customize module instances.

9.3 Conditional Compilation and Execution

A portion of Verilog might be suitable for one environment but not for another. The designer does not wish to create two versions of Verilog design for the two environments. Instead, the designer can specify that the particular portion of the code be compiled only if a certain flag is set. This is called `conditional compilation`.

A designer might also want to execute certain parts of the Verilog design only when a flag is set at run time. This is called `conditional execution`.

9.3.1 Conditional Compilation

Conditional compilation can be accomplished by using compiler directives **`` `ifdef``**, **`` `ifndef``**, **`` `else``**, **`` `elsif``**, and **`` `endif``**. Example 9-5 contains Verilog source code to be compiled conditionally.

Example 9-5 Conditional Compilation

```
//Conditional Compilation
//Example 1
'ifdef TEST //compile module test only if text macro TEST is defined
module test;
...
...
endmodule
'else //compile the module stimulus as default
module stimulus;
...
...
endmodule
'endif //completion of 'ifdef directive

//Example 2
module top;

bus_master b1(); //instantiate module unconditionally
'ifdef ADD_B2
   bus_master b2(); //b2 is instantiated conditionally if text macro
                    //ADD_B2 is defined
'elsif ADD_B3
   bus_master b3(); //b3 is instantiated conditionally if text macro
                    //ADD_B3 is defined
'else
   bus_master b4(); //b4 is instantiate by default
```

Example 9-5 Conditional Compilation (Continued)

```
'endif

'ifndef IGNORE_B5
   bus_master b5(); //b5 is instantiated conditionally if text macro
                    //IGNORE_B5 is not defined
'endif
endmodule
```

The **`ifdef** and **`ifndef** directives can appear anywhere in the design. A designer can conditionally compile statements, modules, blocks, declarations, and other compiler directives. The **`else** directive is optional. A maximum of one **`else** directive can accompany an **`ifdef** or **`ifndef**. Any number of **`elsif** directives can accompany an **`ifdef** or **`ifndef**. An **`ifdef** or **`ifndef** is always closed by a corresponding **`endif**.

The conditional compile flag can be set by using the **`define** statement inside the Verilog file. In the example above, we could define the flags by defining text macros *TEST* and *ADD_B2* at compile time by using the **`define** statement. The Verilog compiler simply skips the portion if the conditional compile flag is not set. A Boolean expression, such as *TEST && ADD_B2*, is not allowed with the **`ifdef** statement.

9.3.2 Conditional Execution

Conditional execution flags allow the designer to control statement execution flow at run time. All statements are compiled but executed conditionally. Conditional execution flags can be used only for behavioral statements. The system task keyword **$test$plusargs** is used for conditional execution.

Consider Example 9-6, which illustrates conditional execution with **$test$plusargs**.

Example 9-6 Conditional Execution with $test$plusargs

```
//Conditional execution
module test;
...
...
initial
begin
   if($test$plusargs("DISPLAY_VAR"))
      $display("Display = %b ", {a,b,c} ); //display only if flag is set
   else
```

Example 9-6 Conditional Execution with $test$plusargs (Continued)

```
//Conditional execution
      $display("No Display"); //otherwise no display
end
endmodule
```

The variables are displayed only if the flag *DISPLAY_VAR* is set at run time. Flags can be set at run time by specifying the option *+DISPLAY_VAR* at run time.

Conditional execution can be further controlled by using the system task keyword **$value$plusargs**. This system task allows testing for arguments to an invocation option. **$value$plusargs** returns a 0 if a matching invocation was not found and non-zero if a matching option was found. Example 9-7 shows an example of **$value$plusargs**.

Example 9-7 Conditional Execution with $value$plusargs

```
//Conditional execution with $value$plusargs
module test;
reg [8*128-1:0] test_string;
integer clk_period;
...
...
initial
begin
   if($value$plusargs("testname=%s", test_string))
      $readmemh(test_string, vectors); //Read test vectors
   else
      //otherwise display error message
      $display("Test name option not specified");

   if($value$plusargs("clk_t=%d", clk_period))
      forever #(clk_period/2) clk = ~clk; //Set up clock
   else
      //otherwise display error message
      $display("Clock period option name not specified");

end

//For example, to invoke the above options invoke simulator with
//+testname=test1.vec +clk_t=10
//Test name = "test1.vec" and clk_period = 10
endmodule
```

9.4 Time Scales

Often, in a single simulation, delay values in one module need to be defined by using a certain time unit, e.g., 1 μs, and delay values in another module need to be defined by using a different time unit, e.g. 100 ns. Verilog HDL allows the reference time unit for modules to be specified with the **`timescale** compiler directive.

Usage: **`timescale** *<reference_time_unit> / <time_precision>*

The *<reference_time_unit>* specifies the unit of measurement for times and delays. The *<time_precision>* specifies the precision to which the delays are rounded off during simulation. Only 1, 10, and 100 are valid integers for specifying time unit and time precision. Consider the two modules, *dummy1* and *dummy2*, in Example 9-8.

Example 9-8 *Time Scales*

```
//Define a time scale for the module dummy1
//Reference time unit is 100 nanoseconds and precision is 1 ns
`timescale 100 ns / 1 ns

module dummy1;

reg toggle;

//initialize toggle
initial
  toggle = 1'b0;

//Flip the toggle register every 5 time units
//In this module 5 time units = 500 ns = .5 µs
always #5
    begin
        toggle = ~toggle;
        $display("%d , In %m toggle = %b ", $time, toggle);
    end

endmodule

//Define a time scale for the module dummy2
//Reference time unit is 1 microsecond and precision is 10 ns
`timescale 1 us / 10 ns

module dummy2;

reg toggle;
```

Example 9-8 *Time Scales (Continued)*

```
//initialize toggle
initial
  toggle = 1'b0;

//Flip the toggle register every 5 time units
//In this module 5 time units = 5 µs  = 5000 ns
always #5
    begin
        toggle = ~toggle;
        $display("%d , In %m toggle = %b ", $time, toggle);
    end

endmodule
```

The two modules *dummy1* and *dummy2* are identical in all respects, except that the time unit for *dummy1* is 100 ns and the time unit for *dummy2* is 1 µs. Thus the **$display** statement in *dummy1* will be executed 10 times for each **$display** executed in *dummy2*. The **$time** task reports the simulation time in terms of the reference time unit for the module in which it is invoked. The first few **$display** statements are shown in the simulation output below to illustrate the effect of the **`timescale** directive.

```
                     5 , In dummy1 toggle = 1
                    10 , In dummy1 toggle = 0
                    15 , In dummy1 toggle = 1
                    20 , In dummy1 toggle = 0
                    25 , In dummy1 toggle = 1
                    30 , In dummy1 toggle = 0
                    35 , In dummy1 toggle = 1
                    40 , In dummy1 toggle = 0
                    45 , In dummy1 toggle = 1
        -->          5 , In dummy2 toggle = 1
                    50 , In dummy1 toggle = 0
                    55 , In dummy1 toggle = 1
```

Notice that the **$display** statement in *dummy2* executes once for every ten **$display** statements in *dummy1*.

9.5 Useful System Tasks

In this section, we discuss the system tasks that are useful for a variety of purposes in Verilog. We discuss system tasks [1] for *file output*, *displaying hierarchy*, *strobing*, *random number generation*, *memory initialization*, and *value change dump*.

9.5.1 File Output

Output from Verilog normally goes to the standard output and the file *verilog.log*. It is possible to redirect the output of Verilog to a chosen file.

Opening a file

A file can be opened with the system task **$fopen**.

Usage: **$fopen**("*<name_of_file>*"); [2]

Usage: *<file_handle>* = **$fopen**("*<name_of_file>*");

The task **$fopen** returns a 32-bit value called a *multichannel descriptor*. [3] Only one bit is set in a multichannel descriptor. The standard output has a multichannel descriptor with the least significant bit (bit 0) set. Standard output is also called channel 0. The standard output is always open. Each successive call to **$fopen** opens a new channel an returns a 32-bit descriptor with bit 1 set, bit 2 set, and so on, up to bit 30 set. Bit 31 is reserved. The channel number corresponds to the individual bit set in the multichannel descriptor. Example 9-9 illustrates the use of file descriptors.

Example 9-9 *File Descriptors*

```
//Multichannel descriptor
integer handle1, handle2, handle3; //integers are 32-bit values

//standard output is open; descriptor = 32'h0000_0001 (bit 0 set)
initial
begin
   handle1 = $fopen("file1.out"); //handle1 = 32'h0000_0002 (bit 1 set)
```

1. Other system tasks such as **$signed** and **$unsigned** used for sign conversion are not discussed in this book. For details, please refer to the "IEEE Standard Verilog Hardware Description Language" document.

2. The "IEEE Standard Verilog Hardware Description Language" document provides additional capabilities for **$fopen**. The **$fopen** syntax mentioned in this book is adequate for most purposes. However, if you need additional capabilities, please refer to the "IEEE Standard Verilog Hardware Description Language" document.

3. The "IEEE Standard Verilog Hardware Description Language" document provides a method for opening up to 2^{30} files by using a single-channel file descriptor. Please refer to it for details.

Example 9-9   File Descriptors

```
    handle2 = $fopen("file2.out"); //handle2 = 32'h0000_0004 (bit 2 set)
    handle3 = $fopen("file3.out"); //handle3 = 32'h0000_0008 (bit 3 set)
end
```

The advantage of multichannel descriptors is that it is possible to selectively write to multiple files at the same time. This is explained below in greater detail.

Writing to files

The system tasks **`$fdisplay`**, **`$fmonitor`**, **`$fwrite`**, and **`$fstrobe`** are used to write to files.[4] Note that these tasks are similar in syntax to regular system tasks **`$display`**, **`$monitor`**, etc., but they provide the additional capability of writing to files.

We will consider only **`$fdisplay`** and **`$fmonitor`** tasks.

Usage: **`$fdisplay`**`(<file_descriptor>, p1, p2 ..., pn);`

`$fmonitor``(<file_descriptor>, p1, p2,..., pn);`

p1, p2, ..., pn can be variables, signal names, or quoted strings. A *file_descriptor* is a multichannel descriptor that can be a file handle or a bitwise combination of file handles. Verilog will write the output to all files that have a 1 associated with them in the file descriptor. We will use the file descriptors defined in Example 9-9 to illustrate the use of the **`$fdisplay`** and **`$fmonitor`** tasks.

```
//All handles defined in Example 9-9
//Writing to files
integer desc1, desc2, desc3; //three file descriptors
initial
begin
    desc1 = handle1 | 1; //bitwise or; desc1 = 32'h0000_0003
    $fdisplay(desc1, "Display 1");//write to files file1.out & stdout

    desc2 = handle2 | handle1; //desc2 = 32'h0000_0006
    $fdisplay(desc2, "Display 2");//write to files file1.out & file2.out
```

4. The "IEEE Standard Verilog Hardware Description Language" document provides many additional capabilities for file output. The file output system tasks mentioned in this book are adequate for most digital designers. However, if you need additional capabilities for file output, please refer to the IEEE Standard Verilog Hardware Description Language document.
Systems tasks for reading files are also provided by the IEEE Standard Verilog Hardware Description Language. These system tasks include **$fgetc**, **$ungetc**, **$fgetc**, **$fscanf**, **$sscanf**, **$fread**, **$ftell**, **$fseek**, **$rewind**, and **$fflush.** However, most digital designers do not need these capabilities frequently. Therefore, they are not covered in this book. If you need to use the file reading capabilities, please refer to the "IEEE Standard Verilog Hardware Description Language" document.

```
(Continued...)
    desc3 = handle3 ; //desc3 = 32'h0000_0008
    $fdisplay(desc3, "Display 3");//write to file file3.out only
end
```

Closing files

Files can be closed with the system task **`$fclose`**.

Usage: **`$fclose`** *`(<file_handle>);`*

```
//Closing Files
$fclose(handle1);
```

A file cannot be written to once it is closed. The corresponding bit in the multichannel descriptor is set to 0. The next **`$fopen`** call can reuse the bit.

9.5.2 Displaying Hierarchy

Hierarchy at any level can be displayed by means of the `%m` option in any of the display tasks, **`$display`**, **`$write`** task, **`$monitor`**, or **`$strobe`** task, as discussed briefly in Section 4.3, `Hierarchical Names`. This is a very useful option. For example, when multiple instances of a module execute the same Verilog code, the `%m` option will distinguish from which module instance the output is coming. No argument is needed for the `%m` option in the display tasks. See Example 9-10.

Example 9-10 Displaying Hierarchy

```
//Displaying hierarchy information
module M;
...
initial
    $display("Displaying in %m");
endmodule

//instantiate module M
module top;
...
M   m1();
M   m2();
```

Example 9-10 Displaying Hierarchy (Continued)

```
//Displaying hierarchy information
M  m3();
endmodule
```

The output from the simulation will look like the following:

```
Displaying in top.m1
Displaying in top.m2
Displaying in top.m3
```

This feature can display full hierarchical names, including module instances, tasks, functions, and named blocks.

9.5.3 Strobing

Strobing is done with the system task keyword **`$strobe`**. This task is very similar to the **`$display`** task except for a slight difference. If many other statements are executed in the same time unit as the **`$display`** task, the order in which the statements and the **`$display`** task are executed is nondeterministic. If **`$strobe`** is used, it is always executed after all other assignment statements in the same time unit have executed. Thus, **`$strobe`** provides a synchronization mechanism to ensure that data is displayed only after all other assignment statements, which change the data in that time step, have executed. See Example 9-11.

Example 9-11 Strobing

```
//Strobing
always @(posedge clock)
begin
    a = b;
    c = d;
end

always @(posedge clock)
    $strobe("Displaying a = %b, c = %b", a, c); // display values at posedge
```

In Example 9-11, the values at positive edge of clock will be displayed only after statements `a = b` and `c = d` execute. If **`$display`** was used, **`$display`** might execute before statements `a = b` and `c = d`, thus displaying different values.

9.5.4 Random Number Generation

Random number generation capabilities are required for generating a random set of test vectors. Random testing is important because it often catches hidden bugs in the design. Random vector generation is also used in performance analysis of chip architectures. The system task **`$random`** is used for generating a random number.

Usage: **`$random`**`;`
`$random``(<seed>);`

The value of `<seed>` is optional and is used to ensure the same random number sequence each time the test is run. The `<seed>` parameter can either be a **`reg`**, **`integer`**, or **`time`** variable. The task **`$random`** returns a 32-bit signed integer. All bits, bit-selects, or part-selects of the 32-bit random number can be used (see Example 9-12).

Example 9-12 *Random Number Generation*

```
//Generate random numbers and apply them to a simple ROM
module test;
integer r_seed;
reg [31:0] addr;//input to ROM
wire [31:0] data;//output from ROM
...
...
ROM rom1(data, addr);

initial
    r_seed = 2; //arbitrarily define the seed as 2.

always @(posedge clock)
    addr = $random(r_seed); //generates random numbers
...
<check output of ROM against expected results>
...
...
endmodule
```

The random number generator is able to generate signed integers. Therefore, depending on the way the **`$random`** task is used, it can generate positive or negative integers. Example 9-13 shows an example of such generation.

Example 9-13 *Generation of Positive and Negative Numbers by $random Task*

```
reg [23:0] rand1, rand2;
rand1 = $random % 60; //Generates a random number between -59 and 59
rand2 = {$random} % 60; //Addition of concatenation operator to
                        //$random generates a positive value between
                        //0 and 59.
```

Note that the algorithm used by **`$random`** is standardized. Therefore, the same simulation test run on different simulators will generate consistent random patterns for the same seed value.

9.5.5 Initializing Memory from File

We discussed how to declare memories in Section 3.2.7, `Memories`. Verilog provides a very useful system task to initialize memories from a data file. Two tasks are provided to read numbers in binary or hexadecimal format. Keywords **`$readmemb`** and **`$readmemh`** are used to initialize memories.

Usage:

```
      $readmemb("<file_name>", <memory_name>);
      $readmemb("<file_name>", <memory_name>, <start_addr>);
      $readmemb("<file_name>", <memory_name>, <start_addr>,
<finish_addr>);
      Identical syntax for $readmemh.
```

The `<file_name>` and `<memory_name>` are mandatory; `<start_addr>` and `<finish_addr>` are optional. Defaults are start index of memory array for `<start_addr>` and end of the data file or memory for `<finish_addr>`. Example 9-14 illustrates how memory is initialized.

Example 9-14 *Initializing Memory*

```
module test;

reg [7:0] memory[0:7]; //declare an 8-byte memory
integer i;

initial
begin
  //read memory file init.dat. address locations given in memory
  $readmemb("init.dat", memory);
```

Example 9-14 Initializing Memory

```
module test;
  //display contents of initialized memory
  for(i=0; i < 8; i = i + 1)
    $display("Memory [%0d] = %b", i, memory[i]);
end

endmodule
```

The file `init.dat` contains the initialization data. Addresses are specified in the data file with *@<address>*. Addresses are specified as hexadecimal numbers. Data is separated by whitespaces. Data can contain **x** or **z**. Uninitialized locations default to **x**. A sample file, *init.dat*, is shown below.

```
@002
11111111 01010101
00000000 10101010

@006
1111zzzz 00001111
```

When the test module is simulated, we will get the following output:

```
Memory [0] = xxxxxxxx
Memory [1] = xxxxxxxx
Memory [2] = 11111111
Memory [3] = 01010101
Memory [4] = 00000000
Memory [5] = 10101010
Memory [6] = 1111zzzz
Memory [7] = 00001111
```

9.5.6 Value Change Dump File

A *value change dump* (*VCD*) is an ASCII file that contains information about simulation time, scope and signal definitions, and signal value changes in the simulation run. All signals or a selected set of signals in a design can be written to a VCD file during simulation. *Postprocessing tools* can take the VCD file as input and visually display hierarchical information, signal values, and signal waveforms. Many postprocessing tools as well as tools integrated into the simulator are now commercially available. For simulation of large designs, designers dump selected signals to a VCD file and use a postprocessing tool to debug, analyze, and verify the simulation output. The use of VCD file in the debug process is shown in Figure 9-1.

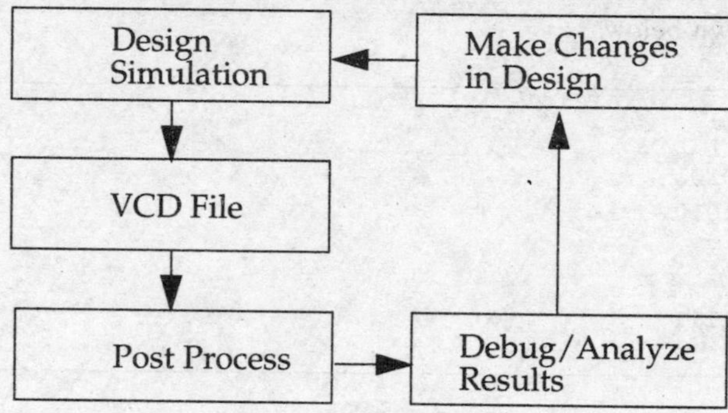

Figure 9-1 Debugging and Analysis of Simulation with VCD File

System tasks are provided for selecting module instances or module instance signals to dump (**$dumpvars**), name of VCD file (**$dumpfile**), starting and stopping the dump process (**$dumpon**, **$dumpoff**), and generating checkpoints (**$dumpall**). The uses of each task are shown in Example 9-15.

Example 9-15 VCD File System Tasks

```
//specify name of VCD file. Otherwise,default name is
//assigned by the simulator.
initial
      $dumpfile("myfile.dmp"); //Simulation info dumped to myfile.dmp

//Dump signals in a module
initial
   $dumpvars; //no arguments, dump all signals in the design
initial
   $dumpvars(1, top); //dump variables in module instance top.
```

Example 9-15 VCD File System Tasks (Continued)

```
                //Number 1 indicates levels of hierarchy. Dump one
                //hierarchy level below top, i.e., dump variables in top,
                //but not signals in modules instantiated by top.
initial
    $dumpvars(2, top.m1);//dump up to 2 levels of hierarchy below top.m1
initial
    $dumpvars(0, top.m1);//Number 0 means dump the entire hierarchy
                         // below top.m1

//Start and stop dump process
initial
begin
    $dumpon;                 //start the dump process.
    #100000 $dumpoff;  //stop the dump process after 100,000 time units
end

//Create a checkpoint. Dump current value of all VCD variables
initial
    $dumpall;
```

The **$dumpfile** and **$dumpvars** tasks are normally specified at the beginning of the simulation. The **$dumpon**, **$dumpoff**, and **$dumpall** tasks control the dump process during the simulation.[5]

Postprocessing tools with graphical displays are commercially available and are now an important part of the simulation and debug process. For large simulation runs, it is very difficult for the designer to analyze the output from **$display** or **$monitor** statements. It is more intuitive to analyze results from graphical waveforms. Formats other than VCD have also emerged, but VCD still remains the popular dump format for Verilog simulators.

However, it is important to note that VCD files can become very large (hundreds of megabytes for large designs). It is important to selectively dump only those signals that need to be examined.

5. Please refer to the "IEEE Standard Verilog Hardware Description Language" document for details on additional tasks such as **$dumpports**, **$dumpportsoff**, **$dumpportson**, **$dumpportsall**, **$dumpportslimit**, and **$dumpportsflush**.

9.6 Summary

In this chapter, we discussed the following aspects of Verilog:

- *Procedural continuous assignments* can be used to override the assignments on registers and nets. **assign** and **deassign** can override assignments on registers. **force** and **release** can override assignments on registers and nets. **assign** and **deassign** are used in the actual design. **force** and **release** are used for debugging.
- Parameters defined in a module can be overridden with the **defparam** statement or by passing a new value during *module instantiation*. During module instantiation, parameter values can be assigned by ordered list or by name. It is recommended to use parameter assignment by name.
- Compilation of parts of the design can be made conditional by using the **\`ifdef**, **\`ifndef**, **\`elsif**, **\`else**, and **\`endif** directives. Compilation flags are defined at compile time by using the **\`define** statement.
- Execution is made conditional in Verilog simulators by means of the **$test$plusargs** system task. The execution flags are defined at run time by *+<flag_name>*.
- Up to 30 files can be opened for writing in Verilog. Each file is assigned a bit in the *multichannel descriptor*. The multichannel descriptor concept can be used to write to multiple files. The *IEEE Standard Verilog Hardware Description Language* document describes more advanced ways of doing file I/O.
- Hierarchy can be displayed with the *%m* option in any display statement.
- *Strobing* is a way to display values at a certain time or event after all other statements in that time unit have executed.
- Random numbers can be generated with the system task **$random**. They are used for random test vector generation. The $**random** task can generate both positive and negative numbers.
- Memory can be initialized from a data file. The data file contains addresses and data. Addresses can also be specified in memory initialization tasks.
- *Value Change Dump* is a popular format used by many designers for debugging with postprocessing tools. Verilog allows all or selected module variables to be dumped to the VCD file. Various system tasks are available for this purpose.

9.7 Exercises

1. Using **assign** and **deassign** statements, design a positive edge-triggered D-flipflop with asynchronous *clear* (*q=0*) and *preset* (*q=1*).

2. Using primitive gates, design a 1-bit full adder *FA*. Instantiate the full adder inside a stimulus module. Force the *sum* output to `a & b & c_in` for the time between 15 and 35 units.

3. A 1-bit full adder *FA* is defined with gates and with delay parameters as shown below.

```
// Define a 1-bit full adder
module fulladd(sum, c_out, a, b, c_in);
parameter d_sum = 0, d_cout = 0;

// I/O port declarations
output sum, c_out;
input a, b, c_in;

// Internal nets
wire s1, c1, c2;

// Instantiate logic gate primitives
xor (s1, a, b);
and (c1, a, b);

xor #(d_sum) (sum, s1, c_in); //delay on output sum is d_sum
and (c2, s1, c_in);

or #(d_cout) (c_out, c2, c1); //delay on output c_out is d_cout

endmodule
```

Define a 4-bit full adder *fulladd4* as shown in Example 5-8 on page 77, but pass the following parameter values to the instances, using the two methods discussed in the book:

Instance	Delay Values
fa0	d_sum=1, d_cout=1
fa1	d_sum=2, d_cout=2
fa2	d_sum=3, d_cout=3
fa3	d_sum=4, d_cout=4

a. Build the *fulladd4* module with **`defparam`** statements to change instance parameter values. Simulate the 4-bit full adder using the stimulus shown in Example 5-9 on page 77. Explain the effect of the full adder delays on the times when outputs of the adder appear. (Use delays of 20 instead of 5 used in this stimulus.)

b. Build the *fulladd4* with delay values passed to instances *fa0, fa1, fa2*, and *fa3* during instantiation. Resimulate the 4-bit adder, using the stimulus above. Check if the results are identical.

4. Create a design that uses the full adder example above. Use a conditional compilation (**`` `ifdef ``**). Compile the *fulladd4* with **defparam** statements if the text macro *DPARAM* is defined by the **`` `define ``** statement; otherwise, compile the *fulladd4* with module instance parameter values.

5. Identify the files to which the following display statements will write:

```
//File output with multi-channel descriptor

module test;

integer handle1,handle2,handle3; //file handles

//open files
initial
begin
  handle1 = $fopen("f1.out");
  handle2 = $fopen("f2.out");
  handle3 = $fopen("f3.out");
end

//Display statements to files
initial
begin
```

```
//File output with multi-channel descriptor
  #5;
  $fdisplay(4, "Display Statement # 1");
  $fdisplay(15, "Display Statement # 2");
  $fdisplay(6, "Display Statement # 3");
  $fdisplay(10, "Display Statement # 4");
  $fdisplay(0, "Display Statement # 5");
end

endmodule
```

6. What will be the output of the **$display** statement shown below?

```
module top;
A a1();
endmodule

module A;
B b1();
endmodule

module B;
initial
    $display("I am inside instance %m");
endmodule
```

7. Consider the 4-bit full adder in Example 6-4 on page 108. Write a stimulus file to do random testing of the full adder. Use a random number generator to generate a 32-bit random number. Pick bits `3:0` and apply them to input *a*; pick bits `7:4` and apply them to input *b*. Use bit `8` and apply it to *c_in*. Apply 20 random test vectors and observe the output.
8. Use the 8-byte memory initialization example in Example 9-14 on page 205. Modify the file to read data in *hexadecimal*. Write a new data file with the following addresses and data values. Unspecified locations are not initialized.

Location Address	Data
1	33
2	66
4	z0
5	0z
6	01

9. Write an **`initial`** block that controls the VCD file. The **`initial`** block must do the following:
    - Set *`myfile.dmp`* as the output VCD file.
    - Dump all variables two levels deep in module instance *`top.a1.b1.c1`*.
    - Stop dumping to VCD at time 200.
    - Start dumping to VCD at time 400.
    - Stop dumping to VCD at time 500.
    - Create a checkpoint. Dump the current value of all VCD variables to the dumpfile.

Part 2 Advanced Verilog Topics

10 **Timing and Delays**
Distributed, lumped and pin-to-pin delays, specify blocks, parallel and full connection, timing checks, delay back-annotation.

11 **Switch-Level Modeling**
MOS and CMOS switches, bidirectional switches, modeling of power and ground, resistive switches, delay specification on switches.

12 **User-Defined Primitives**
Parts of UDP, UDP rules, combinational UDPs, sequential UDPs, shorthand symbols.

13 **Programming Language Interface**
Introduction to PLI, uses of PLI, linking and invocation of PLI tasks, conceptual representation of design, PLI access and utility routines.

14 **Logic Synthesis with Verilog HDL**
Introduction to logic synthesis, impact of logic synthesis, Verilog HDL constructs and operators for logic synthesis, synthesis design flow, verification of synthesized circuits, modeling tips, design partitioning.

15 **Advanced Verification Techniques**
Introduction to a simple verification flow, architectural modeling, test vectors/testbenches, simulation acceleration, emulation, analysis/coverage, assertion checking, formal verification, semi-formal verification, equivalence checking.

Timing and Delays 10

Functional verification of hardware is used to verify functionality of the designed circuit. However, blocks in real hardware have delays associated with the logic elements and paths in them. Therefore, we must also check whether the circuit meets the timing requirements, given the delay specifications for the blocks. Checking timing requirements has become increasingly important as circuits have become smaller and faster. One of the ways to check timing is to do a *timing simulation* that accounts for the delays associated with the block during the simulation.

Techniques other than timing simulation to verify timing have also emerged in the design automation industry. The most popular technique is *static timing verification*. Designers first do a pure functional verification and then verify timing separately with a static timing verification tool. The main advantage of static verification is that it can verify timing in orders of magnitude more quickly than timing simulation. Static timing verification is a separate field of study and is not discussed in this book.

In this chapter, we discuss in detail how timing and delays are controlled and specified in Verilog modules. Thus, by using timing simulation, the designer can verify both functionality and timing of the circuit with Verilog.

Learning Objectives

- Identify types of delay models, *distributed*, *lumped*, and *pin-to-pin (path)* delays used in Verilog simulation.
- Understand how to set path delays in a simulation by using **specify** blocks.
- Explain *parallel connection* and *full connection* between input and output pins.
- Understand how to define parameters inside **specify** blocks by using **specparam** statements.
- Describe state-dependent path delays.
- Explain *rise, fall,* and *turn-off* delays. Understand how to set *min, max,* and *typ* values.

- Define system tasks for timing checks **$setup**, **$hold**, and **$width**.
- Understand *delay back-annotation*.

10.1 Types of Delay Models

There are three types of delay models used in Verilog: *distributed, lumped,* and *pin-to-pin (path)* delays.

10.1.1 Distributed Delay

Distributed delays are specified on a *per element* basis. Delay values are assigned to individual elements in the circuit. An example of distributed delays in module M is shown in Figure 10-1.

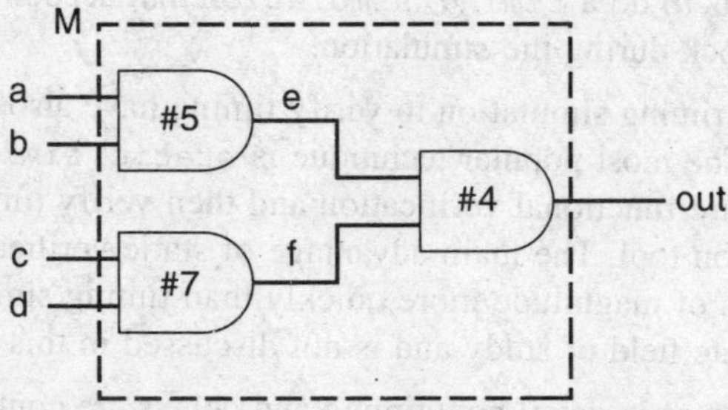

Figure 10-1 Distributed Delay

Distributed delays can be modeled by assigning delay values to individual gates or by using delay values in individual **assign** statements. When inputs of any gate change, the output of the gate changes after the delay value specified. Example 10-1 shows how distributed delays are specified in gates and dataflow description.

Example 10-1 Distributed Delays

```
//Distributed delays in gate-level modules
module M (out, a, b, c, d);
output out;
input a, b, c, d;

wire e, f;

//Delay is distributed to each gate.
and #5 a1(e, a, b);
```

Example 10-1 Distributed Delays (Continued)

```
and #7 a2(f, c, d);
and #4 a3(out, e, f);
endmodule

//Distributed delays in data flow definition of a module
module M (out, a, b, c, d);
output out;
input a, b, c, d;

wire e, f;

//Distributed delay in each expression
assign #5 e = a & b;
assign #7 f = c & d;
assign #4 out = e & f;
endmodule
```

Distributed delays provide detailed delay modeling. Delays in each element of the circuit are specified.

10.1.2 Lumped Delay

Lumped delays are specified on a `per module` basis. They can be specified as a single delay on the output gate of the module. The cumulative delay of all paths is lumped at one location. The example of a lumped delay is shown in Figure 10-2 and Example 10-2.

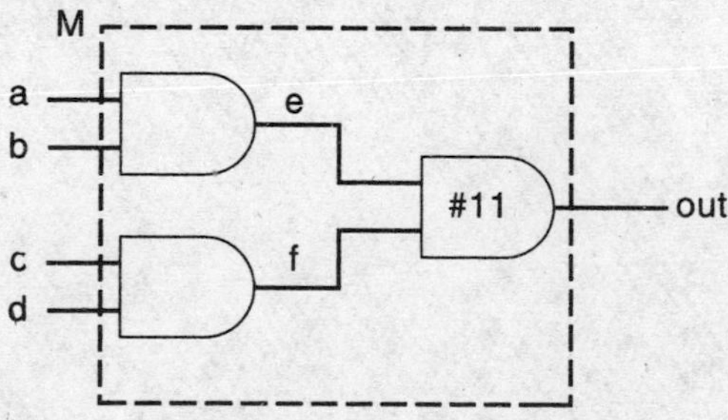

Figure 10-2 Lumped Delay

The previous example is a modification of Figure 10-1. In this example, we computed the maximum delay from any input to the output of Figure 10-1, which is `7 + 4 = 11` units. The entire delay is lumped into the output gate. After a delay, primary output changes after any input to the module *M* changes.

Example 10-2 Lumped Delay

```
//Lumped Delay Model
module M (out, a, b, c, d);
output out;
input a, b, c, d;

wire e, f;

and a1(e, a, b);
and a2(f, c, d);
and #11 a3(out, e, f);//delay only on the output gate
endmodule
```

Lumped delays models are easy to model compared with distributed delays.

10.1.3 Pin-to-Pin Delays

Another method of delay specification for a module is `pin-to-pin` timing. Delays are assigned individually to paths from each input to each output. Thus, delays can be separately specified for each input/output path. In Figure 10-3, we take the example in Figure 10-1 and compute the pin-to-pin delays for each input/output path.

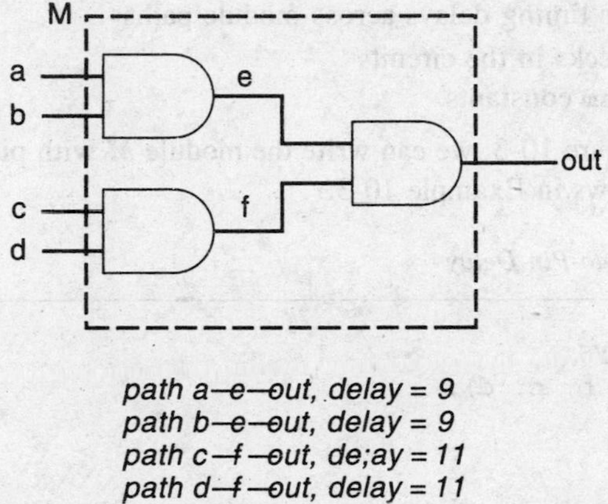

Figure 10-3 Pin-to-Pin Delay

Pin-to-pin delays for standard parts can be directly obtained from data books. Pin-to-pin delays for modules of a digital circuit are obtained by circuit characterization, using a low-level simulator like SPICE.

Although pin-to-pin delays are very detailed, for large circuits they are easier to model than distributed delays because the designer writing delay models needs to know only the I/O pins of the module rather than the internals of the module. The internals of the module may be designed by using gates, data flow, behavioral statements, or mixed design, but the pin-to-pin delay specification remains the same. Pin-to-pin delays are also known as `path delays`. We will use the term "path delays" in the succeeding sections.

We covered distributed and lumped delays in Section 5.2, `Gate Delays`, and in Section 6.2, `Delays`. In the following section, we study path delays in detail.

10.2 Path Delay Modeling

In this section, we discuss various aspects of path delay modeling. In this section, the terms `pin` and `port` are used interchangeably.

10.2.1 Specify Blocks

A delay between a `source` (input or inout) pin and a `destination` (output or inout) pin of a module is called a `module path delay`. Path delays are assigned in Verilog within the keywords **`specify`** and **`endspecify`**. The statements within these keywords constitute a *specify block*.

Specify blocks contain statements to do the following:

- Assign pin-to-pin timing delays across module paths
- Set up timing checks in the circuits
- Define **specparam** constants

For the example in Figure 10-3, we can write the module *M* with pin-to-pin delays, using specify blocks as follows in Example 10-3:

Example 10-3 Pin-to-Pin Delay

```
//Pin-to-pin delays
module M (out, a, b, c, d);
output out;
input a, b, c, d;

wire e, f;

//Specify block with path delay statements
specify
    (a => out) = 9;
    (b => out) = 9;
    (c => out) = 11;
    (d => out) = 11;
endspecify

//gate instantiations
and a1(e, a, b);
and a2(f, c, d);
and a3(out, e, f);
endmodule
```

The specify block is a separate block in the module and does not appear under any other block, such as **initial** or **always**. The meaning of the statements within specify blocks needs to be clarified.

10.2.2 Inside Specify Blocks

In this section, we describe the statements that can be used inside specify blocks.

Parallel connection

As discussed earlier, every path delay statement has a source field and a destination field. In the path delay statements in Example 10-3, *a, b, c,* and *d* are in the position of the source field and *out* is the destination field.

A `parallel connection` is specified by the symbol `=>` and is used as shown below.

Usage: `( <source_field> => <destination_field>) = <delay_value>;`

In a parallel connection, each bit in the source field connects to its corresponding bit in the destination field. If the source and the destination fields are vectors, they must have the same number of bits; otherwise, there is a mismatch. Thus, a parallel connection specifies delays from each bit in source to each bit in destination.

Figure 10-4 shows how bits between the source field and destination field are connected in a parallel connection. Example 10-4 shows the Verilog description for a parallel connection.

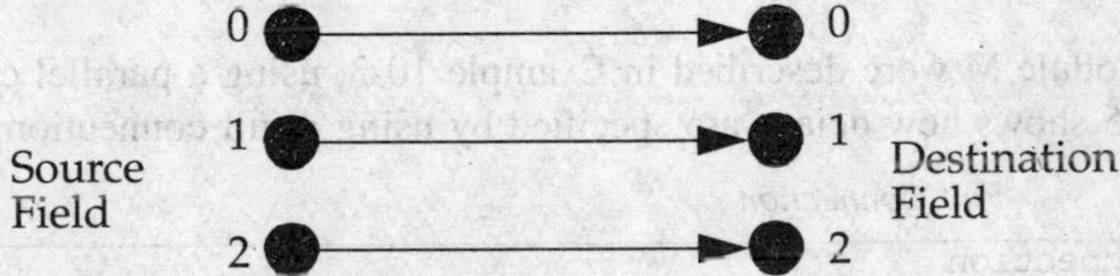

Figure 10-4 Parallel Connection

Example 10-4 Parallel Connection

```
//bit-to-bit connection. both a and out are single-bit
(a => out) = 9;

//vector connection. both a and out are 4-bit vectors a[3:0], out[3:0]
//a is source field, out is destination field.
(a => out) = 9;
//the above statement is shorthand notation
//for four bit-to-bit connection statements
(a[0] => out[0]) = 9;
(a[1] => out[1]) = 9;
(a[2] => out[2]) = 9;
(a[3] => out[3]) = 9;

//illegal connection. a[4:0] is a 5-bit vector, out[3:0] is 4-bit.
//Mismatch between bit width of source and destination fields
(a => out) = 9; //bit width does not match.
```

Full connection

A `full connection` is specified by the symbol `*>` and is used as shown below.

Usage: `( <source_field> *> <destination_field>) = <delay_value>;`

In a full connection, each bit in the source field connects to every bit in the destination field. If the source and the destination are vectors, then they need not have the same number of bits. A full connection describes the delay between each bit of the source and every bit in the destination, as illustrated in Figure 10-5.

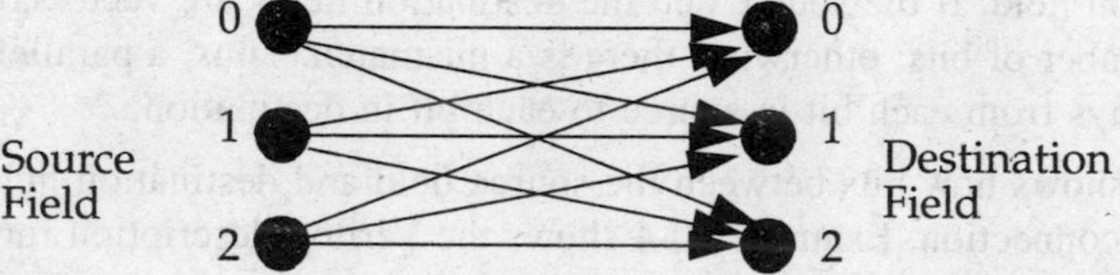

Figure 10-5 Full Connection

Delays for module M were described in Example 10-3, using a parallel connection. Example 10-5 shows how delays are specified by using a full connection.

Example 10-5 Full Connection

```
//Full Connection
module M (out, a, b, c, d);
output out;
input a, b, c, d;

wire e, f;

//full connection
specify
(a,b *> out) = 9;
(c,d *> out) = 11;
endspecify

and a1(e, a, b);

and a2(f, c, d);
and a3(out, e, f);
endmodule
```

The full connection is particularly useful for specifying a delay between each bit of an input vector and every bit in the output vector when bit width of the vectors is large. The following example shows how the full connection sometimes specifies delays very concisely.

```
//a[31:0] is a 32-bit vector and out[15:0] is a 16-bit vector
//Delay of 9 between each bit of a and every bit of out

specify
( a *> out) = 9; // you would need 32 X 16 = 352 parallel connection
            // statements to accomplish the same result! Why?
endspecify
```

Edge-Sensitive Paths

An edge-sensitive path construct is used to model the timing of input to output delays, which occurs only when a specified edge occurs at the source signal.

```
//In this example, at the positive edge of clock, a module path
//extends from clock signal to out signal using a rise delay of 10
//and a fall delay of 8. The data path is from in to out, and the
//in signal is not inverted as it propagates to the out signal.
(posedge clock => (out +: in)) = (10 : 8);
```

specparam statements

Special parameters can be declared for use inside a **specify** block. They are declared by the keyword **specparam**. Instead of using hardcoded delay numbers to specify pin-to-pin delays, it is common to define specify parameters by using **specparam** and then to use those parameters inside the **specify** block. The **specparam** values are often used to store values for nonsimulation tools, such as delay calculators, synthesis tools, and layout estimators. A sample specify block with **specparam** statements is shown in Example 10-6.

Example 10-6 Specparam

```
//Specify parameters using specparam statement
specify
    //define parameters inside the specify block
    specparam d_to_q = 9;
    specparam clk_to_q = 11;
```

Example 10-6 Specparam (Continued)

```
    (d => q) = d_to_q;
    (clk => q) = clk_to_q;
endspecify
```

Note that specify parameters are used only inside their own specify block. They are not general-purpose parameters that are declared by the keyword **`parameter`**. Specify parameters are provided for convenience in assigning delays. It is recommended that all pin-to-pin delay values be expressed in terms of specify parameters instead of hardcoded numbers. Thus, if timing specifications of the circuit change, the user has to change only the values of specify parameters.

Conditional path delays

Based on the states of input signals to a circuit, the pin-to-pin delays might change. Verilog allows path delays to be assigned `conditionally`, based on the value of the signals in the circuit. A conditional path delay is expressed with the **`if`** conditional statement. The operands can be scalar or vector module **`input`** or **`inout`** ports or their bit-selects or part-selects, locally defined registers or nets or their bit-selects or part-selects, or compile time constants (constant numbers and **`specify`** block parameters). The conditional expression can contain any logical, bitwise, reduction, concatenation, or conditional operator shown in Table 6-1 on page 96. The **`else`** construct cannot be used. Conditional path delays are also known as `state dependent path delays (SDPD)`.

Example 10-7 Conditional Path Delays

```
//Conditional Path Delays
module M (out, a, b, c, d);
output out;
input a, b, c, d;

wire e, f;

//specify block with conditional pin-to-pin timing
specify

//different pin-to-pin timing based on state of signal a.
if (a) (a => out) = 9;
if (~a) (a => out) = 10;

//Conditional expression contains two signals b , c.
//If b & c is true, delay = 9,
```

Example 10-7 Conditional Path Delays (Continued)

```
//Conditional Path Delays
//otherwise delay = 13.
if (b & c) (b => out) = 9;
if (~(b & c)) (b => out) = 13;

//Use concatenation operator.
//Use Full connection
if ({c,d} == 2'b01)
        (c,d *> out) = 11;
if ({c,d} != 2'b01)
        (c,d *> out) = 13;

endspecify

and a1(e, a, b);
and a2(f, c, d);
and a3(out, e, f);
endmodule
```

Rise, fall, and turn-off delays

Pin-to-pin timing can also be expressed in more detail by specifying rise, fall, and turn-off delay values (see Example 10-8). `One, two, three, six,` or `twelve` delay values can be specified for any path. `Four, five, seven, eight, nine, ten, or eleven` delay value specification is illegal. The order in which delays are specified must be strictly followed. Rise, fall, and turn-off delay specification for gates was discussed in Section 5.2.1, `Rise, Fall, and Turn-off Delays.` We discuss it in this section in the context of pin-to-pin timing specification.

Example 10-8 Path Delays Specified by Rise, Fall and Turn-off Values

```
//Specify one delay only. Used for all transitions.
specparam t_delay = 11;
(clk => q) = t_delay;

//Specify two delays, rise and fall
//Rise used for transitions 0->1, 0->z, z->1
//Fall used for transitions 1->0, 1->z, z->0
specparam t_rise = 9, t_fall = 13;
(clk => q) = (t_rise, t_fall);

//Specify three delays, rise, fall, and turn-off
```

Example 10-8 Path Delays Specified by Rise, Fall and Turn-off Values (Continued)

```
//Rise used for transitions 0->1, z->1
//Fall used for transitions 1->0, z->0
//Turn-off used for transitions 0->z, 1->z
specparam t_rise = 9, t_fall = 13, t_turnoff = 11;
(clk => q) = (t_rise, t_fall, t_turnoff);

//specify six delays.
//Delays are specified in order
//for transitions 0->1, 1->0, 0->z, z->1, 1->z, z->0. Order
//must be followed strictly.
specparam t_01 = 9, t_10 = 13, t_0z = 11;
specparam t_z1 = 9, t_1z = 11, t_z0 = 13;
(clk => q) = (t_01, t_10, t_0z, t_z1, t_1z, t_z0);

//specify twelve delays.
//Delays are specified in order
//for transitions 0->1, 1->0, 0->z, z->1, 1->z, z->0
//              0->x, x->1, 1->x, x->0, x->z, z->x.
//Order must be followed strictly.
specparam t_01 = 9, t_10 = 13, t_0z = 11;
specparam t_z1 = 9, t_1z = 11, t_z0 = 13;
specparam t_0x = 4, t_x1 = 13, t_1x = 5;
specparam t_x0 = 9, t_xz = 11, t_zx = 7;
(clk => q) = (t_01, t_10, t_0z, t_z1, t_1z, t_z0,
         t_0x, t_x1, t_1x, t_x0, t_xz, t_zx );
```

Min, max, and typical delays

Min, max, and typical delay values were discussed earlier for gates in Section 5.2.2, `Min/Typ/Max Values`. `Min`, `max`, and `typical` values can also be specified for pin-to-pin delays. Any delay value shown in Example 10-8 can be expressed in min, max, typical delay form. Consider the case of the three-delay specification, shown in Example 10-9. Each delay is expressed in `min:typ:max` form.

Example 10-9 Path Delays with Min, Max, and Typical Values

```
//Specify three delays, rise, fall, and turn-off
//Each delay has a min:typ:max value
specparam t_rise = 8:9:10, t_fall = 12:13:14, t_turnoff = 10:11:12;
(clk => q) = (t_rise, t_fall, t_turnoff);
```

As discussed earlier, min, typical, and max values can be typically invoked with the runtime option **+mindelays, +typdelays,** or **+maxdelays** on the Verilog command line. Default is the typical delay value. Invocation may vary with individual simulators.

Handling x transitions

Verilog uses the pessimistic method to compute delays for transitions to the **x** state. The pessimistic approach dictates that if **x** transition delays are not explicitly specified,

- Transitions from **x** to a known state should take the maximum possible time
- Transition from a known state to **x** should take the minimum possible time

A path delay specification with six delays borrowed from Example 10-8 is shown below.

```
//Six delays specified .
//for transitions 0->1, 1->0, 0->z, z->1, 1->z, z->0.

specparam t_01 = 9, t_10 = 13, t_0z = 11;
specparam t_z1 = 9, t_1z = 11, t_z0 = 13;
(clk => q) = (t_01, t_10, t_0z, t_z1, t_1z, t_z0);
```

The computation for transitions to **x** for the above delay specification is shown in the table given here:

Transition	Delay Value
0->x	min(t_01, t_0z) = 9
1->x	min(t_10, t_1z) = 11
z->x	min(t_z0, t_z1) = 9
x->0	max(t_10, t_z0) = 13
x->1	max(t_01, t_z1) = 9
x->z	max(t_1z, t_0z) = 11

10.3 Timing Checks

In the earlier sections of this chapter, we discussed how to specify path delays. The purpose of specifying path delays is to simulate the timing of the actual digital circuit with greater accuracy than gate delays. In this section, we describe how to set up timing checks to see if any timing constraints are violated during simulation. Timing verification is particularly important for timing critical, high-speed sequential circuits such as microprocessors.

System tasks are provided to do timing checks in Verilog. There are many timing check system tasks available in Verilog. We will discuss the three most common timing checks[1] tasks: **$setup**, **$hold**, and **$width**. All timing checks must be inside the *specify* blocks only. Optional notifier arguments used in these timing check system tasks are omitted to simplify the discussion.

10.3.1 $setup and $hold Checks

$setup and **$hold** tasks are used to check the *setup* and *hold* constraints for a sequential element in the design. In a sequential element such as an edge-triggered flipflop, the *setup time* is the minimum time the data must arrive before the active clock edge. The *hold time* is the minimum time the data cannot change after the active clock edge. Setup and hold times are shown in Figure 10-6.

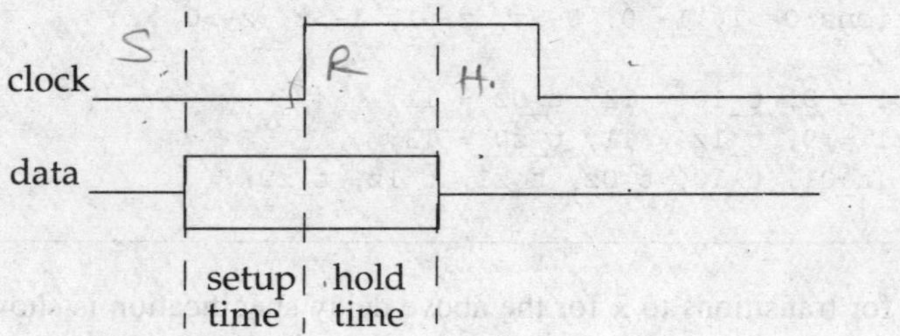

Figure 10-6 Setup and Hold Times

$setup task

Setup checks can be specified with the system task **$setup**.

Usage: **$setup**(data_event, reference_event, limit);

data_event	Signal that is monitored for violations
reference_event	Signal that establishes a reference for monitoring the data_event signal
limit	Minimum time required for setup of data event

Violation is reported if $(T_{reference\_event} - T_{data\_event}) < limit$.

1. The IEEE Standard Verilog Hardware Description Language document provides additional constraint checks, **$removal**, **$recrem**, **$timeskew**, and **$fullskew**. Please refer to it for details. Negative input timing constraints can also be specified.

An example of a setup check is shown below.

```
//Setup check is set.
//clock is the reference
//data is being checked for violations
//Violation reported if Tposedge_clk - Tdata < 3
specify
    $setup(data, posedge clock, 3);
endspecify
```

$hold task

Hold checks can be specified with the system task **`$hold`**.

Usage: **`$hold`** *`(reference_event, data_event, limit);`*

`reference_event`	Signal that establishes a reference for monitoring the *`data_event`* signal
`data_event`	Signal that is monitored for violation
`limit`	Minimum time required for hold of data event

Violation is reported if $(T_{data\_event} - T_{reference\_event}) < limit$.

An example of a hold check is shown below.

```
//Hold check is set.
//clock is the reference
//data is being checked for violations
//Violation reported if Tdata - Tposedge_clk < 5
specify
    $hold(posedge clear, data, 5);
endspecify
```

10.3.2 $width Check

Sometimes it is necessary to check the width of a pulse.

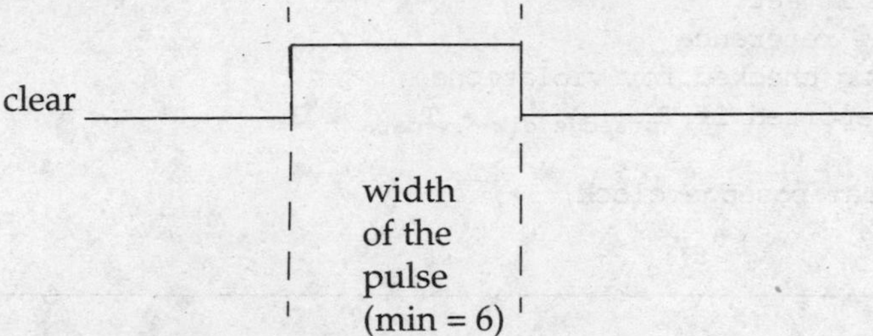

The system task **`$width`** is used to check that the width of a pulse meets the minimum width requirement.

Usage: **`$width`**`(reference_event, limit);`

`reference_event` Edge-triggered event (edge transition of a signal)

`limit` Minimum width of the pulse

The `data_event` is not specified explicitly for **`$width`** but is derived as the next opposite edge of the `reference_event` signal. Thus, the **`$width`** task checks the time between the transition of a signal value to the next opposite transition in the signal value.

Violation is reported if $(T_{data\_event} - T_{reference\_event}) < limit$.

```
//width check is set.
//posedge of clear is the reference_event
//the next negedge of clear is the data_event
//Violation reported if Tdata - Tclk < 6
specify
    $width(posedge clock, 6);
endspecify
```

10.4 Delay Back-Annotation

`Delay back-annotation` is an important and vast topic in timing simulation. An entire book could be devoted to that subject. However, in this section, we introduce the designer to the concept of back-annotation of delays in a simulation. Detailed coverage of this topic is outside the scope of this book. For details, refer to the *IEEE Standard Verilog Hardware Description Language* document.

The various steps in the flow that use delay back-annotation are as follows:

1. The designer writes the RTL description and then performs functional simulation.
2. The RTL description is converted to a gate-level netlist by a logic synthesis tool.
3. The designer obtains `pre-layout` estimates of delays in the chip by using a delay calculator and information about the IC fabrication process. Then, the designer does timing simulation or static timing verification of the gate-level netlist, using these preliminary values to check that the gate-level netlist meets timing constraints.
4. The gate-level netlist is then converted to layout by a place and route tool. The `post-layout` delay values are computed from the resistance (R) and capacitance (C) information in the layout. The R and C information is extracted from factors such as geometry and IC fabrication process.
5. The post layout delay values are *`back-annotated`* to modify the delay estimates for the gate-level netlist. Timing simulation or static timing verification is run again on the gate-level netlist to check if timing constraints are still satisfied.
6. If design changes are required to meet the timing constraints, the designer has to go back to the RTL level, optimize the design for timing, and then repeat Step 2 through Step 5.

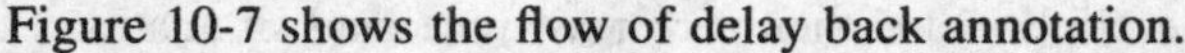

Figure 10-7 shows the flow of delay back annotation.

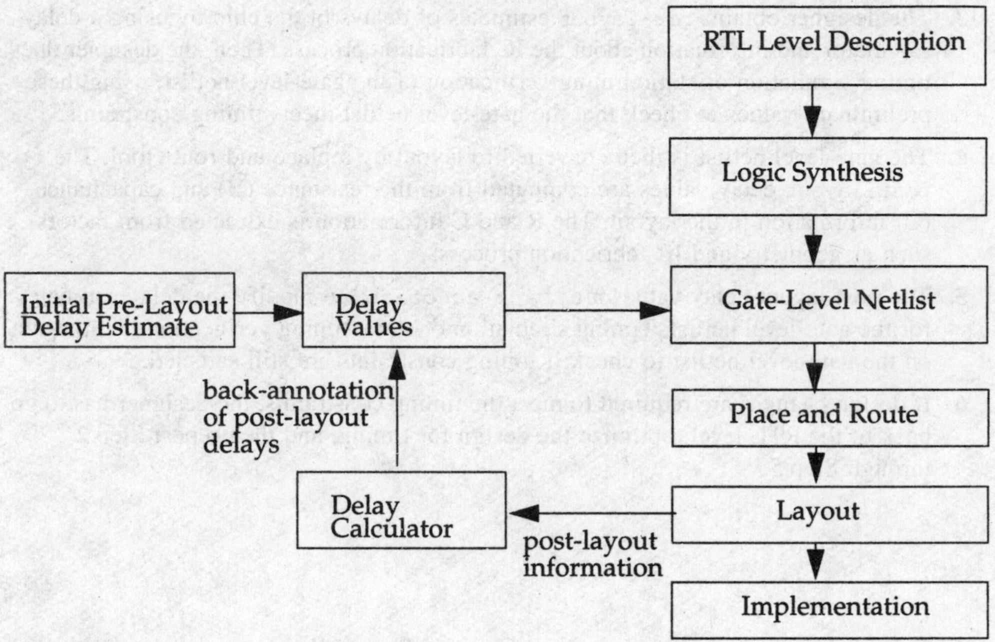

Figure 10-7 Delay Back-Annotation

A standard format called the `Standard Delay Format (SDF)` is popularly used for back-annotation. Details of delay back-annotation are outside the scope of this book and can be obtained from the *IEEE Standard Verilog Hardware Description Language* document.

10.5 Summary

In this chapter, we discussed the following aspects of Verilog:

- There are three types of delay models: `lumped`, `distributed`, and `path delays`. Distributed delays are more accurate than lumped delays but difficult to model for large designs. Lumped delays are relatively simpler to model.
- Path delays, also known as `pin-to-pin` delays, specify delays from input or inout pins to output or inout pins. Path delays provide the most accuracy for modeling delays within a module.

- *Specify* blocks are the basic blocks for expressing path delay information. In modules, *specify* blocks appear separately from initial or always blocks.
- *Parallel connection* and *full connection* are two methods to describe path delays.
- Parameters can be defined inside the *specify* blocks by **specparam** statements.
- Path delays can be conditional or dependent on the values of signals in the circuit. They are known as *State Dependent Path Delays (SDPD).*
- *Rise, fall,* and *turn-off* delays can be described in a path delay. *Min, max,* and *typical* values can also be specified. Transitions to **x** are handled by the pessimistic method.
- *Setup, hold,* and *width* are timing checks that check timing integrity of the digital circuit. Other timing checks are also available but are not discussed in the book.
- *Delay back-annotation* is used to resimulate the digital design with path delays extracted from layout information. This process is used repeatedly to obtain a final circuit that meets all timing requirements.

10.6 Exercises

1. What type of delay model is used in the following circuit? Write the Verilog description for the module *Y*.

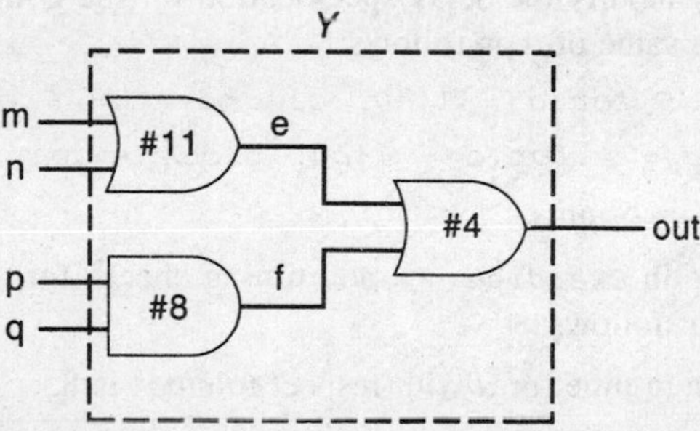

2. Use the largest delay in the module to convert the circuit to a *lumped delay model*. Using a lumped delay model, write the Verilog description for the module *Y*.
3. Compute the delays along each path from input to output for the circuit in *Exercise 1*. Write the Verilog description, using the *path delay model*. Use *specify* blocks.

4. Consider the negative edge triggered with the asynchronous reset D-flipflop shown in the figure below. Write the Verilog description for the module *D_FF*. Show only the I/O ports and path delay specification. Describe path delays, using `parallel connection`.

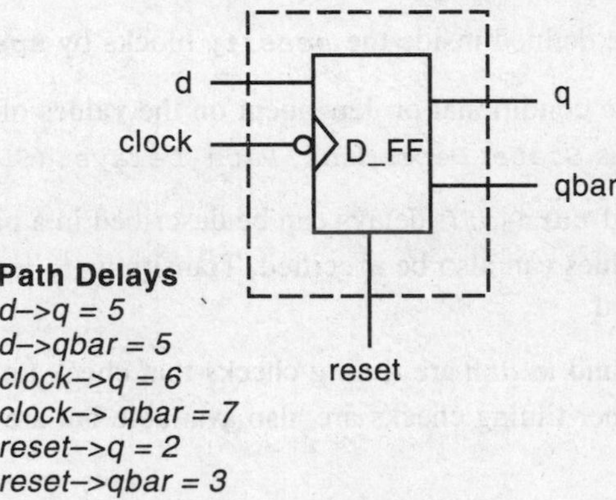

5. Modify the D-flipflop in `Exercise 4` if all path delays are 5 units. Describe the path delays, using `full connections` to *q* and *qbar*.
6. Assume that a six-delay specification is to be specified for all path delays. All path delays are equal. In the `specify` block, define parameters `t_01 = 4, t_10 = 5, t_0z = 7, t_z1 = 2, t_1z = 3, t_z0 = 8`. Use the D-flipflop in `Exercise 4` and write the six-delay specification for all paths, using full connections.
7. In `Exercise 4`, modify the delay specification for the D-flipflop if the delays are dependent on the value of d as follows:

   `clock -> q = 5 for d = 1'b0, clock -> q= 6 otherwise`

   `clock -> qbar = 4 for d = 1'b0, clock ->qbar = 7 otherwise`

   All other delays are 5 units.
8. For the D-flipflop in `Exercise 7`, add timing checks for the D-flipflop in the `specify` block as follows:

   The minimum setup time for *d* with respect to *clock* is 8.

   The minimum hold time for *d* with respect to *clock* is 4.

   The *reset* signal is active high. The minimum width of a *reset* pulse is 42.
9. Describe `delay back-annotation`. Draw the flow diagram for delay back-annotation.

Switch-Level Modeling 11

In *Part 1* of this book, we explained digital design and simulation at a higher level of abstraction such as gates, data flow, and behavior. However, in rare cases designers will choose to design the leaf-level modules, using *transistors*. Verilog provides the ability to design at a MOS-transistor level. Design at this level is becoming rare with the increasing complexity of circuits (millions of transistors) and with the availability of sophisticated CAD tools. Verilog HDL currently provides only digital design capability with logic values `0`, `1`, `x`, `z`, and the drive strengths associated with them. There is no analog capability. Thus, in Verilog HDL, transistors are also known as *switches* that either conduct or are open. In this chapter, we discuss the basic principles of switch-level modeling. For most designers, it is adequate to know only the basics. Detailed information on signal strengths and advanced net definitions is provided in Appendix A, *Strength Modeling and Advanced Net Definitions*. Refer to the *IEEE Standard Verilog Hardware Description Language* document for complete details on switch-level modeling.

Learning Objectives

- Describe basic MOS switches **nmos**, **pmos**, and **cmos**.
- Understand modeling of *bidirectional pass switches, power,* and *ground.*
- Identify resistive MOS switches.
- Explain the method used to specify delays on basic *MOS switches* and *bidirectional pass switches.*
- Build basic switch-level circuits in Verilog, using available switches.

11.1 Switch-Modeling Elements

Verilog provides various constructs to model switch-level circuits. Digital circuits at the MOS-transistor level are described using these elements.[1]

1. Array of instances can be defined for switches. Array of instances is described in Section 5.1.3.

11.1.1 MOS Switches

Two types of MOS switches can be defined with the keywords **nmos** and **pmos**.

```
//MOS switch keywords
nmos              pmos
```

Keyword **nmos** is used to model *NMOS* transistors; keyword **pmos** is used to model ***PMOS*** transistors. The symbols for **nmos** and **pmos** switches are shown in Figure 11-1.

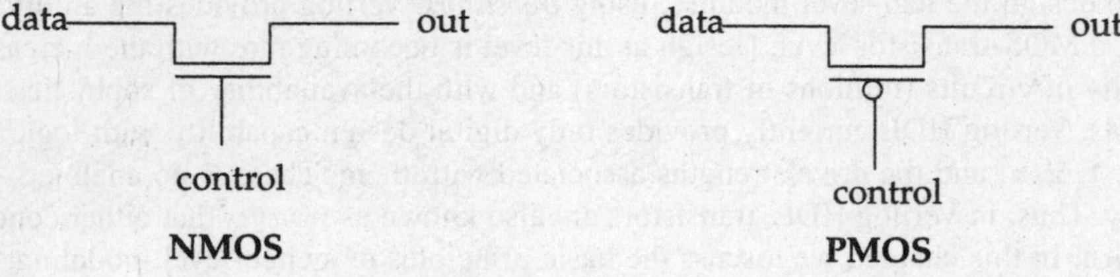

Figure 11-1 NMOS and PMOS Switches

In Verilog, **nmos** and **pmos** switches are instantiated as shown in Example 11-1.

Example 11-1 Instantiation of NMOS and PMOS Switches

```
nmos n1(out, data, control); //instantiate a nmos switch
pmos p1(out, data, control); //instantiate a pmos switch
```

Since switches are Verilog primitives, like logic gates, the name of the instance is optional. Therefore, it is acceptable to instantiate a switch without assigning an instance name.

```
nmos (out, data, control); //instantiate an nmos switch; no instance name
pmos (out, data, control); //instantiate a pmos switch; no instance name
```

The value of the *out* signal is determined from the values of the *data* and *control* signals. Logic tables for *out* are shown in Table 11-1. Some combinations of data and control signals cause the gates to output to either a `1` or `0`, or to a `z` value without a preference for either value. The symbol *L* stands for `0` or `z`; *H* stands for `1` or `z`.

Table 11-1 Logic Tables for NMOS and PMOS

nmos		control 0	1	x	z
data	0	z	0	L	L
	1	z	1	H	H
	x	z	x	x	x
	z	z	z	z	z

pmos		control 0	1	x	z
data	0	0	z	L	L
	1	1	z	H	H
	x	x	z	x	x
	z	z	z	z	z

Thus, the **nmos** switch conducts when its *control* signal is `1`. If the *control* signal is `0`, the output assumes a high impedance value. Similarly, a **pmos** switch conducts if the *control* signal is `0`.

11.1.2 CMOS Switches

CMOS switches are declared with the keyword **cmos**.

A **cmos** device can be modeled with an **nmos** and a **pmos** device. The symbol for a **cmos** switch is shown in Figure 11-2.

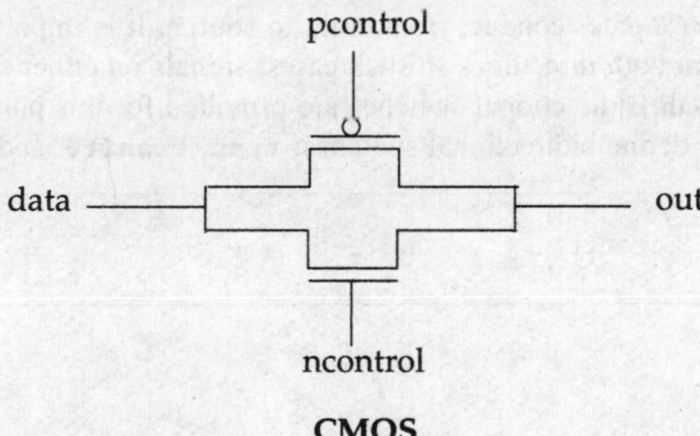

CMOS

Figure 11-2 CMOS Switch

A **cmos** switch is instantiated as shown in Example 11-2.

Example 11-2 Instantiation of a CMOS Switch

```
cmos c1(out, data, ncontrol, pcontrol);//instantiate cmos gate.
            or
cmos (out, data, ncontrol, pcontrol); //no instance name given.
```

The *ncontrol* and *pcontrol* signals are normally complements of each other. When the *ncontrol* signal is `1` and *pcontrol* signal is `0`, the switch conducts. If the *ncontrol* signal is `0` and *pcontrol* is `1`, the output of the switch is high impedance value. The **cmos** gate is essentially a combination of two gates: one **nmos** and one **pmos**. Thus the **cmos** instantiation shown above is equivalent to the following:

```
nmos (out, data, ncontrol); //instantiate a nmos switch
pmos (out, data, pcontrol); //instantiate a pmos switch
```

Since a **cmos** switch is derived from **nmos** and **pmos** switches, it is possible to derive the output value from Table 11-1, given values of *data*, *ncontrol*, and *pcontrol* signals.

11.1.3 Bidirectional Switches

NMOS, *PMOS*, and *CMOS* gates conduct from drain to source. It is important to have devices that conduct in both directions. In such cases, signals on either side of the device can be the driver signal. Bidirectional switches are provided for this purpose. Three keywords are used to define bidirectional switches: **tran**, **tranif0**, and **tranif1**.

```
tran   tranif0   tranif1
```

Symbols for these switches are shown in Figure 11-3 below.

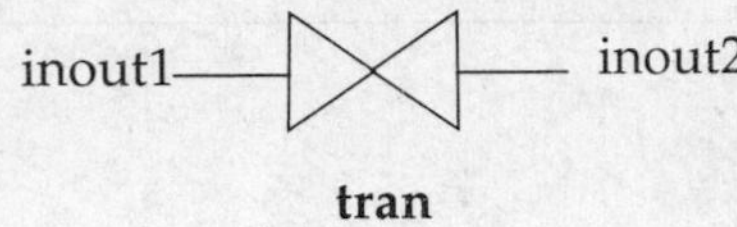

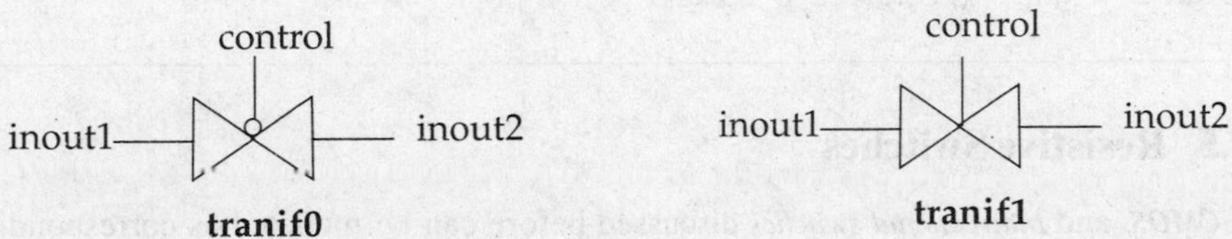

Figure 11-3 Bidirectional Switches

The **tran** switch acts as a buffer between the two signals *inout1* and *inout2*. Either *inout1* or *inout2* can be the driver signal. The *tranif0* switch connects the two signals *inout1* and *inout2* only if the *control* signal is logical **0**. If the *control* signal is a logical **1**, the nondriver signal gets a high impedance value **z**. The driver signal retains value from its driver. The **tranif1** switch conducts if the *control* signal is a logical **1**.

These switches are instantiated as shown in Example 11-3.

Example 11-3 Instantiation of Bidirectional Switches

```
tran t1(inout1, inout2); //instance name t1 is optional
tranif0 (inout1, inout2, control); //instance name is not specified
tranif1 (inout1, inout2, control); //instance name is not specified
```

Bidirectional switches are typically used to provide isolation between buses or signals.

11.1.4 Power and Ground

The power (*Vdd, logic* **1**) and Ground (*Vss, logic* **0**) sources are needed when transistor-level circuits are designed. Power and ground sources are defined with keywords **supply1** and **supply0**.

Sources of type **supply1** are equivalent to *Vdd* in circuits and place a logical **1** on a net. Sources of the type **supply0** are equivalent to *ground* or *Vss* and place a logical **0** on a net. Both **supply1** and **supply0** place logical **1** and **0** continuously on nets throughout the simulation.

Sources **supply1** and **supply0** are shown below.

```
supply1 vdd;
supply0 gnd;

assign a = vdd; //Connect a to vdd
assign b = gnd; //Connect b to gnd
```

11.1.5 Resistive Switches

MOS, CMOS, and *bidirectional switches* discussed before can be modeled as corresponding *resistive* devices. Resistive switches have higher source-to-drain impedance than regular switches and reduce the strength of signals passing through them. Resistive switches are declared with keywords that have an "**r**" prefixed to the corresponding keyword for the regular switch. Resistive switches have the same syntax as regular switches.

```
rnmos    rpmos                    //resistive nmos and pmos switches
rcmos                             //resistive cmos switch
rtran    rtranif0    rtranif1     //resistive bidirectional switches.
```

There are two main differences between regular switches and resistive switches: their source-to-drain impedances and the way they pass signal strengths. Refer to Appendix A, *Strength Modeling and Advanced Net Definitions,* for strength levels in Verilog.

- Resistive devices have a high source-to-drain impedance. Regular switches have a low source-to-drain impedance.
- Resistive switches reduce signal strengths when signals pass through them. The changes are shown below. Regular switches retain strength levels of signals from input to output. The exception is that if the input is of strength **supply**, the output is of **strong** strength. Table 11-2 shows the strength reduction due to resistive switches.

Table 11-2 Strength Reduction by Resistive Switches

Input Strength	Output Strength
supply	pull
strong	pull
pull	weak

Table 11-2 *Strength Reduction by Resistive Switches*

Input Strength	Output Strength
weak	medium
large	medium
medium	small
small	small
high	high

11.1.6 Delay Specification on Switches

MOS and CMOS switches

Delays can be specified for signals that pass through these switch-level elements. Delays are optional and appear immediately after the keyword for the switch. Delay specification is similar to that discussed in Section 5.2.1, *Rise, Fall, and Turn-off Delays. Zero, one, two,* or *three* delays can be specified for switches according to Table 11-3.

Table 11-3 Delay Specification on MOS and CMOS Switches

Switch Element	Delay Specification	Examples

pmos, nmos, rpmos, rnmos	Zero (no delay)
	One (same delay on all transitions)
	Two (rise, fall)
	Three (rise, fall, turnoff)
		pmos p1(out, data, control);
		pmos #(1) p1(out, data, control);
		nmos #(1, 2) p2(out, data, control);
		nmos #(1, 3, 2) p2(out, data, control);

cmos, rcmos	Zero, one, two, or three delays (same as above)	cmos #(5) c2(out, data, nctrl, pctrl); cmos #(1,2) c1(out, data, nctrl, pctrl);

Bidirectional pass switches

Delay specification is interpreted slightly differently for bidirectional pass switches. These switches do not delay signals passing through them. Instead, they have *turn-on* and *turn-off* delays while switching. Zero, one, or two delays can be specified for bidirectional switches, as shown in Table 11-4.

Table 11-4 Delay Specification for Bidirectional Switches

Switch Element	Delay Specification	Examples
tran, rtran	No delay specification allowed	

tranif1, rtranif1
tranif0, rtranif0
	Zero (no delay)
	One (both turn-on and turn-off)
	Two (turn-on, turn-off)
		rtranif0 rt1(inout1, inout2, control);
		tranif0 #(3) T(inout1, inout2, control);
		tranif1 #(1,2) t1(inout1, inout2, control);

Specify blocks

Pin-to-pin delays and timing checks can also be specified for modules designed using switches. Pin-to-pin timing is described, using `specify` blocks. Pin-to-pin delay specification is discussed in detail in Chapter 10, *Timing and Delays*, and is identical for switch-level modules.

11.2 Examples

In this section, we discuss how to build practical digital circuits, using switch-level constructs.

11.2.1 CMOS Nor Gate

Though Verilog has a `nor` gate primitive, let us design our own `nor` gate, using *CMOS* switches. The gate and the switch-level circuit diagram for the `nor` gate are shown in Figure 11-4.

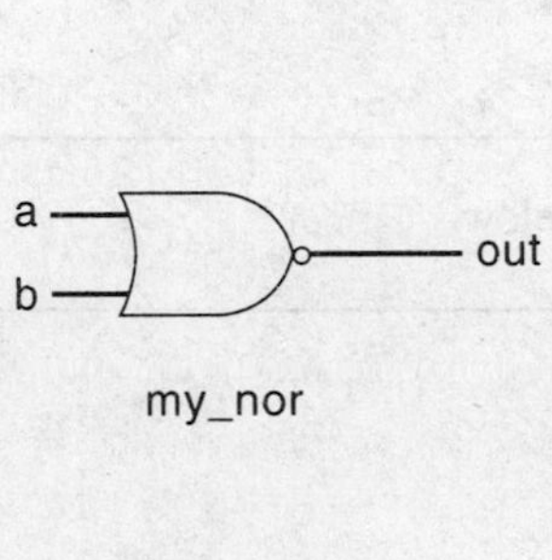

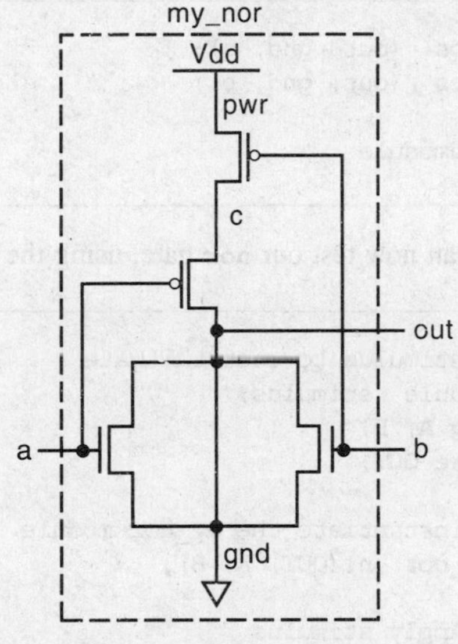

Figure 11-4 Gate and Switch Diagram for Nor Gate

Using the switch primitives discussed in Section 11.1, *Switch-Modeling Elements*, the Verilog description of the circuit is shown in Example 11-4 below.

Example 11-4 Switch-Level Verilog for Nor Gate

```
//Define our own nor gate, my_nor
module my_nor(out, a, b);

output out;
input a, b;

//internal wires
wire c;

//set up power and ground lines
supply1 pwr;      //pwr is connected to Vdd (power supply)
supply0 gnd ;    //gnd is connected to Vss(ground)

//instantiate pmos  switches
pmos  (c, pwr, b);
pmos  (out, c, a);

//instantiate nmos switches
```

Example 11-4 Switch-Level Verilog for Nor Gate (Continued)

```
nmos  (out, gnd, a);
nmos  (out, gnd, b);

endmodule
```

We can now test our **nor** gate, using the stimulus shown below.

```
//stimulus to test the gate
module  stimulus;
reg A, B;
wire OUT;

//instantiate the my_nor module
my_nor  n1(OUT, A, B);

//Apply stimulus
initial
begin
    //test all possible combinations
    A = 1'b0;  B = 1'b0;
    #5 A = 1'b0;  B = 1'b1;
    #5 A = 1'b1;  B = 1'b0;
    #5 A = 1'b1;  B = 1'b1;
end

//check results
initial
    $monitor($time, "  OUT = %b, A = %b, B = %b", OUT, A, B);

endmodule
```

The output of the simulation is shown below.

```
0  OUT = 1, A = 0, B = 0
5  OUT = 0, A = 0, B = 1
10  OUT = 0, A = 1, B = 0
15  OUT = 0, A = 1, B = 1
```

Thus we designed our own **nor** gate. If designers need to customize certain library blocks, they use switch-level modeling.

11.2.2 2-to-1 Multiplexer

A 2-to-1 multiplexer can be defined with *CMOS* switches. We will use the *my_nor* gate declared in Section 11.2.1, *CMOS Nor Gate* to implement the *not* function. The circuit diagram for the multiplexer is shown in Figure 11-5 below.

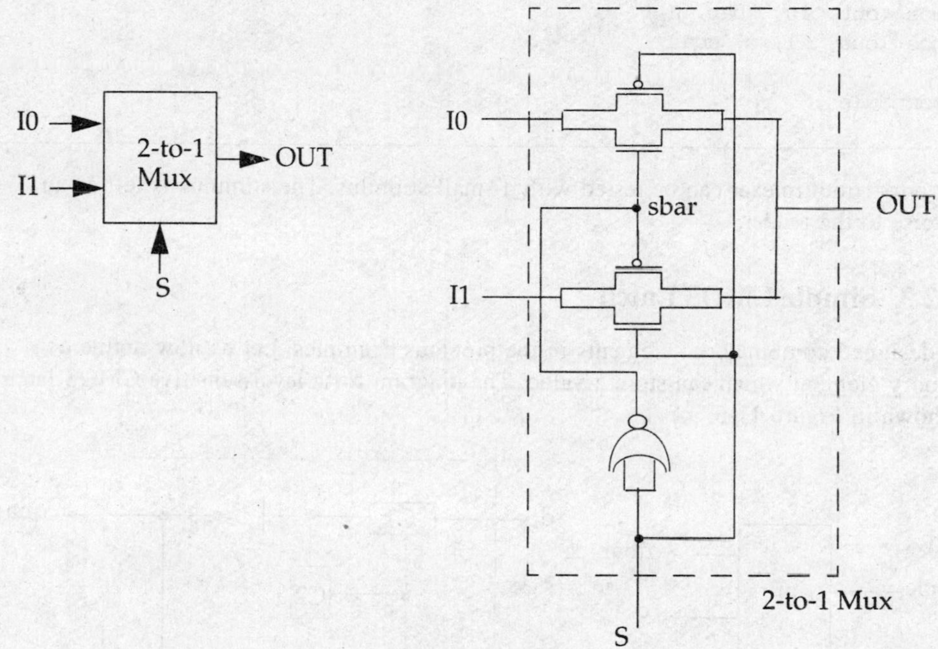

Figure 11-5 2-to-1 Multiplexer, Using Switches

The 2-to-1 multiplexer passes the input *I0* to output *OUT* if *S = 0* and passes *I1* to *OUT* if *S = 1*. The switch-level description for the 2-to-1 multiplexer is shown in Example 11-4.

Example 11-5 Switch-Level Verilog Description of 2-to-1 Multiplexer

```
//Define a 2-to-1 multiplexer using switches
module my_mux (out, s, i0, i1);

output out;
input s, i0, i1;
```

Example 11-5 Switch-Level Verilog Description of 2-to-1 Multiplexer (Continued)

```
//internal wire
wire sbar; //complement of s

//create the complement of s; use my_nor defined previously.
my_nor nt(sbar, s, s); //equivalent to a not gate

//instantiate cmos switches
cmos (out, i0, sbar, s);
cmos (out, i1, s, sbar);

endmodule
```

The 2-to-1 multiplexer can be tested with a small stimulus. The stimulus is left as an exercise to the reader.

11.2.3 Simple CMOS Latch

We designed combinatorial elements in the previous examples. Let us now define a memory element which can store a value. The diagram for a level-sensitive CMOS latch is shown in Figure 11-6.

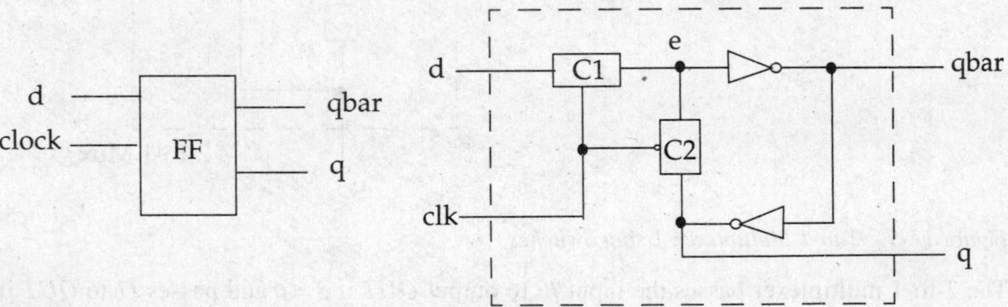

Figure 11-6 CMOS flipflop

The switches *C1* and *C2* are *CMOS* switches, discussed in Section 11.1.2, *CMOS Switches.* Switch *C1* is closed if *clk = 1*, and switch *C2* is closed if *clk = 0*. Complement of the *clk* is fed to the *ncontrol* input of *C2*. The *CMOS* inverters can be defined by using *MOS* switches, as shown in Figure 11-7.

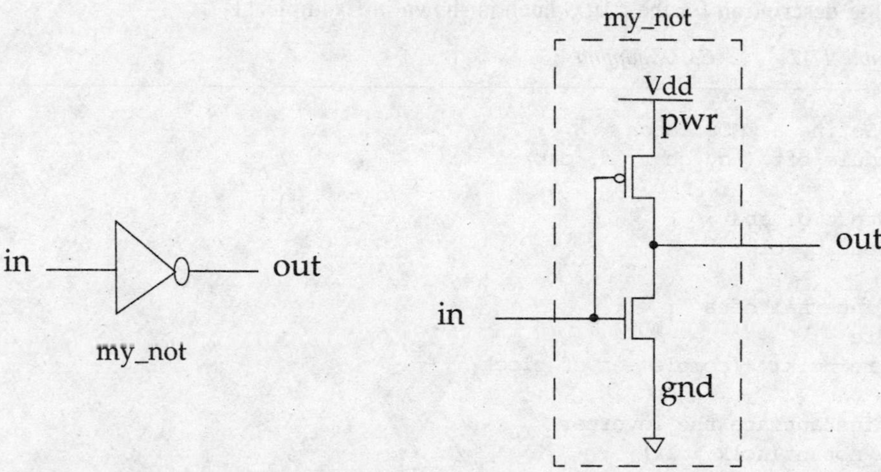

Figure 11-7 CMOS Inverter

We are now ready to write the Verilog description for the CMOS latch. First, we need to design our own inverter *my_not* by using switches. We can write the Verilog module description for the CMOS inverter from the switch-level circuit diagram in Figure 11-7. The Verilog description of the inverter is shown in Example 11-6.

Example 11-6 CMOS Inverter

```
//Define an inverter using MOS switches
module my_not(out, in);

output out;
input in;

//declare power and ground
supply1 pwr;
supply0 gnd;

//instantiate nmos and pmos switches
pmos  (out, pwr, in);
nmos  (out, gnd, in);

endmodule
```

Now, the *CMOS* latch can be defined using the *CMOS* switches and *my_not* inverters. The Verilog description for the *CMOS* latch is shown in Example 11-7.

Example 11-7 *CMOS flipflop*

```
//Define a CMOS latch
module cff ( q, qbar, d, clk);

output q, qbar;
input d, clk;

//internal nets
wire e;
wire nclk; //complement of clock

//instantiate the inverter
my_not nt(nclk, clk);

//instantiate CMOS switches
cmos  (e, d, clk, nclk); //switch C1 closed i.e. e = d, when clk = 1.
cmos  (e, q, nclk, clk); //switch C2 closed i.e. e = q, when clk = 0.

//instantiate the inverters
my_not nt1(qbar, e);
my_not nt2(q, qbar);

endmodule
```

We will leave it as an exercise to the reader to write a small stimulus module and simulate the design to verify the load and store properties of the latch.

11.3 Summary

We discussed the following aspects of Verilog in this chapter:

- Switch-level modeling is at a very low level of design abstraction. Designers use switch modeling in rare cases when they need to customize a leaf cell. Verilog design at this level is becoming less popular with increasing complexity of circuits.
- *MOS, CMOS, bidirectional switches,* and **supply1** and **supply0** sources can be used to design any switch-level circuit. *CMOS* switches are a combination of *MOS* switches.

- Delays can be optionally specified for switch elements. Delays are interpreted differently for bidirectional devices.

11.4 Exercises

1. Draw the circuit diagram for an **xor** gate, using **nmos** and **pmos** switches. Write the Verilog description for the circuit. Apply stimulus and test the design.
2. Draw the circuit diagram for **and** and **or** gates, using **nmos** and **pmos** switches. Write the Verilog description for the circuits. Apply stimulus and test the design.
3. Design the 1-bit full-adder shown below using the **xor**, **and**, and **or** gates built in *Exercise 1* and *Exercise 2* above. Apply stimulus and test the design.

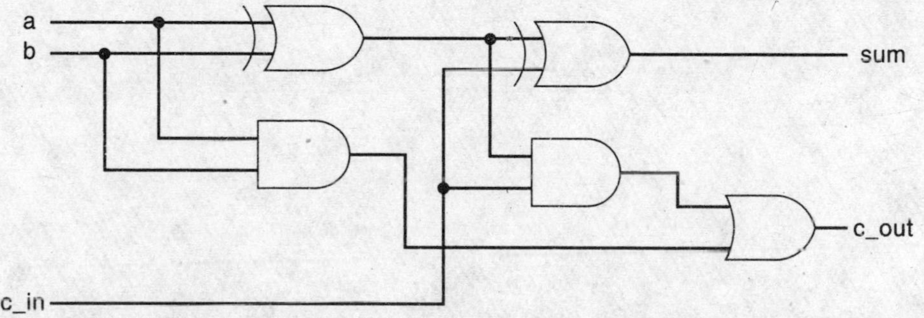

4. Design a 4-bit bidirectional bus switch that has two buses, *BusA* and *BusB*, on one side and a single bus, *BUS*, on the other side. A 1-bit *control* signal is used for switching. *BusA* and *BUS* are connected if *control* = *1*. *BusB* and *BUS* are connected if *control* = *0*. (Hint: Use the switches **tranif0** and **tranif1**.) Apply stimulus and test the design.

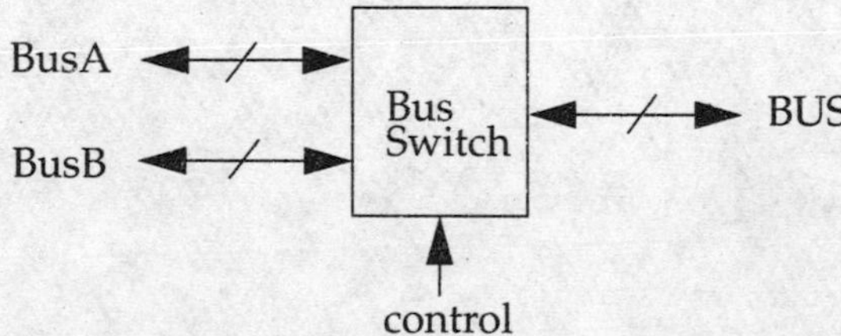

5. Instantiate switches with the following delay specifications. Use your own input/output port names.

a. A **pmos** switch with *rise = 2* and *fall = 3*

b. An **nmos** switch with *rise = 4, fall = 6, turn-off = 5*

c. A **cmos** switch with *delay = 6*

d. A **tranif1** switch with *turn-on = 5, turn-off = 6*

e. A **tranif0** with *delay = 3*

User-Defined Primitives 12

Verilog provides a standard set of primitives, such as **and**, **nand**, **or**, **nor**, and **not**, as a part of the language. These are also commonly known as *built-in* primitives. However, designers occasionally like to use their own custom-built primitives when developing a design. Verilog provides the ability to define *User-Defined Primitives (UDP)*. These primitives are self-contained and do not instantiate other modules or primitives. UDPs are instantiated exactly like gate-level primitives.

There are two types of UDPs: *combinational* and *sequential*.

- Combinational UDPs are defined where the output is solely determined by a logical combination of the inputs. A good example is a 4-to-1 multiplexer.
- Sequential UDPs take the value of the current inputs and the current output to determine the value of the next output. The value of the output is also the internal state of the UDP. Good examples of sequential UDPs are latches and flipflops.

Learning Objectives

- Understand UDP definition rules and parts of a UDP definition.
- Define sequential and combinational UDPs.
- Explain instantiation of UDPs.
- Identify UDP shorthand symbols for more conciseness and better readability.
- Describe the guidelines for UDP design.

12.1 UDP basics

In this section, we describe parts of a UDP definition and rules for UDPs.

12.1.1 Parts of UDP Definition

Figure 12-1 shows the distinct parts of a basic UDP definition in pseudo syntax form. For details, see the formal syntax definition described in Appendix D.

```
//UDP name and terminal list
primitive <udp_name> (
<output_terminal_name> (only one allowed)
<input_terminal_names> );

//Terminal declarations
output <output_terminal_name> ;
input <input_terminal_names> ;
reg <output_terminal_name>; (optional; only for sequential
                                 UDP)

// UDP initialization (optional; only for sequential UD
initial <output_terminal_name> = <value> ;

//UDP state table
table
     <table entries>
endtable

//End of UDP definition

endprimitive
```

Figure 12-1 Parts of UDP Definition

A UDP definition starts with the keyword **`primitive`**. The primitive name, output terminal, and input terminals are specified. Terminals are declared as **`output`** or **`input`** in the terminal declarations section. For a sequential UDP, the output terminal is declared as a **`reg`**. For sequential UDPs, there is an optional **`initial`** statement that initializes the output terminal of the UDP. The UDP state table is most important part of the UDP. It begins with the keyword **`table`** and ends with the keyword **`endtable`**. The table defines how the output will be computed from the inputs and current state. The table is modeled as a lookup table, and the table entries resemble entries in a logic truth table. Primitive definition is completed with the keyword **`endprimitive`**.

12.1.2 UDP Rules

UDP definitions follow certain rules:

1. UDPs can take only scalar input terminals (1 bit). Multiple input terminals are permitted.
2. UDPs can have only one scalar output terminal (1 bit). The output terminal must always appear first in the terminal list. Multiple output terminals are not allowed.
3. In the declarations section, the output terminal is declared with the keyword **`output`**. Since sequential UDPs store state, the output terminal must also be declared as a **`reg`**.
4. The inputs are declared with the keyword **`input`**.
5. The state in a sequential UDP can be initialized with an **`initial`** statement. This statement is optional. A 1-bit value is assigned to the output, which is declared as **`reg`**.
6. The state table entries can contain values **`0`**, **`1`**, or **`x`**. UDPs do not handle **`z`** values. **`z`** values passed to a UDP are treated as **`x`** values.
7. UDPs are defined at the same level as *modules*. UDPs cannot be defined inside modules. They can be *instantiated* only inside modules. UDPs are instantiated exactly like gate primitives.
8. UDPs do not support *inout* ports.

Both combinational and sequential UDPs must follow the above rules. In the following sections, we will discuss the details of combinational and sequential UDPs.

12.2 Combinational UDPs

Combinational UDPs take the inputs and produce the output value by looking up the corresponding entry in the state table.

12.2.1 Combinational UDP Definition

The state table is the most important part of the UDP definition. The best way to explain a state table is to take the example of an **`and`** gate modeled as a UDP. Instead of using the **`and`** gate provided by Verilog, let us define our own **`and`** gate primitive and call it *udp_and*. See Example 12-1.

Example 12-1 Primitive udp_and

```
//Primitive name and terminal list
primitive udp_and(out, a, b);

//Declarations
output out; //must not be declared as reg for combinational UDP
input a, b; //declarations for inputs.

//State table definition; starts with keyword table
table
    //The following comment is for readability only
    //Input entries of the state table must be in the
    //same order as the input terminal list.
   // a   b   :   out;
      0   0   :   0;
      0   1   :   0;
      1   0   :   0;
      1   1   :   1;
endtable //end state table definition

endprimitive //end of udp_and definition
```

Compare parts of *udp_and* defined above with the parts discussed in Figure 12-1. The missing parts are that the output is not declared as **reg** and the **initial** statement is absent. Note that these missing parts are used only for sequential UDPs, which are discussed later in the chapter.

ANSI C style declarations for UDPs are also supported. This style allows the declarations of a primitive port to be combined with the port list. Example 12-2 shows an example of an ANSI C style UDP declaration.

Example 12-2 ANSI C Style UDP Declaration

```
//Primitive name and terminal list
primitive udp_and(output out,
                  input a,
                  input b);
--
```

```
--
endprimitive //end of udp_and definition
```

12.2.2 State Table Entries

In order to understand how state table entries are specified, let us take a closer look at the state table for *udp_and*. Each entry in the state table in a combinational UDP has the following pseudosyntax:

```
<input1> <input2> ..... <inputN> : <output>;
```

Note the following points about state table entries:

1. The *<input#>* values in a state table entry must appear in the same order as they appear in the input terminal list. It is important to keep this in mind while designing UDPs, because designers frequently make mistakes in the input order and get incorrect results.
2. Inputs and output are separated by a "**:**".
3. A state table entry ends with a "**;**".
4. All possible combinations of inputs, where the output produces a known value, must be explicitly specified. Otherwise, if a certain combination occurs and the corresponding entry is not in the table, the output is **x**. Use of default **x** output is frequently used in commercial models. Note that the table for *udp_and* does not handle the case when *a* or *b* is **x**.

In the Verilog **and** gate, if $a = x$ and $b = 0$, the result should be `0`, but *udp_and* will give an **x** as output because the corresponding entry was not found in the state table, that is, the state table was incompletely specified. To understand how to completely specify all possible combinations in a UDP, let us define our own **or** gate *udp_or,* which completely specifies all possible cases. The UDP definition for *udp_or* is shown in Example 12-3.

Example 12-3 *Primitive udp_or*

```
primitive udp_or(out, a, b);

output out;
input a, b;

table
```

Example 12-3 Primitive udp_or (Continued)

```
   // a    b    :    out;
      0    0    :    0;
      0    1    :    1;
      1    0    :    1;
      1    1    :    1;
      x    1    :    1;
      1    x    :    1;
endtable

endprimitive
```

Notice that the above example covers all possible combinations of *a* and *b* where the output is not **x**. The value **z** is not allowed in a UDP. The **z** values on inputs are treated as **x** values.

12.2.3 Shorthand Notation for Don't Cares

In the above example, whenever one input is **1**, the result of the OR operation is **1**, regardless of the value of the other input. The **?** symbol is used for a *don't care* condition. A **?** symbol is automatically expanded to **0**, **1**, or **x**. The **or** gate described above can be rewritten with the **?** symbol.

```
primitive udp_or(out, a, b);

output out;
input a, b;

table
   // a    b    :    out;
      0    0    :    0;
      1    ?    :    1; //? expanded to 0, 1, x
      ?    1    :    1; //? expanded to 0, 1, x
      0    x    :    x;
      x    0    :    x;
endtable

endprimitive
```

12.2.4 Instantiating UDP Primitives

Having discussed how to define combinational UDPs, let us take a look at how UDPs are instantiated. UDPs are instantiated exactly like Verilog gate primitives. Let us design a 1-bit full adder with the *udp_and* and *udp_or* primitives defined earlier. The 1-bit full adder code shown in Example 12-4 is identical to Example 5-7 on page 75 except that the standard Verilog primitives **and** and **or** are replaced with *udp_and* and *upd_or* primitives.

Example 12-4 Instantiation of udp Primitives

```
// Define a 1-bit full adder
module fulladd(sum, c_out, a, b, c_in);

// I/O port declarations
output sum, c_out;
input a, b, c_in;

// Internal nets
wire s1, c1, c2;

// Instantiate logic gate primitives
xor (s1, a, b);//use Verilog primitive
udp_and (c1, a, b); //use UDP

xor (sum, s1, c_in); //use Verilog primitive
udp_and (c2, s1, c_in); //use UDP

udp_or  (c_out, c2, c1);//use UDP

endmodule
```

12.2.5 Example of a Combinational UDP

We discussed two small examples of combinational UDPs: *udp_and* and *udp_or*. Let us design a bigger combinational UDP, a *4-to-1 multiplexer*. A 4-to-1 multiplexer was designed with gates in Section 5.1.4, *Examples*. In this section, we describe the multiplexer as a UDP. Note that the multiplexer is ideal because it has only one **output** terminal. The block diagram and truth table for the multiplexer are shown in Figure 12-2.

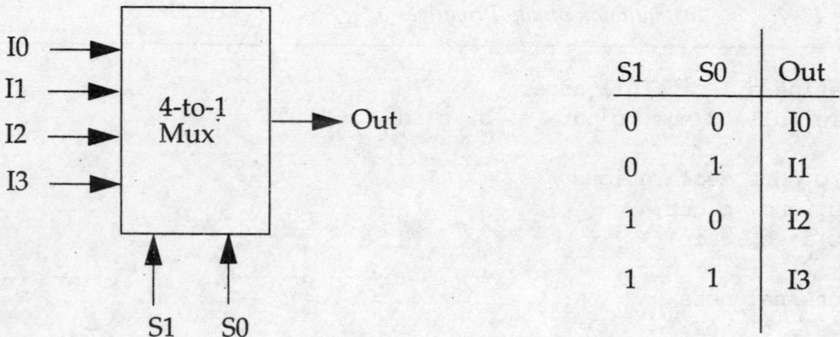

S1	S0	Out
0	0	I0
0	1	I1
1	0	I2
1	1	I3

Figure 12-2 4-to-1 Multiplexer with UDP

The multiplexer has six inputs and one output. The Verilog UDP description for the multiplexer is shown in Example 12-5.

Example 12-5 Verilog Description of 4-to-1 Multiplexer with UDP

```
// 4-to-1 multiplexer. Define it as a primitive
primitive mux4_to_1 ( output out,
                      input i0, i1, i2, i3, s1, s0);
table
  //  i0  i1  i2  i3, s1  s0  : out
      1   ?   ?   ?   0   0   : 1 ;
      0   ?   ?   ?   0   0   : 0 ;
      ?   1   ?   ?   0   1   : 1 ;
      ?   0   ?   ?   0   1   : 0 ;
      ?   ?   1   ?   1   0   : 1 ;
      ?   ?   0   ?   1   0   : 0 ;
      ?   ?   ?   1   1   1   : 1 ;
      ?   ?   ?   0   1   1   : 0 ;
      ?   ?   ?   ?   x   ?   : x ;
      ?   ?   ?   ?   ?   x   : x ;
endtable
```

Example 12-5 Verilog Description of 4-to-1 Multiplexer with UDP (Continued)

```
endprimitive
```

It is important to note that the state table becomes large very quickly as the number of inputs increases. Memory requirements to simulate UDPs increase exponentially with the number of inputs to the UDP. However, UDPs offer a convenient feature to implement an arbitrary function whose truth table is known, without extracting actual logic and by using logic gates to implement the circuit.

The stimulus shown in Example 12-6 is applied to test the multiplexer.

Example 12-6 Stimulus for 4-to-1 Multiplexer with UDP

```
// Define the stimulus module (no ports)
module stimulus;

// Declare variables to be connected
// to inputs
reg IN0, IN1, IN2, IN3;
reg S1, S0;

// Declare output wire
wire OUTPUT;

// Instantiate the multiplexer
mux4_to_1 mymux(OUTPUT, IN0, IN1, IN2, IN3, S1, S0);

// Stimulate the inputs
initial
begin
  // set input lines
  IN0 = 1; IN1 = 0; IN2 = 1; IN3 = 0;
  #1 $display("IN0= %b, IN1= %b, IN2= %b, IN3= %b\n",IN0,IN1,IN2,IN3);
// choose IN0
  S1 = 0; S0 = 0;
  #1 $display("S1 = %b, S0 = %b, OUTPUT = %b \n", S1, S0, OUTPUT);

  // choose IN1
  S1 = 0; S0 = 1;
  #1 $display("S1 = %b, S0 = %b, OUTPUT = %b \n", S1, S0, OUTPUT);

  // choose IN2
```

Example 12-6 Stimulus for 4-to-1 Multiplexer with UDP (Continued)

```
  S1 = 1; S0 = 0;
  #1 $display("S1 = %b, S0 = %b, OUTPUT = %b \n", S1, S0, OUTPUT);

  // choose IN3
  S1 = 1; S0 = 1;
  #1 $display("S1 = %b, S0 = %b, OUTPUT = %b \n", S1, S0, OUTPUT);
end

endmodule
```

The output of the simulation is shown below.

```
IN0= 1, IN1= 0, IN2= 1, IN3= 0

S1 = 0, S0 = 0, OUTPUT = 1

S1 = 0, S0 = 1, OUTPUT = 0

S1 = 1, S0 = 0, OUTPUT = 1

S1 = 1, S0 = 1, OUTPUT = 0
```

12.3 Sequential UDPs

Sequential UDPs differ from combinational UDPs in their definition and behavior. Sequential UDPs have the following differences:

- The output of a sequential UDP is always declared as a **reg**.
- An **initial** statement can be used to initialize output of sequential UDPs.
- The format of a state table entry is slightly different.

```
<input1> <input2> ..... <inputN> : <current_state> : <next_state>;
```

- There are three sections in a state table entry: *inputs*, *current state*, and *next state*. The three sections are separated by a *colon* (**:**) symbol.

- The input specification of state table entries can be in terms of *input levels* or *edge transitions*.
- The *current state* is the current value of the output register.
- The *next state* is computed based on inputs and the current state. The next state becomes the new value of the output register.
- All possible combinations of inputs must be specified to avoid *unknown* output values.

If a sequential UDP is sensitive to input levels, it is called a *level-sensitive sequential UDP*. If a sequential UDP is sensitive to edge transitions on inputs, it is called an *edge-sensitive sequential UDP*.

12.3.1 Level-Sensitive Sequential UDPs

Level-sensitive UDPs change state based on *input levels*. Latches are the most common example of level-sensitive UDPs. A simple latch with *clear* is shown in Figure 12-3

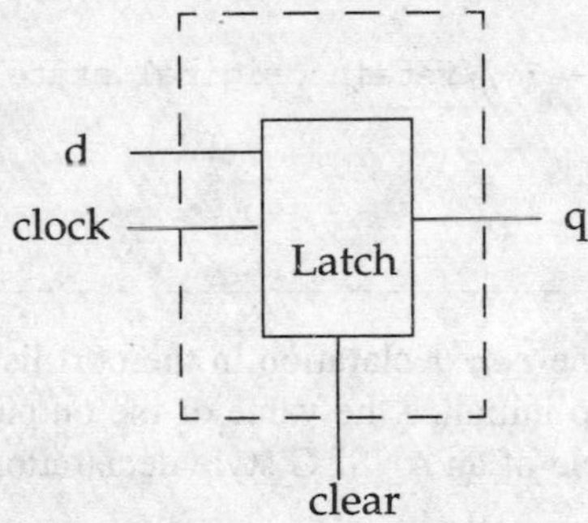

Figure 12-3 Level-Sensitive Latch with clear

In the level-sensitive latch shown above, if the *clear* input is `1`, the output *q* is always `0`. If *clear* is `0`, *q = d* when *clock = 1*. If *clock = 0*, *q* retains its value. The latch can be described as a UDP as shown in Example 12-7. Note that the *dash* "-" symbol is used to denote *no change* in the state of the latch.

Example 12-7 Verilog Description of Level-Sensitive UDP

```
//Define level-sensitive latch by using UDP.
primitive latch(q, d, clock, clear);

//declarations
```

Example 12-7 Verilog Description of Level-Sensitive UDP (Continued)

```
output q;
reg q; //q declared as reg to create internal storage
input d, clock, clear;

//sequential UDP initialization
//only one initial statement allowed
initial
    q = 0; //initialize output to value 0

//state table
table
  //d clock clear : q : q+ ;

    ?   ?   1     : ? : 0 ; //clear condition;
                            //q+ is the new output value

    1   1   0     : ? : 1 ; //latch q = data  = 1
    0   1   0     : ? : 0 ; //latch q = data  = 0

    ?   0   0     : ? : - ; //retain original state if clock = 0
endtable

endprimitive
```

Sequential UDPs can include the **reg** declaration in the port list using an ANSI C style UDP declaration. They can also initialize the value of the output in the port declaration. Example 12-8 shows an example of an ANSI C style declaration for sequential UDPs.

Example 12-8 ANSI C Style Port Declaration for Sequential UDP

```
//Define level-sensitive latch by using UDP.
primitive latch(output reg q = 0,
                input d, clock, clear);
--
--
--
endprimitive
```

12.3.2 Edge-Sensitive Sequential UDPs

Edge-sensitive sequential UDPs change state based on *edge transitions* and/or *input levels.* Edge-triggered flipflops are the most common example of edge-sensitive sequential UDPs. Consider the negative edge-triggered D-flipflop with *clear* shown in Figure 12-4.

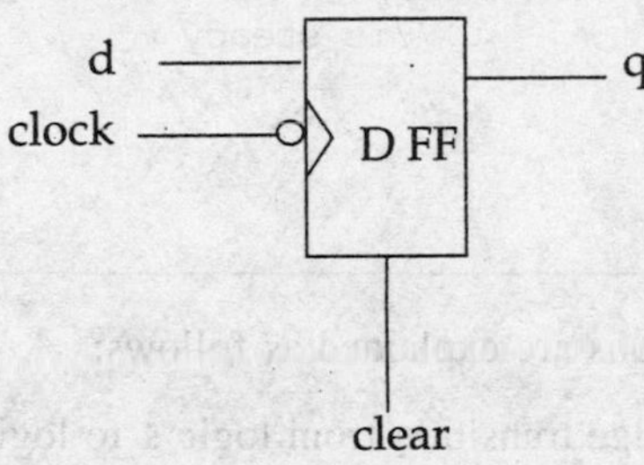

Figure 12-4 Edge-Sensitive D-flipflop with clear

In the edge-sensitive flipflop shown above, if *clear =1*, the output *q* is always `0`. If *clear = 0*, the D-flipflop functions normally. On the negative edge of *clock*, i.e., transition from `1` to `0`, *q* gets the value of *d*. If *clock* transitions to an unknown state or on a positive edge of *clock*, do not change the value of *q*. Also, if *d* changes when *clock* is steady, hold the value of *q*.

The Verilog UDP description for the D flipflop is shown in Example 12-9.

Example 12-9 Negative Edge-Triggered D-flipflop with clear

```
//Define an edge-sensitive sequential UDP;
primitive edge_dff(output reg q = 0,
                   input d, clock, clear);


table
    //  d clock clear : q : q+  ;

        ?   ?     1   : ? : 0 ; //output = 0 if clear = 1
        ?   ?    (10) : ? : - ; //ignore negative transition of clear

        1  (10)   0   : ? : 1 ; //latch data on negative transition of
        0  (10)   0   : ? : 0 ; //clock

        ?  (1x)   0   : ? : - ; //hold q if clock transitions to unknown
                                //state
```

Example 12-9 Negative Edge-Triggered D-flipflop with clear (Continued)

```
        ?   (0?)  0   : ? : - ; //ignore positive transitions of clock
        ?   (x1)  0   : ? : - ; //ignore positive transitions of clock

        (??) ?    0     : ? : - ; //ignore any change in d when clock
                                  //is steady
endtable

endprimitive
```

In Example 12-9, edge transitions are explained as follows:

- *(10)* denotes a negative edge transition from logic **1** to logic **0**.
- *(1x)* denotes a transition from logic **1** to unknown **x** state.
- *(0?)* denotes a transition from **0** to **0**, **1**, or **x**. Potential positive-edge transition.
- *(??)* denotes any transition in signal value **0**,**1**, or **x** to **0**,**1**, or **x**.

It is important to completely specify the UDP by covering all possible combinations of transitions and levels in the state table for which the outputs have a known value. Otherwise, some combinations may result in an unknown value. Only one edge specification is allowed per table entry. More than one edge specification in a single table entry, as shown below, is illegal in Verilog.

```
table
...

        (01) (10) 0 : ? :1 ; //illegal;two edge transitions in an entry
...
endtable
```

12.3.3 Example of a Sequential UDP

We discussed small examples of sequential UDPs. Let us now describe a slightly bigger example, a *4-bit binary ripple counter.* A 4-bit binary ripple counter was designed with T-flipflops in Section 6.5.3, *Ripple Counter.* The T-flipflops were built with negative edge-triggered D-flipflops. Instead, let us define the T-flipflop directly as a UDP primitive. The UDP definition for the T-flipflop is shown in Example 12-10.

Example 12-10 T-flipflop with UDP

```
// Edge-triggered T-flipflop
primitive T_FF(output reg q,
          input clk, clear);

//no initialization of q; TFF will be initialized with clear signal

table
  //   clk   clear :   q   : q+ ;
       //asynchronous clear condition
       ?       1   :   ?   : 0 ;

       //ignore negative edge of clear
       ?     (10)  :   ?   : - ;

       //toggle flipflop at negative edge of clk
       (10)    0   :   1   : 0 ;
       (10)    0   :   0   : 1 ;

       //ignore positive edge of clk
       (0?)    0   :   ?   : - ;
endtable
endprimitive
```

To build the ripple counter with T-flipflops, four T-flipflops are instantiated in the ripple counter, as shown in Example 12-11.

Example 12-11 Instantiation of T_FF UDP in Ripple Counter

```
// Ripple counter
module counter(Q , clock, clear);

// I/O ports
output [3:0] Q;
```

Example 12-11 Instantiation of T_FF UDP in Ripple Counter (Continued)

```
input clock, clear;

// Instantiate the T flipflops
// Instance names are optional
T_FF tff0(Q[0], clock, clear);
T_FF tff1(Q[1], Q[0], clear);
T_FF tff2(Q[2], Q[1], clear);
T_FF tff3(Q[3], Q[2], clear);

endmodule
```

If stimulus shown in Example 6-9 on page 113 is applied to the counter, identical simulation output will be obtained.

12.4 UDP Table Shorthand Symbols

Shorthand symbols for levels and edge transitions are provided so UDP tables can be written in a concise manner. We already discussed the symbols `?` and `-`. A summary of all shorthand symbols and their meanings is shown in Table 12-1.

Table 12-1 UDP Table Shorthand Symbols

Shorthand Symbols	Meaning	Explanation
`?`	0, 1, x	Cannot be specified in an output field
`b`	0, 1	Cannot be specified in an output field
`-`	No change in state value	Can be specified only in output field of a sequential UDP
`r`	(01)	Rising edge of signal
`f`	(10)	Falling edge of signal
`p`	(01), (0x) or (x1)	Potential rising edge of signal
`n`	(10), (1x) or (x0)	Potential falling edge of signal
`*`	(??)	Any value change in signal

Using the shorthand symbols, we can rewrite the table entries in Example 12-9 on page 263 as follows.

```
table
  //  d clock clear : q : q+  ;

      ?   ?     1    : ? : 0 ; //output = 0 if clear = 1
      ?   ?     f    : ? : - ; //ignore negative transition of clear

      1   f     0    : ? : 1 ; //latch data on negative transition of
      0   f     0    : ? : 0 ; //clock

      ?   (1x)  0    : ? : - ; //hold q if clock transitions to unknown
                                //state

      ?   p     0    : ? : - ; //ignore positive transitions of clock

      *   ?     0    : ? : - ; //ignore any change in d when
                           //clock is steady
endtable
```

Note that the use of shorthand symbols makes the entries more readable and more concise.

12.5 Guidelines for UDP Design

When designing a functional block, it is important to decide whether to model it as a module or as a user-defined primitive. Here are some guidelines used to make that decision.

- UDPs model functionality only. They do not model timing or process technology (such as CMOS, TTL, ECL). The primary purpose of a UDP is to define in a simple and concise form the functional portion of a block. A module is always used to model a complete block that has timing and process technology.
- A block can modeled as a UDP only if it has exactly one output terminal. If the block to be designed has more than one output, it has to be modeled as a module.
- The limit on the maximum number of inputs of a UDP is specific to the Verilog simulator being used. However, Verilog simulators are required to allow a minimum of 9 inputs for sequential UDPs and 10 for combinational UDPs.

- A UDP is typically implemented as a lookup table in memory. As the number of inputs increases, the number of table entries grows exponentially. Thus, the memory requirement for a UDP grows exponentially in relation to the number of inputs. It is not advisable to design a block with a large number of inputs as a UDP.
- UDPs are not always the appropriate method to design a block. Sometimes it is easier to design blocks as a module. For example, it is not advisable to design an 8-to-1 multiplexer as a UDP because of the large number of table entries. Instead, the data flow or behavioral representation would be much simpler. It is important to consider complexity trade-offs to decide whether to use UDP to represent a block.

There are also some guidelines for writing the UDP state table.

- The UDP state table should be specified as completely as possible. All possible input combinations for which the output is known should be covered. If a certain combination of inputs is not specified, the default output value for that combination will be **x**. This feature is used frequently in commercial libraries to reduce the number of table entries.
- Shorthand symbols should be used to combine table entries wherever possible. Shorthand symbols make the UDP description more concise. However, the Verilog simulator may internally expand the table entries. Thus, there is no memory requirement reduction by using shorthand symbols.
- Level-sensitive entries take precedence over edge-sensitive entries. If edge-sensitive and level-sensitive entries clash on the same inputs, the output is determined by the level-sensitive entry because it has precedence over the edge-sensitive entry.

12.6 Summary

We discussed the following aspects of Verilog in this chapter:

- *User-defined primitives (UDP)* are used to define custom Verilog primitives by the use of lookup tables. UDPs offer a convenient way to design certain functional blocks.
- UDPs can have only one output terminal. UDPs are defined at the same level as modules. UDPs are instantiated exactly like gate primitives. A *state table* is the most important component of UDP specification.
- UDPs can be *combinational* or *sequential*. Sequential UDPs can be *edge-* or *level-sensitive*.

- *Combinational UDPs* are used to describe combinational circuits where the output is purely a logical combination of the inputs.
- *Sequential UDPs* are used to define blocks with timing controls. Blocks such as latches or flipflops can be described with sequential UDPs. Sequential UDPs are modeled like state machines. There is a present state and a next state. The next state is also the output of the UDP. Edge- and level-sensitive descriptions can be mixed.
- Shorthand symbols are provided to make UDP state table entries more concise. Shorthand notation should be used wherever possible.
- It is important to decide whether a functional block should be described as a UDP or as a module. Memory requirements and complexity trade-offs must be considered.

12.7 Exercises

1. Design a 2-to-1 multiplexer by using UDP. The select signal is *s*, inputs are *i0, i1,* and the output is *out*. If the select signal *s* = **x**, the output *out* is always `0`. If *s* = `0`, then *out* = *i0*. If s = 1, then out = i1.
2. Write the truth table for the Boolean function *Y = (A & B) | (C ^ D)*. Define a UDP that implements this Boolean function. Assume that the inputs will never take the value **x**.
3. Define a level-sensitive latch with a preset signal. Inputs are *d, clock,* and *preset*. Output is *q*. If *clock = 0,* then *q = d.* If *clock* = `1` or **x**, then *q* is unchanged. If *preset* = `1`, then *q = 1.* If *preset = 0,* then *q* is decided by *clock* and *d* signals. If *preset = x,* then *q = x.*

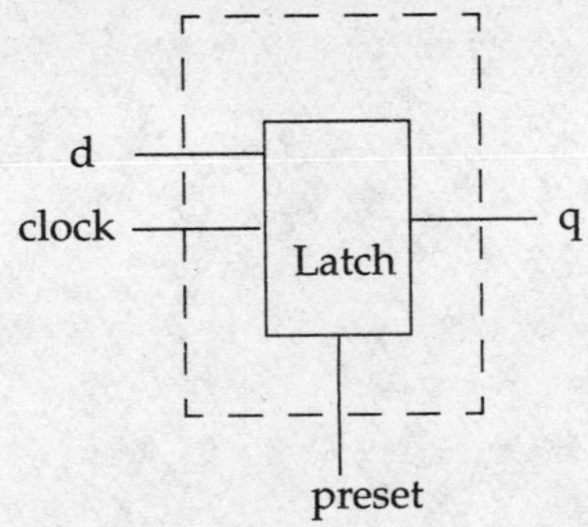

4. Define a positive edge-triggered D-flipflop with *clear* as a UDP. Signal *clear* is active low. Use Example 12-9 on page 263 as a guideline. Use shorthand notation wherever possible.

5. Define a negative edge-triggered JK flipflop, *jk_ff* with asynchronous *preset* and *clear* as a UDP. $q = 1$ when $preset = 1$ and $q = 0$ when $clear = 1$.

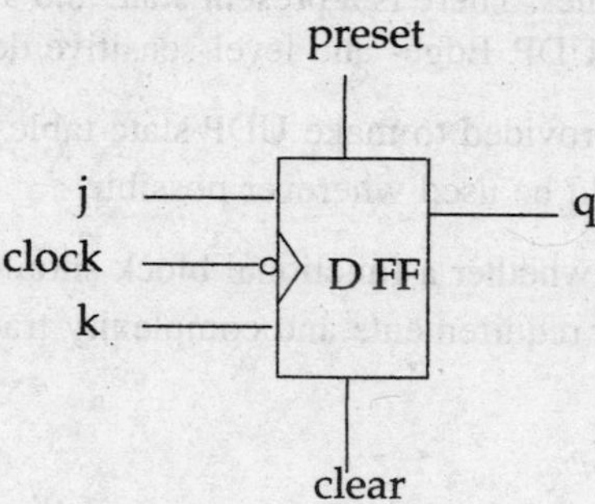

The table for a JK flipflop is shown below.

J	K	q_{n+1}
0	0	q_n
0	1	0
1	0	1
1	1	$\overline{q_n}$

6. Design the 4-bit synchronous counter shown below. Use the UDP *jk_ff* that was defined above.

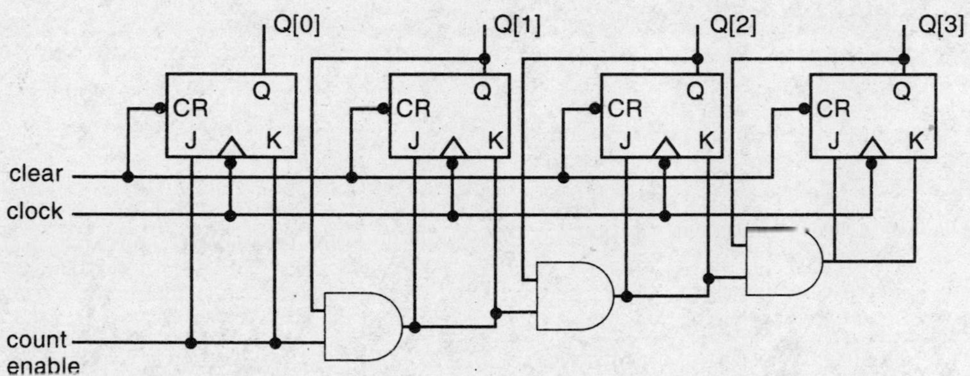

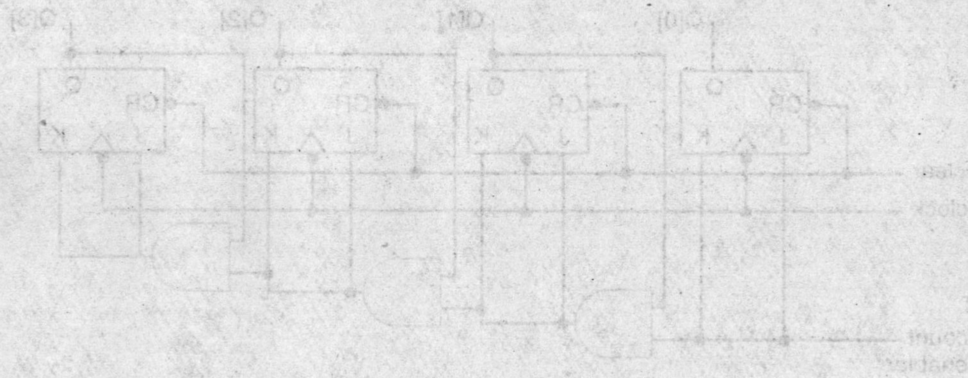

Programming Language Interface 13

Verilog provides the set of standard system tasks and functions defined in Appendix C, *List of Keywords, System Tasks, and Compiler Directives*. However, designers frequently need to customize the capability of the Verilog language by defining their own system tasks and functions. To do this, the designers need to interact with the internal representation of the design and the simulation environment in the Verilog simulator. The *Programming Language Interface (PLI)* provides a set of interface routines to read internal data representation, write to internal data representation, and extract information about the simulation environment. *User-defined system tasks and functions* can be created with this predefined set of PLI interface routines.

Verilog Programming Language Interface is a very broad area of study. Thus, only the basics of Verilog PLI are covered in this chapter. Designers should consult the *IEEE Standard Verilog Hardware Description Language* document for complete details of the PLI.

There are three generations of the Verilog PLI.

1. *Task/Function* (`tf_`) routines make up the first generation PLI. These routines are primarily used for operations involving user-defined task/function arguments, utility functions, callback mechanism, and writing data to output devices.
2. *Access* (`acc_`) routines make up the second-generation PLI. These routines provide object-oriented access directly into a Verilog HDL structural description. These routines can be used to access and modify a wide variety of objects in the Verilog HDL description.
3. *Verilog Procedural Interface* (`vpi_`) routines make up the third-generation PLI. These routines are a superset of the functionality of `acc_` and `tf_` routines.

For the sake of simplicity, we will discuss only `acc_` and `tf_` routines in this chapter.

Learning Objectives

- Explain how PLI routines are used in a Verilog simulation.
- Describe the uses of the PLI.

- Define *user-defined system tasks and functions* and *user-defined C routines.*
- Understand linking and invocation of user-defined system tasks.
- Explain how the PLI is represented conceptually inside a Verilog simulator.
- Identify and describe how to use the two classes of PLI library routines: *access* routines and *utility* routines.
- Learn to create *user-defined system tasks and functions* and use them in simulation.

The first step is to understand how PLI tasks fit into the Verilog simulation. A sample simulation flow using PLI routines is shown in Figure 13-1.

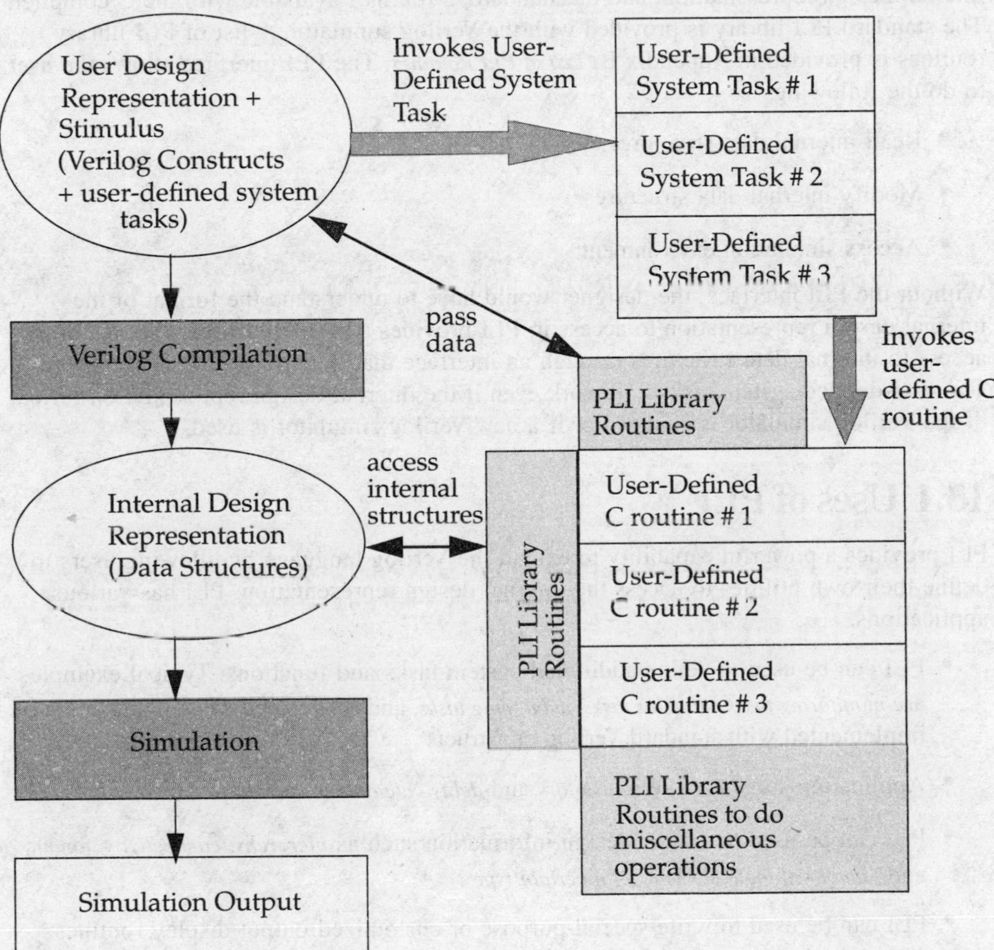

Figure 13-1 PLI Interface

A designer describes the design and stimulus by using standard Verilog constructs and system tasks. In addition, *user-defined system tasks* can also be invoked in the design and stimulus. The design and stimulus are compiled and converted to an internal design representation. The internal design representation is typically in the Verilog simulator proprietary format and is incomprehensible to the designer. The internal representation is then used to run the actual simulation and produce output.

Each of the user-defined system tasks is linked to a *user-defined C routine*. The C routines are described by means of a *standard library* of PLI interface routines, which can access the internal design representation, and the standard C routines available with the C compiler. The standard PLI library is provided with the Verilog simulator. A list of PLI library routines is provided in Appendix B, *List of PLI Routines*. The PLI interface allows the user to do the following:

- Read internal data structures
- Modify internal data structures
- Access simulation environment

Without the PLI interface, the designer would have to understand the format of the internal design representation to access it. PLI provides a layer of abstraction that allows access to internal data structures through an interface that is uniform for all simulators. The user-defined system tasks will work even if the internal design representation format of the Verilog simulator is changed or if a new Verilog simulator is used.

13.1 Uses of PLI

PLI provides a powerful capability to extend the Verilog language by allowing users to define their own utilities to access the internal design representation. PLI has various applications.

- PLI can be used to define additional system tasks and functions. Typical examples are *monitoring tasks, stimulus tasks, debugging tasks,* and *complex operations* that cannot be implemented with standard Verilog constructs.
- Application software like *translators* and *delay calculators* can be written with PLI.
- PLI can be used to extract design information such as *hierarchy, connectivity, fanout,* and *number of logic elements of a certain type* .
- PLI can be used to write special-purpose or customized output display routines. Waveform viewers can use this file to generate *waveforms, logic connectivity, source level browsers,* and *hierarchy information.*
- Routines that provide stimulus to the simulation can be written with PLI. The stimulus could be automatically generated or translated from some other form of stimulus.
- General Verilog-based application software can be written with PLI routines. This software will work with all Verilog simulators because of the uniform access provided by the PLI interface.

13.2 Linking and Invocation of PLI Tasks

Designers can write their own user-defined system tasks by using PLI library routines. However, the Verilog simulator must know about the *existence* of the user-defined system task and its corresponding user-defined C function. This is done by linking the user-defined system task into the Verilog simulator.

To understand the process, let us consider the example of a simple system task *$hello_verilog*. When invoked, the task simply prints out a message "Hello Verilog World". First, the C routine that implements the task must be defined with PLI library routines. The C routine *hello_verilog* in the file *hello_verilog.c* is shown below.

```
#include "veriuser.h" /*include the file provided in release dir*/

int hello_verilog()
{
    io_printf("Hello Verilog World\n");
}
```

The *hello_verilog* routine is fairly straightforward. The *io_printf* is a PLI library routine that works exactly like *printf.*

The following sections show the steps involved in defining and using the new *$hello_verilog* system task.

13.2.1 Linking PLI Tasks

Whenever the task *$hello_verilog* is invoked in the Verilog code, the C routine *hello_verilog* must be executed. The simulator needs to be aware that a new system task called *$hello_verilog* exists and is linked to the C routine *hello_verilog*. This process is called *linking* the PLI routines into the Verilog simulator. Different simulators provide different mechanisms to link PLI routines. Also, though the exact mechanics of the linking process might be different for simulators, the fundamentals of the linking process remain the same. For details, refer to the latest reference manuals available with your simulator.

At the end of the linking step, a special binary executable containing the new *$hello_verilog* system task is created. For example, instead of the usual simulator binary executable, a new binary executable *hverilog* is produced. To simulate, run **hverilog** instead of your usual simulator executable file.

13.2.2 Invoking PLI Tasks

Once the user-defined task has been linked into the Verilog simulator, it can be invoked like any Verilog system task by the keyword **`$hello_verilog`**. A Verilog module *hello_top,* which calls the task *$hello_verilog,* is defined in file *hello.v* as shown below.

```
module hello_top;

initial
    $hello_verilog; //Invoke the user-defined task $hello_verilog

endmodule
```

Output of the simulation is as follows:

```
Hello Verilog World
```

13.2.3 General Flow of PLI Task Addition and Invocation

We discussed a simple example to illustrate how a user-defined system task is named, implemented in terms of a user-defined C routine, linked into the simulator, and invoked in the Verilog code. More complex PLI tasks discussed in the following sections will follow the same process. Figure 13-2 summarizes the general process of adding and invoking a user-defined system task.

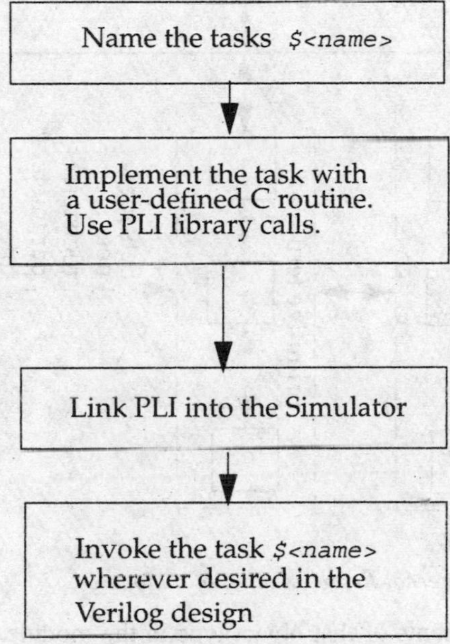

Figure 13-2 General Flow of PLI Task Addition and Invocation

13.3 Internal Data Representation

Before we understand how to use PLI library routines, it is first necessary to describe how a design is viewed internally in the simulator. Each module is viewed as a collection of *object types*. Object types are elements defined in Verilog, such as:

- Module instances, module ports, module pin-to-pin paths, and intermodule paths
- Top-level modules
- Primitive instances, and primitive terminals
- Nets, registers, parameters, and specparams
- Integer, time, and real variables
- Timing checks
- Named events

Each object type has a corresponding set that identifies all objects of that type in the module. Sets of all object types are interconnected.

A conceptual internal representation of a module is shown in Figure 13-3.

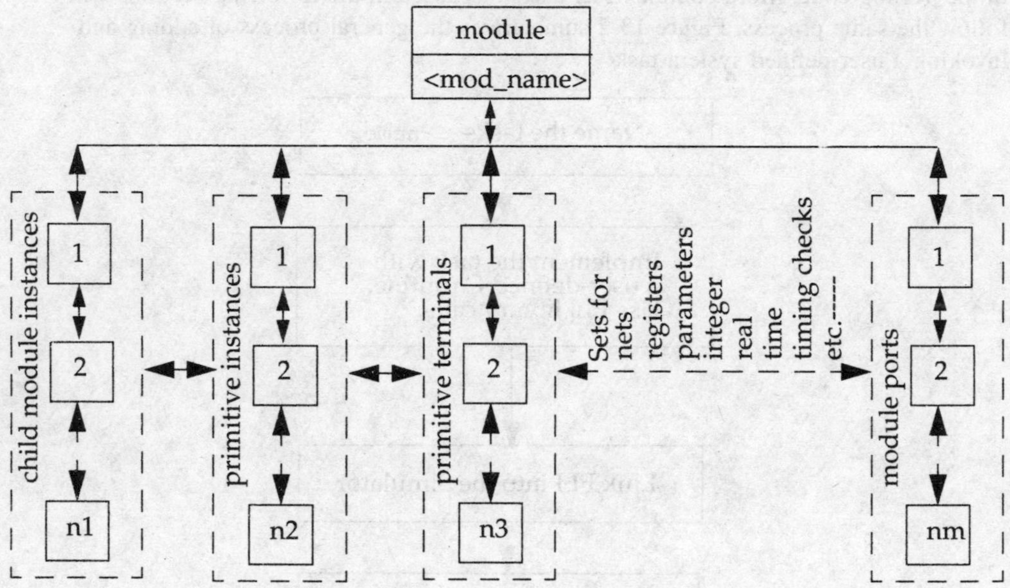

Figure 13-3 Conceptual Internal Representation of a Module

Each set contains all elements of that object type in the module. All sets are interconnected. The connections between the sets are bidirectional. The entire internal representation can be traversed by using PLI library routines to obtain information about the module. PLI library routines are discussed later in the chapter.

To illustrate the internal data representation, consider the example of a simple 2-to-1 multiplexer whose gate level circuit is shown in Figure 13-4.

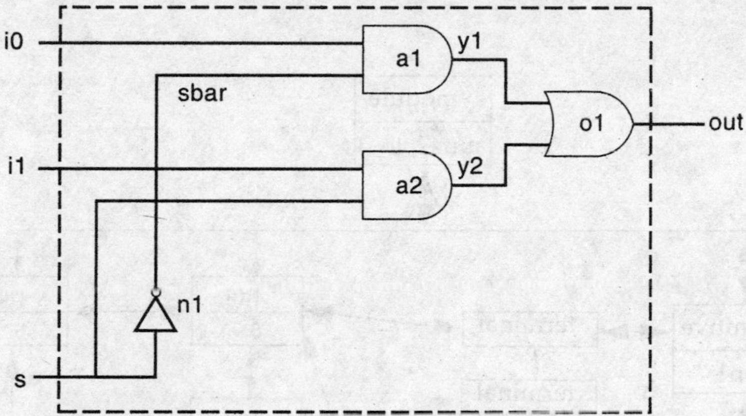

Figure 13-4 2-to-1 Multiplexer

The Verilog description of the circuit is shown in Example 13-1.

Example 13-1 Verilog Description of 2-to-1 Multiplexer

```
module mux2_to_1(out, i0, i1, s);

output out; //output port
input i0, i1; //input ports
input s;

wire sbar, y1, y2; //internal nets

//Gate Instantiations
not n1(sbar, s);
and a1(y1, i0, sbar);
and a2(y2, i1, s);
or o1(out, y1, y2);

endmodule
```

The internal data representation for the 2-to-1 multiplexer is shown in Figure 13-5. Sets are shown for primitive instances, primitive instance terminals, module ports, and nets. Other object types are not present in this module.

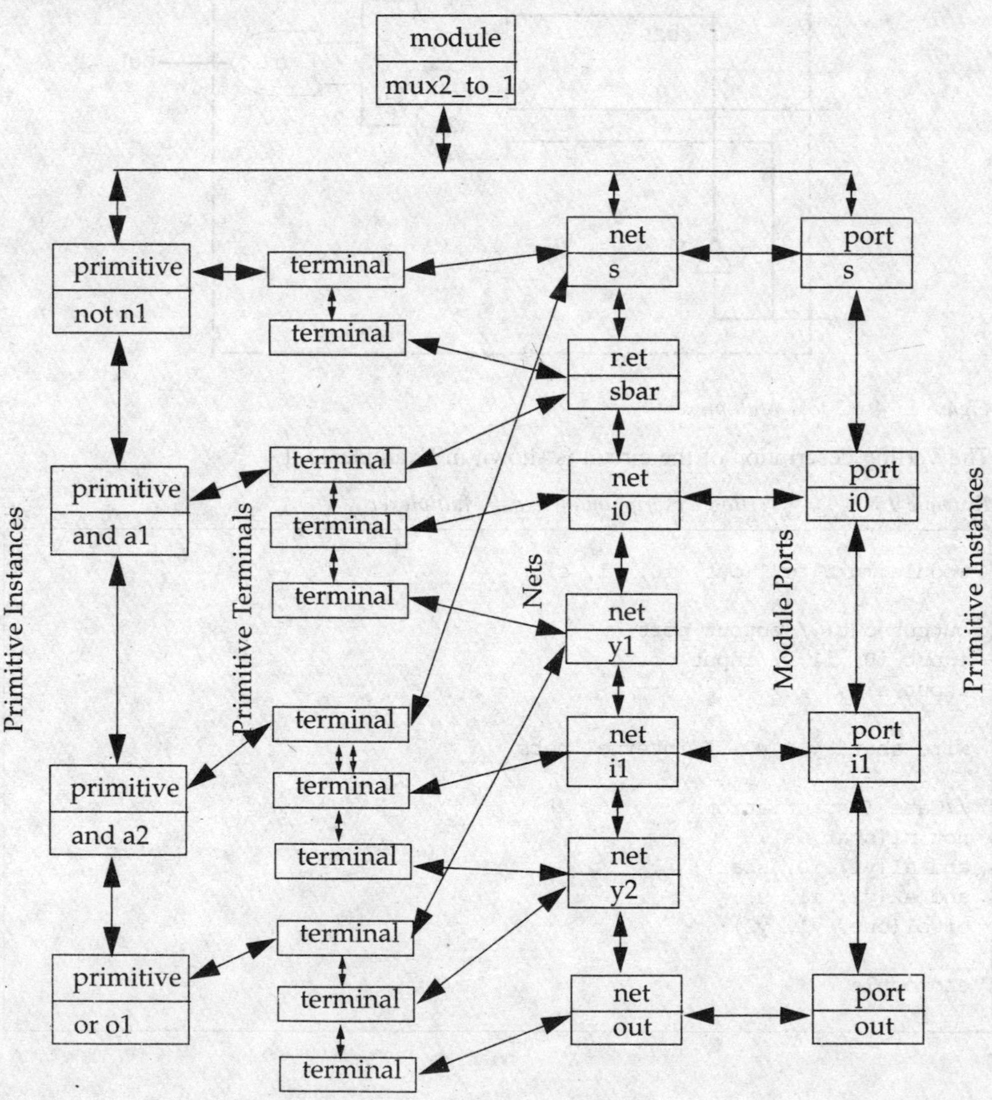

Figure 13-5 Internal Data Representation of 2-to-1 Multiplexer

The example shown above does not contain register, integers, module instances, and other object types. If they are present in a module definition, they are also represented in terms of sets. This description is a conceptual view of the internal structures. The exact implementation of data structures is simulator-dependent.

13.4 PLI Library Routines

PLI library routines provide a standard interface to the internal data representation of the design. The user-defined C routines for user-defined system tasks are written by using PLI library routines. In the example in Section 13.2, *Linking and Invocation of PLI Tasks*, *$hello_verilog* is the user-defined system task, *hello_verilog* is the user defined C routine, and *io_printf* is a PLI library routine.

There are two broad classes of PLI library routines: access routines and utility routines. (Note that **vpi_** routines are a superset of access and utility routines and are not discussed in this book.)

Access routines provide access to information about the internal data representation; they allow the user C routine to traverse the data structure and extract information about the design. Utility routines are mainly used for passing data across the Verilog/Programming Language Boundary and for miscellaneous housekeeping functions. Figure 13-6 shows the role of access and utility routines in PLI.

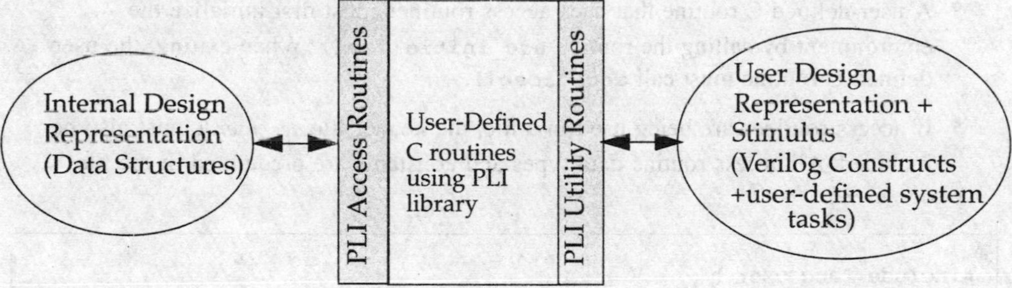

Figure 13-6 Role of Access and Utility Routines

A complete list of PLI library routines is provided in Appendix B, *List of PLI Routines*. The function and usage of each routine are also specified.

13.4.1 Access Routines

Access routines are also popularly called *acc* routines. Access routines can do the following:

- Read information about a particular object from the internal data representation
- Write information about a particular object into the internal data representation

We will discuss only reading of information from the design. Information about modifying internal design representation can be found in the *Programming Language Interface (PLI) Manual.* However, reading of information is adequate for most practical purposes.

Access routines can read information about objects in the design. Objects can be one of the following types:

- Module instances, module ports, module pin-to-pin paths, and intermodule paths
- Top-level modules
- Primitive instances, and primitive terminals
- Nets, registers, parameters, and specparams
- Integer, time, and real variables
- Timing checks
- Named events

Mechanics of access routines

Some observations about access routines are listed below.

- Access routines always start with the prefix **acc_**.
- A user-defined C routine that uses access routines must first initialize the environment by calling the routine **acc_initialize()**. When exiting, the user-defined C routine must call **acc_close()**.
- If access routines are being used in a file, the header file *acc_user.h* must also be included. All access routine data types and constants are predefined in the file *acc_user.h.*

```
#include "acc_user.h"
```

 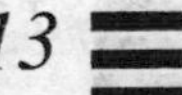

- Access routines use the concept of a *handle* to access an object. Handles are predefined data types that point to specific objects in the design. Any information about the object can be obtained once the object handle is obtained. This is similar to the concept of file handles for accessing files in C programs. An object handle identifier is declared with the keyword **handle**.

```
handle top_handle;
```

Types of access routines

We discuss six types of access routines.

- *Handle routines.* They return handles to objects in the design. The name of handle routines always starts with the prefix **acc_handle_**.
- *Next routines.* They return the handle to the next object in the set of a given object type in a design. Next routines always start with the prefix **acc_next_** and accept reference objects as arguments.
- *Value Change Link (VCL) routines.* They allow the user system task to add and delete objects from the list of objects that are monitored for value changes. VCL routines always begin with the prefix **acc_vcl_** and do not return a value.
- *Fetch routines.* They can extract a variety of information about objects. Information such as full hierarchical path name, relative name, and other attributes can be obtained. Fetch routines always start with the prefix **acc_fetch_**.
- *Utility access routines.* They perform miscellaneous operations related to access routines. For example, **acc_initialize()** and **acc_close()** are utility routines.
- *Modify routines.* They can modify internal data structures. We do not discuss them in this book. Refer to the *IEEE Standard Verilog Hardware Description Language* document for details about modify routines.

A complete list of access routines and their usage is provided in Appendix B, *List of PLI Routines*.

Examples of access routines

We will discuss two examples that illustrate the use of access routines. The first example is a user-defined system task to find names of all ports in a module and count the number of ports. The second example is a user-defined system task that monitors the changes in values of nets.

Example 1: Get Module Port List

Let us write a user-defined system task *$get_ports* to find complete hierarchical names of input, output, and inout ports in a module and to count the number of input, output, and inout ports. The user-defined system task will be invoked in Verilog as *$get_ports("<hierarchical_module_name>").* The user-defined C routine *get_ports,* which implements the task *$get_ports,* is described in file *get_ports.c*. The file *get_ports.c* is shown in Example 13-2.

Example 13-2 PLI Routine to get Module Port List

```
#include "acc_user.h"

int get_ports()
{
  handle  mod, port;
  int input_ctr = 0;
  int output_ctr = 0;
  int inout_ctr = 0;

  acc_initialize();

  mod = acc_handle_tfarg(1); /* get a handle to the module instance
                                first argument in the system task argument
                                list */

  port = acc_handle_port(mod, 0); /* get the first port of the module */

  while( port != null ) /* loop for all ports */
  {
    if (acc_fetch_direction(port) == accInput) /* Input port */
    {
        io_printf("Input Port %s \n", acc_fetch_fullname(port));
                                        /* full hierarchical name */

        input_ctr++;
    }
    else if (acc_fetch_direction(port) == accOutput) /* Output port */
    {
        io_printf("Output Port %s \n", acc_fetch_fullname(port));
        output_ctr++;
    }
    else if (acc_fetch_direction(port) == accInout) /* Inout port */
{
        io_printf("Inout Port %s \n", acc_fetch_fullname(port));
        inout_ctr++;
```

Example 13-2 PLI Routine to get Module Port List (Continued)

```
    }

    port = acc_next_port(mod, port); /* go to the next port */
  }

  io_printf("Input Ports = %d Output Ports = %d, Inout ports = %d\n\n",
                          input_ctr, output_ctr, inout_ctr);
  acc_close();

}
```

Notice that *handle, fetch, next,* and *utility access* routines are used to write the user C routine.

Link the new task into the Verilog simulator as described in Section 13.2.1, *Linking PLI Tasks*. To check the newly defined task, we will use it to find out the port list of the module *mux2_to_1* described in Example 13-1. A top-level module that instantiates the 2-to-1 multiplexer and invokes the *$get_ports* task is shown below.

```
module top;
wire OUT;
reg I0, I1, S;

mux2_to_1 my_mux(OUT, I0, I1, S); /*Instantiate the 2-to-1 mux*/

initial
begin
  $get_ports("top.my_mux"); /*invoke task $get_ports to get port list*/
end

endmodule
```

Invocation of *$get_ports* causes the user C routine *$get_ports* to be executed. The output of the simulation is shown below.

```
Output Port top.my_mux.out
Input Port top.my_mux.i0
Input Port top.my_mux.i1
```

```
(Continued...)
Input Port top.my_mux.s
Input Ports = 3 Output Ports = 1, Inout ports = 0
```

Example 2: Monitor Nets for Value Changes

This example highlights the use of *Value Change Link (VCL)* routines. Instead of using the *$monitor* task provided with the Verilog simulator, let us define our own task to monitor specific nets in the design for value changes. The task *$my_monitor("<net_name>");* is to be invoked to add a *<net_name>* to the monitoring list.

The user-defined C routine *my_monitor,* which implements the user-defined system task, is shown in Example 13-3.

Example 13-3 PLI Routine to Monitor Nets for Value Changes

```
#include "acc_user.h"

char convert_to_char();
int display_net();

int my_monitor()
{
  handle net;
  char *netname ; /*pointer to store names of nets*/
  char *malloc();

  acc_initialize(); /*initialize environment*/

  net = acc_handle_tfarg(1); /*get a handle to the net to be monitored*/

  /*Find hierarchical name of net and store it*/
  netname = malloc(strlen(acc_fetch_fullname(net)));
  strcpy(netname,  acc_fetch_fullname(net));

  /* Call the VCL routine to add a signal to the monitoring list*/
  /* Pass four arguments to acc_vcl_add task*/
  /* 1st : handle to the monitored object (net)
     2nd : Consumer C routine to call when the object value changes
(display_net)
     3rd : String to be passed to consumer C routine (netname)
     4th : Predefined VCL flags: vcl_verilog_logic for logic monitoring
                          vcl_verilog_strength for strength monitoring*/
  acc_vcl_add(net, display_net, netname, vcl_verilog_logic);
```

Example 13-3 PLI Routine to Monitor Nets for Value Changes (Continued)

```
  acc_close();
}
```

Notice that the net is added to the monitoring list with the routine *acc_vcl_add*. A consumer routine *display_net* is an argument to *acc_vcl_add*. Whenever the value of the net changes, the *acc_vcl_add* calls the consumer routine *display_net* and passes a pointer to a data structure of the type *p_vc_record*. A *consumer routine* is a C routine that performs an action determined by the user whenever *acc_vcl_add* calls it. The *p_vc_record* is predefined in the *acc_user.h* file, as shown below.

```
typedef struct t_vc_record{
    int vc_reason;      /*reason for value change*/
    int vc_hightime;    /*Higher 32 bits of 64-bit simulation time*/
    int vc_lowtime;     /*Lower 32 bits of 64-bit simulation time*/
    char *user_data;    /*String passed in 3rd argument of acc_vcl_add*/
    union  {            /*New value of the monitored signal*/
        unsigned char        logic_value;
        double               real_value;
        handle               vector_handle;
        s_strengths          strengths_s;
    } out_value;
} *p_vc_record;
```

The consumer routine *display_net* simply displays the *time of change, name of net,* and *new value of the net*. The consumer routine is written as shown in Example 13-4. Another routine, *convert_to_char*, is defined to convert the logic value constants to an ASCII character.

Example 13-4 Consumer Routine for VCL Example

```
/*Consumer routine. Called whenever any monitored net changes*/
display_net(vc_record)
p_vc_record vc_record; /*Structure p_vc_record predefined in
                          acc_user.h*/
{

  /*Print time, name, and new value of the changed net */
  io_printf("%d New value of net %s is %c \n",
```

Example 13-4 *Consumer Routine for VCL Example (Continued)*

```
                        vc_record->vc_lowtime,
                        vc_record->user_data,
                        convert_to_char(vc_record->out_value.logic_value));
}

/*Miscellaneous routine to convert predefined character constant to
  ASCII character*/
char convert_to_char(logic_val)
char logic_val;
{
  char temp;

  switch(logic_val)
  {
    /*vcl0, vcl1, vclX and vclZ are predefined in acc_user.h*/
    case vcl0: temp='0';
               break;
    case vcl1: temp='1';
               break;
    case vclX: temp='X';
               break;
    case vclZ: temp='Z';
               break;
  }
  return(temp);
}
```

Link the new task into the Verilog simulator as described in Section 13.2.1, *Linking PLI Tasks*. To check the newly defined task, we will use it to monitor nets *sbar* and *y1* when stimulus is applied to module *mux*2_to_1 described in Example 13-1 on page 281. A top-level module that instantiates the 2-to-1 multiplexer, applies stimulus, and invokes the *$my_monitor* task is shown below.

```
module top;
wire OUT;
reg I0, I1, S;

mux2_to_1 my_mux(OUT, I0, I1, S); //Instantiate the module mux2_to_1

initial //Add nets to the monitoring list
begin
```

```
(Continued...)
  $my_monitor("top.my_mux.sbar");
  $my_monitor("top.my_mux.y1");
end

initial //Apply Stimulus
begin
  I0=1'b0; I1=1'b1; S = 1'b0;
  #5 I0=1'b1; I1=1'b1; S = 1'b1;
  #5 I0=1'b0; I1=1'b1; S = 1'bx;
  #5 I0=1'b1; I1=1'b1; S = 1'b1;
end

endmodule
```

The output of the simulation is shown below.

```
0 New value of net top.my_mux.y1 is 0
0 New value of net top.my_mux.sbar is 1
5 New value of net top.my_mux.y1 is 1
5 New value of net top.my_mux.sbar is 0
5 New value of net top.my_mux.y1 is 0
10 New value of net top.my_mux.sbar is X
15 New value of net top.my_mux.y1 is X
15 New value of net top.my_mux.sbar is 0
15 New value of net top.my_mux.y1 is 0
```

13.4.2 Utility Routines

Utility routines are miscellaneous PLI routines that pass data in both directions across the Verilog/user C routine boundary. Utility routines are also popularly called "*tf*" routines.

Mechanics of utility routines

Some observations about utility routines are listed below.

- Utility routines always start with the prefix *tf_*.

- If utility routines are being used in a file, the header file *veriuser.h* must be included. All utility routine data types and constants are predefined in *veriuser.h*.

```
#include "veriuser.h"
```

Types of utility routines

Utility routines are available for the following purposes:

- Get information about the Verilog system task invocation
- Get argument list information
- Get values of arguments
- Pass back new values of arguments to calling system task
- Monitor changes in values of arguments
- Get information about simulation time and scheduled events
- Perform housekeeping tasks, such as saving work areas, and storing pointers to tasks
- Do long arithmetic
- Display messages
- Halt, terminate, save, and restore simulation

A list of utility routines, their function, and usage is provided in Appendix B.

Example of utility routines

Until now we encountered only one utility routine, **`io_printf()`**. Now we will look at a few more utility routines that allow passing of data between the Verilog design and the user-defined C routines.

Verilog provides the system tasks **`$stop`** and **`$finish`** that suspend and terminate the simulation. Let us define our own system task, *$my_stop_finish,* which does both stopping and finishing based on the arguments passed to it. The complete specifications for the user-defined system task *$my_stop_finish* are shown in Table 13-1.

Table 13-1 Specifications for $my_stop_finish

1st Argument	2nd Argument	Action
0	none	Stop simulation. Display simulation time and message.
1	none	Finish simulation. Display simulation time and message.
0	any value	Stop simulation. Display simulation time, module instance from which stop was called, and message.
1	any value	Finish simulation. Display simulation time, module instance from which stop was called, and message.

The source code for the user-defined C routine *my_stop_finish* is shown in Example 13-5.

Example 13-5 User C Routine my_stop_finish Using Utility Routines

```
#include "veriuser.h"

int my_stop_finish()
{

  if(tf_nump() == 1) /* if 1 argument is passed to the my_stop_finish
                       task, display only simulation time and message*/
  {
    if(tf_getp(1) == 0) /* get value of argument. If the argument
                          is 0, then stop the simulation*/
    {
      io_printf("Mymessage: Simulation stopped at time %d\n",
                               tf_gettime());
      tf_dostop(); /*stop the simulation*/
    }
    else if(tf_getp(1) == 1)  /* if the argument is 0 then terminate
                              the simulation*/
    {
      io_printf("Mymessage: Simulation finished at time %d\n",
                               tf_gettime());
      tf_dofinish(); /*terminate the simulation*/
    }
    else
      /* Pass warning message */
      tf_warning("Bad arguments to \$my_stop_finish at time %d\n",
                                              tf_gettime());
  }

  else if(tf_nump() == 2) /* if 1 argument is passed to the my_stop_finish
                       task, then print module instance from which the
                       task was called, time and message */
  {
    if(tf_getp(1) == 0) /* if the argument is 0 then stop
                          the simulation*/
    {
      io_printf
       ("Mymessage: Simulation stopped at time %d in instance  %s \n",
                               tf_gettime(), tf_mipname());
      tf_dostop(); /*stop the simulation*/
    }
    else if(tf_getp(1) == 1)  /* if the argument is 0 then terminate
```

Example 13-5 User C Routine my_stop_finish Using Utility Routines (Continued)

```
                              the simulation*/
    {
      io_printf
       ("Mymessage: Simulation finished at time %d in instance  %s \n",
                                     tf_gettime(), tf_mipname());
      tf_dofinish(); /*terminate the simulation*/
    }
    else
      /* Pass warning message */
      tf_warning("Bad arguments to \$my_stop_finish at time %d\n",
                                                 tf_gettime());
  }

}
```

Link the new task into the Verilog simulator as described in Section 13.2.1, *Linking PLI Tasks*. To check the newly defined task *$my_stop_finish*, a stimulus in which *$my_stop_finish* is called with all possible combinations of arguments is applied to the **module** *mux2_to_1* described in Example 13-1 on page 281. A top-level module that instantiates the 2-to-1 multiplexer, applies stimulus, and invokes the *$my_stop_finish* task is shown below.

```
module top;
wire OUT;
reg I0, I1, S;

mux2_to_1 my_mux(OUT, I0, I1, S); //Instantiate the module mux2_to_1

initial //Apply Stimulus
begin
  I0=1'b0; I1=1'b1; S = 1'b0;
  $my_stop_finish(0); //Stop simulation. Don't print module instance name
  #5 I0=1'b1; I1=1'b1; S = 1'b1;
  $my_stop_finish(0,1); //Stop simulation. Print module instance name
  #5 I0=1'b0; I1=1'b1; S = 1'bx;
  $my_stop_finish(2,1); //Pass bad argument 2 to the task
  #5 I0=1'b1; I1=1'b1; S = 1'b1;
  $my_stop_finish(1,1); //Terminate simulation. Print module instance
                        //name
end
```

```
endmodule
```

The output of the simulation with a Verilog simulator is shown below.

```
Mymessage: Simulation stopped at time 0
Type ? for help
C1 > .
Mymessage: Simulation stopped at time 5 in instance  top
C1 > .
"my_stop_finish.v", 14: warning! Bad arguments to $my_stop_finish at time
10

Mymessage: Simulation finished at time 15 in instance  top
```

13.5 Summary

In this chapter, we described the Programming Language Interface (PLI) for Verilog. The following aspects were discussed:

- PLI Interface provides a set of C interface routines to read, write, and extract information about the internal data structures of the design. Designers can write their own system tasks to do various useful functions.
- PLI Interface can be used for monitors, debuggers, translators, delay calculators, automatic stimulus generators, dump file generators, and other useful utilities.
- A *user-defined system task* is implemented with a corresponding *user-defined C routine*. The C routine uses PLI library calls.
- The process of informing the simulator that a new user-defined system task is attached to a corresponding user C routine is called *linking*. Different simulators handle the linking process differently.
- User-defined system tasks are invoked like standard Verilog system tasks, e.g., *$hello_verilog(); .* The corresponding user C routine *hello_verilog* is executed whenever the task is invoked.
- A design is represented internally in a Verilog simulator as a big data structure with sets for objects. PLI library routines allow access to the internal data structures.

- *Access (acc) routines* and *utility (tf) routines* are two types of PLI library routines.
- Utility routines represent the *first* generation of Verilog PLI. Utility routines are used to pass data back and forth across the boundary of user C routines and the original Verilog design. Utility routines start with the prefix *tf_*. Utility routines do not interact with object handles.
- Access routines represent the *second* generation of Verilog PLI. Access routines can read and write information about a particular object from/to the design. Access routines start with the prefix *acc_*. Access routines are used primarily across the boundary of user C routines and internal data representation. Access routines interact with object handles.
- *Value change link (VCL)* is a special category of access routines that allows monitoring of objects in a design. A consumer routine is executed whenever the monitored object value changes.
- Verilog Procedural Interface (VPI) routines represent the *third* generation of Verilog PLI. VPI routines provide a superset of the functionality of **`acc_`** and **`tf_`** routines. VPI routines are not covered in this book.

Programming Language Interface is a very broad area of study. Thus, only the basics of Verilog PLI are covered in this chapter. Designers should consult the *IEEE Standard Verilog Hardware Description Language* document for details of PLI.

13.6 Exercises

Refer to Appendix B, *List of PLI Routines,* and the *IEEE Standard Verilog Hardware Description Language* document for a list of PLI access and utility routines, their function, and usage. You will need to use some PLI library calls that were not discussed in this chapter.

1. Write a user-defined system task, *$get_in_ports,* that gets full hierarchical names of only the input ports of a module instance. Hierarchical module instance name is the input to the task. (Hint: Use the C routine in Example 13-2 as a reference.) Link the task into the Verilog simulator. Find the input ports of the 1-bit full adder defined in Example 5-7 on page 75.
2. Write a user-defined system task, *$count_and_gates,* which counts the number of **`and`** gate primitives in a module instance. Hierarchical module instance name is the input to the task. Use this task to count the number of **`and`** gates in the 4-to-1 multiplexer in Example 5-5.

3. Create a user-defined system task, *$monitor_mod_output,* that finds out all the output signals of a module instance and adds them to a monitoring list. The line "*Output signal has changed*" should appear whenever any output signal of the module changes value. (Hint: Use *VCL* routines.) Use the 2-to-1 multiplexer in Example 13-1. Add output signals to the monitoring list by using *$monitor_mod_output*. Check results by applying stimulus.

Logic Synthesis with Verilog HDL 14

Advances in logic synthesis have pushed HDLs into the forefront of digital design technology. Logic synthesis tools have cut design cycle times significantly. Designers can design at a high level of abstraction and thus reduce design time. In this chapter, we discuss logic synthesis with Verilog HDL. Synopsys synthesis products were used for the examples in this chapter, and results for individual examples may vary with synthesis tools. However, the concepts discussed in this chapter are general enough to be applied to any logic synthesis tool.[1] This chapter is intended to give the reader a basic understanding of the mechanics and issues involved in logic synthesis. It is not intended to be comprehensive material on logic synthesis. Detailed knowledge of logic synthesis can be obtained from reference manuals, logic synthesis books, and by attending training classes.

Learning Objectives

- Define logic synthesis and explain the benefits of logic synthesis.
- Identify Verilog HDL constructs and operators accepted in logic synthesis. Understand how the logic synthesis tool interprets these constructs.
- Explain a typical design flow, using logic synthesis. Describe the components in the logic synthesis-based design flow.
- Describe verification of the gate-level netlist produced by logic synthesis.
- Understand techniques for writing efficient RTL descriptions.
- Describe partitioning techniques to help logic synthesis provide the optimal gate-level netlist.
- Design combinational and sequential circuits, using logic synthesis.

1. Many EDA vendors now offer logic synthesis tools. Please see the reference documentation provided with your logic synthesis tool for details on how to synthesize RTL to gates. There may be minor variations from the material presented in this chapter.

14

14.1 What Is Logic Synthesis?

Simply speaking, *logic synthesis* is the process of converting a high-level description of the design into an optimized gate-level representation, given a *standard cell library* and certain design constraints. A standard cell library can have simple cells, such as basic logic gates like **`and`**, **`or`**, and **`nor`**, or macro cells, such as adders, muxes, and special flip-flops. A standard cell library is also known as the *technology library*. It is discussed in detail later in this chapter.

Logic synthesis always existed even in the days of schematic gate-level design, but it was always done inside the designer's mind. The designer would first understand the architectural description. Then he would consider design constraints such as *timing, area, testability,* and *power*. The designer would partition the design into high-level blocks, draw them on a piece of paper or a computer terminal, and describe the functionality of the circuit. This was the *high-level description.* Finally, each block would be implemented on a hand-drawn schematic, using the cells available in the standard cell library. The last step was the most complex process in the design flow and required several time-consuming design iterations before an optimized gate-level representation that met all design constraints was obtained. Thus, the *designer's mind* was used as the logic synthesis tool, as illustrated in Figure 14-1.

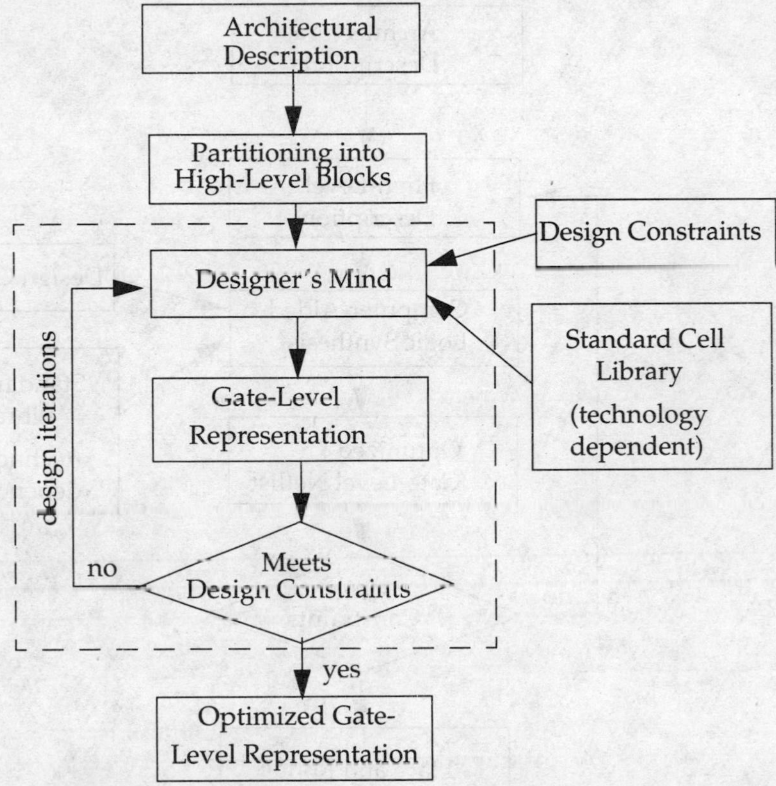

Figure 14-1 Designer's Mind as the Logic Synthesis Tool

The advent of *computer-aided logic synthesis tools* has automated the process of converting the high-level description to logic gates. Instead of trying to perform logic synthesis in their minds, designers can now concentrate on the architectural trade-offs, high-level description of the design, accurate design constraints, and optimization of cells in the standard cell library. These are fed to the computer-aided logic synthesis tool, which performs several iterations internally and generates the optimized gate-level description. Also, instead of drawing the high-level description on a screen or a piece of paper, designers describe the high-level design in terms of HDLs. Verilog HDL has become one of the popular HDLs for the writing of high-level descriptions. Figure 14-2 illustrates the process.

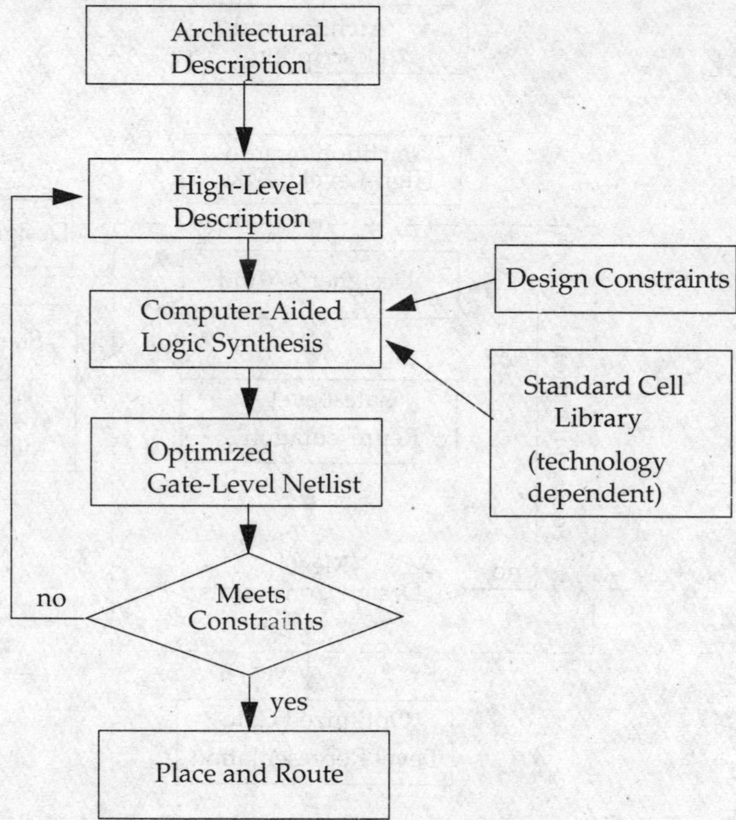

Figure 14-2 Basic Computer-Aided Logic Synthesis Process

Automated logic synthesis has significantly reduced time for conversion from high-level design representation to gates. This has allowed designers to spend more time on designing at a higher level of representation, because less time is required for converting the design to gates.

14.2 Impact of Logic Synthesis

Logic synthesis has revolutionized the digital design industry by significantly improving productivity and by reducing design cycle time. Before the days of automated logic synthesis, when designs were converted to gates manually, the design process had the following limitations:

- For large designs, manual conversion was prone to human error. A small gate missed somewhere could mean redesign of entire blocks.
- The designer could never be sure that the design constraints were going to be met until the gate-level implementation was completed and tested.
- A significant portion of the design cycle was dominated by the time taken to convert a high-level design into gates.
- If the gate-level design did not meet requirements, the turnaround time for redesign of blocks was very high.
- *What-if* scenarios were hard to verify. For example, the designer designed a block in gates that could run at a cycle time of 20 ns. If the designer wanted to find out whether the circuit could be optimized to run faster at 15 ns, the entire block had to be redesigned. Thus, redesign was needed to verify *what-if* scenarios.
- Each designer would implement design blocks differently. There was little consistency in design styles. For large designs, this could mean that smaller blocks were optimized, but the overall design was not optimal.
- If a bug was found in the final, gate-level design, this would sometimes require the redesign of thousands of gates.
- Timing, area, and power dissipation in library cells are fabrication-technology specific. Thus if the company changed the IC fabrication vendor after the gate-level design was complete, this would mean the redesign of the entire circuit and a possible change in design methodology.
- Design reuse was not possible. Designs were technology-specific, hard to port, and very difficult to reuse.

Automated logic synthesis tools addressed these problems as follows:

- High-level design is less prone to human error because designs are described at a higher level of abstraction.

- High-level design is done without significant concern about design constraints. Logic synthesis will convert a high-level design to a gate-level netlist and ensure that all constraints have been met. If not, the designer goes back, modifies the high-level design and repeats the process until a gate-level netlist that satisfies timing, area, and power constraints is obtained.
- Conversion from high-level design to gates is fast. With this improvement, design cycle times are shortened considerably. What took months before can now be done in hours or days.
- Turnaround time for redesign of blocks is shorter because changes are required only at the register-transfer level; then, the design is simply resynthesized to obtain the gate-level netlist.
- *What-if* scenarios are easy to verify. The high-level description does not change. The designer has merely to change the timing constraint from 20 ns to 15 ns and resynthesize the design to get the new gate-level netlist that is optimized to achieve a cycle time of 15 ns.
- Logic synthesis tools optimize the design as a whole. This removes the problem with varied designer styles for the different blocks in the design and suboptimal designs.
- If a bug is found in the gate-level design, the designer goes back and changes the high-level description to eliminate the bug. Then, the high-level description is again read into the logic synthesis tool to automatically generate a new gate-level description.
- Logic synthesis tools allow *technology-independent* design. A high-level description may be written without the IC fabrication technology in mind. Logic synthesis tools convert the design to gates, using cells in the standard cell library provided by an IC fabrication vendor. If the technology changes or the IC fabrication vendor changes, designers simply use logic synthesis to retarget the design to gates, using the standard cell library for the new technology.
- Design reuse is possible for technology-independent descriptions. For example, if the functionality of the I/O block in a microprocessor does not change, the RTL description of the I/O block can be reused in the design of derivative microprocessors. If the technology changes, the synthesis tool simply maps to the desired technology.

14.3 Verilog HDL Synthesis

For the purpose of logic synthesis, designs are currently written in an HDL at a *register transfer level (RTL)*. The term RTL is used for an HDL description style that utilizes a combination of data flow and behavioral constructs. Logic synthesis tools take the register transfer-level HDL description and convert it to an optimized gate-level netlist. Verilog and VHDL are the two most popular HDLs used to describe the functionality at the RTL level. In this chapter, we discuss RTL-based logic synthesis with Verilog HDL. Behavioral synthesis tools that convert a behavioral description into an RTL description are slowly evolving, but RTL-based synthesis is currently the most popular design method. Thus, we will address only RTL-based synthesis in this chapter.

14.3.1 Verilog Constructs

Not all constructs can be used when writing a description for a logic synthesis tool. In general, any construct that is used to define a cycle-by-cycle RTL description is acceptable to the logic synthesis tool. A list of constructs that are typically accepted by logic synthesis tools is given in Table 14-1. The capabilities of individual logic synthesis tools may vary. The constructs that are typically acceptable to logic synthesis tools are also shown.

Table 14-1 Verilog HDL Constructs for Logic Synthesis

Construct Type	Keyword or Description	Notes
ports	input, inout, output	
parameters	parameter	
module definition	module	
signals and variables	wire, reg, tri	Vectors are allowed
instantiation	module instances, primitive gate instances	E.g., mymux m1(out, i0, i1, s); E.g., nand (out, a, b);
functions and tasks	function, task	Timing constructs ignored
procedural	always, if, then, else, case, casex, casez	initial is not supported
procedural blocks	begin, end, named blocks, disable	Disabling of named blocks allowed
data flow	assign	Delay information is ignored
loops	for, while, forever,	while and forever loops must contain @(posedge clk) or @(negedge clk)

Remember that we are providing a cycle-by-cycle RTL description of the circuit. Hence, there are restrictions on the way these constructs are used for the logic synthesis tool. For example, the **while** and **forever** loops must be broken by a @ *(posedge clock)* or @ *(negedge clock)* statement to enforce cycle-by-cycle behavior and to prevent combinational feedback. Another restriction is that logic synthesis ignores all timing delays specified by #<*delay*> construct. Therefore, pre- and post-synthesis Verilog simulation results may not match. The designer must use a description style that eliminates these mismatches. Also, the **initial** construct is not supported by logic synthesis tools. Instead, the designer must use a reset mechanism to initialize the signals in the circuit.

It is recommended that all signal widths and variable widths be explicitly specified. Defining unsized variables can result in large, gate-level netlists because synthesis tools can infer unnecessary logic based on the variable definition.

14.3.2 Verilog Operators

Almost all operators in Verilog are allowed for logic synthesis. Table 14-2 is a list of the operators allowed. Only operators such as **===** and **!==** that are related to **x** and **z** are not allowed, because equality with **x** and **z** does not have much meaning in logic synthesis. While writing expressions, it is recommended that you use parentheses to group logic the way you want it to appear. If you rely on operator precedence, logic synthesis tools might produce an undesirable logic structure.

Table 14-2 Verilog HDL Operators for Logic Synthesis

<table>
<tr><th>Operator Type</th><th>Operator Symbol</th><th>Operation Performed</th></tr>
<tr><td>Arithmetic</td><td>*</td><td>multiply</td></tr>
<tr><td></td><td>/</td><td>divide</td></tr>
<tr><td></td><td>+</td><td>add</td></tr>
<tr><td></td><td>-</td><td>subtract</td></tr>
<tr><td></td><td>%</td><td>modulus</td></tr>
<tr><td></td><td>+</td><td>unary plus</td></tr>
<tr><td></td><td>-</td><td>unary minus</td></tr>
<tr><td>Logical</td><td>!</td><td>logical negation</td></tr>
<tr><td></td><td>&&</td><td>logical and</td></tr>
<tr><td></td><td>||</td><td>logical or</td></tr>
<tr><td>Relational</td><td>></td><td>greater than</td></tr>
<tr><td></td><td><</td><td>less than</td></tr>
<tr><td></td><td>>=</td><td>greater than or equal</td></tr>
<tr><td></td><td><=</td><td>less than or equal</td></tr>
<tr><td>Equality</td><td>==</td><td>equality</td></tr>
<tr><td></td><td>!=</td><td>inequality</td></tr>
<tr><td>Bit-wise</td><td>~</td><td>bitwise negation</td></tr>
<tr><td></td><td>&</td><td>bitwise and</td></tr>
<tr><td></td><td>|</td><td>bitwise or</td></tr>
<tr><td></td><td>^</td><td>bitwise ex-or</td></tr>
<tr><td></td><td>^~ or ~^</td><td>bitwise ex-nor</td></tr>
</table>

Table 14-2 Verilog HDL Operators for Logic Synthesis (Continued)

Reduction	`&`
	`~&`
	`|`
	`~|`
	`^`
	`^~` or `~^`
		reduction and
		reduction nand
		reduction or
		reduction nor
		reduction ex-or
		reduction ex-nor

Shift	`>>`
	`<<`
	`>>>`
	`<<<`
		right shift
		left shift
		arithmetic right shift
		arithmetic left shift

Concatenation	`{ }`	concatenation
Conditional	`?:`	conditional

14.3.3 Interpretation of a Few Verilog Constructs

Having described the basic Verilog constructs, let us try to understand how logic synthesis tools frequently interpret these constructs and translate them to logic gates.

The assign statement

The **`assign`** construct is the most fundamental construct used to describe combinational logic at an RTL level. Given below is a logic expression that uses the **`assign`** statement.

```
assign out - (a & b) | c;
```

This will frequently translate to the following gate-level representation:

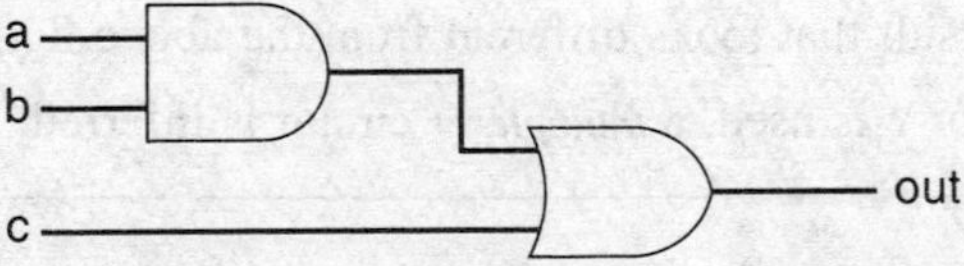

If *a, b, c,* and *out* are 2-bit vectors *[1:0]*, then the above **assign** statement will frequently translate to two identical circuits for each bit.

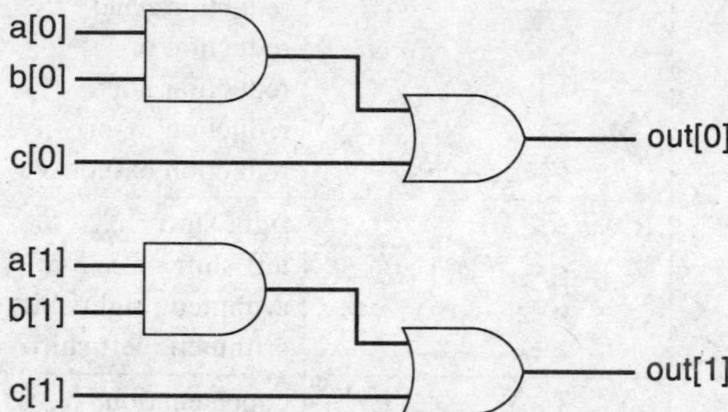

If arithmetic operators are used, each arithmetic operator is implemented in terms of arithmetic hardware blocks available to the logic synthesis tool. A 1-bit full adder is implemented below.

```
assign {c_out, sum} = a + b + c_in;
```

Assuming that the 1-bit full adder is available internally in the logic synthesis tool, the above **assign** statement is often interpreted by logic synthesis tools as follows:

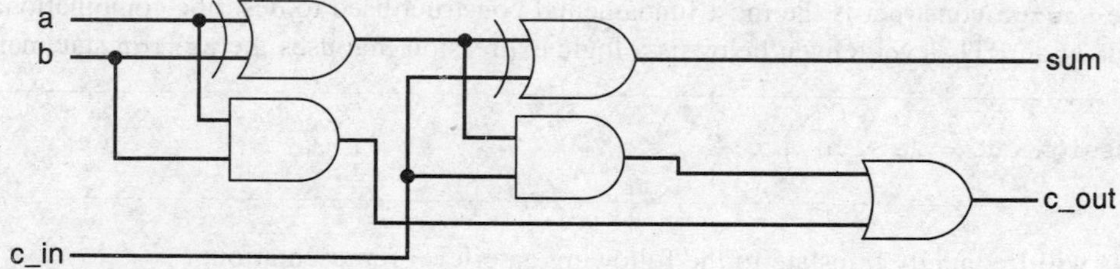

If a multiple-bit adder is synthesized, the synthesis tool will perform optimization and the designer might get a result that looks different from the above figure.

If a conditional operator **?** is used, a *multiplexer* circuit is inferred.

```
assign out = (s) ? i1 : i0;
```

It frequently translates to the gate-level representation shown in Figure 14-3.

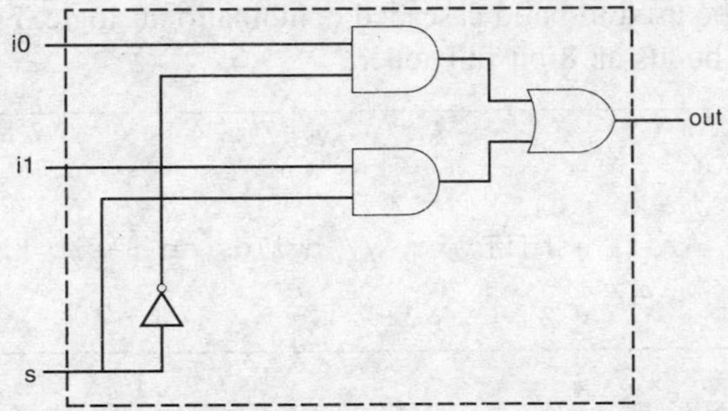

Figure 14-3 Multiplexer Description

The if-else statement

Single *if-else* statements translate to multiplexers where the control signal is the signal or variable in the **if** clause.

```
if(s)
    out = i1;
else
    out = i0;
```

The above statement will frequently translate to the gate-level description shown in Figure 14-3. In general, multiple *if-else-if* statements do not synthesize to large multiplexers.

The case statement

The **case** statement also can be used to infer multiplexers. The above multiplexer would have been inferred from the following description that uses **case** statements:

```
case (s)
    1'b0 : out = i0;
    1'b1 : out = i1;
endcase
```

Large **case** statements may be used to infer large multiplexers.

for loops

The **for** loops can be used to build cascaded combinational logic. For example, the following **for** loop builds an 8-bit full adder:

```
c = c_in;
for(i=0; i <=7; i = i + 1)
    {c, sum[i]} = a[i] + b[i] + c; // builds an 8-bit ripple adder
c_out = c;
```

The always statement

The **always** statement can be used to infer sequential and combinational logic. For sequential logic, the **always** statement must be controlled by the change in the value of a clock signal *clk*.

```
always @(posedge clk)
        q <= d;
```

This is inferred as a positive edge-triggered D-flipflop with *d* as input, *q* as output, and *clk* as the clocking signal.

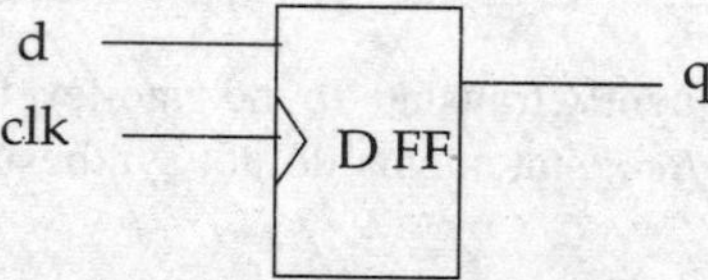

Similarly, the following Verilog description creates a level-sensitive latch:

```
always @(clk or d)
      if (clk)
          q <= d;
```

For combinational logic, the **always** statement must be triggered by a signal other than the *clk*, *reset,* or *preset*. For example, the following block will be interpreted as a 1-bit full adder:

```
always @(a or b or c_in)
        {c_out, sum} = a + b + c_in;
```

The function statement

Functions synthesize to combinational blocks with one output variable. The output might be scalar or vector. A 4-bit full adder is implemented as a function in the Verilog description below. The most significant bit of the function is used for the carry bit.

```
function [4:0] fulladd;
input [3:0] a, b;
input c_in;
begin
   fulladd = a + b + c_in; //bit 4 of fulladd for carry, bits[3:0] for sum.
end
endfunction
```

14.4 Synthesis Design Flow

Having understood how basic Verilog constructs are interpreted by the logic synthesis tool, let us now discuss the synthesis design flow from an RTL description to an optimized gate-level description.

14.4.1 RTL to Gates

To fully utilize the benefits of logic synthesis, the designer must first understand the flow from the high-level RTL description to a gate-level netlist. Figure 14-4 explains that flow.

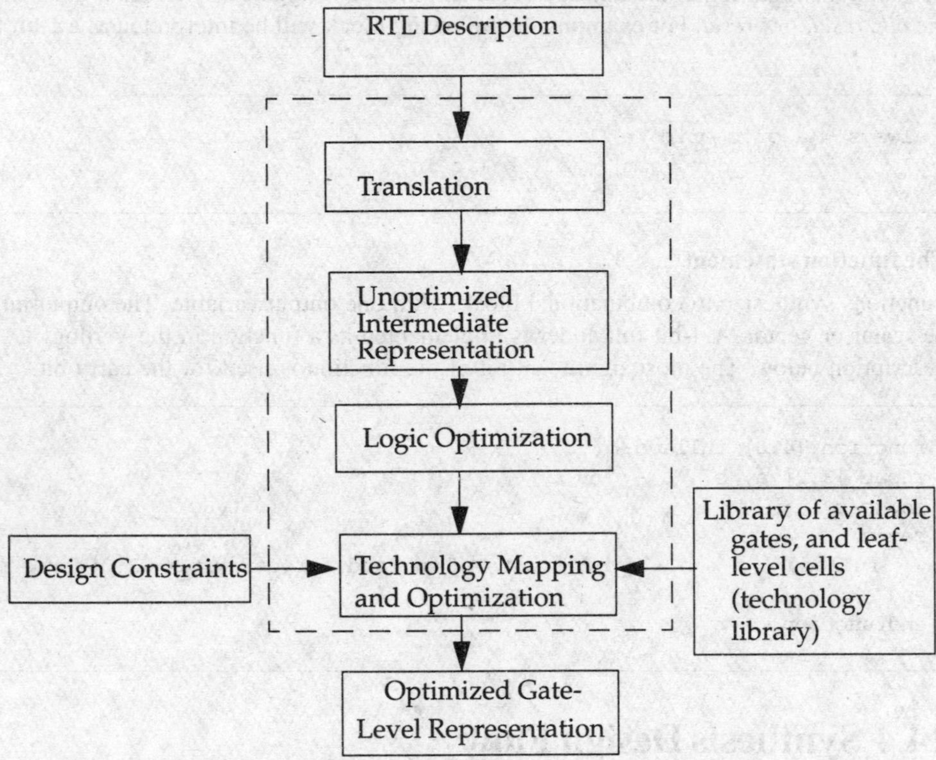

Figure 14-4 Logic Synthesis Flow from RTL to Gates

Let us discuss each component of the flow in detail.

RTL description

The designer describes the design at a high level by using RTL constructs. The designer spends time in functional verification to ensure that the RTL description functions correctly. After the functionality is verified, the RTL description is input to the logic synthesis tool.

Translation

The RTL description is converted by the logic synthesis tool to an unoptimized, intermediate, internal representation. This process is called *translation*. Translation is relatively simple and uses techniques similar to those discussed in Section 14.3.3, *Interpretation of a Few Verilog Constructs*. The translator understands the basic primitives and operators in the Verilog RTL description. Design constraints such as area, timing, and power are not considered in the translation process. At this point, the logic synthesis tool does a simple allocation of internal resources.

Unoptimized intermediate representation

The translation process yields an *unoptimized intermediate representation* of the design. The design is represented internally by the logic synthesis tool in terms of internal data structures. The unoptimized intermediate representation is incomprehensible to the user.

Logic optimization

The logic is now optimized to remove redundant logic. Various technology-independent boolean logic optimization techniques are used. This process is called *logic optimization*. It is a very important step in logic synthesis, and it yields an *optimized internal representation* of the design.

Technology mapping and optimization

Until this step, the design description is independent of a specific *target technology*. In this step, the synthesis tool takes the internal representation and implements the representation in gates, using the cells provided in the technology library. In other words, the design is *mapped* to the desired *target technology*.

Suppose you want to get your IC chip fabricated at ABC Inc. ABC Inc. has 0.65 micron CMOS technology, which it calls *abc_100* technology. Then, abc_100 becomes the target technology. You must therefore implement your internal design representation in gates, using the cells provided inthe abc_100 technology library. This is called *technology mapping*. Also, the implementation should satisfy such design constraints as timing, area, and power. Some local optimizations are done to achieve the best results for the target technology. This is called *technology optimization* or *technology-dependent optimization.*

Technology library

The *technology library* contains *library cells* provided by ABC Inc. The term *standard cell library* used earlier in the chapter and the term *technology library* are identical and are used interchangeably.

To build a technology library, ABC Inc. decides on the range of functionality to provide in its library cells. As discussed earlier, library cells can be basic logic gates or macro cells such as adders, ALUs, multiplexers, and special flipflops. The library cells are the basic building blocks that ABC Inc. will use for IC fabrication. Physical layout of library cells is done first. Then, the area of each cell is computed from the cell layout. Next, modeling techniques are used to estimate the timing and power characteristics of each library cell. This process is called *cell characterization.*

Finally, each cell is described in a format that is understood by the synthesis tool. The cell description contains information about the following:

- Functionality of the cell
- Area of the cell layout
- Timing information about the cell
- Power information about the cell

A collection of these cells is called the *technology library*. The synthesis tool uses these cells to implement the design. The quality of results from synthesis tools will typically be dominated by the cells available in the technology library. If the choice of cells in the technology library is limited, the synthesis tool cannot do much in terms of optimization for timing, area, and power.

Design constraints

Design constraints typically include the following:

- *Timing*—The circuit must meet certain timing requirements. An internal static timing analyzer checks timing.
- *Area*—The area of the final layout must not exceed a limit.
- *Power*—The power dissipation in the circuit must not exceed a threshold.

In general, there is an inverse relationship between area and timing constraints. For a given technology library, to optimize timing (faster circuits), the design has to be parallelized, which typically means that larger circuits have to be built. To build smaller circuits, designers must generally compromise on circuit speed. The inverse relationship is shown in Figure 14-5.

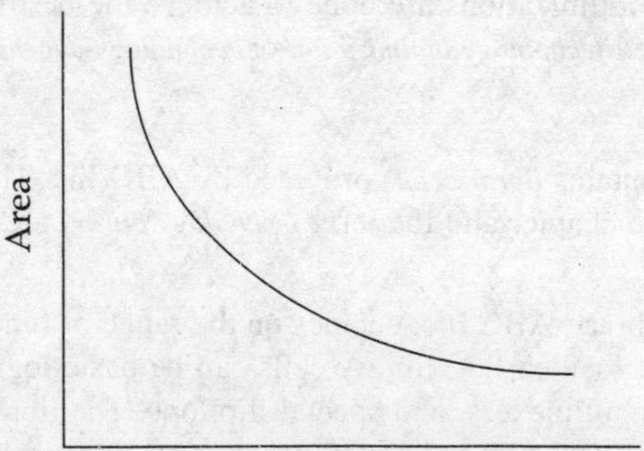

Figure 14-5 Area vs. Timing Trade-off

On top of design constraints, *operating environment factors,* such as input and output delays, drive strengths, and loads, will affect the optimization for the target technology. Operating environment factors must be input to the logic synthesis tool to ensure that circuits are optimized for the required operating environment.

Optimized gate-level description

After the technology mapping is complete, an optimized gate-level netlist described in terms of target technology components is produced. If this netlist meets the required constraints, it is handed to ABC Inc. for final layout. Otherwise, the designer modifies the RTL or reconstrains the design to achieve the desired results. This process is iterated until the netlist meets the required constraints. ABC Inc. will do the layout, do timing checks to ensure that the circuit meets required timing after layout, and then fabricate the IC chip for you.

There are three points to note about the synthesis flow.

1. For very high-speed circuits like microprocessors, vendor technology libraries may yield nonoptimal results. Instead, design groups obtain information about the fabrication process used by the vendor, for example, 0.65 micron CMOS process, and build their own technology library components. Cell characterization is done by the designers. Discussion about building technology libraries and cell characterization is beyond the scope of this book.
2. Translation, logic optimization, and technology mapping are done *internally* in the logic synthesis tool and are not visible to the designer. The technology library is given to the designer. Once the technology is chosen, the designer can control only the input RTL description and design constraint specification. Thus, writing efficient RTL descriptions, specifying design constraints accurately, evaluating design trade-offs, and having a good technology library are very important to produce optimal digital circuits when using logic synthesis.
3. For submicron designs, interconnect delays are becoming a dominating factor in the overall delay. Therefore, as geometries shrink, in order to accurately model interconnect delays, synthesis tools will need to have a tighter link to layout, right at the RTL level. Timing analyzers built into synthesis tools will have to account for interconnect delays in the total delay calculation.

14.4.2 An Example of RTL-to-Gates

Let us discuss synthesis of a 4-bit magnitude comparator to understand each step in the synthesis flow. Steps of the synthesis flow such as translation, logic optimization, and technology mapping are not visible to us as designers. Therefore, we will concentrate on the components that are visible to the designer, such as the RTL description, technology library, design constraints, and the final, optimized, gate-level description.

Design specification

A magnitude comparator checks if one number is greater than, equal to, or less than another number. Design a 4-bit magnitude comparator IC chip that has the following specifications:

- The name of the design is magnitude_comparator
- Inputs *A* and *B* are 4-bit inputs. No **x** or **z** values will appear on *A* and *B* inputs
- Output *A_gt_B* is true if *A is greater than B*
- Output *A_lt_B* is true if *A is less than B*
- Output *A_eq_B* is true if *A is equal to B*
- The magnitude comparator circuit must be as fast as possible. Area can be compromised for speed.

RTL description

The RTL description that describes the magnitude comparator is shown in Example 14-1. This is a technology-independent description. The designer does not have to worry about the target technology at this point.

Example 14-1 RTL for Magnitude Comparator

```
//Module magnitude comparator
module magnitude_comparator(A_gt_B, A_lt_B, A_eq_B, A, B);

//Comparison output
output A_gt_B, A_lt_B, A_eq_B;

//4-bits numbers input
input [3:0] A, B;

assign A_gt_B = (A > B); //A greater than B
assign A_lt_B = (A < B); //A less than B
assign A_eq_B = (A == B); //A equal to B

endmodule
```

Notice that the RTL description is very concise.

Technology library

We decide to use the 0.65 micron CMOS process called *abc_100* used by ABC Inc. to make our IC chip. ABC Inc. supplies a technology library for synthesis. The library contains the following library cells. The library cells are defined in a format understood by the synthesis tool.

```
//Library cells for abc_100 technology

VNAND//2-input nand gate
```

```
(Continued...)
VAND//2-input and gate
VNOR//2-input nor gate
VOR//2-input or gate
VNOT//not gate
VBUF//buffer
NDFF//Negative edge triggered D flipflop
PDFF//Positive edge triggered D flipflop
```

Functionality, timing, area, and power dissipation information of each library cell are specified in the technology library.

Design constraints

According to the specification, the design should be as fast as possible for the target technology, abc_100. There are no area constraints. Thus, there is only one design constraint.

- Optimize the final circuit for fastest timing

Logic synthesis

The RTL description of the magnitude comparator is read by the logic synthesis tool. The design constraints and technology library for abc_100 are provided to the logic synthesis tool. The logic synthesis tool performs the necessary optimizations and produces a gate-level description optimized for abc_100 technology.

Final, Optimized, Gate-Level Description

The logic synthesis tool produces a final, gate-level description. The schematic for the gate-level circuit is shown in Figure 14-6.

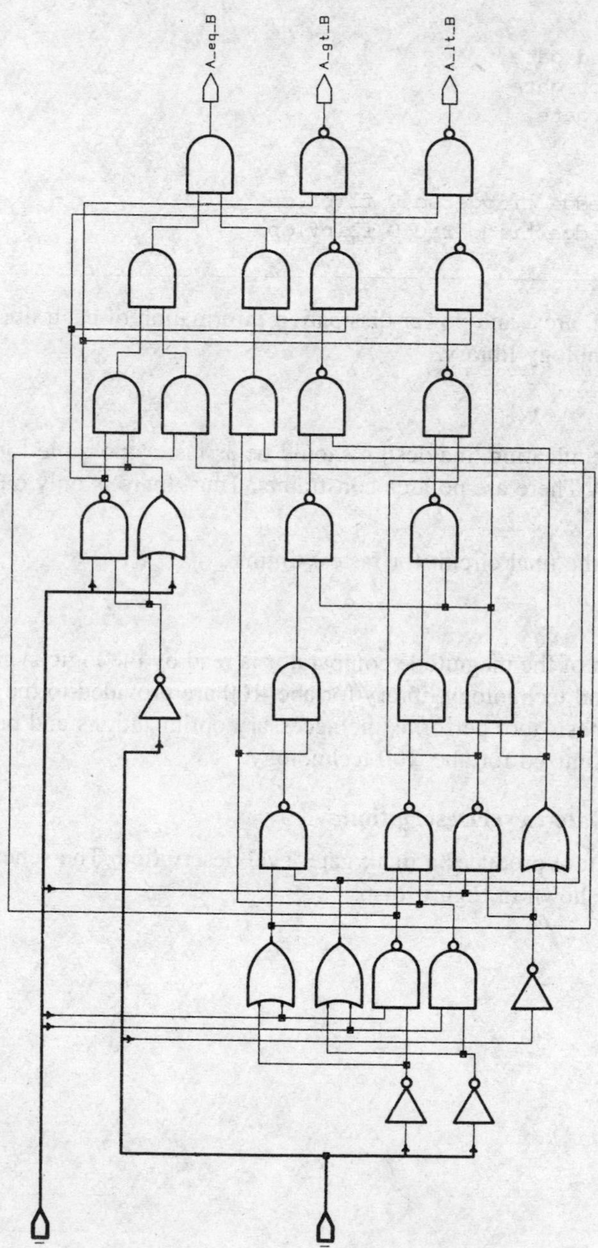

Figure 14-6 Gate-Level Schematic for the Magnitude Comparator

The gate-level Verilog description produced by the logic synthesis tool for the circuit is shown in Example 14-2. Ports are connected *by name.*

Example 14-2 Gate-Level Description for the Magnitude Comparator

```
module magnitude_comparator ( A_gt_B, A_lt_B, A_eq_B, A, B );
input  [3:0] A;
input  [3:0] B;
output A_gt_B, A_lt_B, A_eq_B;
    wire n60, n61, n62, n50, n63, n51, n64, n52, n65, n40, n53,
         n41, n54, n42, n55, n43, n56, n44, n57, n45, n58, n46,
         n59, n47, n48, n49, n38, n39;
    VAND U7 ( .in0(n48), .in1(n49), .out(n38) );
    VAND U8 ( .in0(n51), .in1(n52), .out(n50) );
    VAND U9 ( .in0(n54), .in1(n55), .out(n53) );
    VNOT U30 ( .in(A[2]), .out(n62) );
    VNOT U31 ( .in(A[1]), .out(n59) );
    VNOT U32 ( .in(A[0]), .out(n60) );
    VNAND U20 ( .in0(B[2]), .in1(n62), .out(n45) );
    VNAND U21 ( .in0(n61), .in1(n45), .out(n63) );
    VNAND U22 ( .in0(n63), .in1(n42), .out(n41) );
    VAND U10 ( .in0(n55), .in1(n52), .out(n47) );
    VOR U23 ( .in0(n60), .in1(B[0]), .out(n57) );
    VAND U11 ( .in0(n56), .in1(n57), .out(n49) );
    VNAND U24 ( .in0(n57), .in1(n52), .out(n54) );
    VAND U12 ( .in0(n40), .in1(n42), .out(n48) );
    VNAND U25 ( .in0(n53), .in1(n44), .out(n64) );
    VOR U13 ( .in0(n58), .in1(B[3]), .out(n42) );
    VOR U26 ( .in0(n62), .in1(B[2]), .out(n46) );
    VNAND U14 ( .in0(B[3]), .in1(n58), .out(n40) );
    VNAND U27 ( .in0(n64), .in1(n46), .out(n65) );
    VNAND U15 ( .in0(B[1]), .in1(n59), .out(n55) );
    VNAND U28 ( .in0(n65), .in1(n40), .out(n43) );
    VOR U16 ( .in0(n59), .in1(B[1]), .out(n52) );
   VNOT U29 ( .in(A[3]), .out(n58) );
    VNAND U17 ( .in0(B[0]), .in1(n60), .out(n56) );
    VNAND U18 ( .in0(n56), .in1(n55), .out(n51) );
    VNAND U19 ( .in0(n50), .in1(n44), .out(n61) );
    VAND U2 ( .in0(n38), .in1(n39), .out(A_eq_B) );
    VNAND U3 ( .in0(n40), .in1(n41), .out(A_lt_B) );
    VNAND U4 ( .in0(n42), .in1(n43), .out(A_gt_B) );
    VAND U5 ( .in0(n45), .in1(n46), .out(n44) );
    VAND U6 ( .in0(n47), .in1(n44), .out(n39) );
endmodule
```

If the designer decides to use another technology, say, *xyz_100* from XYZ Inc., because it is a better technology, the RTL description and design constraints do not change. Only the technology library changes. Thus, to map to a new technology, a logic synthesis tool simply reads the unchanged RTL description, unchanged design constraints, and new technology library and creates a new, optimized, gate-level netlist.

Note that if automated logic synthesis were not available, choosing a new technology would require the designer to redesign and reoptimize by hand the gate-level netlist in Example 14-2.

IC Fabrication

The gate-level netlist is verified for functionality and timing and then submitted to ABC Inc. ABC Inc. does the chip layout, checks that the post-layout circuit meets timing requirements, and then fabricates the IC chip, using abc_100 technology.

14.5 Verification of the Gate-Level Netlist

The optimized gate-level netlist produced by the logic synthesis tool must be verified for functionality. Also, the synthesis tool may not always be able to meet both timing and area requirements if they are too stringent. Thus, a separate timing verification can be done on the gate-level netlist.

14.5.1 Functional Verification

Identical stimulus is run with the original RTL and synthesized gate-level descriptions of the design. The output is compared to find any mismatches. For the magnitude comparator, a sample stimulus file is shown in Example 14-3.

Example 14-3 Stimulus for Magnitude Comparator

```
module stimulus;

reg [3:0] A, B;
wire A_GT_B, A_LT_B, A_EQ_B;

//Instantiate the magnitude comparator
magnitude_comparator MC(A_GT_B, A_LT_B, A_EQ_B, A, B);

initial
  $monitor($time," A = %b, B = %b, A_GT_B = %b, A_LT_B = %b, A_EQ_B = %b",
        A, B, A_GT_B, A_LT_B, A_EQ_B);

//stimulate the magnitude comparator.
```

Example 14-3 *Stimulus for Magnitude Comparator (Continued)*

```
initial
begin
  A = 4'b1010; B = 4'b1001;
  # 10 A = 4'b1110; B = 4'b1111;
  # 10 A = 4'b0000; B = 4'b0000;
  # 10 A = 4'b1000; B = 4'b1100;
  # 10 A = 4'b0110; B = 4'b1110;
  # 10 A = 4'b1110; B = 4'b1110;
end

endmodule
```

The same stimulus is applied to both the RTL description in Example 14-1 and the synthesized gate-level description in Example 14-2, and the simulation output is compared for mismatches. However, there is an additional consideration. The gate-level description is in terms of library cells *VAND, VNAND,* etc. Verilog simulators do not understand the meaning of these cells. Thus, to simulate the gate level description, a *simulation library, abc_100.v*, must be provided by ABC Inc. The simulation library must describe cells *VAND, VNAND,* etc., in terms of Verilog HDL primitives **and**, **nand**, etc. For example, the *VAND* cell will be defined in the simulation library as shown in Example 14-4.

Example 14-4 *Simulation Library*

```
//Simulation Library abc_100.v. Extremely simple. No timing checks.

module VAND (out, in0, in1);
input in0;
input in1;
output out;

//timing information, rise/fall and min:typ:max
specify
(in0 => out) = (0.260604:0.513000:0.955206, 0.255524:0.503000:0.936586);
(in1 => out) = (0.260604:0.513000:0.955206, 0.255524:0.503000:0.936586);
endspecify

//instantiate a Verilog HDL primitive
and (out, in0, in1);
endmodule
...
```

Example 14-4 *Simulation Library (Continued)*

```
//All library cells will have corresponding module definitions
//in terms of Verilog primitives.
...
```

Stimulus is applied to the RTL description and the gate-level description. A typical invocation with a Verilog simulator is shown below.

```
//Apply stimulus to RTL description
> verilog stimulus.v mag_compare.v

//Apply stimulus to gate-level description.
//Include simulation library "abc_100.v" using the -v option
> verilog stimulus.v mag_compare.gv -v abc_100.v
```

The simulation output must be identical for the two simulations. In our case, the output is identical. For the example of the magnitude comparator, the output is shown in Example 14-5.

Example 14-5 *Output from Simulation of Magnitude Comparator*

```
 0 A = 1010, B = 1001, A_GT_B = 1, A_LT_B = 0, A_EQ_B = 0
10 A = 1110, B = 1111, A_GT_B = 0, A_LT_B = 1, A_EQ_B = 0
20 A = 0000, B = 0000, A_GT_B = 0, A_LT_B = 0, A_EQ_B = 1
30 A = 1000, B = 1100, A_GT_B = 0, A_LT_B = 1, A_EQ_B = 0
40 A = 0110, B = 1110, A_GT_B = 0, A_LT_B = 1, A_EQ_B = 0
50 A = 1110, B = 1110, A_GT_B = 0, A_LT_B = 0, A_EQ_B = 1
```

If the output is not identical, the designer needs to check for any potential bugs and rerun the whole flow until all bugs are eliminated.

Comparing simulation output of an RTL and a gate-level netlist is only a part of the functional verification process. Various techniques are used to ensure that the gate-level netlist produced by logic synthesis is functionally correct. One technique is to write a high-level architectural description in C++. The output obtained by executing the high-level architectural description is compared against the simulation output of the RTL or the gate-level description. Another technique called *equivalence checking* is also frequently used. It is discussed in greater detail in Section 15.3.2, *Equivalence Checking*, in this book.

Timing verification

The gate-level netlist is typically checked for timing by use of *timing simulation* or by a *static timing verifier*. If any timing constraints are violated, the designer must either redesign part of the RTL or make trade-offs in design constraints for logic synthesis. The entire flow is iterated until timing requirements are met. Details of static timing verifiers are beyond the scope of this book. Timing simulation is discussed in Chapter 10, *Timing and Delays*.

14.6 Modeling Tips for Logic Synthesis

The Verilog RTL design style used by the designer affects the final gate-level netlist produced by logic synthesis. Logic synthesis can produce efficient or inefficient gate-level netlists, based on the style of RTL descriptions. Hence, the designer must be aware of techniques used to write efficient circuit descriptions. In this section, we provide tips about modeling trade-offs, for the designer to write efficient, synthesizable Verilog descriptions.

14.6.1 Verilog Coding Style[2]

The style of the Verilog description greatly affects the final design. For logic synthesis, it is important to consider actual hardware implementation issues. The RTL specification should be as close to the desired structure as possible without sacrificing the benefits of a high level of abstraction. There is a trade-off between the level of design abstraction and control over the structure of the logic synthesis output. Designing at a very high level of abstraction can cause logic with undesirable structure to be generated by the synthesis tool. Designing at a very low level (e.g., hand instantiation of each cell) causes the designer to lose the benefits of high-level design and technology independence. Also, a "good" style will vary among logic synthesis tools. However, many principles are common across logic synthesis tools. Listed below are some guidelines that the designer should consider while designing at the RTL level.

---

2. Verilog coding style suggestions may vary slightly based on your logic synthesis tool. However, the suggestions included in this chapter are applicable to most cases. The "IEEE Standard Verilog Hardware Description Language" document also adds a new language construct called `attribute`. Attributes such as full_case, parallel_case, state_variable, and optimize can be included in the Verilog HDL specification of the design. These attributes are used by synthesis tools to guide the synthesis process.

Use meaningful names for signals and variables

Names of signals and variables should be meaningful so that the code becomes self-commented and readable.

Avoid mixing positive and negative edge-triggered flipflops

Mixing positive and negative edge-triggered flipflops may introduce inverters and buffers into the clock tree. This is often undesirable because clock skews are introduced in the circuit.

Use basic building blocks vs. use continuous assign statements

Trade-offs exist between using basic building blocks versus using continuous **assign** statements in the RTL description. Continuous **assign** statements are a very concise way of representing the functionality and they generally do a good job of generating random logic. However, the final logic structure is not necessarily symmetrical. Instantiation of basic building blocks creates symmetric designs, and the logic synthesis tool is able to optimize smaller modules more effectively. However, instantiation of building blocks is not a concise way to describe the design; it inhibits retargeting to alternate technologies, and generally there is a degradation in simulator performance.

Assume that a 2-to-1, 8-bit multiplexer is defined as a module *mux2_1L8* in the design. If a 32-bit multiplexer is needed, it can be built by instantiating 8-bit multiplexers rather than by using the **assign** statement.

```
//Style 1: 32-bit mux using assign statement
module mux2_1L32(out, a, b, select);
output [31:0] out;
input [31:0] a, b;
wire select;

assign out = select ? a : b;
endmodule

//Style 2: 32-bit multiplexer using basic building blocks
//If 8-bit muxes are defined earlier in the design, instantiating
//these muxes is more efficient for
//synthesis. Fewer gates, faster design.
//Less efficient for simulation
module mux2_1L32(out, a, b, select);
output [31:0] out;
input [31:0] a, b;
wire select;
```

```
(Continued...)
mux2_1L8 m0(out[7:0], a[7:0], b[7:0], select); //bits 7 through 0
mux2_1L8 m1(out[15:7], a[15:7], b[ 15:7], select); //bits 15 through 7
mux2_1L8 m2(out[23:16], a[23:16], b[23:16], select); //bits 23 through 16
mux2_1L8 m3(out[31:24], a[31:24], b[31:24], select); //bits 31 through 24

endmodule
```

Instantiate multiplexers vs. use if-else or case statements

We discussed in Section 14.3.3, *Interpretation of a Few Verilog Constructs*, that **`if-else`** and **`case`** statements are frequently synthesized to multiplexers in hardware. If a structured implementation is needed, it is better to implement a block directly by using multiplexers, because **`if-else`** or **`case`** statements can cause undesired random logic to be generated by the synthesis tool. Instantiating a multiplexer gives better control and faster synthesis, but it has the disadvantage of technology dependence and a longer RTL description. On the other hand, **`if-else`** and **`case`** statements can represent multiplexers very concisely and are used to create technology-independent RTL descriptions.

Use parentheses to optimize logic structure

The designer can control the final structure of logic by using parentheses to group logic. Using parentheses also improves readability of the Verilog description.

```
//translates to 3 adders in series
out = a + b + c + d;

//translates to 2 adders in parallel with one final adder to sum results
out = (a + b) + (c + d) ;
```

Use arithmetic operators *, /, and % vs. design building blocks

Multiply, divide, and modulo operators are very expensive to implement in terms of logic and area. However, these arithmetic operators can be used to implement the desired functionality concisely and in a technology-independent manner. On the other hand, designing custom blocks to do multiplication, division, or modulo operation can take a longer time, and the RTL description becomes more technology-dependent.

Be careful with multiple assignments to the same variable

Multiple assignments to the same variable can cause undesired logic to be generated. The previous assignment might be ignored, and only the last assignment would be used.

```
//two assignments to the same variable
always @(posedge clk)
        if(load1) q <= a1;

always @(posedge clk)
        if(load2) q <= a2;
```

The synthesis tool infers two flipflops with the outputs **and**ed together to produce the *q* output. The designer needs to be careful about such situations.

Define if-else or case statements explicitly

Branches for all possible conditions must be specified in the **if-else** or **case** statements. Otherwise, level-sensitive latches may be inferred instead of multiplexers. Refer to Section 14.3.3, *Interpretation of a Few Verilog Constructs*, for the discussion on latch inference.

```
//latch is inferred; incomplete specification.
//whenever control = 1, out = a which implies a latch behavior.
//no branch for control = 0
always @(control or a)
    if (control)
        out <= a;

//multiplexer is inferred. complete specification for all values of
//control
always @(control or a or b)
    if (control)
        out = a;
    else
        out = b;
```

Similarly, for **case** statements, all possible branches, including the **default** statement, must be specified.

14.6.2 Design Partitioning

Design partitioning is another important factor for efficient logic synthesis. The way the designer partitions the design can greatly affect the output of the logic synthesis tool. Various partitioning techniques can be used.

Horizontal partitioning

Use bit slices to give the logic synthesis tool a smaller block to optimize. This is called *horizontal partitioning*. It reduces complexity of the problem and produces more optimal results for each block. For example, instead of directly designing a 16-bit ALU, design a 4-bit ALU and build the 16-bit ALU with four 4-bit ALUs. Thus, the logic synthesis tool has to optimize only the 4-bit ALU, which is a smaller problem than optimizing the 16-bit ALU. The partitioning of the ALU is shown in Figure 14-7.

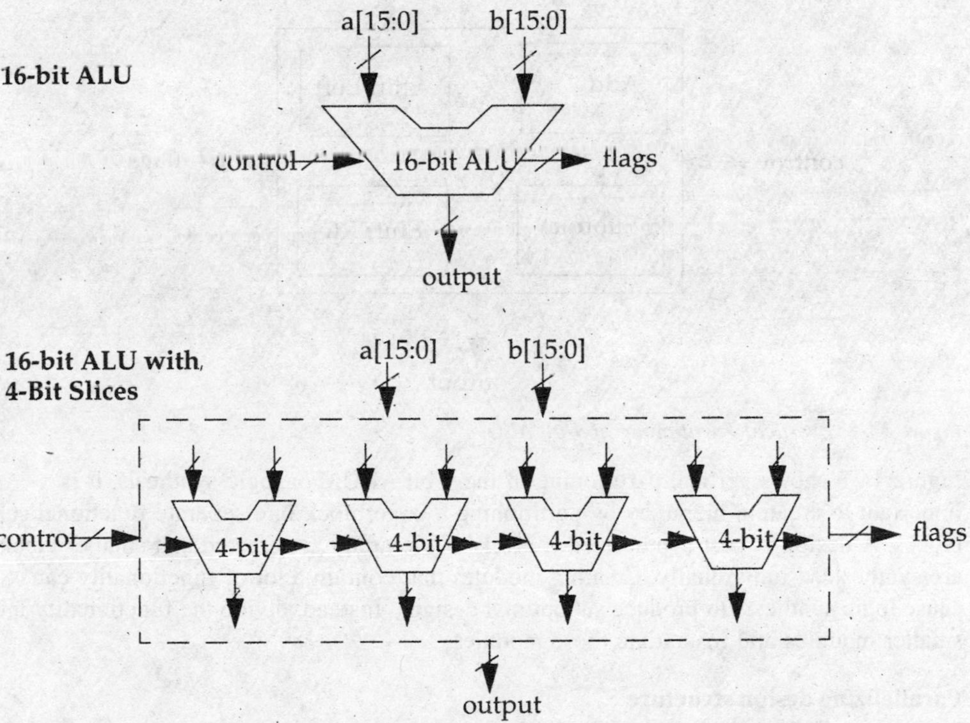

Figure 14-7 Horizontal Partitioning of 16-bit ALU

The downside of horizontal partitioning is that global minima can often be different local minima. Thus, by use of bit slices, each block is optimized individually, but there may be some global redundancies that the synthesis tool may not be able to eliminate.

Vertical Partitioning

Vertical partitioning implies that the functionality of a block is divided into smaller submodules. This is different from horizontal partitioning. In horizontal partitioning, all blocks do the same function. In vertical partitioning, each block does a different function. Assume that the 4-bit ALU described earlier is a four-function ALU with functions *add, subtract, shift right,* and *shift left*. Each block is distinct in function. This is vertical partitioning. Vertical partitioning of the 4-bit ALU is shown in Figure 14-8.

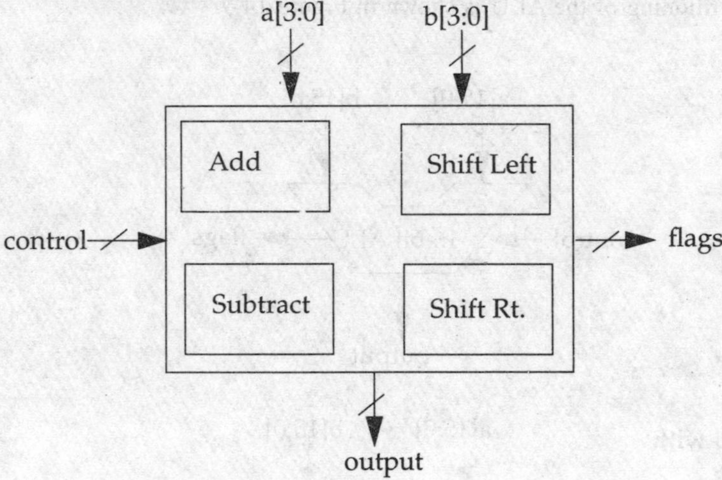

Figure 14-8 Vertical Partitioning of 4-bit ALU

Figure 14-8 shows vertical partitioning of the 4-bit ALU. For logic synthesis, it is important to create a hierarchy by partitioning a large block into separate functional sub-blocks. A design is best synthesized if levels of hierarchy are created and smaller blocks are synthesized individually. Creating modules that contain a lot of functionality can cause logic synthesis to produce suboptimal designs. Instead, divide the functionality into smaller modules and instantiate those modules.

Parallelizing design structure

In this technique, we use more resources to produce faster designs. We convert *sequential* operations into *parallel* operations by using more logic. A good example is the carry lookahead full adder.

Contrast the carry lookahead adder with a ripple carry adder. A ripple carry adder is serial in nature. A 4-bit ripple carry adder requires 9 gate delays to generate all sum and carry bits. On the other hand, assuming that up to 5-input `and` and `or` gates are available, a carry lookahead adder generates the sum and carry bits in 4 gate delays. Thus, we use more logic gates to build a carry lookahead unit, which is faster compared to an n-bit ripple carry adder. See Figure 14-9.

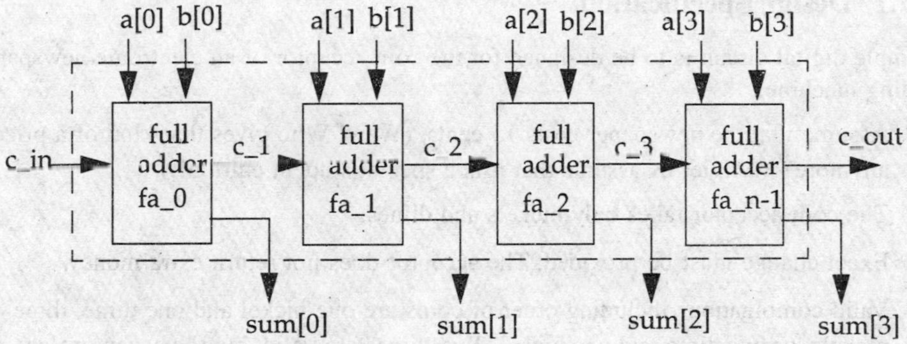

(a) Ripple Carry Adder (n-bit) , Delay = `9 gate delays, fewer logic gat`

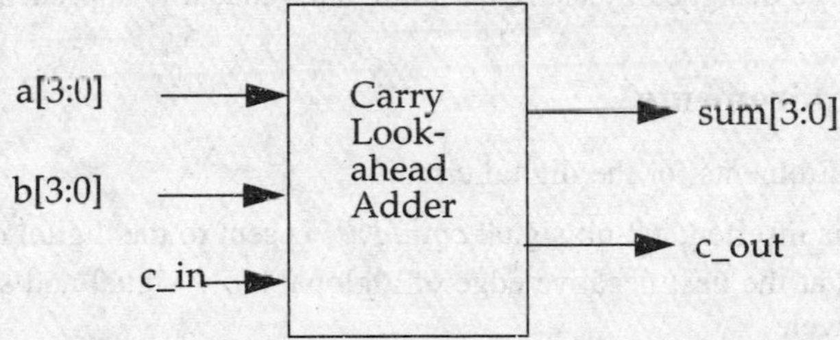

(b) Carry Lookahead Adder, Delay = `4 gate delays, more logic gates`

Figure 14-9 Parallelizing the Operation of an Adder

14.6.3 Design Constraint Specification

Design constraints are as important as efficient HDL descriptions in producing optimal designs. Accurate specification of timing, area, power, and environmental parameters such as input drive strengths, output loads, input arrival times, etc., are crucial to produce a gate-level netlist that is optimal. A deviation from the correct constraints or omission of a constraint can lead to nonoptimal designs. Careful attention must be given to specifying design constraints.

14.7 Example of Sequential Circuit Synthesis

In Section 14.4.2, *An Example of RTL-to-Gates*, we synthesized a combinational circuit. Let us now consider an example of sequential circuit synthesis. Specifically, we will design finite state machines.

14.7.1 Design Specification

A simple digital circuit is to be designed for the coin acceptor of an electronic newspaper vending machine.

- Assume that the newspaper costs 15 cents. (Wow! Who gives that kind of a price anymore? Well, let us assume that it is a special student edition!!)
- The coin acceptor takes only nickels and dimes.
- Exact change must be provided. The acceptor does not return extra money.
- Valid combinations including order of coins are one nickel and one dime, three nickels, or one dime and one nickel. Two dimes are valid, but the acceptor does not return money.

This digital circuit can be designed by using the finite state machine approach.

14.7.2 Circuit Requirements

We must set some requirements for the digital circuit.

- When each coin is inserted, a 2-bit signal *coin[1:0]* is sent to the digital circuit. The signal is asserted at the next negative edge of a global *clock* signal and stays up for exactly 1 clock cycle.
- The output of the digital circuit is a single bit. Each time the total amount inserted is 15 cents or more, an output signal *newspaper* goes high for exactly one clock cycle and the vending machine door is released.
- A *reset* signal can be used to reset the finite state machine. We assume *synchronous reset*.

14.7.3 Finite State Machine (FSM)

We can represent the functionality of the digital circuit with a finite state machine.

- input : 2-bit, *coin[1:0]*—no coin *x0= 2'b00*, nickel *x5 = 2'b01*, dime *x10 = 2'b10.*
- output: 1-bit, *newspaper*—release door when *newspaper = 1'b1*
- states: 4 states—*s0 = 0 cents; s5 = 5 cents; s10 = 10 cents; s15 = 15 cents*

The bubble diagram for the finite state machine is shown in Figure 14-10. Each arc in the FSM is labeled with a label *<input>/<output>* where input is 2-bit and output is 1-bit. For example, *x5/0* means transition to the state pointed to by the arc, when input is *x5 (2'b01)*, and set the output to `0`.

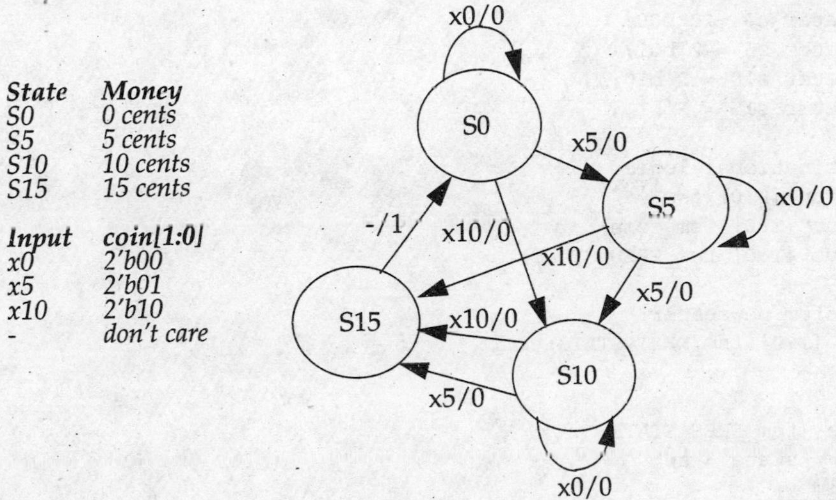

Figure 14-10 Finite State Machine for Newspaper Vending Machine

14.7.4 Verilog Description

The Verilog RTL description for the finite state machine is shown in Example 14-6.

Example 14-6 RTL Description for Newspaper Vending Machine FSM

```
//Design the newspaper vending machine coin acceptor
//using a FSM approach
module vend( coin, clock, reset, newspaper);

//Input output port declarations
input [1:0] coin;
input clock;
input reset;
output newspaper;
wire newspaper;

//internal FSM state declarations
wire [1:0] NEXT_STATE;
```

Example 14-6 RTL Description for Newspaper Vending Machine FSM (Continued)

```
reg [1:0] PRES_STATE;

//state encodings
parameter s0 = 2'b00;
parameter s5 = 2'b01;
parameter s10 = 2'b10;
parameter s15 = 2'b11;

//Combinational logic
function [2:0] fsm;
  input [1:0] fsm_coin;
  input [1:0] fsm_PRES_STATE;

  reg fsm_newspaper;
  reg [1:0] fsm_NEXT_STATE;

begin
  case (fsm_PRES_STATE)
  s0: //state = s0
  begin
    if (fsm_coin == 2'b10)
    begin
      fsm_newspaper = 1'b0;
      fsm_NEXT_STATE = s10;
    end
    else if (fsm_coin == 2'b01)
    begin
      fsm_newspaper = 1'b0;
      fsm_NEXT_STATE = s5;
    end
    else
    begin
      fsm_newspaper = 1'b0;
      fsm_NEXT_STATE = s0;
    end
  end

 s5: //state = s5
 begin
   if (fsm_coin == 2'b10)
   begin
     fsm_newspaper = 1'b0;
     fsm_NEXT_STATE = s15;
```

Example 14-6 RTL Description for Newspaper Vending Machine FSM (Continued)

```
        end
        else if (fsm_coin == 2'b01)
        begin
          fsm_newspaper = 1'b0;
          fsm_NEXT_STATE = s10;
        end
        else
        begin
          fsm_newspaper = 1'b0;
          fsm_NEXT_STATE = s5;
        end

    s10: //state = s10
      begin
        if (fsm_coin == 2'b10)
        begin
          fsm_newspaper = 1'b0;
          fsm_NEXT_STATE = s15;
        end
        else if (fsm_coin == 2'b01)
        begin
          fsm_newspaper = 1'b0;
          fsm_NEXT_STATE = s15;
        end
        else
        begin
          fsm_newspaper = 1'b0;
          fsm_NEXT_STATE = s10;
        end
      end
      s15: //state = s15
      begin
        fsm_newspaper = 1'b1;
        fsm_NEXT_STATE = s0;
      end
      endcase
      fsm = {fsm_newspaper, fsm_NEXT_STATE};
    end
    endfunction

    //Reevaluate combinational logic each time a coin
    //is put or the present state changes
    assign {newspaper, NEXT_STATE} = fsm(coin, PRES_STATE);
```

Example 14-6 RTL Description for Newspaper Vending Machine FSM (Continued)

```
//clock the state flipflops.
//use synchronous reset
always @(posedge clock)
begin
  if (reset == 1'b1)
    PRES_STATE <=  s0;
  else
    PRES_STATE <=  NEXT_STATE;
end

endmodule
```

14.7.5 Technology Library

We defined abc_100 technology in Section 14.4.1, *RTL to Gates*. We will use abc_100 as the target technology library. abc_100 contains the following library cells:

```
//Library cells for abc_100 technology

VNAND//2-input nand gate
VAND//2-input and gate
VNOR//2-input nor gate
VOR//2-input or gate
VNOT//not gate
VBUF//buffer
NDFF//Negative edge triggered D flipflop
PDFF//Positive edge triggered D flipflop
```

14.7.6 Design Constraints

Timing critical is the only design constraint we used in this design. Typically, design constraints are more elaborate.

14.7.7 Logic Synthesis

We synthesize the RTL description by using the specified design constraints and technology library and obtain the optimized gate-level netlist.

14.7.8 Optimized Gate-Level Netlist

We use logic synthesis to map the RTL description to the abc_100 technology. The optimized gate-level netlist produced is shown in Example 14-7.

Example 14-7 *Optimized Gate-Level Netlist for Newspaper Vending Machine FSM*

```
module vend ( coin, clock, reset, newspaper );
input  [1:0] coin;
input  clock, reset;
output newspaper;
    wire \PRES_STATE[1] , n289, n300, n301, n302, \PRES_STATE243[1] ,
         n303, n304, \PRES_STATE[0] , n290, n291, n292, n293, n294,
         n295, n296, n297, n298, n299, \PRES_STATE243[0] ;
    PDFF \PRES_STATE_reg[1]  ( .clk(clock), .d(\PRES_STATE243[1] ),
                    .clrbar( 1'b1), .prebar(1'b1), .q(\PRES_STATE[1] ) );
    PDFF \PRES_STATE_reg[0]  ( .clk(clock), .d(\PRES_STATE243[0] ),
                    .clrbar( 1'b1), .prebar(1'b1), .q(\PRES_STATE[0] ) );
    VOR U119 ( .in0(n292), .in1(n295), .out(n302) );
    VAND U118 ( .in0(\PRES_STATE[0] ), .in1(\PRES_STATE[1] ),
                  .out(newspaper));
    VNAND U117 ( .in0(n300), .in1(n301), .out(n291) );
    VNOR U116 ( .in0(n298), .in1(coin[0]), .out(n299) );
    VNOR U115 ( .in0(reset), .in1(newspaper), .out(n289) );
    VNOT U128 ( .in(\PRES_STATE[1] ), .out(n298) );
    VAND U114 ( .in0(n297), .in1(n298), .out(n296) );
    VNOT U127 ( .in(\PRES_STATE[0] ), .out(n295) );
    VAND U113 ( .in0(n295), .in1(n292), .out(n294) );
    VNOT U126 ( .in(coin[1]), .out(n293) );
    VNAND U112 ( .in0(coin[0]), .in1(n293), .out(n292) );
    VNAND U125 ( .in0(n294), .in1(n303), .out(n300) );
    VNOR U111 ( .in0(n291), .in1(reset), .out(\PRES_STATE243[0] ) );
    VNAND U124 ( .in0(\PRES_STATE[0] ), .in1(n304), .out(n301) );
    VAND U110 ( .in0(n289), .in1(n290), .out(\PRES_STATE243[1] ) );
    VNAND U123 ( .in0(n292), .in1(n298), .out(n304) );
    VNAND U122 ( .in0(n299), .in1(coin[1]), .out(n303) );
    VNAND U121 ( .in0(n296), .in1(n302), .out(n290) );
    VOR U120 ( .in0(n293), .in1(coin[0]), .out(n297) );
endmodule
```

The schematic diagram for the gate-level netlist is shown in Figure 14-11.

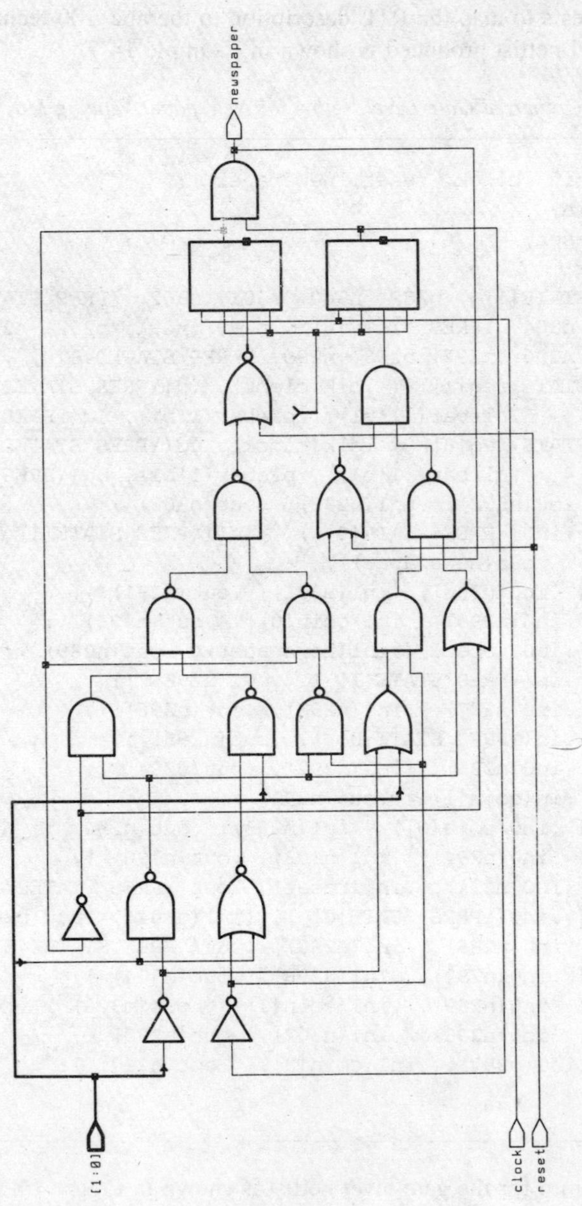

Figure 14-11 Gate-Level Schematic for the Vending Machine

14.7.9 Verification

Stimulus is applied to the original RTL description to test all possible combinations of coins. The same stimulus is applied to test the optimized gate-level netlist. Stimulus applied to both the RTL and gate-level netlist is shown in Example 14-8.

Example 14-8 Stimulus for Newspaper Vending Machine FSM

```
module stimulus;
reg clock;
reg [1:0] coin;
reg reset;
wire newspaper;

//instantiate the vending state machine
vend vendY (coin, clock, reset, newspaper);

//Display the output
initial
begin
  $display("\t\tTime  Reset Newspaper\n");
  $monitor("%d  %d  %d", $time, reset, newspaper);
end

//Apply stimulus to the vending machine
initial
begin
  clock = 0;
  coin = 0;
  reset = 1;
  #50 reset = 0;
  @(negedge clock); //wait until negative edge of clock

  //Put 3 nickels to get newspaper
  #80 coin = 1; #40 coin = 0;
  #80 coin = 1; #40 coin = 0;
  #80 coin = 1; #40 coin = 0;

 //Put one nickel and then one dime to get newspaper
  #180 coin = 1; #40 coin = 0;
  #80 coin = 2; #40 coin = 0;

  //Put two dimes; machine does not return a nickel to get newspaper
  #180 coin = 2; #40 coin = 0;
  #80 coin = 2; #40 coin = 0;
```

Example 14-8 *Stimulus for Newspaper Vending Machine FSM (Continued)*

```
  //Put one dime and then one nickel to get newspaper
  #180 coin = 2; #40 coin = 0;
  #80 coin = 1; #40 coin = 0;

  #80 $finish;
end

//setup clock; cycle time = 40 units
always
begin
  #20 clock = ~clock;
end

endmodule
```

The outputs from the simulation of RTL and the gate-level netlist are compared. In our case, Example 14-9, the outputs are identical. Thus, the gate-level netlist is verified.

Example 14-9 *Output of Newspaper Vending Machine FSM*

```
        Time Reset Newspaper

           0    1       x
          20    1       0
          50    0       0
         420    0       1
         460    0       0
         780    0       1
         820    0       0
        1100    0       1
        1140    0       0
        1460    0       1
        1500    0       0
```

The gate-level netlist is sent to ABC Inc., which does the layout, checks that the layout meets the timing requirements, and then fabricates the IC chip.

14.8 Summary

In this chapter, we discussed the following aspects of logic synthesis with Verilog HDL:

- *Logic synthesis* is the process of converting a high-level description of the design into an optimized, gate-level representation, using the cells in the technology library.
- *Computer-aided logic synthesis tools* have greatly reduced the design cycle time and have improved productivity. They allow designers to write technology-independent, high-level descriptions and produce technology-dependent, optimized, gate-level netlists. Both *combinational* and *sequential* RTL descriptions can be synthesized.
- Logic synthesis tools accept high-level descriptions at the *register transfer level (RTL)*. Thus, not all Verilog constructs are acceptable to a logic synthesis tool. We discussed the acceptable Verilog constructs and operators and their interpretation in terms of digital circuit elements.
- A logic synthesis tool accepts an *RTL description, design constraints,* and a *technology library* and produces an *optimized gate-level netlist. Translation, logic optimization*, and *technology mapping* are the internal processes in a logic synthesis tool and are normally invisible to the user.
- Functional verification of the optimized gate-level netlist is done by applying the same stimulus to the RTL description and the gate-level netlist and comparing the output. Timing is verified with *timing simulation* or *static timing verification.*
- Proper Verilog coding techniques must be used to write efficient RTL descriptions, and various design trade-offs must be evaluated. Guidelines for writing efficient RTL descriptions were discussed.
- *Design partitioning* is an important technique used to break the design into smaller blocks. Smaller blocks reduce the complexity of optimization for the logic synthesis tool.
- Accurate specification of design constraints is an important part of logic synthesis.

High-level synthesis tools allow the designer to write designs at an algorithmic level. However, high-level synthesis is still an emerging design paradigm, and RTL remains the popular high-level description method for logic synthesis tools.

14.9 Exercises

1. A 4-bit full adder with carry lookahead was defined in Example 6-5 on page 109, using an RTL description. Synthesize the full adder, using a technology library available to you. Optimize for fastest timing. Apply identical stimulus to the RTL and the gate-level netlist and compare the output.

2. A 1-bit full subtractor has three inputs *x, y,* and *z* (*previous borrow*) and two outputs *D*(difference) and *B*(borrow). The logic equations for *D* and *B* are as follows:

```
D = x'y'z + x'yz' + xy'z' + xyz
B = x'y + x'z +yz
```

   Write the Verilog RTL description for the full subtractor. Synthesize the full subtractor, using any technology library available to you. Optimize for fastest timing. Apply identical stimulus to the RTL and the gate-level netlist and compare the output.

3. Design a 3-to-8 decoder, using a Verilog RTL description. A 3-bit input *a[2:0]* is provided to the decoder. The output of the decoder is *out[7:0]*. The output bit indexed by *a[2:0]* gets the value `1`, the other bits are `0`. Synthesize the decoder, using any technology library available to you. Optimize for smallest area. Apply identical stimulus to the RTL and the gate-level netlist and compare the outputs.

4. Write the Verilog RTL description for a 4-bit binary counter with synchronous reset that is active high. (Hint: Use **`always`** loop with the *@(posedge clock)* statement.) Synthesize the counter, using any technology library available to you. Optimize for smallest area. Apply identical stimulus to the RTL and the gate-level netlist and compare the outputs.

5. Using a synchronous finite-state machine approach, design a circuit that takes a single-bit stream as an input at the pin *in*. An output pin *match* is asserted high each time a pattern 10101 is detected. A *reset* pin initializes the circuit synchronously. Input pin *clk* is used to clock the circuit. Synthesize the circuit, using any technology library available to you. Optimize for fastest timing. Apply identical stimulus to the RTL and the gate-level netlist and compare the outputs.

Advanced Verification Techniques

15

Verilog HDL was traditionally used both as a simulation modeling language and as a hardware description language. Verilog HDL was heavily used in verification and simulation for testbenches, test environments, simulation models, and architectural models. This approach worked well for smaller designs and simpler test environments.

As the average gate count for designs began to approach or exceed one million, verification soon became the main bottleneck in the design process. Design teams started spending 50-70% of their time in verifying designs rather than creating new ones.

Designers quickly realized that to verify complex designs, they needed to use tools that contained enhanced verification capabilities. They needed tools that could automate some of the tedious processes. Moreover, it was important to find bugs the very first time to avoid expensive chip re-spins.

To address these needs, a variety of verification methodologies and tools has emerged over the past few years. The latest addition to verification methodology is assertion-based verification. However, Verilog HDL remains the focal point in the design process. These new developments enhance the productivity of verifying Verilog HDL-based designs. This chapter gives the reader a basic understanding of these verification concepts that complement Verilog HDL.

Learning Objectives

- Define the components of a traditional verification flow.
- Understand architectural modeling concepts.
- Explain the use of high-level verification languages (HVLs).
- Describe different techniques for effective simulation.
- Explain the methods for analysis of simulation results.
- Describe coverage techniques.
- Understand assertion-checking techniques.
- Understand formal verification techniques.

- Describe semi-formal verification techniques.
- Define equivalence checking.

15.1 Traditional Verification Flow

A traditional verification flow consisting of certain standard components is illustrated in Figure 15-1. This flow addresses only the verification perspective. It assumes that logic design is done separately.

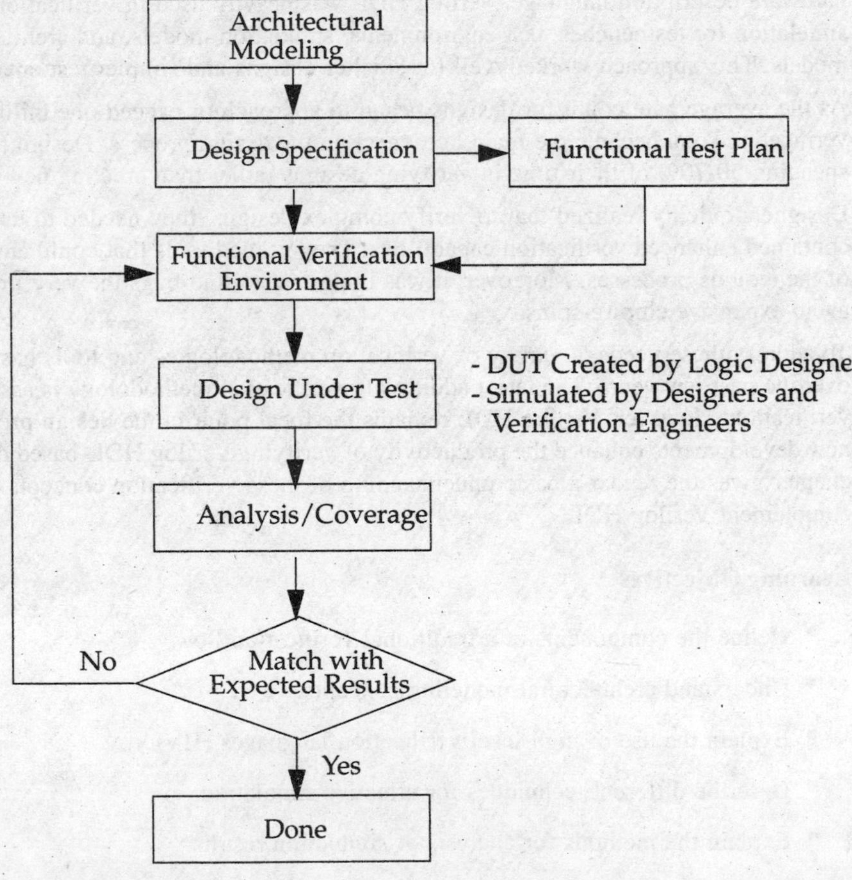

Figure 15-1 Traditional Verification Flow

As shown in Figure 15-1, the traditional verification flow consists of the following steps:

1. The chip architect first needs to create a design specification. In order to create a good specification, an analysis of architectural trade-offs has to be performed so that the best possible architecture can be chosen. This is usually done by simulating architectural models of the design. At the end of this step, the design specification is complete.
2. When the specification is ready, a functional test plan is created based on the design specification. This test plan forms the fundamental framework of the functional verification environment. Based on the test plan, test vectors are applied to the design-under-test (DUT), which is written in Verilog HDL. Functional test environments are needed to apply these test vectors. There are many tools available for generating and applying test vectors. These tools also allow the efficient creation of test environments.
3. The DUT is then simulated using traditional software simulators. (The DUT is normally created by logic designers. Verification engineers simulate the DUT.)
4. The output is then analyzed and checked against the expected results. This can be done manually using waveform viewers and debugging tools. Alternately, analysis can be automated by the test environment checking the output of the DUT or by parsing the log files using a language like PERL. In addition, coverage results are analyzed to ensure that the tests have exercised the design thoroughly and that the verification goals are met. If the output matches the expected results and the coverage goals are met, then the verification is complete.
5. Optionally, additional steps can be taken to decrease the risk of a future design re-spin. These steps include Hardware Acceleration, Hardware Emulation, and Assertion-based Verification.

Earlier, each step in the traditional verification flow was accomplished with Verilog HDL. Though Verilog HDL remains the dominant method for creating the DUT, many advances have occurred in the other steps of the verification flow. The following sections describe these advances in detail.

15.1.1 Architectural Modeling

This stage includes design exploration by the architects. The initial model typically does not capture exact design behavior, except to the extent required for the initial design decisions. For example, a fundamental algorithm like an MPEG decoder might be implemented, but the processor-to-memory bandwidth is not specified. The architect tries out several different variations of the model and makes some fundamental decisions about the system. These decisions may include the number of processors, algorithms implemented in hardware, memory architecture, and so on. These trade-offs will affect the eventual implementation of the target design.

Architectural models are often written using C and C++. Though C++ has the advantage of object-oriented constructs, it does not implement concepts such as parallelism and timing that were found in HDLs. Thus, creators of architectural models have to implement these concepts in their models. This is very cumbersome, resulting in long development times for architectural models.

To solve this problem, architectural modeling languages were invented. These languages have both the object-oriented constructs found in C++ as well as parallelism and timing constructs found in HDLs. Thus, they are well-suited for high-level architectural models.

A likely advancement in the future is the design of chips at the architectural-modeling level rather than at the RTL level. High-level synthesis tools will convert architectural models to Verilog RTL design implementations based on the trade-off inputs. These RTL designs can then go through the standard ASIC design and verification flow. Figure 15-2 shows an example of such a flow.

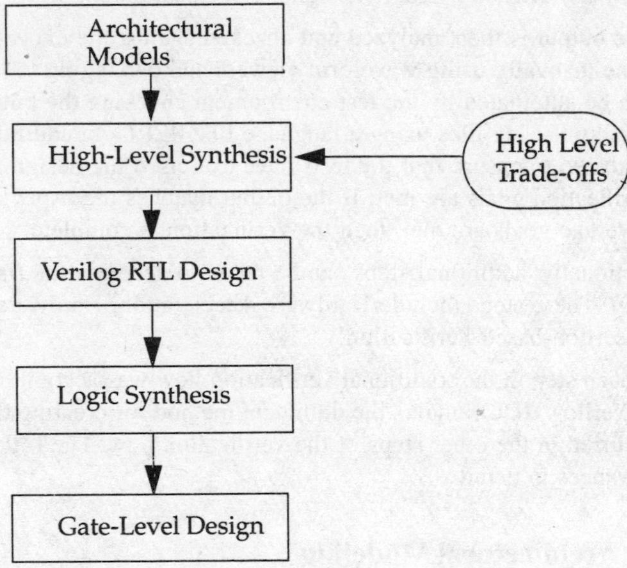

Figure 15-2 Architectural Modeling

Appendix E, *Verilog Tidbits*, contains further information on popular architectural modeling languages.

15.1.2 Functional Verification Environment

The functional verification of a chip can be divided into three phases.

- *Block-level verification:* Block-level verification is usually done by the block designer using Verilog for both design and verification. A number of simple test cases are executed to ensure that the block functions well enough for chip integration.
- *Full-ChipVerification*: The goal of full-chip verification is to ensure that all of the features of the full chip described in the functional test plan are covered.
- *Extended Verification:* The objective of the extended verification is to find all corner case bugs in the design. This phase of verification is lengthy since the set of tests is not predetermined and it may continue past tape-out.

During the functional verification phase, a combination of directed and random simulation is used. Directed tests are written by the verification engineers to test a specific behavior of the design. They may use random data, but the sequence of events is predetermined. Random sequences of legal input transactions are used toward the end of functional verification and during the extended verification phases in order to simulate corner cases which the designer may have missed.

As Verilog HDL became popular, designers[1] started using Verilog HDL for both the DUT and its surrounding functional verification environment. In a typical HDL-based verification environment,

- The testbench consisted of HDL procedures that wrote data to the DUT or read data from it.
- The tests, which called the testbench procedures in sequence to apply manually selected input stimuli to the DUT and checked the results, were directed only toward specific features of the design as described in the functional test plan.

However, as design sizes exceeded one million gates, this approach became less effective because

- The tests became harder and more time-consuming to write because of decreasing controllability of the design.
- Verifying correct behavior became difficult due to decreasing observability into internal design states.
- The tests became difficult to read and maintain.

1. In this chapter, the words "designer" and "verification engineer" have been used interchangeably. This is because logic designers perform block-level verification and are often involved in the full-chip verification process.

- There were too many corner cases for the available labor.
- Multiple environments became difficult to create and maintain because they used little shared code.

To make the test environment more reusable and readable, verification engineers needed to write the tests and the test environment code in an object-oriented programming language. *High-Level Verification Languages (HVLs)* were created to address this need. Appendix E, *Verilog Tidbits*, contains further information on popular HVLs.

HVLs are powerful because they combine the object-oriented approach of C++ with the parallelism and timing constructs in HDLs and are thus best suited for verification. HVLs also help in the automatic generation of test stimuli and provide an integrated environment for functional verification, including input drivers, output drivers, data checking, protocol checking, and coverage. Thus, HVLs maximize productivity for creating and maintaining verification environments.

Figure 15-3 shows the various components of a typical functional verification environment. HVLs greatly improve the designer's ability to create and maintain each test component. Note that Verilog HDL is still the primary method of creating a DUT.

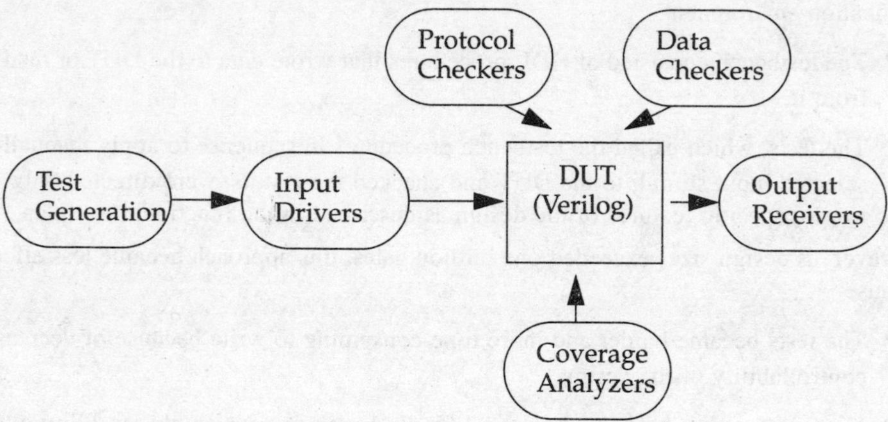

Figure 15-3 Components of a Functional Verification Environment

In an HVL-based methodology, the verification components are simulated in the HVL simulator and the DUT is simulated with a Verilog simulator. The HVL simulator and the Verilog simulator interact with each other to produce the simulation results. Figure 15-4 shows an example of such an interaction. The HVL simulator and Verilog simulator are run as two separate processes and communicate through the Verilog PLI interface. The

HVL simulator is primarily responsible for all verification components, including test generation, input driver, output receiver, data checker, protocol checker, and coverage analyzer. The Verilog simulator is responsible for simulating the DUT.

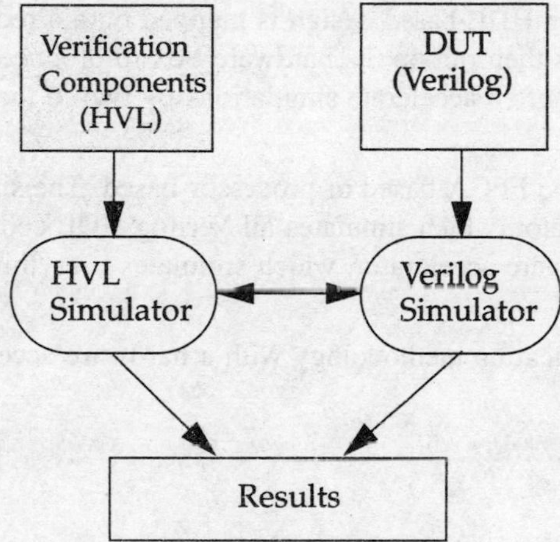

Figure 15-4 Interaction between HVL and Verilog Simulators

The future trend in HVLs is to apply acceleration techniques to HVL simulators to greatly speed up the simulations. These acceleration techniques are similar to those used for Verilog HDL simulators and are discussed in Section 15.1.3, *Simulation*.

15.1.3 Simulation

There are three ways to simulate a design: software simulation, hardware acceleration, and hardware emulation.

Software Simulation

Software simulators were typically used to run Verilog HDL-based designs. Software simulators run on a generic computer or server. They load the Verilog HDL code and simulate the behavior in software. Appendix E, *Verilog Tidbits*, contains further information on popular software simulators.

However, when designs started exceeding one million gates, software simulations began to consume large amounts of time and became a bottleneck in the verification process. Thus, various techniques emerged to accelerate these simulations. Two techniques, hardware acceleration and emulation, were invented.

Hardware Acceleration

Hardware acceleration is used to speed up existing simulations and to run long sequences of random transactions during functional and extended verification phases.

In this technique, the Verilog HDL-based design is mapped onto a reconfigurable hardware box. The design is then run on the hardware box to produce simulation results. Hardware acceleration[2] can often accelerate simulations by two to three orders of magnitude.

Hardware accelerators can be FPGA-based or processor-based. The simulation is divided between the software simulator, which simulates all Verilog HDL code that is not synthesizable, and the hardware accelerator, which simulates everything that is synthesizable.

Figure 15-5 shows the verification methodology with a hardware accelerator.

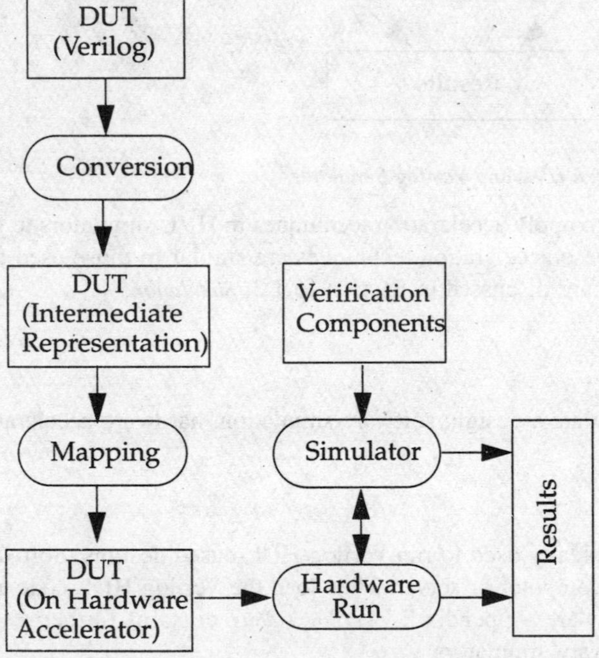

Figure 15-5 Hardware Acceleration

2. Also known as "Simulation Acceleration."

 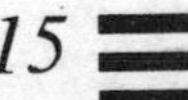

Verification components may be simulated using a Verilog simulator or an HVL simulator. The simulator and the hardware accelerator interact with each other to produce results.

Hardware accelerators can cut simulation times from a matter of days to a few hours. Therefore, they can greatly shorten the verification timeline. However, they are expensive and need significant set-up time. Another drawback is that they usually require long compilation times, which means that they are most useful only for long regression simulations. As a result, smaller designs still employ software simulation as the simulation technique of choice.

Appendix E, *Verilog Tidbits*, contains further information on popular hardware accelerators.

Hardware Emulation

Hardware emulation[3] is used to verify the design in a real-life environment with real system software running on the system. HW emulation is used during the extended verification phase since the design must be pretty stable.

One of the major benefits of hardware emulation is that hardware software integration can start before the actual hardware is available, thus saving time in the schedule. By running real-life software, conditions that are very difficult to set up in a simulation environment can be tested.

When the design is complete, software engineers often want to run their software on the design before the design is realized on a chip. Here are a few examples of what the designer of a chip might want to do before a chip is sent for fabrication:

1. Designers of a microprocessor want to try booting the UNIX operating system.
2. Designers of an MPEG decoder want to have live frames decoded and shown on a screen.
3. Designers of a graphics chip want actual frame renderings to show up on the screen in real time.

Running live systems with the design is an important verification step that reduces the possibility of bugs and a design re-spin. However, software simulators and hardware accelerators cannot be used for this purpose because they are too slow and do not have the necessary hooks to run a live system. For example, to boot UNIX with a software simulation of a design may take many years. Hardware emulation can boot UNIX in a few hours.

3. Also known as "In-Circuit Emulation."

Figure 15-6 shows the setup of a typical emulation system. Emulation is done so that the software application runs exactly as it would on the real chip in a real circuit. The software application is oblivious to the fact that it is running on an emulator rather than the actual chip.

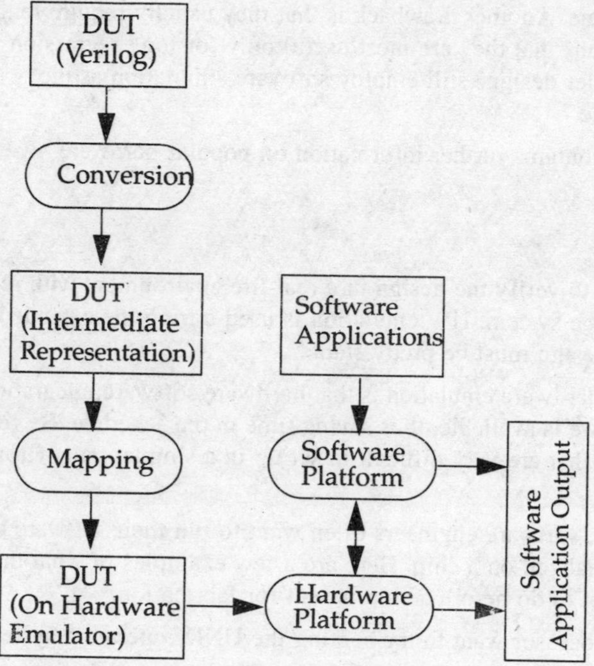

Figure 15-6 Hardware Emulation

Hardware emulators typically run at megahertz speeds. However, they are very expensive and require significant setup time. As a result, smaller designs still employ software simulation as the simulation technique of choice.

Appendix E, *Verilog Tidbits*, contains further information on popular hardware emulators.

15.1.4 Analysis

An important step in the traditional verification flow is to analyze the design to check the following items:

1. Was the data received equal to the expected data?
2. Was the data received correctly according to the interface protocol?

To analyze the correctness of the data value and the data protocol, various methods are used.

1. *Waveform Viewers* are used to see the dump files. The designer visually goes through the dump files from various tests and ensures that the data value and the data protocol are both correct.
2. *Log Files* contain traces of the simulation run. The designer visually looks at the log files from various tests and determines the correctness of the data value and the data protocol based on the simulation messages.

These methods are extremely tedious and time-consuming. Every time a test is run, the designers have to manually look through the dump files and log files. This method breaks down when a large number of simulation runs needs to be analyzed. Therefore, it is advisable to make your test environment self checking. Two components are required for building a self-checking test environment:

1. Data Checker
2. Protocol Checker

Data checkers compare each value output from the simulation and check the value on-the-fly against the expected output. If there is a mismatch, the simulation can be stopped immediately to display an error message. If there are no error messages, the simulation is deemed to complete successfully. *Scoreboards* are often used to implement data checkers. Scoreboards are often used to indicate the completion of transactions and to verify that data is received on the correct interface. Scoreboards also ensure that data is not lost in the DUT, even if the protocol is followed, and that the data received is correct.

Protocol checkers check on-the-fly whether the data protocol is followed at each input and output interface. If there is a violation of protocol, the simulation can be stopped immediately to display an error message. If there are no error messages, the simulation is deemed to complete successfully.

A self-checking methodology allows the designer to run thousands of tests without having to analyze each test for correctness. If there is a failure, the designer can probe further into the dump files and the log files to determine the cause of the error.

15.1.5 Coverage

Coverage helps the designer determine when verification is complete. Various methods have been developed and used to quantify the verification progress. There are two types of coverage: structural and functional.

Structural Coverage

Structural coverage deals with the structure of the Verilog HDL code and tells when key portions of that structure have been covered. There are three main types of structural coverage:

1. *Code coverage*: The basic assumption of code coverage is that unexercised code potentially bears bugs. However, code coverage checks how well RTL code was exercised rather than design functionality. Code coverage does not tell whether the verification is complete. It simply tells that verification is not complete until 100% code coverage is achieved. Therefore, code coverage is useful but it is not a complete metric.
2. *Toggle coverage*: This is one of the oldest coverage measurements. It was historically used for manufacturing tests. Toggle coverage monitors the bits of logic that have toggled during simulation. If a bit does not toggle from 0 to 1, or from 1 to 0, it has not been adequately verified.

   Toggle coverage does not ensure completeness. It cannot assure that a specific bit toggle sequence that represents high-level functionality has occurred. Toggle coverage does not shorten the verification process. It may even prolong the verification process as engineers try to toggle a bit, which cannot toggle according to the specification. Toggle coverage is very low-level coverage and it is cumbersome to relate a specific bit to a high-level test plan item.
3. *Branch coverage*: Branch coverage checks if all possible branches in a control flow are taken. This coverage metric is necessary but not sufficient.

Functional Coverage

Functional coverage perceives the design from a system point of view. Functional coverage ensures that all possible legal values of input stimuli are exercised in all possible combinations at all possible times. Moreover, functional coverage also provides finite state machine coverage, including states and state transitions.

Functional coverage can be enhanced with implementation coverage by inserting coverage points or assertions in the RTL code. For example, it enhances the functional coverage metric by determining if all transactions have been tested while receiving an interrupt or when one of the internal FIFOs is full.

Appendix E, *Verilog Tidbits*, contains further information on popular coverage tools.

15.2 Assertion Checking

The traditional verification flow discussed in the previous section is a *black box* approach, i.e., verification relies only on the knowledge of the input and output behavior of the system.

Many other verification methodologies have evolved over the past few years to complement the traditional verification flow discussed in the previous section. In this section and the following sections, we explain some of these new verification methodologies that use the *white box* verification approach, i.e., knowledge of the internal structure of the design is needed for verification.

Assertion checking is a form of white box verification. It requires knowledge of internal structures of the design. The main purpose of assertion checkers is to improve observability.

Assertions are statements about a design's intended behavior. There are two types of assertions:

- *Temporal assertions* – they describe the timing relationship between signals.
- *Static assertions* – they describe a property of a signal that is always true or false.

Assertions may be used in the RTL code to describe the intended behavior of a piece of Verilog HDL code. The following are examples of such behavior:

- An FSM state register should always be one-hot.
- The full and empty flags of a FIFO should never be asserted at the same time.

Assertions can also be used to describe the behavior of the internal or external interface of a chip. For example, the acknowledge signal should always be asserted within five cycles of the request signal. Assertions may be verified in simulation or by using formal methods.

Assertions do not contribute to the element being designed; they are usually treated as comments for logic synthesis. Their sole purpose is to ensure consistency between the designer's intention and the design that is created. Figure 15-7 shows the interfaces at which assertions could be placed in a FIFO-based design.

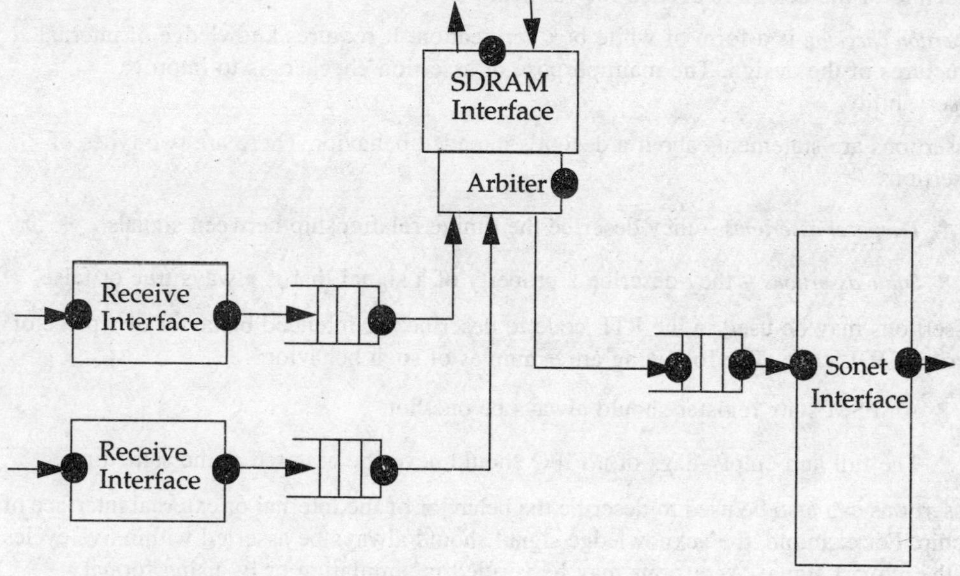

Figure 15-7 Assertion Checks

Assertion checks can be used with the traditional verification flow described in Section 15.1, *Traditional Verification Flow*. Assertion checks are placed by the designer at critical points in the design. During simulation, if there is a failure at that point, the designer is notified.

Assertion-based verification (ABV) has the following advantages:

1. ABV improves observability. It isolates the problem close to the source.
2. ABV improves verification efficiency. It reduces the number of engineers involved in the debugging process. Engineers are notified when there are bugs. This eliminates their having to look through waveforms and log files for hours to find bugs. Thus, the debug process is greatly simplified.

Appendix E, *Verilog Tidbits*, contains further information on popular assertion-checking tools.

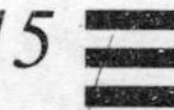

15.3 Formal Verification

A well-known white-box approach is *formal verification*, in which mathematical techniques are used to prove an assertion or a property of the design. The property to be proven may be related to the chip's overall functional specification, or it may represent internal design behavior. Detailed knowledge of the behavior of design structures is often required to specify useful properties that are worth proving. Thus, one can prove the correctness of a design without doing simulations. Another application of formal verification is to prove that the architectural specifications of a design are sound before starting with the RTL implementation.

A formal verification tool proves a design property by exploring all possible ways to manipulate a design. All input changes must conform to the constraints for legal behavior. Assertions on interfaces act as constraints to the formal tool to constrain what is legal behavior on the inputs. Attempts are then made to prove the assertions in the RTL code to be true or false. If the constraints on the inputs are too loose, then the formal verification tool can generate counter-examples that rely on illegal input sequences that would not occur in the design. If the constraints are too tight, then the tool will not explore all possible behavior and will wrongly report the design as "proven."

Figure 15-8 shows the verification flow with a formal verification tool. In the best case, the tool either proves a particular assertion absolutely or provides a counter-example to show the circumstances under which the assertion[4] is not met.

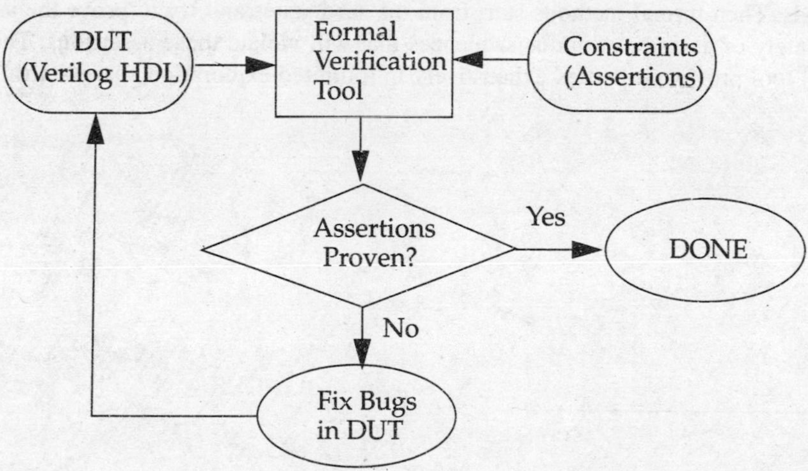

Figure 15-8 Formal Verification Flow

Since formal verification tools explore a design exhaustively, they can run only on designs that are limited in size. Typically, beyond 10,000 gates, absolute formal proofs become too hard and the tool blows up in terms of computation time and memory usage.

The limitations on formal verification tools are not based on the number of lines. They are based on the complexity of the assertions being proven and the design structure. The limitation lies in the number of cycles the algorithm can reach from the seed state (formal verifications tools often use reset as the seed state).

To circumvent the problems of formal verification, semi-formal techniques are used.

15.3.1 Semi-formal Verification

Semi-formal verification combines the traditional verification flow using test vectors with the power and thoroughness of formal verification. Semi-formal techniques have the following components:

1. Semi-formal methods supplement, but do not replace, simulation with test vectors.
2. Embedded assertion checks define the properties targeted by formal methods.
3. Embedded assertion checks define the input constraints.
4. Semi-formal methods explore a limited state space exhaustively from the states reached by simulation, thus maximizing the effect of simulation. The exploration is limited to a certain point around the state reached by simulation.

During a Verilog simulation, *seed* states are captured to serve as starting points for formal methods. Then formal methods start from the seed states and try to prove the assertions completely or describe stimulus sequences that will violate these assertions. The semi-formal tool proves properties exhaustively in a limited exploration space starting from

4. Assertions are not used simply to increase observability. In formal verification, they are used as constraints. The formal verification tool explores the state space such that it proves the assertion absolutely or produces a counter-example. Thus, assertions also increase controllability, i.e., they control how the formal verification tool explores the state space to prove a property.

these seed states, thus quickly identifying many corner-cases that would have been detected only by extensive simulation test suites. Figure 15-9 shows the verification flow with a semi-formal tool.

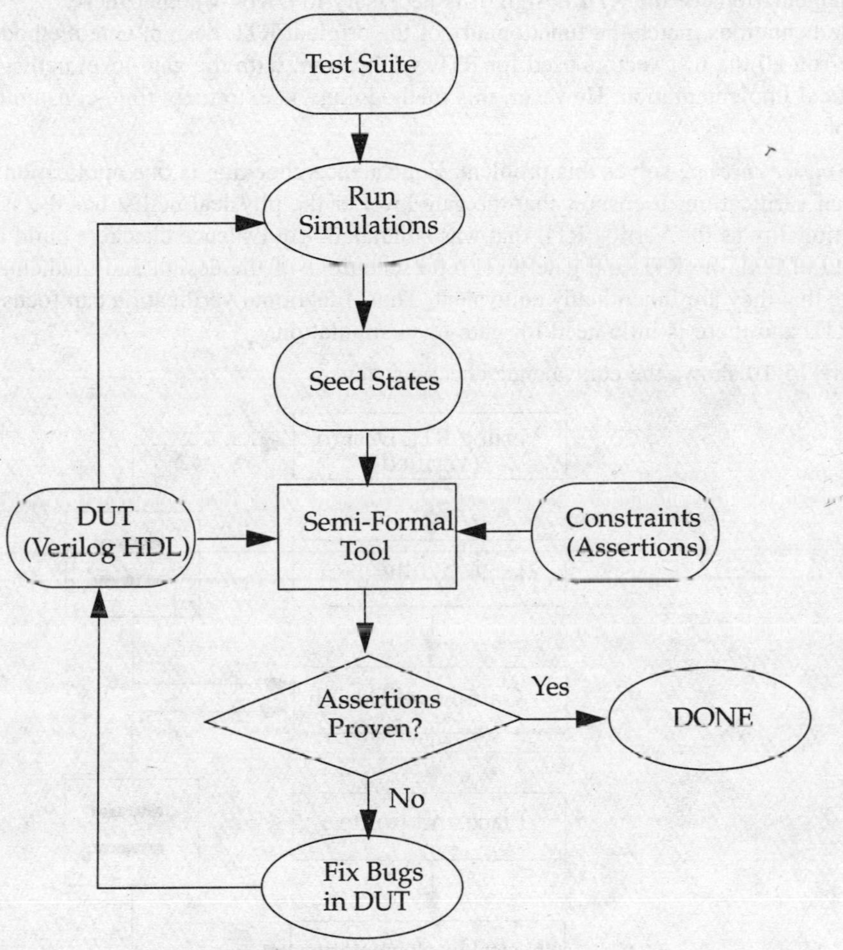

Figure 15-9 Semi-formal Verification Flow

Formal and semi-formal verification methods have recently received a lot of attention because of the increasing complexity of designs. Appendix E, *Verilog Tidbits*, contains further information on popular tools that employ formal and semi-formal verification methods.

15.3.2 Equivalence Checking

After logic synthesis and place and route tools create a gate-level netlist and physical implementations of the RTL design, it is necessary to check whether these implementations match the functionality of the original RTL design. One methodology is to re-run all the test vectors used for RTL verification, with the gate-level netlist and the physical implementation. However, this methodology is extremely time-consuming and tedious.

Equivalence checking solves this problem. Equivalence checking is one application of formal verification. It ensures that the gate level or the physical netlist has the same functionality as the Verilog RTL that was simulated. Equivalence checkers build a logical model of both the RTL and gate-level representations of the design and mathematically prove that they are functionally equivalent. Thus, functional verification can focus entirely on RTL and there is little need for gate-level simulation.

Figure 15-10 shows the equivalence checking flow.

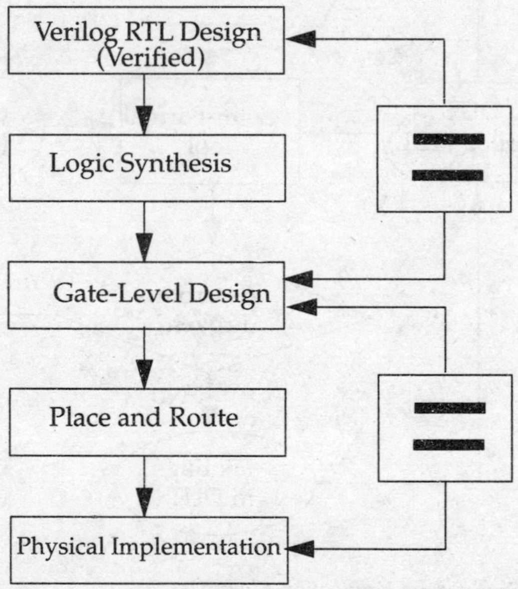

Figure 15-10 Equivalence Checking

Appendix E, *Verilog Tidbits*, contains further information on popular equivalence checking tools.

15.4 Summary

- A traditional verification flow contains a test-vector-based approach. An architectural model is developed to analyze design trade-offs. Once the design is finalized, it is verified using test vectors and simulation. Then the results are analyzed and coverage is measured. If the analysis meets the verification goals, the design is deemed verified.
- *Architectural modeling* is used by architects for design exploration. The initial model of the design typically does not capture exact design behavior, except to the extent required for the initial design decisions. Architectural modeling languages are suitable for building architectural models.
- Functional verification environments often contain test generators, input drivers, output receivers, data checkers, protocol checkers, and coverage analyzers. *High-level verification languages* (HVLs) can be used to effectively create and maintain these environments.
- Software simulators are the most popular tools for simulating Verilog HDL designs. *Hardware accelerators* are used to accelerate simulation by a few orders of magnitude. *Hardware emulators* run in the megahertz range and are used to run software applications as if they were running on the real chip.
- Waveforms and log files are the most common methods to analyze the output from a simulation. For effective analysis, it is important to build automatic data checker and protocol checker modules. If there is a violation of data value or protocol, the simulation is stopped immediately and an error message is displayed. A self-checking methodology allows the designer to run thousands of tests without having to analyze each test for correctness.
- *Toggle coverage*, *code coverage,* and *branch coverage* are three types of *structural coverage* techniques. *Functional coverage* perceives the design from a system point of view. Functional coverage also provides finite state machine coverage, including states and state transitions. A combination of functional coverage and other coverage techniques is recommended.
- *Assertion checking* is a form of white-box verification. It requires knowledge of the internal structures of the design. Assertion checking improves observability and verification efficiency. Assertion checks are placed by the designer at critical points in the design. If there is a failure at that point, the designer is notified.
- *Formal verification* is a white-box approach in which mathematical techniques are used to exhaustively prove an assertion or a property of the design. *Semi-formal verification* combines the traditional verification flow using test vectors with the

power and thoroughness of formal verification. *Equivalence checking* is an application of formal verification that examines the RTL representation of the design and checks to see if it matches the gate-level and physical implementations of the design.

Part 3 Appendices

Strength Modeling and Advanced Net Definitions A

A.1 Strength Levels

Verilog allows signals to have logic values and strength values. Logic values are `0`, `1`, `x`, and `z`. Logic strength values are used to resolve combinations of multiple signals and to represent behavior of actual hardware elements as accurately as possible. Several logic strengths are available. Table A-1 shows the strength levels for signals. Driving strengths are used for signal values that are driven on a net. Storage strengths are used to model charge storage in `trireg` type nets, which are discussed later in this appendix.

Table A-1 Strength Levels

Strength Level	Abbreviation	Degree	Strength Type
supply1	Su1	strongest 1	driving
strong1	St1		driving
pull1	Pu1	↑	driving
large1	La1		storage
weak1	We1		driving
medium1	Me1		storage
small1	Sm1		storage
highz1	HiZ1	weakest 1	high impedance
highz	HiZ0	weakest 0	high impedance
small0	Sm0		storage
medium0	Me0		storage
weak0	We0		driving
large0	La0		storage
pull0	Pu0	↓	driving
strong0	St0		driving
supply0	Su0	strongest 0	driving

A.2 Signal Contention

Logic strength values can be used to resolve signal contention on nets that have multiple drivers. There are many rules applicable to resolution of contention. However, two cases of interest that are most commonly used are described below.

A.2.1 Multiple Signals with the Same Value and Different Strength

If two signals with the same known value and different strength drive the same net, the signal with the higher strength wins.

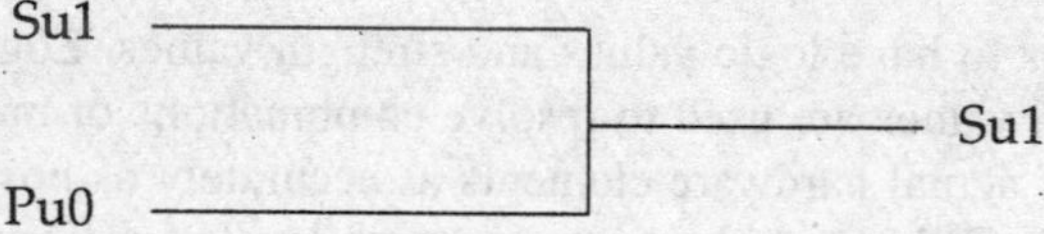

In the example shown, **supply** strength is greater than **pull**. Hence, *Su1* wins.

A.2.2 Multiple Signals with Opposite Value and Same Strength

When two signals with opposite value and same strength combine, the resulting value is **x**.

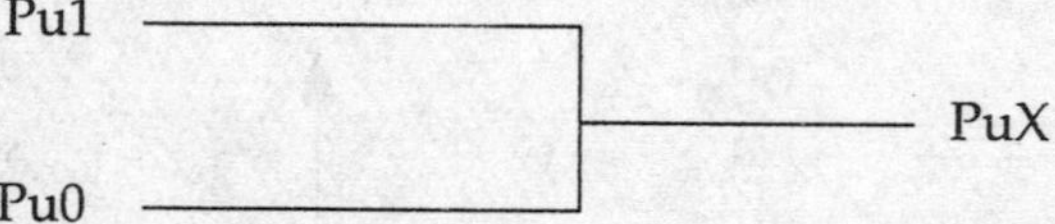

A.3 Advanced Net Types

We discussed resolution of signal contention by using strength levels. There are other methods to resolve contention without using strength levels. Verilog provides advanced net declarations to model logic contention.

A.3.1 tri

The keywords **wire** and **tri** have identical syntax and function. However, separate names are provided to indicate the purpose of the net. Keyword **wire** denotes nets with single drivers, and **tri** is denotes nets that have multiple drivers. A multiplexer, as defined below, uses the **tri** declaration.

```
module mux(out, a, b, control);
output out;
input a, b, control;
tri out;
wire a, b, control;

bufif0 b1(out, a, control); //drives a when control = 0; z otherwise
bufif1 b2(out, b, control); //drives b when control = 1; z otherwise

endmodule
```

The net is driven by *b1* and *b2* in a complementary manner. When *b1* drives *a*, *b2* is tristated; when *b2* drives *b*, *b1* is tristated. Thus, there is no logic contention. If there is contention on a **tri** net, it is resolved by using strength levels. If there are two signals of opposite values and same strength, the resulting value of the **tri** net is **x**.

A.3.2 trireg

Keyword **trireg** is used to model nets having capacitance that stores values. The default strength for **trireg** nets is **medium**. Nets of type **trireg** are in one of two states:

- *Driven state*—At least one driver drives a **0**, **1**, or **x** value on the net. The value is continuously stored in the **trireg** net. It takes the strength of the driver.
- *Capacitive state*—All drivers on the net have high impedance (**z**) value. The net holds the last driven value. The strength is **small**, **medium**, or **large** (default is **medium**).

```
trireg (large) out;
wire a, control;

bufif1 (out, a, control); // net out gets value of a when control = 1;
                          //when control = 0, out retains last value of a
                          //instead of going to z. strength is large.
```

A.3.3 tri0 and tri1

Keywords **tri0** and **tri1** are used to model resistive **pulldown** and **pullup** devices. A **tri0** net has a value **0** if nothing is driving the net. Similarly, **tri1** net has a value **1** if nothing is driving the net. The default strength is **pull**.

```
tri0 out;
wire a, control;

bufif1 (out, a, control); //net out gets the value of a when control = 1;
                          //when control = 0, out gets the value 0 instead
                          //of z. If out were declared as tri1, the
                          //default value of out would be 1 instead of 0.
```

A.3.4 supply0 and supply1

Keyword **supply1** is used to model a power supply. Keyword **supply0** is used to model ground. Nets declared as **supply1** or **supply0** have constant logic value and a strength level **supply** (strongest strength level).

```
supply1 vcc;   //all nets connected to vcc are connected to power supply
supply0 gnd;   //all nets connected to gnd are connected to ground
```

A.3.5 wor, wand, trior, and triand

When there is logic contention, if we simply use a **tri** net, we will get an **x**. This could be indicative of a design problem. However, sometimes the designer needs to resolve the final logic value when there are multiple drivers on the net, without using strength levels. Keywords **wor**, **wand**, **trior**, and **triand** are used to resolve such conflicts. Net **wand** performs the *and* operation on multiple driver logic values. If any value is **0**, the value of the net **wand** is **0**. Net **wor** performs the *or* operation on multiple driver values. If any value is **1**, the net **wor** is **1**. Nets **triand** and **trior** have the same syntax and function as the nets **wor** and **wand**. The example below explains the function.

```
wand out1;
wor out2;

buf (out1, 1'b0);
buf (out1, 1'b1); //out1 is a wand net; gets the final value 1'b0
```

```
buf (out2, 1'b0);
buf (out2, 1'b1); //out2 is a wor net; gets the final value 1'b1
```

List of PLI Routines

A list of PLI `acc_` and `tf_` routines is provided. VPI routines are not listed.[1] Names, the argument list, and a brief description of the routine are shown for each PLI routine. For details regarding the use of each PLI routine, refer to the *IEEE Standard Verilog Hardware Description Language* document.

B.1 Conventions

Conventions to be used for arguments are shown below.

Convention	Meaning
char *format	Pass formatted string
char *	Pass name of object as a string
underlined arguments	Arguments are optional
*	Pointer to the data type
....	More arguments of the same type

B.2 Access Routines

Access routines are classified into five categories: handle, next, value change link, fetch, and modify routines.

B.2.1 Handle Routines

Handle routines return handles to objects in the design. The names of handle routines always starts with the prefix `acc_handle_`. See Table B-1.

1. See the "IEEE Standard Verilog Hardware Description Language" document for details on VPI routines.

Table B-1 Handle Routines

Return Type	Name	Argument List	Description
handle	acc_handle_by_name	(char *name, handle scope)	Object from name relative to scope.
handle	acc_handle_condition	(handle object)	Conditional expression for module path or timing check handle.
handle	acc_handle_conn	(handle terminal);	Get net connected to a primitive, module path, or timing check terminal.
handle	acc_handle_datapath	(handle modpath);	Get the handle to data path for an edge-sensitive module path.
handle	acc_handle_hiconn	(handle port);	Get hierarchically higher net connection to a module port.
handle	acc_handle _interactive_scope	( );	Get the handle to the current simulation interactive scope.
handle	acc_handle_loconn	(handle port);	Get hierarchically lower net connection to a module port.
handle	acc_handle_modpath	(handle module, char *src, char *dest); or (handle module, handle src, handle dest);	Get the handle to module path whose source and destination are specified. Module path can be specified by names or handles.
handle	acc_handle_notifier	(handle tchk);	Get notifier register associated with a particular timing check.
handle	acc_handle_object	(char *name);	Get the handle for any object, given its full or relative hierarchical path name.
handle	acc_handle_parent	(handle object);	Get the handle for own primitive or containing module or an object.
handle	acc_handle_path	(handle outport, handle inport);	Get the handle to path from output port of a module to input port of ' another module.
handle	acc_handle_pathin	(handle modpath);	Get the handle for first net connected to the input of a module path.
handle	acc_handle_pathout	(handle modpath);	Get the handle for first net connected to the output of a module path.
handle	acc_handle_port	(handle module, int port#);	Get the handle for module port. Port# is the position from the left in the module definition (starting with 0).

Table B-1 Handle Routines (Continued)

Return Type	Name	Argument List	Description
handle	acc_handle_scope	(handle object);	Get the handle to the scope containing an object.
handle	acc_handle _simulated_net	(handle collapsed_net_handle);	Get the handle to the net associated with a collapsed net.
handle	acc_handle_tchk	(handle module, int tchk_type, char *netname1, int edge1, ...);	Get the handle for a specified timing check of a module or cell.
handle	acc_handle_tchkarg1	(handle tchk);	Get net connected to the first argument of a timing check.
handle	acc_handle_tchkarg2	(handle tchk);	Get net connected to the second argument of a timing check.
handle	acc_handle_terminal	(handle primitive, int terminal#);	Get the handle for a primitive terminal. Terminal# is the position in the argument list.
handle	acc_handle_tfarg	(int arg#);	Get the handle to argument arg# of calling system task or function that invokes the PLI routine.
handle	acc_handle_tfinst	( );	Get the handle to the current user defined system task or function.

B.2.2 Next Routines

Next routines return the handle to the next object in the linked list of a given object type in a design. Next routines always start with the prefix **`acc_next_`** and accept reference objects as arguments. Reference objects are shown with a prefix *current_*. See Table B-2.

Table B-2 Next Routines

Return Type	Name	Argument List	Description
handle	acc_next	(int obj_type_array[], handle module, handle current_object);	Get next object of a certain type within a scope. Object types such as accNet or accRegister are defined in obj_type_array.
handle	acc_next_bit	(handle vector, handle current_bit);	Get next bit in a vector port or array.
handle	acc_next_cell	(handle module, handle current_cell);	Get next cell instance in a module. Cells are defined in a library.
handle	acc_next_cell_load	(handle net, handle current_cell_load);	Get next cell load on a net.

Table B-2 Next Routines (Continued)

Return Type	Name	Argument List	Description
handle	acc_next_child	(handle module, handle current_child);	Get next module instance appearing in this module
handle	acc_next_driver	(handle net, handle current_driver_terminal);	Get next primitive terminal driver that drives the net.
handle	acc_next_hiconn	(handle port, handle current_net);	Get next higher net connection.
handle	acc_next_input	(handle path_or_tchk, handle current_terminal);	Get next input terminal of a specified module path or timing check.
handle	acc_next_load	(handle net, handle current_load);	Get next primitive terminal driven by a net independent of hierarchy.
handle	acc_next_loconn	(handle port, handle current_net);	Get next lower net connection to a module port.
handle	acc_next_modpath	(handle module, handle path);	Get next path within a module.
handle	acc_next_net	(handle module, handle current_net);	Get the next net in a module.
handle	acc_next output	(handle path, handle current_terminal);	Get next output terminal of a module path or data path.
handle	acc_next_parameter	(handle module, handle current_parameter);	Get next parameter in a module.
handle	acc_next_port	(handle module, handle current_port);	Get the next port in a module port list.
handle	acc_next_portout	(handle module, handle current_port);	Get next output or inout port of a module.
handle	acc_next_primitive	(handle module, handle current_primitive);	Get next primitive in a module.
handle	acc_next_scope	(handle scope, handle current_scope);	Get next hierarchy scope within a certain scope.
handle	acc_next_specparam	(handle module, handle current_specparam);	Get next specparam declared in a module.
handle	acc_next_tchk	(handle module, handle current_tchk);	Get next timing check in a module.
handle	acc_next_terminal	(handle primitive, handle current_terminal);	Get next terminal of a primitive.
handle	acc_next_topmod	(handle current_topmod);	Get next top level module in the design.

B.2.3 Value Change Link (VCL) Routines

VCL routines allow the user system task to add and delete objects from the list of objects that are monitored for value changes. VCL routines always begin with the prefix **acc_vcl_** and do not return a value. See Table B-3.

Table B-3 Value Change Link Routines

Return Type	Name	Argument List	Description
void	acc_vcl_add	(handle object, int (*consumer_routine) (), char *user_data, int VCL_flags);	Tell the Verilog simulator to call the consumer routine with value change information whenever the value of an object changes.
void	acc_vcl_delete	(handle object, int (*consumer_routine) (), char *user_data, int VCL_flags);	Tell the Verilog simulator to stop calling the consumer routine when the value of an object changes.

B.2.4 Fetch Routines

Fetch routines can extract a variety of information about objects. Information such as full hierarchical path name, relative name, and other attributes can be obtained. Fetch routines always start with the prefix **acc_fetch_**. See Table B-4.

Table B-4 Fetch Routines

Return Type	Name	Argument List	Description
int	acc_fetch_argc	( );	Get the number of invocation command-line arguments.
char **	acc_fetch_argv	( );	Get the array of invocation command-line arguments.
double	acc_fetch_attribute	(handle object, char *attribute, double default);	Get the attribute of a parameter or specparam.
char *	acc_fetch_defname	(handle object);	Get the defining name of a module or a primitive instance.
int	acc_fetch_delay_mode	(handle module);	Get delay mode of a module instance.
bool	acc_fetch_delays	(handle object, double *rise, double *fall, double *turnoff); (handle object, double *d1, *d2, *d3, *d4 *d5, *d6);	Get typical delay values for primitives, module paths, timing checks, or module input ports.
int	acc_fetch_direction	(handle object);	Get the direction of a port or terminal, i.e., input, output, or inout.

Table B-4 Fetch Routines (Continued)

Return Type	Name	Argument List	Description
int	acc_fetch_edge	(handle path_or_tchk_term);	Get the edge specifier type of a path input or output terminal or a timing check input terminal.
char *	acc_fetch_fullname	(handle object);	Get the full hierarchical name of any name object or module path.
int	acc_fetch_fulltype	(handle object);	Get the type of the object. Return a predefined integer constant that tells type.
int	acc_fetch_index	(handle port_or_terminal);	Get the index for a port or terminal for gate, switch, UDP instance, module, etc. Zero returned for the first terminal.
void	acc_fetch_location	(p_location loc_p, handle object);	Get the location of an object in a Verilog source file. p_location is a predefined data structure that has file name and line number in the file.
char *	acc_fetch_name	(handle object);	Get instance of object or module path within a module.
int	acc_fetch_paramtype	(handle parameter);	Get the data type of parameter, integer, string, real, etc.
double	acc_fetch_paramval	(handle parameter);	Get value of parameter or specparam. Must cast return values to integer, string, or double.
int	acc_fetch_polarity	(handle path);	Get polarity of a path.
int	acc_fetch_precision	( );	Get the simulation time precision.
bool	acc_fetch_pulsere	(handle path, double *r1, double *e1,double *r2, double *e2.........)	Get pulse control values for module paths based on reject values and e_values for transitions.
int	acc_fetch_range	(handle vector, int *msb, int *lsb);	Get the most significant bit and least significant bit range values of a vector.
int	acc_fetch_size	(handle object);	Get number of bits in a net, register, or port.
double	acc_fetch_tfarg	(int arg#);	Get value of system task or function argument indexed by arg#.

Table B-4 Fetch Routines (Continued)

Return Type	Name	Argument List	Description
int	acc_fetch_tfarg_int	(int arg#);	Get integer value of system task or function argument indexed by arg#.
char *	acc_fetch_tfarg_str	(int arg#);	Get string value of system task or function argument indexed by arg#.
void	acc_fetch _timescale_info	(handle object, p_timescale_info timescale_p);	Get the time scale information for an object. p_timescale_info is a pointer to a predefined time scale data structure.
int	acc_fetch_type	(handle object);	Get the type of object. Return a predefined integer constant such as accIntegerVar, accModule, etc.
char *	acc_fetch_type_str	(handle object);	Get the type of object in string format. Return a string of type accIntegerVar, accParameter, etc.
char *	acc_fetch_value	(handle object, char *format);	Get the logic or strength value of a net, register, or variable in the specified format.

B.2.5 Utility Access Routines

Utility access routines perform miscellaneous operations related to access routines. See Table B-5.

Table B-5 Utility Access Routines

Return Type	Name	Argument List	Description
void	acc_close	( );	Free internal memory used by access routines and reset all configuration parameters to default values.
handle *	acc_collect	(handle *next_routine, handle ref_object, int *count);	Collect all objects related to a particular reference object by successive calls to an acc_next routine. Return an array of handles.
bool	acc_compare_handles	(handle object1, handle object2);	Return true if both handles refer to the same object.
void	acc_configure	(int config_param, char *config_value);	Set parameters that control the operation of various access routines.
int	acc_count	(handle *next_routine, handle ref_object);	Count the number of objects in a reference object such as a module. The objects are counted by successive calls to the acc_next routine
void	acc_free	(handle *object_handles);	Free memory allocated by acc_collect for storing object handles.
void	acc_initialize	( );	Reset all access routine configuration parameters. Call when entering a user-defined PLI routine.
bool	acc_object_in_typelist	(handle object, int object_types[]);	Match the object type or property against an array of listed types or properties.
bool	acc_object_of_type	(handle object, int object_type);	Match the object type or property against a specific type or property.
int	acc_product_type	( );	Get the type of software product being used.
char *	acc_product_version	( );	Get the version of software product being used.
int	acc_release_object	(handle object);	Deallocate memory associated with an input or output terminal path.

Table B-5 Utility Access Routines (Continued)

Return Type	Name	Argument List	Description
void	acc_reset_buffer	( );	Reset the string buffer.
handle	acc_set _interactive_scope	( );	Set the interactive scope of a software implementation.
void	acc_set_scope	(handle module, char *module_name);	Set the scope for searching for objects in a design hierarchy.
char *	acc_version	( );	Get the version of access routines being used.

B.2.6 Modify Routines

Modify routines can modify internal data structures. See Table B-6.

Table B-6 Modify Routines

Return Type	Name	Argument List	Description
void	acc_append_delays	(handle object, double rise, double fall, double z); or (handle object, double d1, ..., double d6); or (handle object, double limit); or (handle object double delay[]);	Add delays to existing delay values for primitives, module paths, timing checks, or module input ports. Can specify rise/fall/turn-off or 6 delay or timing check or min:typ:max format.
bool	acc_append_pulsere	(handle path, double r1, ..., double r12, double e1, ..., double e12);	Add to the existing pulse control values of a module path.
void	acc_replace_delays	(handle object, double rise, double fall, double z); or (handle object, double d1, ..., double d6); or (handle object, double limit); or (handle object double delay[]);	Replace delay values for primitives, module paths, timing checks, or module input ports. Can specify rise/fall/turn-off or 6 delay or timing check or min:typ:max format.
bool	acc_replace_pulsere	(handle path, double r1, ..., double r12, double e1, ..., double e12);	Set pulse control values of a module path as a percentage of path delays.
void	acc_set_pulsere	(handle path, double reject, double e);	Set pulse control percentages for a module path.
void	acc_set_value	(handle object, p_setval_value value_P, p_setval_delay delay_P);	Set value for a register or a sequential UDP.

B.3 Utility (tf_) Routines

Utility (`tf_`) routines are used to pass data in both directions across the Verilog/user C routine boundary. All the `tf_` routines assume that operations are being performed on current instances. Each `tf_` routine has a `tf_i` counterpart in which the instance pointer where the operations take place has to be passed as an additional argument at the end of the argument list. See Table B-7 through B-16.

B.3.1 Get Calling Task/Function Information

Table B-7 Get Calling Task/Function Information

Return Type	Name	Argument List	Description
char *	tf_getinstance	( );	Get the pointer to the current instance of the simulation task or function that called the user's PLI application program.
char *	tf_mipname	( );	Get the Verilog hierarchical path name of the simulation module containing the call to the user's PI application program.
char *	tf_ispname	( )	Get the Verilog hierarchical path name of the scope containing the call to the user's PLI application program.

B.3.2 Get Argument List Information

Table B-8 Get Argument List Information

Return Type	Name	Argument List	Description
int	tf_nump	( );	Get the number of parameters in the argument list.
int	tf_typep	(int param_index#);	Get the type of a particular parameter in the argument list.
int	tf_sizep	(int param_index#);	Get the length of a parameter in bits.
t_tfexprinfo *	tf_expinfo	(int param_index#, struct t_tfexprinfo *exprinfo_p);	Get information about a parameter expression.
t_tfexprinfo *	tf_nodeinfo	(int param_index#, struct t_tfexprinfo *exprinfo_p);	Get information about a node value parameter.

B.3.3 Get Parameter Values

Table B-9 Get Parameter Values

Return Type	Name	Argument List	Description
int	tf_getp	(int param_index#);	Get the value of parameter in integer form.
double	tf_getrealp	(int param_index#);	Get the value of a parameter in double-precision floating-point form.
int	tf_getlongp	(int *aof_highvalue, int para_index#);	Get parameter value in long 64-bit integer form.
char *	tf_strgetp	(int param_index#, char format_character);	Get parameter value as a formatted character string.
char *	tf_getcstringp	(int param_index#);	Get parameter value as a C character string.
void	tf_evaluatep	(int param_index#);	Evaluate a parameter expression and get the result.

B.3.4 Put Parameter Value

Table B-10 Put Parameter Values

Return Type	Name	Argument List	Description
void	tf_putp	(int param_index#, int value);	Pass back an integer value to the calling task or function.
void	tf_putrealp	(int param_index#, double value;	Pass back a double-precision floating-point value to the calling task or function.
void	tf_putlongp	(int param_index#, int lowvalue, int highvalue);	Pass back a double-precision 64-bit integer value to the calling task or function.
void	tf_propagatep	(int param_index#);	Propagate a node parameter value.
int	tf_strdelputp	(int param_index#, int bitlength, char format_char, int delay, int delaytype, char *value_p);	Pass back a value and schedule an event on the parameter. The value is expressed as a formatted character string, and the delay, as an integer value.
int	tf_strrealdelputp	(int param_index#, int bitlength, char format_char, int delay, double delaytype, char *value_p);	Pass back a string value with an attached real delay.
int	tf_strlongdelputp	(int param_index#, int bitlength, char format_char, int lowdelay,int highdelay, int delaytype, char *value_p);	Pass back a string value with an attached long delay.

B.3.5 Monitor Parameter Value Changes

Table B-11 Monitor Parameter Value Changes

Return Type	Name	Argument List	Description
void	tf_asynchon	( );	Enable a user PLI routine to be called whenever a parameter changes value.
void	tf_asynchoff	( );	Disable asynchronous calling.
void	tf_synchronize	( );	Synchronize parameter value changes to the end of the current simulation time slot.
void	tf_rosynchronize	( );	Synchronize parameter value changes and suppress new event generation during current simulation time slot.
int	tf_getpchange	(int param_index#);	Get the number of the parameter that changed value.
int	tf_copypvc_flag	(int param_index#);	Copy a parameter value change flag.
int	tf_movepvc_flag	(int param_index#);	Save a parameter value change flag.
int	tf_testpvc_flag	(int param_index#);	Test a parameter value change flag.

B.3.6 Synchronize Tasks

Table B-12 Synchronize Tasks

Return Type	Name	Argument List	Description
int	tf_gettime	( );	Get current simulation time in integer form.
	tf_getrealtime		
int	tf_getlongtime	(int *aof_hightime);	Get current simulation time in long integer form.
char *	tf_strgettime	( );	Get current simulation time as a character string.
int	tf_getnextlongtime	(int *aof_lowtime, int *aof_hightime);	Get time of the next scheduled simulation event.
int	tf_setdelay	(int delay);	Cause user task to be reactivated at a future simulation time expressed as an integer value delay.
int	tf_setlongdelay	(int lowdelay, int highdelay);	Cause user task to be reactivated after a long integer value delay.
int	tf_setrealdelay	(double delay, char *instance);	Activate the misctf application at a particular simulation time.

Table B-12 Synchronize Tasks (Continued)

Return Type	Name	Argument List	Description
void	tf_scale_longdelay	(char *instance, int lowdelay, int hidelay, int *aof_lowtime, int *aof_hightime);	Convert a 64-bit integer delay to internal simulation time units.
void	tf_scale_realdelay	(char *instance, double delay, double *aof_realdelay);	Convert a double-precision floating-point delay to internal simulation time units.
void	tf_unscale_longdelay	(char *instance, int lowdelay, int hidelay, int *aof_lowtime, int *aof_hightime);	Convert a delay from internal simulation time units to the time scale of a particular module.
void	tf_unscale_realdelay	(char *instance, double delay, double *aof_realdelay);	Convert a delay from internal simulation time units to the time scale of a particular module.
void	tf_clearalldelays	( );	Clear all reactivation delays.
int	tf_strdelputp	(int param_index#, int bitlength, char format_char, int delay, int delaytype, char *value_p);	Pass back a value and schedule an event on the parameter. The value is expressed as a formatted character string and the delay as an integer value.
int	tf_strrealdelputp	(int param_index#, int bitlength, char format_char, int delay, double delaytype, char *value_p);	Pass back a string value with an attached real delay.
int	tf_strlongdelputp	(int param_index#, int bitlength, char format_char, int lowdelay,int highdelay, int delaytype, char *value_p);	Pass back a string value with an attached long delay.

B.3.7 Long Arithmetic

Table B-13 Long Arithmetic

Return Type	Name	Argument List	Description
void	tf_add_long	(int *aof_low1, int *aof_high1, int low2, int high2);	Add two 64-bit long values.
void	tf_subtract_long	(int *aof_low1, int *aof_high1, int low2, int high2);	Subtract one long value from another.
void	tf_multiply_long	(int *aof_low1, int *aof_high1, int low2, int high2);	Multiply two long values.
void	tf_divide_long	(int *aof_low1, int *aof_high1, int low2, int high2);	Divide one long value by another.
int	tf_compare_long	(int low1, int high1, int low2, int high2);	Compare two long values.
char *	tf_longtime_tostr	(int lowtime, int hightime);	Convert a long value to a character string.
void	tf_real_to_long	(double real, int *aof_low, int *aof_high);	Convert a real number to a 64-bit integer.
void	tf_long_to_real	(int low, int high, double *aof_real);	Convert a long integer to a real number.

B.3.8 Display Messages

Table B-14 Display Messages

Return Type	Name	Argument List	Description
void	io_printf	(char *format, arg1,......);	Write messages to the standard output and log file.
void	io_mcdprintf	(char *format, arg1,......);	Write messages to multiple-channel descriptor files.
void	tf_error	(char *format, arg1,......);	Print error message.
void	tf_warning	(char *format, arg1,......);	Print warning message.
void	tf_message	(int level, char facility, char code, char *message, arg1, ...);	Print error and warning messages, using the Verilog simulator's standard error handling facility.
void	tf_text	(char *format, arg1, ...);	Store error message information in a buffer. Displayed when tf_message is called.

B.3.9 Miscellaneous Utility Routines

Table B-15 Miscellaneous Utility Routines

Return Type	Name	Argument List	Description
void	tf_dostop	( );	Halt the simulation and put the system in interactive mode.
void	tf_dofinish	( );	Terminate the simulation.
char *	mc_scanplus_args	(char *startarg);	Get command line plus (+) options entered by the user in interactive mode.
void	tf_write_save	(char *blockptr, int blocklength);	Write PLI application data to a save file.
int	tf_read_restart	(char *blockptr, int block_length);	Get a block of data from a previously written save file.
void	tf_read_restore	(char *blockptr, int blocklength);	Retrieve data from a save file.
void	tf_dumpflush	( );	Dump parameter value changes to a system dump file.
char *	tf_dumpfilename	( );	Get name of system dump file.

B.3.10 Housekeeping Tasks

Table B-16 Housekeeping Tasks

Return Type	Name	Argument List	Description
void	tf_setworkarea	(char *workarea);	Save a pointer to the work area of a PLI application task/function instance.
char *	tf_getworkarea	( );	Retrieve pointer to a work area.
void	tf_setroutine	(char (*routine) ());	Store pointer to a PLI application task/function.
char *	tf_getroutine	( );	Retrieve pointer to a PLI application task/function.
void	tf_settflist	(char *tflist);	Store pointer to a PLI application task/function instance.
char *	tf_gettflist	( );	Retrieve pointer to a PLI application task/function instance.

List of Keywords, System Tasks, and Compiler Directives

C 

C.1 Keywords

Keywords[1] are predefined, nonescaped identifiers that define the language constructs. An escaped identifier is never treated as a keyword. All keywords are defined in lowercase.

1. From IEEE Std. 1364-2001.

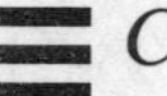 C

The list is sorted in alphabetical order.

```
always          ifnone                  rnmos
and             incdir                  rpmos
assign          include                 rtran
automatic       initial                 rtranif0
begin           inout                   rtranif1
buf             input                   scalared
bufif0          instance                showcancelled
bufif1          integer                 signed
case            join                    small
casex           large                   specify
casez           liblist                 specparam
cell            library                 strong0
cmos            localparam              strong1
config          macromodule             supply0
deassign        medium                  supply1
default         module                  table
defparam        nand                    task
design          negedge                 time
disable         nmos                    tran
edge            nor                     tranif0
else            noshowcancelled         tranif1
end             not                     tri
endcase         notif0                  tri0
endconfig       notif1                  tri1
endfunction     or                      triand
endgenerate     output                  trior
endmodule       parameter               trireg
endprimitive    pmos                    unsigned
endspecify      posedge                 use
endtable        primitive               vectored
endtask         pull0                   wait
event           pull1                   wand
for             pulldown                weak0
force           pullup                  weak1
forever         pulsestyle_onevent      while
fork            pulsestyle_ondetect     wire
function        rcmos                   wor
generate        real                    xnor
genvar          realtime                xor
highz0          reg
highz1          release
if              repeat
```

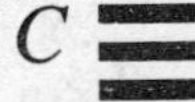

C.2 System Tasks and Functions

The following is a list of keywords frequently used by Verilog simulators for names of system tasks and functions. Not all system tasks and functions are explained in this book. For details, refer to the *IEEE Standard Verilog Hardware Description Language* document. This list is sorted in alphabetical order.

```
$bitstoreal     $countdrivers    $display       $fclose
$fdisplay       $fmonitor        $fopen         $fstrobe
$fwrite         $finish          $getpattern    $history
$incsave        $input           $itor          $key
$list           $log             $monitor       $monitoroff
$monitoron      $nokey
```

C.3 Compiler Directives

The following is a list of keywords frequently used by Verilog simulators for specifying compiler directives. Only the most frequently used directives are discussed in the book. For details, refer to the *IEEE Standard Verilog Hardware Description Language* document. This list is sorted in alphabetical order.

```
`accelerate            `autoexpand_vectornets    `celldefine
`default_nettype       `define                   `define
`else                  `elsif                    `endcelldefine
`endif                 `endprotect               `endprotected
`expand_vectornets     `ifdef                    `ifndef
`include               `no accelerate            `noexpand_vectornets
`noremove_gatenames    `nounconnected_drive      `protect
`protected             `remove_gatenames         `remove_netnames
`resetall              `timescale                `unconnected_drive
```

Formal Syntax Definition D

This appendix contains the formal definition[1] of the Verilog-2001 standard in Backus-Naur Form (BNF). The formal definition contains a description of every possible usage of Verilog HDL. Therefore, it is very useful if there is a doubt on the usage of certain Verilog HDL syntax.

Though the BNF may be hard to understand initially, the following summary may help the reader better understand the formal syntax definition:

1. Bold text represents literal words themselves (these are called terminals). Example: **module**.
2. Non-bold text (possibly with underscores) represents syntactic categories (these are called non terminals). Example: port_identifier.
3. Syntactic categories are defined using the form: syntactic_category ::= definition
4. [ ] square brackets (non-bold) surround optional items.
5. { } curly brackets (non-bold) surround items that can repeat zero or more times.
6. | vertical line (non-bold) separates alternatives.

1. From IEEE Std. 1364-2001.

D.1 Source Text

D.1.1 Library Source Text

library_text ::= { library_descriptions }
library_descriptions ::=
library_declaration
| include_statement
| config_declaration
library_declaration ::=
library library_identifier file_path_spec [{ **,** file_path_spec }]
[**-incdir** file_path_spec [{ **,** file_path_spec }] **;**
file_path_spec ::= file_path
include_statement ::= **include** <file_path_spec> **;**

D.1.2 Configuration Source Text

config_declaration ::=
config config_identifier **;**
design_statement
{config_rule_statement}
endconfig
design_statement ::= **design** { [library_identifier**.**]cell_identifier } **;**
config_rule_statement ::=
default_clause liblist_clause
| inst_clause liblist_clause
| inst_clause use_clause
| cell_clause liblist_clause
| cell_clause use_clause
default_clause ::= **default**
inst_clause ::= **instance** inst_name
inst_name ::= topmodule_identifier{**.**instance_identifier}
cell_clause ::= **cell** [library_identifier**.**]cell_identifier
liblist_clause ::= **liblist** [{library_identifier}]
use_clause ::= **use** [library_identifier**.**]cell_identifier[**:config**]

D.1.3 Module and Primitive Source Text

source_text ::= { description }

description ::=
    module_declaration
  | udp_declaration
module_declaration ::=
  { attribute_instance } module_keyword module_identifier [module_parameter_port_list]
      [list_of_ports] ; { module_item }
      endmodule
  | { attribute_instance } module_keyword module_identifier [module_parameter_port_list]
      [list_of_port_declarations] ; { non_port_module_item }
      endmodule
module_keyword ::= **module** | **macromodule**

D.1.4 Module Parameters and Ports

module_parameter_port_list ::= **#** (parameter_declaration { , parameter_declaration })
list_of_ports ::= (port { , port })
list_of_port_declarations ::=
    (port_declaration { , port_declaration })
  | ( )
port ::=
    [port_expression]
  | . port_identifier ([port_expression])
port_expression ::=
    port_reference
  | { port_reference { , port_reference } }
port_reference ::=
    port_identifier
  | port_identifier [constant_expression]
  | port_identifier [range_expression]
port_declaration ::=
    {attribute_instance} inout_declaration
  | {attribute_instance} input_declaration
  | {attribute_instance} output_declaration

D.1.5 Module Items

module_item ::=

module_or_generate_item
| port_declaration ;
| { attribute_instance } generated_instantiation
| { attribute_instance } local_parameter_declaration
| { attribute_instance } parameter_declaration
| { attribute_instance } specify_block
| { attribute_instance } specparam_declaration

module_or_generate_item ::=
{ attribute_instance } module_or_generate_item_declaration
| { attribute_instance } parameter_override
| { attribute_instance } continuous_assign
| { attribute_instance } gate_instantiation
| { attribute_instance } udp_instantiation
| { attribute_instance } module_instantiation
| { attribute_instance } initial_construct
| { attribute_instance } always_construct

module_or_generate_item_declaration ::=
net_declaration
| reg_declaration
| integer_declaration
| real_declaration
| time_declaration
| realtime_declaration
| event_declaration
| genvar_declaration
| task_declaration
| function_declaration

non_port_module_item ::=
{ attribute_instance } generated_instantiation
| { attribute_instance } local_parameter_declaration
| { attribute_instance } module_or_generate_item
| { attribute_instance } parameter_declaration
| { attribute_instance } specify_block
| { attribute_instance } specparam_declaration

parameter_override ::= **defparam** list_of_param_assignments ;

D.2 Declarations

D.2.1 Declaration Types

Module parameter declarations

local_parameter_declaration ::=
    localparam [**signed**] [range] list_of_param_assignments ;
  | **localparam integer** list_of_param_assignments ;
  | **localparam real** list_of_param_assignments ;
  | **localparam realtime** list_of_param_assignments ;
  | **localparam time** list_of_param_assignments ;
parameter_declaration ::=
    parameter [**signed**] [range] list_of_param_assignments ;
  | **parameter integer** list_of_param_assignments ;
  | **parameter real** list_of_param_assignments ;
  | **parameter realtime** list_of_param_assignments ;
  | **parameter time** list_of_param_assignments ;
specparam_declaration ::= **specparam** [range] list_of_specparam_assignments ;

Port declarations

inout_declaration ::= **inout** [net_type] [**signed**] [range]
        list_of_port_identifiers
input_declaration ::= **input** [net_type] [**signed**] [range]
        list_of_port_identifiers
output_declaration ::=
    output [net_type] [**signed**] [range]
        list_of_port_identifiers
  | **output** [**reg**] [**signed**] [range]
        list_of_port_identifiers
  | **output reg** [**signed**] [range]
        list_of_variable_port_identifiers
  | **output** [output_variable_type]
        list_of_port_identifiers
  | **output** output_variable_type
        list_of_variable_port_identifiers

Type declarations

event_declaration ::= **event** list_of_event_identifiers ;
genvar_declaration ::= **genvar** list_of_genvar_identifiers ;
integer_declaration ::= **integer** list_of_variable_identifiers ;
net_declaration ::=
    net_type [**signed**]
        [delay3] list_of_net_identifiers ;
    | net_type [drive_strength] [**signed**]
        [delay3] list_of_net_decl_assignments ;
    | net_type [**vectored** | **scalared**] [**signed**]
        range [delay3] list_of_net_identifiers ;
    | net_type [drive_strength] [**vectored** | **scalared**] [**signed**]
        range [delay3] list_of_net_decl_assignments ;
    | **trireg** [charge_strength] [**signed**]
        [delay3] list_of_net_identifiers ;
    | **trireg** [drive_strength] [**signed**]
        [delay3] list_of_net_decl_assignments ;
    | **trireg** [charge_strength] [**vectored** | **scalared**] [**signed**]
        range [delay3] list_of_net_identifiers ;
    | **trireg** [drive_strength] [**vectored** | **scalared**] [**signed**]
        range [delay3] list_of_net_decl_assignments ;
real_declaration ::= **real** list_of_real_identifiers ;
realtime_declaration ::= **realtime** list_of_real_identifiers ;
reg_declaration ::= **reg** [**signed**] [range]
        list_of_variable_identifiers ;
time_declaration ::= **time** list_of_variable_identifiers ;

D.2.2 Declaration Data Types

Net and variable types

net_type ::=
    supply0 | **supply1**
    | **tri** | **triand** | **trior** | **tri0** | **tri1**
    | **wire** | **wand** | **wor**
output_variable_type ::= **integer** | **time**
real_type ::=
    real_identifier [= constant_expression]

| real_identifier dimension { dimension }
variable_type ::=
variable_identifier [= constant_expression]
| variable_identifier dimension { dimension }

Strengths

drive_strength ::=
(strength0 , strength1)
| (strength1 , strength0)
| (strength0 , **highz1**)
| (strength1 , **highz0**)
| (**highz0** , strength1)
| (**highz1** , strength0)
strength0 ::= **supply0** | **strong0** | **pull0** | **weak0**
strength1 ::= **supply1** | **strong1** | **pull1** | **weak1**
charge_strength ::= **(small)** | **(medium)** | **(large)**

Delays

delay3 ::= # delay_value | # (delay_value [, delay_value [, delay_value]])
delay2 ::= # delay_value | # (delay_value [, delay_value])
delay_value ::=
unsigned_number
| parameter_identifier
| specparam_identifier
| mintypmax_expression

D.2.3 Declaration Lists

list_of_event_identifiers ::= event_identifier [dimension { dimension }]
{ , event_identifier [dimension { dimension }] }
list_of_genvar_identifiers ::= genvar_identifier { , genvar_identifier }
list_of_net_decl_assignments ::= net_decl_assignment { , net_decl_assignment }
list_of_net_identifiers ::= net_identifier [dimension { dimension }]
{ , net_identifier [dimension { dimension }] }
list_of_param_assignments ::= param_assignment { , param_assignment }
list_of_port_identifiers ::= port_identifier { , port_identifier }
list_of_real_identifiers ::= real_type { , real_type }
list_of_specparam_assignments ::= specparam_assignment { , specparam_assignment }

list_of_variable_identifiers ::= variable_type { , variable_type }
list_of_variable_port_identifiers ::= port_identifier [= constant_expression]
{ , port_identifier [= constant_expression] }

D.2.4 Declaration Assignments

net_decl_assignment ::= net_identifier = expression
param_assignment ::= parameter_identifier = constant_expression
specparam_assignment ::=
specparam_identifier = constant_mintypmax_expression
| pulse_control_specparam
pulse_control_specparam ::=
PATHPULSE$ = (reject_limit_value [, error_limit_value]) ;
| **PATHPULSE$**specify_input_terminal_descriptor$specify_output_terminal_descriptor
= (reject_limit_value [, error_limit_value]) ;
error_limit_value ::= limit_value
reject_limit_value ::= limit_value
limit_value ::= constant_mintypmax_expression

D.2.5 Declaration Ranges

dimension ::= [dimension_constant_expression : dimension_constant_expression]
range ::= [msb_constant_expression : lsb_constant_expression]

D.2.6 Function Declarations

function_declaration ::=
function [**automatic**] [**signed**] [range_or_type] function_identifier ;
function_item_declaration { function_item_declaration }
function_statement
endfunction
| **function** [**automatic**] [**signed**] [range_or_type] function_identifier (
function_port_list) ;
block_item_declaration { block_item_declaration }
function_statement
endfunction
function_item_declaration ::=
block_item_declaration
| tf_input_declaration ;
function_port_list ::= { attribute_instance } tf_input_declaration { , { attribute_instance }

tf_input_declaration }

range_or_type ::= range | **integer** | **real** | **realtime** | **time**

D.2.7 Task Declarations

task_declaration ::=
task [**automatic**] task_identifier **;**
{ task_item_declaration }
statement
endtask
| **task** [**automatic**] task_identifier (task_port_list) **;**
{ block_item_declaration }
statement
endtask

task_item_declaration ::=
block_item_declaration
| { attribute_instance } tf_input_declaration **;**
| { attribute_instance } tf_output_declaration **;**
| { attribute_instance } tf_inout_declaration **;**

task_port_list ::= task_port_item { **,** task_port_item }

task_port_item ::=
{ attribute_instance } tf_input_declaration
| { attribute_instance } tf_output_declaration
| { attribute_instance } tf_inout_declaration

tf_input_declaration ::=
input [**reg**] [**signed**] [range] list_of_port_identifiers
| **input** [task_port_type] list_of_port_identifiers

tf_output_declaration ::=
output [**reg**] [**signed**] [range] list_of_port_identifiers
| **output** [task_port_type] list_of_port_identifiers

tf_inout_declaration ::=
inout [**reg**] [**signed**] [range] list_of_port_identifiers
| **inout** [task_port_type] list_of_port_identifiers

task_port_type ::=
time | **real** | **realtime** | **integer**

D.2.8 Block Item Declarations

block_item_declaration ::=
  { attribute_instance } block_reg_declaration
  | { attribute_instance } event_declaration
  | { attribute_instance } integer_declaration
  | { attribute_instance } local_parameter_declaration
  | { attribute_instance } parameter_declaration
  | { attribute_instance } real_declaration
  | { attribute_instance } realtime_declaration
  | { attribute_instance } time_declaration

block_reg_declaration ::= **reg** [**signed**] [range]
    list_of_block_variable_identifiers **;**

list_of_block_variable_identifiers ::=
    block_variable_type { **,** block_variable_type }

block_variable_type ::=
  variable_identifier
  | variable_identifier dimension { dimension }

D.3 Primitive Instances

D.3.1 Primitive Instantiation and Instances

gate_instantiation ::=
  cmos_switchtype [delay3]
    cmos_switch_instance { **,** cmos_switch_instance } **;**
  | enable_gatetype [drive_strength] [delay3]
    enable_gate_instance { **,** enable_gate_instance } **;**
  | mos_switchtype [delay3]
    mos_switch_instance { **,** mos_switch_instance } **;**
  | n_input_gatetype [drive_strength] [delay2]
    n_input_gate_instance { **,** n_input_gate_instance } **;**
  | n_output_gatetype [drive_strength] [delay2]
    n_output_gate_instance { **,** n_output_gate_instance } **;**

  | pass_en_switchtype [delay2]
    pass_enable_switch_instance { **,** pass_enable_switch_instance } **;**
  | pass_switchtype

pass_switch_instance { , pass_switch_instance } ;
| **pulldown** [pulldown_strength]
pull_gate_instance { , pull_gate_instance } ;
| **pullup** [pullup_strength]
pull_gate_instance { , pull_gate_instance } ;

cmos_switch_instance ::= [name_of_gate_instance] (output_terminal , input_terminal , ncontrol_terminal , pcontrol_terminal)

enable_gate_instance ::= [name_of_gate_instance] (output_terminal , input_terminal , enable_terminal)

mos_switch_instance ::= [name_of_gate_instance] (output_terminal , input_terminal , enable_terminal)

n_input_gate_instance ::= [name_of_gate_instance] (output_terminal , input_terminal { , input_terminal })

n_output_gate_instance ::= [name_of_gate_instance] (output_terminal { , output_terminal } , input_terminal)

pass_switch_instance ::= [name_of_gate_instance] (inout_terminal , inout_terminal)

pass_enable_switch_instance ::= [name_of_gate_instance] (inout_terminal , inout_terminal , enable_terminal)

pull_gate_instance ::= [name_of_gate_instance] (output_terminal)

name_of_gate_instance ::= gate_instance_identifier [range]

D.3.2 Primitive Strengths

pulldown_strength ::=
(strength0 , strength1)
| (strength1 , strength0)
| (strength0)

pullup_strength ::=
(strength0 , strength1)
| (strength1 , strength0)
| (strength1)

D.3.3 Primitive Terminals

enable_terminal ::= expression
inout_terminal ::= net_lvalue
input_terminal ::= expression
ncontrol_terminal ::= expression
output_terminal ::= net_lvalue
pcontrol_terminal ::= expression

D.3.4 Primitive Gate and Switch Types

cmos_switchtype ::= **cmos** | **rcmos**
enable_gatetype ::= **bufif0** | **bufif1** | **notif0** | **notif1**
mos_switchtype ::= **nmos** | **pmos** | **rnmos** | **rpmos**
n_input_gatetype ::= **and** | **nand** | **or** | **nor** | **xor** | **xnor**
n_output_gatetype ::= **buf** | **not**
pass_en_switchtype ::= **tranif0** | **tranif1** | **rtranif1** | **rtranif0**
pass_switchtype ::= **tran** | **rtran**

D.4 Module and Generated Instantiation

D.4.1 Module Instantiation

module_instantiation ::=
    module_identifier [parameter_value_assignment]
        module_instance { , module_instance } ;
parameter_value_assignment ::= **#** (list_of_parameter_assignments)
list_of_parameter_assignments ::=
    ordered_parameter_assignment { , ordered_parameter_assignment } |
    named_parameter_assignment { , named_parameter_assignment }
ordered_parameter_assignment ::= expression
named_parameter_assignment ::= **.** parameter_identifier ([expression])
module_instance ::= name_of_instance ([list_of_port_connections])
name_of_instance ::= module_instance_identifier [range]
list_of_port_connections ::=
    ordered_port_connection { , ordered_port_connection }
    | named_port_connection { , named_port_connection }
ordered_port_connection ::= { attribute_instance } [expression]
named_port_connection ::= { attribute_instance } .port_identifier ([expression])

D.4.2 Generated Instantiation

generated_instantiation ::= **generate** { generate_item } **endgenerate**
generate_item_or_null ::= generate_item | ;
generate_item ::=
    generate_conditional_statement
    | generate_case_statement
    | generate_loop_statement

| generate_block
| module_or_generate_item
generate_conditional_statement ::=
if (constant_expression) generate_item_or_null [**else** generate_item_or_null]
generate_case_statement ::= **case** (constant_expression)
genvar_case_item { genvar_case_item } **endcase**
genvar_case_item ::= constant_expression { , constant_expression } **:**
generate_item_or_null | **default** [**:**] generate_item_or_null
generate_loop_statement ::= **for** (genvar_assignment **;** constant_expression **;**
genvar_assignment)
begin : generate_block_identifier { generate_item } **end**
genvar_assignment ::= genvar_identifier = constant_expression
generate_block ::= **begin** [**:** generate_block_identifier] { generate_item } **end**

D.5 UDP Declaration and Instantiation

D.5.1 UDP Declaration

udp_declaration ::=
{ attribute_instance } **primitive** udp_identifier (udp_port list) **;**
udp_port_declaration { udp_port_declaration }
udp_body
endprimitive
| { attribute_instance } **primitive** udp_identifier (udp_declaration_port_list) **;**
udp_body
endprimitive

D.5.2 UDP Ports

udp_port_list ::= output_port_identifier **,** input_port_identifier { **,** input_port_identifier }
udp_declaration_port_list ::=
udp_output_declaration **,** udp_input_declaration { **,** udp_input_declaration }
udp_port_declaration ::=
udp_output_declaration **;**
| udp_input_declaration **;**
| udp_reg_declaration **;**
udp_output_declaration ::=
{ attribute_instance } **output** port_identifier
| { attribute_instance } **output reg** port_identifier [= constant_expression]

udp_input_declaration ::= { attribute_instance } **input** list_of_port_identifiers
udp_reg_declaration ::= { attribute_instance } **reg** variable_identifier

D.5.3 UDP Body

udp_body ::= combinational_body | sequential_body
combinational_body ::= **table** combinational_entry { combinational_entry } **endtable**
combinational_entry ::= level_input_list : output_symbol ;
sequential_body ::= [udp_initial_statement] **table** sequential_entry { sequential_entry } **endtable**
udp_initial_statement ::= **initial** output_port_identifier = init_val ;
init_val ::= **1'b0 | 1'b1 | 1'bx | 1'bX | 1'B0 | 1'B1 | 1'Bx | 1'BX | 1 | 0**
sequential_entry ::= seq_input_list : current_state : next_state ;
seq_input_list ::= level_input_list | edge_input_list
level_input_list ::= level_symbol { level_symbol }
edge_input_list ::= { level_symbol } edge_indicator { level_symbol }
edge_indicator ::= (level_symbol level_symbol) | edge_symbol
current_state ::= level_symbol
next_state ::= output_symbol | -
output_symbol ::= **0 | 1 | x | X**
level_symbol ::= **0 | 1 | x | X | ? | b | B**
edge_symbol ::= **r | R | f | F | p | P | n | N | ***

D.5.4 UDP Instantiation

udp_instantiation ::= udp_identifier [drive_strength] [delay2] udp_instance { , udp_instance } ;
udp_instance ::= [name_of_udp_instance] (output_terminal , input_terminal { , input_terminal })
name_of_udp_instance ::= udp_instance_identifier [range]

D.6 Behavioral Statements

D.6.1 Continuous Assignment Statements

continuous_assign ::= **assign** [drive_strength] [delay3] list_of_net_assignments ;
list_of_net_assignments ::= net_assignment { , net_assignment }
net_assignment ::= net_lvalue = expression

D.6.2 Procedural Blocks and Assignments

initial_construct ::= **initial** statement
always_construct ::= **always** statement
blocking_assignment ::= variable_lvalue = [delay_or_event_control] expression
nonblocking_assignment ::= variable_lvalue <= [delay_or_event_control] expression
procedural_continuous_assignments ::=
 assign variable_assignment
 | **deassign** variable_lvalue
 | **force** variable_assignment
 | **force** net_assignment
 | **release** variable_lvalue
 | **release** net_lvalue
function_blocking_assignment ::= variable_lvalue = expression
function_statement_or_null ::=
 function_statement
 | { attribute_instance } **;**

D.6.3 Parallel and Sequential Blocks

function_seq_block ::= **begin** [**:** block_identifier
 { block_item_declaration }] { function_statement } **end**
variable_assignment ::= variable_lvalue = expression
par_block ::= **fork** [**:** block_identifier
 { block_item_declaration }] { statement } **join**
seq_block ::= **begin** [**:** block_identifier
 { block_item_declaration }] { statement } **end**

D.6.4 Statements

statement ::=
 { attribute_instance } blocking_assignment **;**
 | { attribute_instance } case_statement
 | { attribute_instance } conditional_statement
 | { attribute_instance } disable_statement
 | { attribute_instance } event_trigger
 | { attribute_instance } loop_statement
 | { attribute_instance } nonblocking_assignment **;**
 | { attribute_instance } par_block
 | { attribute_instance } procedural_continuous_assignments **;**

| { attribute_instance } procedural_timing_control_statement
| { attribute_instance } seq_block
| { attribute_instance } system_task_enable
| { attribute_instance } task_enable
| { attribute_instance } wait_statement

statement_or_null ::=
statement
| { attribute_instance } ;

function_statement ::=
{ attribute_instance } function_blocking_assignment ;
| { attribute_instance } function_case_statement
| { attribute_instance } function_conditional_statement
| { attribute_instance } function_loop_statement
| { attribute_instance } function_seq_block
| { attribute_instance } disable_statement
| { attribute_instance } system_task_enable

D.6.5 Timing Control Statements

delay_control ::=
delay_value
| # (mintypmax_expression)

delay_or_event_control ::=
delay_control
| event_control
| **repeat** (expression) event_control

disable_statement ::=
disable hierarchical_task_identifier ;
| **disable** hierarchical_block_identifier ;

event_control ::=
@ event_identifier
| @ (event_expression)
| @*
| @ (*)

event_trigger ::=
-> hierarchical_event_identifier ;

event_expression ::=
expression
| hierarchical_identifier

| **posedge** expression
| **negedge** expression
| event_expression **or** event_expression
| event_expression , event_expression
procedural_timing_control_statement ::=
delay_or_event_control statement_or_null
wait_statement ::=
wait (expression) statement_or_null

D.6.6 Conditional Statements

conditional_statement ::=
if (expression)
statement_or_null [**else** statement_or_null]
| if_else_if_statement
if_else_if_statement ::=
if (expression) statement_or_null
{ **else if** (expression) statement_or_null }
[**else** statement_or_null]
function_conditional_statement ::=
if (expression) function_statement_or_null
[**else** function_statement_or_null]
| function_if_else_if_statement
function_if_else_if_statement ::=
if (expression) function_statement_or_null
{ **else if** (expression) function_statement_or_null }
[**else** function_statement_or_null]

D.6.7 Case Statements

case_statement ::=
case (expression)
case_item { case_item } **endcase**
| **casez** (expression)
case_item { case_item } **endcase**
| **casex** (expression)
case_item { case_item } **endcase**
case_item ::=
expression { , expression } : statement_or_null

| **default** [**:**] statement_or_null
function_case_statement ::=
case (expression)
function_case_item { function_case_item } **endcase**
| **casez** (expression)
function_case_item { function_case_item } **endcase**
| **casex** (expression)
function_case_item { function_case_item } **endcase**
function_case_item ::=
expression { , expression } **:** function_statement_or_null
| **default** [**:**] function_statement_or_null

D.6.8 Looping Statements

function_loop_statement ::=
forever function_statement
| **repeat** (expression) function_statement
| **while** (expression) function_statement

| **for** (variable_assignment ; expression ; variable_assignment)
function_statement
loop_statement ::=
forever statement
| **repeat** (expression) statement
| **while** (expression) statement
| **for** (variable_assignment ; expression ; variable_assignment)
statement

D.6.9 Task Enable Statements

system_task_enable ::= system_task_identifier [(expression { , expression })] **;**
task_enable ::= hierarchical_task_identifier [(expression { , expression })] **;**

D.7 Specify Section

D.7.1 Specify Block Declaration

specify_block ::= **specify** { specify_item } **endspecify**
specify_item ::=

```
        specparam_declaration
      | pulsestyle_declaration
      | showcancelled_declaration
      | path_declaration
      | system_timing_check
pulsestyle_declaration ::=
        pulsestyle_onevent list_of_path_outputs ;
      | pulsestyle_ondetect list_of_path_outputs ;
showcancelled_declaration ::=
        showcancelled list_of_path_outputs ;
      | noshowcancelled list_of_path_outputs ;
```

D.7.2 Specify Path Declarations

```
path_declaration ::=
        simple_path_declaration ;
      | edge_sensitive_path_declaration ;
      | state_dependent_path_declaration ;
simple_path_declaration ::=
        parallel_path_description = path_delay_value
      | full_path_description = path_delay_value
parallel_path_description ::=
      ( specify_input_terminal_descriptor [ polarity_operator ] =>
                specify_output_terminal_descriptor )
full_path_description ::=
      ( list_of_path_inputs [ polarity_operator ] *> list_of_path_outputs )
list_of_path_inputs ::=
        specify_input_terminal_descriptor { , specify_input_terminal_descriptor }

list_of_path_outputs ::=
        specify_output_terminal_descriptor { , specify_output_terminal_descriptor }
```

D.7.3 Specify Block Terminals

```
specify_input_terminal_descriptor ::=
        input_identifier
      | input_identifier [ constant_expression ]
      | input_identifier [ range_expression ]
specify_output_terminal_descriptor ::=
```

```
        output_identifier
        | output_identifier [ constant_expression ]
        | output_identifier [ range_expression ]
input_identifier ::= input_port_identifier | inout_port_identifier
output_identifier ::= output_port_identifier | inout_port_identifier
```

D.7.4 Specify Path Delays

```
path_delay_value ::=
        list_of_path_delay_expressions
        | ( list_of_path_delay_expressions )
list_of_path_delay_expressions ::=
        t_path_delay_expression
        | trise_path_delay_expression , tfall_path_delay_expression
        | trise_path_delay_expression , tfall_path_delay_expression , tz_path_delay_expression
        | t01_path_delay_expression , t10_path_delay_expression , t0z_path_delay_expression ,
          tz1_path_delay_expression , t1z_path_delay_expression , tz0_path_delay_expression
        | t01_path_delay_expression , t10_path_delay_expression , t0z_path_delay_expression ,
          tz1_path_delay_expression , t1z_path_delay_expression , tz0_path_delay_expression
          t0x_path_delay_expression , tx1_path_delay_expression , t1x_path_delay_expression ,
          tx0_path_delay_expression , txz_path_delay_expression , tzx_path_delay_expression
t_path_delay_expression ::= path_delay_expression
trise_path_delay_expression ::= path_delay_expression
tfall_path_delay_expression ::= path_delay_expression
tz_path_delay_expression ::= path_delay_expression
t01_path_delay_expression ::= path_delay_expression
t10_path_delay_expression ::= path_delay_expression
t0z_path_delay_expression ::= path_delay_expression
tz1_path_delay_expression ::= path_delay_expression
t1z_path_delay_expression ::= path_delay_expression
tz0_path_delay_expression ::= path_delay_expression
t0x_path_delay_expression ::= path_delay_expression
tx1_path_delay_expression ::= path_delay_expression
t1x_path_delay_expression ::= path_delay_expression
tx0_path_delay_expression ::= path_delay_expression
txz_path_delay_expression ::= path_delay_expression
tzx_path_delay_expression ::= path_delay_expression
path_delay_expression ::= constant_mintypmax_expression
```

edge_sensitive_path_declaration ::=
    parallel_edge_sensitive_path_description = path_delay_value
    | full_edge_sensitive_path_description = path_delay_value
parallel_edge_sensitive_path_description ::=
    ([edge_identifier] specify_input_terminal_descriptor =>
        specify_output_terminal_descriptor [polarity_operator] : data_source_expression)
full_edge_sensitive_path_description ::=
    ([edge_identifier] list_of_path_inputs *>
        list_of_path_outputs [polarity_operator] : data_source_expression)
data_source_expression ::= expression
edge_identifier ::= **posedge** | **negedge**
state_dependent_path_declaration ::=
    if (module_path_expression) simple_path_declaration
    | **if** (module_path_cxpression) edge_sensitive_path_declaration
    | **ifnone** simple_path_declaration
polarity_operator ::= + | -

D.7.5 System Timing Checks

System timing check commands

system_timing_check ::=
    $setup_timing_check
    | $hold _timing_check
    | $setuphold_timing_check
    | $recovery_timing_check
    | $removal_timing_check
    | $recrem_timing_check
    | $skew_timing_check
    | $timeskew_timing_check
    | $fullskew_timing_check
    | $period_timing_check
    | $width_timing_check
    | $nochange_timing_check
$setup_timing_check ::=
    $setup (data_event , reference_event , timing_check_limit [, [notify_reg]]) ;
$hold _timing_check ::=
    $hold (reference_event , data_event , timing_check_limit [, [notify_reg]]) ;
$setuphold_timing_check ::=

```
    $setuphold ( reference_event , data_event , timing_check_limit , timing_check_limit
                  [ , [ notify_reg ] [ , [ stamptime_condition ] [ , [ checktime_condition ]
                  [ , [ delayed_reference ] [ , [ delayed_data ] ] ] ] ] ] ) ;
$recovery_timing_check ::=
    $recovery ( reference_event , data_event , timing_check_limit [ , [ notify_reg ] ] ) ;
$removal_timing_check ::=
    $removal ( reference_event , data_event , timing_check_limit [ , [ notify_reg ] ] ) ;
$recrem_timing_check ::=
    $recrem ( reference_event , data_event , timing_check_limit , timing_check_limit
                  [ , [ notify_reg ] [ , [ stamptime_condition ] [ , [ checktime_condition ]
                  [ , [ delayed_reference ] [ , [ delayed_data ] ] ] ] ] ] ) ;
$skew_timing_check ::=
    $skew ( reference_event , data_event , timing_check_limit [ , [ notify_reg ] ] ) ;
$timeskew_timing_check ::=
    $timeskew ( reference_event , data_event , timing_check_limit
                  [ , [ notify_reg ] [ , [ event_based_flag ] [ , [ remain_active_flag ] ] ] ] ) ;
$fullskew_timing_check ::=
    $fullskew ( reference_event , data_event , timing_check_limit , timing_check_limit
                  [ , [ notify_reg ] [ , [ event_based_flag ] [ , [ remain_active_flag ] ] ] ] ) ;
$period_timing_check ::=
    $period ( controlled_reference_event , timing_check_limit [ , [ notify_reg ] ] ) ;
$width_timing_check ::=
    $width ( controlled_reference_event , timing_check_limit ,
                  threshold [ , [ notify_reg ] ] ) ;
$nochange_timing_check ::=
    $nochange ( reference_event , data_event , start_edge_offset ,
                  end_edge_offset [ , [ notify_reg ] ] ) ;
```

System timing check command arguments

```
checktime_condition ::= mintypmax_expression
controlled_reference_event ::= controlled_timing_check_event
data_event ::= timing_check_event
delayed_data ::=
      terminal_identifier
    | terminal_identifier [ constant_mintypmax_expression ]
delayed_reference ::=
      terminal_identifier
    | terminal_identifier [ constant_mintypmax_expression ]
```

end_edge_offset ::= mintypmax_expression
event_based_flag ::= constant_expression
notify_reg ::= variable_identifier
reference_event ::= timing_check_event
remain_active_flag ::= constant_mintypmax_expression
stamptime_condition ::= mintypmax_expression
start_edge_offset ::= mintypmax_expression
threshold ::=constant_expression
timing_check_limit ::= expression

System timing check event definitions

timing_check_event ::=
    [timing_check_event_control] specify_terminal_descriptor [**&&&**
        timing_check_condition]
controlled_timing_check_event ::=
    timing_check_event_control specify_terminal_descriptor [**&&&**
        timing_check_condition]
timing_check_event_control ::=
    posedge
    | **negedge**
    | edge_control_specifier
specify_terminal_descriptor ::=
    specify_input_terminal_descriptor
    | specify_output_terminal_descriptor
edge_control_specifier ::= **edge** [edge_descriptor [, edge_descriptor]]
edge_descriptor[1] ::=
    01
    | **10**
    | z_or_x zero_or_one
    | zero_or_one z_or_x
zero_or_one ::= **0** | **1**
z_or_x ::= **x** | **X** | **z** | **Z**
timing_check_condition ::=
    scalar_timing_check_condition
    | (scalar_timing_check_condition)
scalar_timing_check_condition ::=
    expression
    | ~ expression

| expression == scalar_constant
| expression === scalar_constant
| expression != scalar_constant
| expression !== scalar_constant
scalar_constant ::=
1'b0 | 1'b1 | 1'B0 | 1'B1 | 'b0 | 'b1 | 'B0 | 'B1 | 1 | 0

D.8 Expressions

D.8.1 Concatenations

concatenation ::= **{** expression { **,** expression } **}**
constant_concatenation ::= **{** constant_expression { **,** constant_expression } **}**
constant_multiple_concatenation ::= **{** constant_expression constant_concatenation **}**
module_path_concatenation ::= **{** module_path_expression { **,** module_path_expression } **}**
module_path_multiple_concatenation ::= **{** constant_expression module_path_concatenation **}**
multiple_concatenation ::= **{** constant_expression concatenation **}**
net_concatenation ::= **{** net_concatenation_value { **,** net_concatenation_value } **}**
net_concatenation_value ::=
hierarchical_net_identifier
| hierarchical_net_identifier **[** expression **]** { **[** expression **]** }
| hierarchical_net_identifier **[** expression **]** { **[** expression **]** } **[** range_expression **]**
| hierarchical_net_identifier **[** range_expression **]**
| net_concatenation
variable_concatenation ::= **{** variable_concatenation_value { **,** variable_concatenation_value } **}**
variable_concatenation_value ::=
hierarchical_variable_identifier
| hierarchical_variable_identifier **[** expression **]** { **[** expression **]** }
| hierarchical_variable_identifier **[** expression **]** { **[** expression **]** } **[** range_expression **]**
| hierarchical_variable_identifier **[** range_expression **]**
| variable_concatenation

D.8.2 Function calls

constant_function_call ::= function_identifier { attribute_instance }
(constant_expression { **,** constant_expression } **)**
function_call ::= hierarchical_function_identifier{ attribute_instance }

(expression { , expression })
genvar_function_call ::= genvar_function_identifier { attribute_instance }
(constant_expression { , constant_expression })
system_function_call ::= system_function_identifier
[(expression { , expression })]

D.8.3 Expressions

base_expression ::= expression
conditional_expression ::= expression1 **?** { attribute_instance } expression2 **:** expression3
constant_base_expression ::= constant_expression
constant_expression ::=
constant_primary
| unary_operator { attribute_instance } constant_primary
| constant_expression binary_operator { attribute_instance } constant_expression
| constant_expression **?** { attribute_instance } constant_expression **:** constant_expression
| string
constant_mintypmax_expression ::=
constant_expression
| constant_expression **:** constant_expression **:** constant_expression
constant_range_expression ::=
constant_expression
| msb_constant_expression **:** lsb_constant_expression
| constant_base_expression **+:** width_constant_expression
| constant_base_expression **-:** width_constant_expression
dimension_constant_expression ::= constant_expression
expression1 ::= expression
expression2 ::= expression
expression3 ::= expression
expression ::=
primary
| unary_operator { attribute_instance } primary
| expression binary_operator { attribute_instance } expression
| conditional_expression
| string
lsb_constant_expression ::= constant_expression
mintypmax_expression ::=
expression
| expression **:** expression **:** expression

module_path_conditional_expression ::= module_path_expression **?** { attribute_instance }
module_path_expression **:** module_path_expression

module_path_expression ::=
module_path_primary
| unary_module_path_operator { attribute_instance } module_path_primary

| module_path_expression binary_module_path_operator { attribute_instance }
module_path_expression
| module_path_conditional_expression

module_path_mintypmax_expression ::=
module_path_expression
| module_path_expression **:** module_path_expression **:** module_path_expression

msb_constant_expression ::= constant_expression

range_expression ::=
expression
| msb_constant_expression **:** lsb_constant_expression
| base_expression **+:** width_constant_expression
| base_expression **-:** width_constant_expression

width_constant_expression ::= constant_expression

D.8.4 Primaries

constant_primary ::=
constant_concatenation
| constant_function_call
| (constant_mintypmax_expression)
| constant_multiple_concatenation
| genvar_identifier
| number
| parameter_identifier
| specparam_identifier

module_path_primary ::=
number
| identifier
| module_path_concatenation
| module_path_multiple_concatenation
| function_call
| system_function_call
| constant_function_call

| (module_path_mintypmax_expression)

primary ::=

number

| hierarchical_identifier

| hierarchical_identifier [expression] { [expression] }

| hierarchical_identifier [expression] { [expression] } [range_expression]

| hierarchical_identifier [range_expression]

| concatenation

| multiple_concatenation

| function_call

| system_function_call

| constant_function_call

| (mintypmax_expression)

D.8.5 Expression Left-Side Values

net_lvalue ::=

hierarchical_net_identifier

| hierarchical_net_identifier [constant_expression] { [constant_expression] }

| hierarchical_net_identifier [constant_expression] { [constant_expression] } [constant_range_expression]

| hierarchical_net_identifier [constant_range_expression]

| net_concatenation

variable_lvalue ::=

hierarchical_variable_identifier

| hierarchical_variable_identifier [expression] { [expression] }

| hierarchical_variable_identifier [expression] { [expression] } [range_expression]

| hierarchical_variable_identifier [range_expression]

| variable_concatenation

D.8.6 Operators

unary_operator ::=

+ | - | ! | ~ | & | ~& | | | ~| | ^ | ~^ | ^~

binary_operator ::=

+ | - | * | / | % | == | != | === | !== | && | || | **

| < | <= | > | >= | & | | | ^ | ^~ | ~^ | >> | << | >>> | <<<

unary_module_path_operator ::=

! | ~ | & | ~& | | | ~| | ^ | ~^ | ^~

binary_module_path_operator ::=
 == | != | && | || | & | | | ^ | ^~ | ~^

D.8.7 Numbers

number ::=
 decimal_number
 | octal_number
 | binary_number
 | hex_number
 | real_number
real_number[1] ::=
 unsigned_number **.** unsigned_number
 | unsigned_number [**.** unsigned_number] exp [sign] unsigned_number
exp ::= **e** | **E**
decimal_number ::=
 unsigned_number
 | [size] decimal_base unsigned_number
 | [size] decimal_base x_digit { _ }
 | [size] decimal_base z_digit { _ }
binary_number ::= [size] binary_base binary_value
octal_number ::= [size] octal_base octal_value
hex_number ::= [size] hex_base hex_value
sign ::= **+** | **-**
size ::= non_zero_unsigned_number
non_zero_unsigned_number[1] ::= non_zero_decimal_digit { _ | decimal_digit}
unsigned_number[1] ::= decimal_digit { _ | decimal_digit }
binary_value[1] ::= binary_digit { _ | binary_digit }
octal_value[1] ::= octal_digit { _ | octal_digit }
hex_value[1] ::= hex_digit { _ | hex_digit }
decimal_base[1] ::= **'[s|S]d** | **'[s|S]D**
binary_base[1] ::= **'[s|S]b** | **'[s|S]B**
octal_base[1] ::= **'[s|S]o** | **'[s|S]O**
hex_base[1] ::= **'[s|S]h** | **'[s|S]H**
non_zero_decimal_digit ::= **1** | **2** | **3** | **4** | **5** | **6** | **7** | **8** | **9**
decimal_digit ::= **0** | **1** | **2** | **3** | **4** | **5** | **6** | **7** | **8** | **9**
binary_digit ::= x_digit | z_digit | **0** | **1**
octal_digit ::= x_digit | z_digit | **0** | **1** | **2** | **3** | **4** | **5** | **6** | **7**

hex_digit ::=
    x_digit | z_digit | **0** | **1** | **2** | **3** | **4** | **5** | **6** | **7** | **8** | **9**
    | **a** | **b** | **c** | **d** | **e** | **f** | **A** | **B** | **C** | **D** | **E** | **F**
x_digit ::= **x** | **X**
z_digit ::= **z** | **Z** | **?**

D.8.8 Strings

string ::= " { Any_ASCII_Characters_except_new_line } "

D.9 General

D.9.1 Attributes

attribute_instance ::= **(*** attr_spec { **,** attr_spec } ***)**
attr_spec ::=
    attr_name = constant_expression
    | attr_name
attr_namc ::= identifier

D.9.2 Comments

comment ::=
    one_line_comment
    | block_comment
one_line_comment ::= **//** comment_text **\n**
block_comment ::= **/*** comment_text ***/**
comment_text ::= { Any_ASCII_character }

D.9.3 Identifiers

arrayed_identifier ::=
    simple_arrayed_identifier
    | escaped_arrayed_identifier
block_identifier ::= identifier
cell_identifier ::= identifier
config_identifier ::= identifier
escaped_arrayed_identifier ::= escaped_identifier [range]
escaped_hierarchical_identifier[4] ::=

escaped_hierarchical_branch
{ .simple_hierarchical_branch | .escaped_hierarchical_branch }
escaped_identifier ::= \ {Any_ASCII_character_except_white_space} white_space
event_identifier ::= identifier
function_identifier ::= identifier
gate_instance_identifier ::= arrayed_identifier
generate_block_identifier ::= identifier
genvar_function_identifier ::= identifier /* Hierarchy disallowed */
genvar_identifier ::= identifier
hierarchical_block_identifier ::= hierarchical_identifier
hierarchical_event_identifier ::= hierarchical_identifier
hierarchical_function_identifier ::= hierarchical_identifier
hierarchical_identifier ::=
simple_hierarchical_identifier
| escaped_hierarchical_identifier
hierarchical_net_identifier ::= hierarchical_identifier
hierarchical_variable_identifier ::= hierarchical_identifier
hierarchical_task_identifier ::= hierarchical_identifier
identifier ::=
simple_identifier
| escaped_identifier
inout_port_identifier ::= identifier
input_port_identifier ::= identifier
instance_identifier ::= identifier
library_identifier ::= identifier
memory_identifier ::= identifier
module_identifier ::= identifier
module_instance_identifier ::= arrayed_identifier
net_identifier ::= identifier
output_port_identifier ::= identifier
parameter_identifier ::= identifier
port_identifier ::= identifier
real_identifier ::= identifier
simple_arrayed_identifier ::= simple_identifier [range]
simple_hierarchical_identifier[3] ::=
simple_hierarchical_branch [.escaped_identifier]
simple_identifier[2] ::= [**a-zA-Z_**] { [**a-zA-Z0-9_$**] }
specparam_identifier ::= identifier

system_function_identifier[5] ::= **$[a-zA-Z0-9_$]{ [a-zA-Z0-9_$] }**
system_task_identifier[5] ::= **$[a-zA-Z0-9_$]{ [a-zA-Z0-9_$] }**
task_identifier ::= identifier
terminal_identifier ::= identifier
text_macro_identifier ::= simple_identifier
topmodule_identifier ::= identifier
udp_identifier ::= identifier
udp_instance_identifier ::= arrayed_identifier
variable_identifier ::= identifier

D.9.4 Identifier Branches

simple_hierarchical_branch[3] ::=
simple_identifier [[unsigned_number]]
[{ .simple_identifier [[unsigned_number]] }]
escaped_hierarchical_branch[4] ::=
escaped_identifier [[unsigned_number]]
[{ .escaped_identifier [[unsigned_number]] }]

D.9.5 Whitespace

white_space ::= space | tab | newline | eof[6]

NOTES

1) Embedded spaces are illegal.
2) A simple_identifier and arrayed_reference shall start with an alpha or underscore (_) character, shall have at least one character, and shall not have any spaces.
3) The period (.) in simple_hierarchical_identifier and simple_hierarchical_branch shall not be preceded or followed by white_space.
4) The period in escaped_hierarchical_identifier and escaped_hierarchical_branch shall be preceded by white_space, but shall not be followed by white_space.
5) The $ character in a system_function_identifier or system_task_identifier shall not be followed by white_space. A system_function_identifier or system_task_identifier shall not be escaped.
6) End of file.

Verilog Tidbits

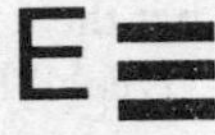

Answers to common Verilog questions are provided in this appendix.

Origins of Verilog HDL

Verilog HDL originated around 1983 at Gateway Design Automation, which was then located in Acton, Massachusetts. The language that most influenced Verilog HDL was HILO-2, which was developed at Brunel University in England under contract to produce a test generation system for the British Ministry of Defense. HILO-2 successfully combined the gate and register transfer levels of abstraction and supported verification simulation, timing analysis, fault simulation, and test generation.

Gateway Design Automation was privately held at that time and was headed by Dr. Prabhu Goel, the inventor of the PODEM test generation algorithm. Verilog HDL was introduced into the EDA market in 1985 as a simulator product. Verilog HDL was designed by Phil Moorby, who was later to become the Chief Designer for *Verilog-XL* and the first Corporate Fellow at Cadence Design Systems. Gateway Design Automation grew rapidly with the success of *Verilog-XL* and was finally acquired by Cadence Design Systems, San Jose, CA, in 1989.

Verilog HDL was opened to the public by Cadence Design Systems in 1990. Open Verilog Internation(OVI) was formed to standardize and promote Verilog HDL and related design automation products.

In 1992, the Board of Directors of OVI began an effort to establish Verilog HDL as an IEEE standard. In 1993, the first IEEE Working Group was formed and, after 18 months of focused efforts, Verilog became the IEEE Standard 1364-1995.

After the standardization process was complete, the 1364 Working Group started looking for feedback from 1364 users worldwide so that the standard could be enhanced and modified accordingly. This led to a five-year effort to create a much better Verilog standard IEEE 1364-2001.

Interpreted, Compiled, Native Compiled Simulators

Verilog simulators come in three flavors, based on the way they perform the simulation.

Interpreted simulators read in the Verilog HDL design, create data structures in memory, and run the simulation interpretively. A compile is performed each time the simulation is run, but the compile is usually very fast. An example of an interpreted simulator is Cadence *Verilog-XL* simulator.

Compiled code simulators read in the Verilog HDL design and convert it to equivalent C code (or some other programming language). The C code is then compiled by a standard C compiler to get the binary executable. The binary is executed to run the simulation. Compile time is usually long for compiled code simulators, but, in general, the execution speed is faster compared to interpreted simulators. An example of compiled code simulator is Synopsys *VCS* simulator.

Native compiled code simulators read in the Verilog HDL design and convert it directly to binary code for a specific machine platform. The compilation is optimized and tuned separately for each machine platform. Of course, that means that a native compiled code simulator for a Sun workstation will not run on an HP workstation, and vice versa. Because of fine tuning, native compiled code simulators can yield significant performance benefits. An example of a native compiled code simulator is Cadence *Verilog-NC* simulator.

Event-Driven Simulation, Oblivious Simulation

Verilog simulators typically use an *event-driven* or an *oblivious simulation* algorithm. An event-driven algorithm processes elements in the design only when signals at the inputs of these elements change. Intelligent scheduling is required to process elements. Oblivious algorithms process all elements in the design, irrespective of changes in signals. Little or no scheduling is required to process elements.

Cycle-Based Simulation

Cycle-based simulation is useful for synchronous designs where operations happen only at active clock edges. Cycle simulators work on a cycle-by-cycle basis. Timing information between two clock edges is lost. Significant performance advantages can be obtained by using cycle simulation.

Fault Simulation

Fault simulation is used to deliberately insert *stuck-at* or *bridging* faults in the reference circuit. Then, a test pattern is applied and the outputs of the faulty circuit and the reference circuit are compared. The fault is said to be *detected* if the outputs mismatch. A set of test patterns is developed for testing the circuit.

General Verilog Web sites

The following sites provide interesting information related toVerilog HDL.

1. Verilog—*http://www.verilog.com*
2. Cadence—*http://www.cadence.com/*
3. EE Times—*http://www.eetimes.com*
4. Synopsys—*http://www.synopsys.com/*
5. DVCon (Conference for HDL and HVL Users)—*http://www.dvcon.org*
6. Verification Guild—*http://www.janick.bergeron.com/guild/default.htm*
7. Deep Chip—*http://www.deepchip.com*

Architectural Modeling Tools

1. For details on System C, see *http://www.systemc.org*

High-Level Verification Languages

1. Information on *e* is available at *http://www.verisity.com*
2. Information on *Vera* is available at *http://www.open-vera.com*
3. Information on *SuperLog* is available at *http://www.synopsys.com*
4. Information on *SystemVerilog* is available at *http://www.accellera.org*

Simulation Tools

1. Information on *Verilog-XL* and *Verilog-NC* is available at *http://www.cadence.com*
2. Information on *VCS* is available at *http://www.synopsys.com*

Hardware Acceleration Tools

Information on hardware acceleration tools is available at the Web sites of the following companies:

1. *http://www.cadence.com*
2. *http://www.aptix.com*
3. *http://www.mentorg.com*
4. *http://www.axiscorp.com*
5. *http://www.tharas.com*

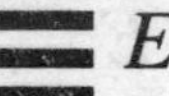

In-Circuit Emulation Tools

Information on in-circuit emulation tools is available at the Web sites of the following companies.

1. *http://www.cadence.com*
2. *http://www.mentorg.com*

Coverage Tools

Information on coverage tools is available at the Web sites of the following companies:

1. *http://www.verisity.com*
2. *http://www.synopsys.com*

Assertion Checking Tools

Information on assertion checking tools is available at the Web sites of the following companies:

1. Information on *e* is available at *http://www.verisity.com*
2. Information on *Vera* is available at *http://www.open-vera.com*
3. Information on *SystemVerilog* is available at *http://www.accellera.org*
4. *http://www.0-in.com*
5. *http://www.verplex.com*
6. Information on Open Verification Library is available at *http://www.accellera.org*

Equivalence Checking Tools

1. Information on equivalence checking tools is available at *http://www.verplex.com*
2. Information on equivalence checking tools is available at *http://www.synopsys.com*

Formal Verification Tools

Information on formal verification tools is available at the Web sites of the following companies:

1. *http://www.verplex.com*
2. *http://www.realintent.com*
3. *http://www.synopsys.com*
4. *http://www.athdl.com*
5. *http://www.0-in.com*

Verilog Examples

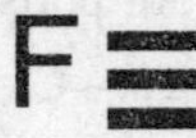

This appendix contains the source code for two examples.

- The first example is a synthesizable model of a FIFO implomentation
- The second example is a behavioral model of a 256K × 16 DRAM.

These examples are provided to give the reader a flavor of real-life Verilog HDL usage. The reader is encouraged to look through the source code to understand coding style and the usage of Verilog HDL constructs.

F.1 Synthesizable FIFO Model

This example describes a synthesizable implementation of a FIFO. The FIFO depth and FIFO width in bits can be modified by simply changing the value of two parameters, *`FWIDTH* and *`FDEPTH*. For this example, the FIFO depth is 4 and the FIFO width is 32 bits. The input/output ports of the FIFO are shown in Figure F-1.

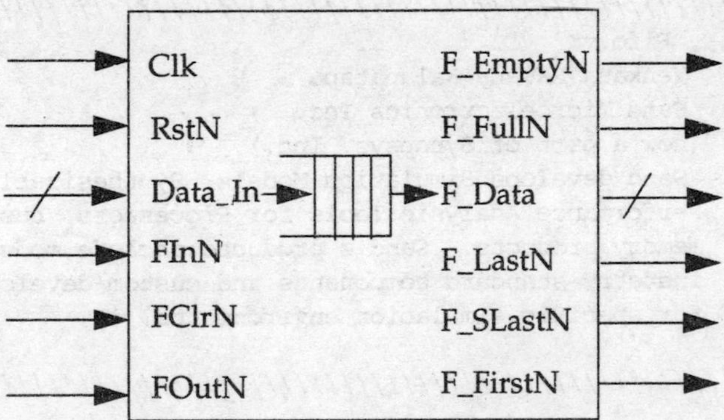

Figure F-1 FIFO Input/Output Ports

Input ports

All ports with a suffix "N" are low-asserted.

Clk—Clock signal

RstN—Reset signal

Data_In—32-bit data into the FIFO

FInN—Write into FIFO signal

FClrN—Clear signal to FIFO

FOutN—Read from FIFO signal

Output ports

F_Data—32-bit output data from FIFO

F_FullN—Signal indicating that FIFO is full

F_EmptyN—Signal indicating that FIFO is empty

F_LastN—Signal indicating that FIFO has space for one data value

F_SLastN—Signal indicating that FIFO has space for two data values

F_FirstN—Signal indicating that there is only one data value in FIFO

The Verilog HDL code for the FIFO implementation is shown in Code Example F-1.

Code Example F-1 Synthesizable FIFO Model

```
/////////////////////////////////////////////////////////////////////////
// FileName:  "Fifo.v"
// Author  :  Venkata Ramana Kalapatapu
// Company :  Sand Microelectronics Inc.
//            (now a part of Synopsys, Inc.),
// Profile :  Sand develops Simulation Models, Synthesizable Cores and
//           Performance Analysis Tools for Processors, buses and
//           memory products.  Sand's products include models for
//           industry-standard components and custom-developed models
//           for specific simulation environments.
//
/////////////////////////////////////////////////////////////////////////


`define  FWIDTH      32             // Width of the FIFO.
`define  FDEPTH      4              // Depth of the FIFO.
`define  FCWIDTH     2              // Counter Width of the FIFO 2 to power
                                    // FCWIDTH = FDEPTH.
```

Code Example F-1 Synthesizable FIFO Model (Continued)

```
module FIFO(  Clk,
              RstN,
              Data_In,
              FClrN,
              FInN,
              FOutN,

              F_Data,
              F_FullN,
              F_LastN,
              F_SLastN,
              F_FirstN,
              F_EmptyN
          );


input                        Clk;      // CLK signal.
input                        RstN;     // Low Asserted Reset signal.
input [(`FWIDTH-1):0]        Data_In;  // Data into FIFO.
input                        FInN;     // Write into FIFO Signal.
input                        FClrN;    // Clear signal to FIFO.
input                        FOutN;    // Read from FIFO signal.

output [(`FWIDTH-1):0]       F_Data;   // FIFO data out.
output                       F_FullN;  // FIFO full indicating signal.
output                       F_EmptyN; // FIFO empty indicating signal.
output                       F_LastN;  // FIFO Last but one signal.
output                       F_SLastN; // FIFO SLast but one signal.
output                       F_FirstN; // Signal indicating only one
                                       // word in FIFO.


reg                F_FullN;
reg                F_EmptyN;
reg                F_LastN;
reg                F_SLastN;
reg                F_FirstN;

reg    [`FCWIDTH:0]        fcounter; //counter indicates num of data in FIFO
reg    [(`FCWIDTH-1):0]    rd_ptr;       // Current read pointer.
reg    [(`FCWIDTH-1):0]    wr_ptr;       // Current write pointer.
wire   [(`FWIDTH-1):0]     FIFODataOut; // Data out from FIFO MemBlk
```

Code Example F-1 Synthesizable FIFO Model (Continued)

```
wire   [(`FWIDTH-1):0]     FIFODataIn;  // Data into FIFO MemBlk

wire   ReadN  = FOutN;
wire   WriteN = FInN;

assign F_Data      = FIFODataOut;
assign FIFODataIn = Data_In;


    FIFO_MEM_BLK memblk(.clk(Clk),
                        .writeN(WriteN),
                        .rd_addr(rd_ptr),
                        .wr_addr(wr_ptr),
                        .data_in(FIFODataIn),
                        .data_out(FIFODataOut)
                       );


    // Control circuitry for FIFO. If reset or clr signal is asserted,
    // all the counters are set to 0. If write only the write counter
    // is incremented else if read only read counter is incremented
    // else if both, read and write counters are incremented.
    // fcounter indicates the num of items in the FIFO. Write only
    // increments the fcounter, read only decrements the counter, and
    // read && write doesn't change the counter value.
    always @(posedge Clk or negedge RstN)
    begin

       if(!RstN) begin
          fcounter     <= 0;
          rd_ptr       <= 0;
          wr_ptr       <= 0;
       end
       else begin

          if(!FClrN ) begin
             fcounter     <= 0;
             rd_ptr       <= 0;
             wr_ptr       <= 0;
          end
          else begin
```

Code Example F-1 Synthesizable FIFO Model (Continued)

```
         if(!WriteN && F_FullN)
            wr_ptr <= wr_ptr + 1;

         if(!ReadN && F_EmptyN)
            rd_ptr <= rd_ptr + 1;

         if(!WriteN && ReadN && F_FullN)
            fcounter <= fcounter + 1;

         else if(WriteN && !ReadN && F_EmptyN)
            fcounter <= fcounter - 1;

      end
   end
end


// All the FIFO status signals depends on the value of fcounter.
// If the fcounter is equal to fdepth, indicates FIFO is full.
// If the fcounter is equal to zero, indicates the FIFO is empty.



// F_EmptyN signal indicates FIFO Empty Status. By default it is
// asserted, indicating the FIFO is empty. After the First Data is
// put into the FIFO the signal is deasserted.
always @(posedge Clk or negedge RstN)
begin

   if(!RstN)
      F_EmptyN <= 1'b0;

   else begin
      if(FClrN==1'b1) begin

         if(F_EmptyN==1'b0 && WriteN==1'b0)

            F_EmptyN <= 1'b1;

         else if(F_FirstN==1'b0 && ReadN==1'b0 && WriteN==1'b1)

            F_EmptyN <= 1'b0;
      end
```

Code Example F-1 Synthesizable FIFO Model (Continued)

```
        else
            F_EmptyN <= 1'b0;
    end
end

// F_FirstN signal indicates that there is only one datum sitting
// in the FIFO. When the FIFO is empty and a write to FIFO occurs,
// this signal gets asserted.
always @(posedge Clk or negedge RstN)
begin

    if(!RstN)

        F_FirstN <= 1'b1;

    else begin
        if(FClrN==1'b1) begin

            if((F_EmptyN==1'b0 && WriteN==1'b0) ||
                (fcounter==2 && ReadN==1'b0 && WriteN==1'b1))

                    F_FirstN <= 1'b0;

            else if (F_FirstN==1'b0 && (WriteN ^ ReadN))
                    F_FirstN <= 1'b1;
        end
        else begin

            F_FirstN <= 1'b1;
        end
    end
end


// F_SLastN indicates that there is space for only two data words
//in the FIFO.
always @(posedge Clk or negedge RstN)
begin

    if(!RstN)

        F_SLastN <= 1'b1;
```

Code Example F-1 Synthesizable FIFO Model (Continued)

```
    else begin

        if(FClrN==1'b1) begin

            if( (F_LastN==1'b0 && ReadN==1'b0 && WriteN==1'b1) ||
                (fcounter == (`FDEPTH-3) && WriteN==1'b0 && ReadN==1'b1))

                F_SLastN <= 1'b0;


            else if(F_SLastN==1'b0 && (ReadN ^ WriteN) )
                F_SLastN <= 1'b1;

        end
        else
            F_SLastN <= 1'b1;

    end
end

// F_LastN indicates that there is one space for only one data
// word in the FIFO.
always @(posedge Clk or negedge RstN)
begin

    if(!RstN)

        F_LastN <= 1'b1;

    else begin
        if(FClrN==1'b1) begin

            if ((F_FullN==1'b0 && ReadN==1'b0)  ||
                (fcounter == (`FDEPTH-2) && WriteN==1'b0 && ReadN==1'b1))

                F_LastN <= 1'b0;

            else if(F_LastN==1'b0 && (ReadN ^ WriteN) )
                F_LastN <= 1'b1;
        end
        else
            F_LastN <= 1'b1;
    end
```

Code Example F-1   Synthesizable FIFO Model (Continued)

```
   end


   // F_FullN indicates that the FIFO is full.
   always @(posedge Clk or negedge RstN)
   begin

      if(!RstN)

          F_FullN <= 1'b1;

      else begin
          if(FClrN==1'b1)  begin

              if (F_LastN==1'b0 && WriteN==1'b0 && ReadN==1'b1)

                   F_FullN <= 1'b0;

              else if(F_FullN==1'b0 && ReadN==1'b0)

                   F_FullN <= 1'b1;
          end
          else
              F_FullN <= 1'b1;

      end
   end

endmodule


//////////////////////////////////////////////////////////////////////
//
//
//   Configurable memory block for fifo. The width of the mem
//   block is configured via FWIDTH. All the data into fifo is done
//   synchronous to block.
//
//   Author : Venkata Ramana Kalapatapu
//
//////////////////////////////////////////////////////////////////////
```

Code Example F-1 Synthesizable FIFO Model (Continued)

```
module FIFO_MEM_BLK( clk,
                     writeN,
                     wr_addr,
                     rd_addr,
                     data_in,
                     data_out
                   );


input                  clk;     // input clk.
input  writeN;   // Write Signal to put data into fifo.
input  [(`FCWIDTH-1):0]  wr_addr;   // Write Address.
input  [(`FCWIDTH-1):0]  rd_addr;   // Read Address.
input  [(`FWIDTH-1):0]   data_in;   // DataIn in to Memory Block

output [(`FWIDTH-1):0]   data_out; // Data Out from the Memory
                                   // Block(FIFO)

wire   [(`FWIDTH-1):0] data_out;

reg    [(`FWIDTH-1):0] FIFO[0:(`FDEPTH-1)];


assign data_out  = FIFO[rd_addr];

always @(posedge clk)
begin

   if(writeN==1'b0)
      FIFO[wr_addr] <= data_in;
end

endmodule
```

F.2 Behavioral DRAM Model

This example describes a behavioral implementation of a 256K × 16 DRAM. The DRAM has 256K 16-bit memory locations. The input/output ports of the DRAM are shown in Figure F-2.

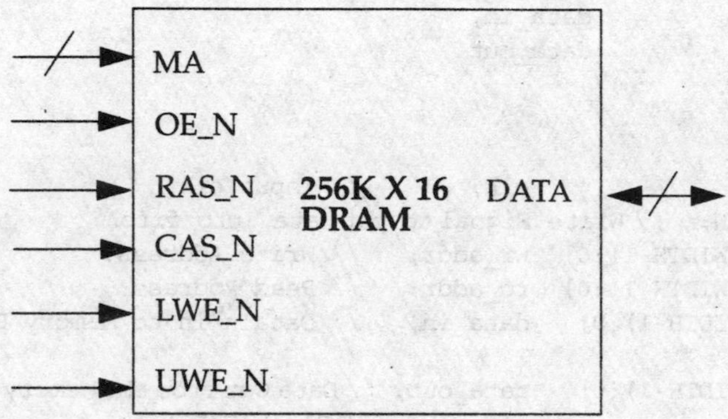

Figure F-2 DRAM Input/Output Ports

Input ports

All ports with a suffix "N" are low-asserted.

MA—10-bit memory address

OE_N—Output enable for reading data

RAS_N—Row address strobe for asserting row address

CAS_N—Column address strobe for asserting column address

LWE_N—Lower write enable to write lower 8 bits of DATA into memory

UWE_N—Upper write enable to write upper 8 bits of DATA into memory

Inout ports

DATA—16-bit data as input or output. Write input if *LWE_N* or *UWE_N* is asserted. Read output if *OE_N* is asserted.

The Verilog HDL code for the DRAM implementation is shown in Code Example F-1.

Code Example F-2 Behavioral DRAM Model

```
///////////////////////////////////////////////////////////////////////
// FileName:  "dram.v" - functional model of a 256K x 16 DRAM
// Author  :  Venkata Ramana Kalapatapu
// Company :  Sand Microelectronics Inc.(now a part of Synopsys, Inc.)
// Profile :  Sand develops Simulation Models, Synthesizable Cores, and
//            Performance Analysis Tools for Processors, buses and
//            memory products. Sand's products include models for
//            industry-standard components and custom-developed
//            models for specific simulation environments.
//
///////////////////////////////////////////////////////////////////////

module DRAM( DATA,
             MA,
             RAS_N,
             CAS_N,
             LWE_N,
             UWE_N,
             OE_N);

   inout [15:0]    DATA;
   input [9:0]     MA;
   input           RAS_N;
   input           CAS_N;
   input           LWE_N;
   input           UWE_N;
   input           OE_N;

   reg   [15:0]  memblk [0:262143];  // Memory Block. 256K x 16.
   reg   [9:0]   rowadd;             // RowAddress Upper 10 bits of MA.
   reg   [7:0]   coladd;             // ColAddress Lower 8 bits of MA.
   reg   [15:0]  rd_data;            // Read Data.
   reg   [15:0]  temp_reg;

   reg        hidden_ref;
   reg        last_lwe;
   reg        last_uwe;
   reg        cas_bef_ras_ref;
   reg        end_cas_bef_ras_ref;
   reg        last_cas;
   reg        read;
   reg        rmw;
```

Code Example F-2 Behavioral DRAM Model (Continued)

```
reg        output_disable_check;
integer    page_mode;

assign #5 DATA=(OE_N===1'b0 && CAS_N===1'b0) ? rd_data : 16'bz;

parameter infile = "ini_file"; //Input file for preloading the Dram.

initial
begin
   $readmemh(infile, memblk);
end


always @(RAS_N)
begin

   if(RAS_N == 1'b0 ) begin
       if(CAS_N == 1'b1 ) begin
           rowadd = MA;
       end
       else
           hidden_ref = 1'b1;
   end
   else
           hidden_ref = 1'b0;
end


always @(CAS_N)
   #1 last_cas = CAS_N;


always @(CAS_N or LWE_N or UWE_N)
begin

   if(RAS_N===1'b0 && CAS_N===1'b0 ) begin

       if(last_cas==1'b1)
           coladd = MA[7:0];

       if(LWE_N!==1'b0 && UWE_N!==1'b0)  begin  // Read Cycle.

           rd_data = memblk[{rowadd, coladd}];
```

Code Example F-2 Behavioral DRAM Model (Continued)

```
          $display("READ : address = %b, Data = %b",
         {rowadd,coladd}, rd_data );
      end
      else if(LWE_N===1'b0 && UWE_N===1'b0) begin
                                               // Write Cycle both bytes.
          memblk[{rowadd,coladd}] = DATA;
          $display("WRITE: address = %b, Data = %b",
         {rowadd,coladd}, DATA );
      end
      else if(LWE N===1'b0 && UWE_N===1'b1) begin
                                               // Lower Byte Write Cycle.

          temp_reg = memblk[{rowadd, coladd}];
          temp_reg[7:0] = DATA[7:0];
          memblk[{rowadd,coladd}] = temp_reg;
      end
      else if(LWE_N===1'b1 && UWE_N===1'b0) begin
                                               // Upper Byte Write Cycle.

          temp_reg = memblk[{rowadd, coladd}];
          temp_reg[15:8] = DATA[15:8];
          memblk[{rowadd,coladd}] = temp_reg;
      end
   end
end


// Refresh.
always @(CAS_N or RAS_N)
begin

     if(CAS_N==1'b0  && last_cas===1'b1 && RAS_N===1'b1) begin
         cas_bef_ras_ref = 1'b1;
     end

     if(CAS_N===1'b1 && RAS_N===1'b1 && cas_bef_ras_ref==1'b1) begin
         end_cas_bef_ras_ref = 1'b1;
         cas_bef_ras_ref = 1'b0;
     end

     if( (CAS_N===1'b0 && RAS_N===1'b0) && end_cas_bef_ras_ref==1'b1 )
         end_cas_bef_ras_ref = 1'b0;
```

Code Example F-2 Behavioral DRAM Model (Continued)

```
  end

endmodule
```

Index

C

D

E

F

G

H

I

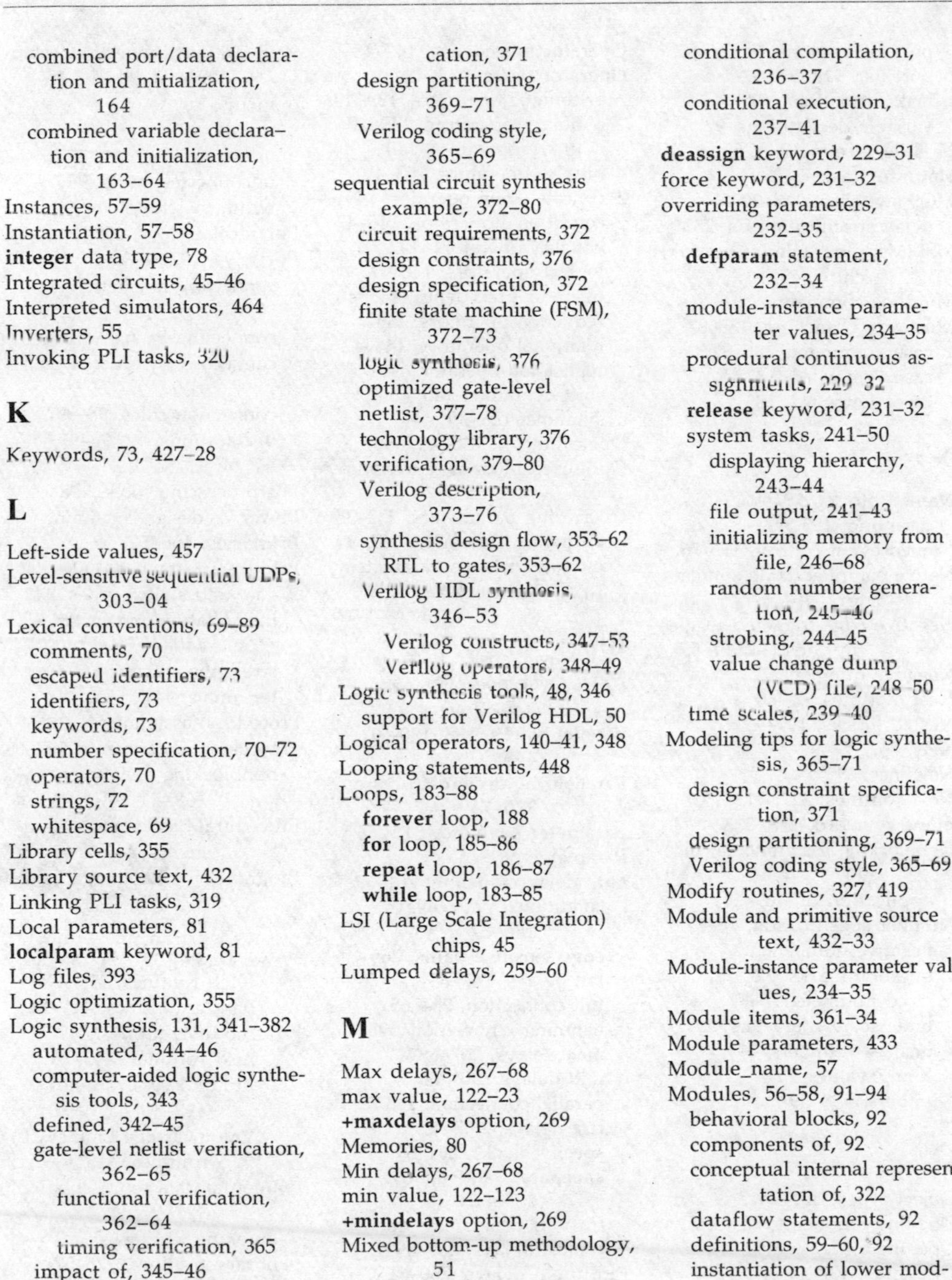

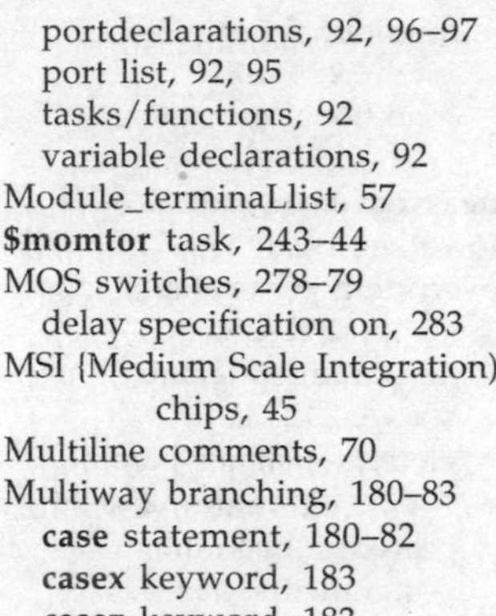

Q

R

S

T

W

X

About the CD-ROM

Using the CD-ROM

The CD that accompanies this book contains a demonstration version of the SILOS 2001 Verilog HDL Toolbox for Microsoft® Windows (98/98SE/ME/NT/2000/XP). To run it, please follow these instructions—

1. Insert CD into CD-ROM drive.
2. Run D:\SETUP.EXE (where D: is the letter of your CD drive).
3. Copy D:\VERILOG_BOOK_EXAMPLES directory to hard drive and make the folder writable.
4. See D:\README.TXT for further instructions.

If you are a Unix user, please do the following—

1. Go to `http://authors.phptr.com/palnitkar/`.
2. Binary.
3. Get file VERILOG_BOOK_EXAMPLES.tar.
4. Get file README.txt.
5. Tar xvf VERILOG_BOOK_EXAMPLES.tar.
6. See README.txt for details.